Modern
Jews
Engage
the New
Testament

Modern Jews Engage the New Testament

Enhancing Jewish Well-Being in a Christian Environment

Rabbi Michael J. Cook, PhD

For People of All Faiths, All Backgrounds

JEWISH LIGHTS Publishing

Woodstock, Vermont

Modern Jews Engage the New Testament:
Enhancing Jewish Well-Being in a Christian Environment

2012 Hardcover Edition, Third Printing

Image of *Synagoga* © Mary Ann Sullivan, Bluffton University

Library of Congress Cataloging-in-Publication Data
Cook, Michael J., Rabbi.
  Modern Jews engage the New Testament: enhancing Jewish well-being in a Christian environment / by Michael J. Cook.
    p. cm.
  Includes bibliographical references and index.
  ISBN-13: 978-1-58023-313-2
  ISBN-10: 1-58023-313-9
  1. Jesus Christ—Jewish interpretations. 2. Bible. N.T.—Criticism, interpretation, etc. 3. Judaism—Relations—Christianity. 4. Christianity and other religions—Judaism. I. Title.
  BM620.C625 2008
  225.602'4296—dc22

                                                          2007046948

10 9 8 7 6 5 4 3

Manufactured in the United States of America
❀ Printed on recycled paper.

Jacket Design: Tim Holtz

For People of All Faiths, All Backgrounds
Published by Jewish Lights Publishing
A Division of LongHill Partners, Inc.
Sunset Farm Offices, Route 4, P.O. Box 237
Woodstock, VT 05091
Tel: (802) 457-4000   Fax: (802) 457-4004
www.jewishlights.com

To Judy,
for sharing in this book, and for always opening my eyes,
and to *Synagoga*,
for her daring, through this book, at last to open hers.

I do not feel obliged to believe that the same God who has endowed us with sense, reason, and intellect has intended us to forgo their use....
　　　　　—Galileo Galilei[1]

Contents

Before We Proceed

How to Read This Book

Most Jews are wary of, even intimidated by, the New Testament. Yet most Christians would be astonished at how anyone could be alienated from their sacred scripture. I intend to explain how these circumstances developed and to offer new ways of reaching the heart of these problems. As such, I present less a survey or introduction to the New Testament than a manual for managing it, a book that is:

- primarily for lay readers but also for those of a scholarly bent.
- primarily for Jews but also for interested Gentiles.
- primarily for religionists but also for secularists.

Beyond these general readerships, I also have the following ones in mind:

- *Jewish professionals (rabbis, cantors, educators, and communal service workers)*—for use as their class text in their adult-education, teacher-training, religious school, and conversion courses; in counseling the intermarried; and in interacting with Christian clergy, with churches and sectarian colleges, and with the Christian community at large.
- *Academicians, seminarians, and college students*—in their courses on the New Testament, on its understanding by Jews, and on its impact on Jewish history.
- *Christian clergy*—in seeking guidance for how to reread New Testament texts that have an effect on Jews and Judaism.
- *Centers for Christian-Jewish Learning*—as a text in their programming on the New Testament in relation to Jewish concerns.
- *Jewish, interfaith, and blended relationships and their households, and Jews-by-Choice*—in seeking greater ease to engage in reasoned and informed interchange on religious issues and differences within relationships and families.

- *Jewish youth programmers*—in imparting information about Jesus and the Gospels that is cogent, balanced, and helpful to youngsters who are vulnerable to Christian missionaries and millennialists.
- *Generalists with special interest in the dynamics of religious texts.*

Accommodating These Differing Readerships

Because this book combines material that is vital to the novice with analyses that are potentially useful for scholars, certain devices are used to bridge widely differing interest levels:

Multidirectional reading options. For newcomers to this subject, chapters are arranged in a logical progression and are best addressed as sequenced. Yet, each is also written to stand on its own, so readers can productively approach them in any sequence.

Multipurpose applicability. This book is envisioned also for programming use, for example, weekly adult-education classes, synagogue Institutes for Christian clergy and seminarians, religious studies department courses in colleges, interfaith sessions at Centers for Christian-Jewish Learning, and so on. Accordingly, I provide my personal recommendations as to which chapters best lend themselves to which programming. (For these suggestions, see "Suitability Index for Using This Multipurpose Book: Matching Contents to Occasion.")

Two types of endnotes. Because some readers consult endnotes as they go while others do so on a delayed basis or not at all, standard superscripts ([1]) indicate conventional endnotes, but underlined superscripts ([1]) indicate those endnotes that I believe readers might profit from consulting immediately.

Chapter-ending tools. Most of Chapters 9 through 20 (Parts Four through Six of the book) end with sections that are pedagogical tools:

1. "The Most Valuable Ideas in This Chapter May Be"
2. "What Gospel Dynamics Have We Recognized in This Chapter?"
3. "Loose Ends Worth Tying"

Some readers may prefer to examine the first two items even before beginning these chapters. The third item draws attention to materials that are additional or tangential to the chapter's primary focus. The superscript (→) within chapter texts signals that a subject just mentioned will receive elaboration in the "Loose Ends Worth Tying" section.

- *Rearranged Synoptic Columns.* To aid those who are unfamiliar with reading Gospel texts in parallel columns, I display Matthew, Mark, and

Preface Fig. 1—Resequencing Synoptic Columns

Customary Sequencing   **Our Sequencing**

Text of Matthew ca. 85	Text of Mark ca. 72 (earliest Gospel)	Text of Luke ca. 94+

Text of Mark ca. 72 (earliest Gospel)	Text of Matthew ca. 85	Text of Luke ca. 94+

Luke not in their customary New Testament order of appearance but in their order of *composition*. The accompanying figure shows an example of what this looks like.

Other Matters

Chapter 21 outlines some of the ideas that animate my conclusions throughout this volume. This summary occurs late in the book because novice readers will find it more helpful after they have covered the earlier material. Nonetheless, as with each chapter, Chapter 21 stands on its own and can be read at any time. It opens with my views on the sensitive matter of Jews venturing to analyze sacred Christian texts.

All quotations from scholars in this book are appropriately noted in corresponding endnotes. But, given the special nature and purposes of this volume, I do not name the scholars within the body of the text if it might prove distracting to new learners.

Cross-referencing of chapters, notes, and illustrative materials is included especially to accommodate those who wish to read chapters out of order. In the titles of charts, diagrams, and so on (e.g., Fig. 5.3), the first number indicates the chapter while the second number indicates where in the sequence of figures in that chapter this figure appears. (See also "Listing of Figures.")

Biblical quotations are from *The Holy Bible: Revised Standard Version* (New York: Division of Christian Education of the National Council of Churches of Christ in the United States of America, 1965; with permission), with any emphases (italicized words) added. Chapter and verse citations usually appear within the main text, but in some cases strings of citations have been shifted to endnotes. (For abbreviations of biblical books, and other ancient writings, see "Abbreviations" in the back matter of this book.)

With regard to Hebrew transliterations, I depart from standard transliterations if alternatives are already more familiar, for example, *tikkun olam* ("repairing the world"), instead of *tiqqun olam*.

I have selected those materials and approaches that I believe will best help accomplish the goals set forth in the Introduction. As an example, each of the five chapters on Paul and the Gospels features the one constellation of factors that I feel is indispensable for readers to know.

"Notes on Terminology—Keeping Our Referents Straight" follows the Introduction. I strongly recommend that readers fully examine this section before delving into the rest of the book. When an expression explained in the "Notes on Terminology" appears in other chapters, it may be signaled by an asterisk (*).

Key to Superscripts

[1] Conventional endnote

[1] An endnote worth reading immediately

→ See "Loose Ends Worth Tying"

* Consult "Notes on Terminology"

Introduction

Reversing "Statuary Blindness"—the Goal That Distinguishes This Book

A lthough the New Testament has exerted the most harmful impact on the Jewish people's history, Jews have always opted to remain ignorant about it. This is the glaring exception to the time-honored Jewish approach to problem-solving, which is to amass—not shun—knowledge. As a result of not knowing how to engage the New Testament, Jews have allowed problems that began after the mid-first century not only to recur frequently but also to intensify and fester. These problems have persisted into modern times, continuing to destabilize Jews' well-being on a communal as well as an individual basis.

Over the course of my teaching career, I have witnessed a reversal of this age-old aversion. Increasingly, but only gradually, Jews are coming to recognize how opting for ignorance about the New Testament indeed has been to their detriment. The purpose of this book is to accelerate this long overdue change in attitude.

But the primary goal here is not for readers to learn the New Testament's *content*. Rather, it is that they develop the ability to discern the *dynamics*—the problem-solving techniques—that underlie this content. (The rationale for this is explained most broadly in Chaps. 8 and 23.) I believe that many Christians, too, may profit from approaching their scripture in the fashion I propose.

Having taught the New Testament on the graduate school and rabbinical seminary level for several decades, I realize that, by now, more than a thousand of my students are Jewish professionals (rabbis, cantors, educators, communal service leaders, camp directors) who are active in North America and abroad. From them continue to come testimonials as to how indispensable training in New Testament dynamics has been in

enhancing the well-being of their constituents, and it is with their urging that Cincinnati's campus of the Hebrew Union College-Jewish Institute of Religion has become the first rabbinical seminary in history to make substantive training in the New Testament's textual and technical dynamics a requirement for ordination. From these former students also come requests for this very book as a tool for expanding this same kind of knowledge to a larger Jewish population, notwithstanding the Jewish community's initial resistance.

Initial resistance? Of course. I know it well, having once embodied it myself. Perhaps my own case will be instructive.

Statuary Blindness

I first encountered "statuary blindness" during my freshman year at Haverford College. In a course on medieval Church art in Europe, I

Intro. Fig. 1
Synagoga

chanced upon a sculpture of a blindfolded woman oddly captioned *Synagoga*—"Synagogue" (Intro. Fig. 1[1]). Upon further research, I discovered that representations of *Synagoga* were legion, not only in statuary but also in Bible illuminations, ivory book covers, paintings, and stained-glass windows. Her blindfold suggested Judaism's opaqueness to the truths of Christianity. Her obtuseness seemed willful, because not only did her blindfold appear easy to remove, but in some depictions it was also so gauze-like that if *Synagoga* simply opened her eyes she would see straight through it.

Often accompanying *Synagoga* was a clear-sighted female counterpart, *Ecclesia* ("Church"). Usually the two women stood flanking Jesus from below as he died atop the cross. Typically, he looked down toward *Ecclesia*, positioned on *his* right, as she devoutly held up a chalice to catch the blood streaming from his rib cage. Meanwhile, *Synagoga* stood—usually ignored—on Jesus' left ("sinister," in Latin).

Only in rare depictions did *Synagoga*'s prospects for recovering her sight seem promising, as when a hand was extended from "Christ" to remove her blindfold, signaling that the Jews would eventually accept him.[2] Usually, however, her malady seemed permanent—as when she was shot in the eye (directly through the blindfold) by a Satanic arrow, or she was stabbed by a sword emanating from the crossbeam above, piercing her skull and exiting her throat! Here *Synagoga*'s obtuseness

was deemed so hopeless that patience, presumably God's, must have run out.[3] In jousting matches with *Ecclesia*, she might sit atop a lame ass,[4] holding a broken lance (to suggest her powerlessness) or a goat's head[5] (to symbolize the Temple cult or to mark her as lustful and unchaste[6]), with the odds of her prevailing over her opponent nil.

Even more distasteful were images of *Synagoga* wielding her staff to penetrate Christ clear through. It is in the course of perforating his left side that her staff splinters; then, in exiting his right side, it opens the wound that spurts his blood into *Ecclesia's* waiting chalice. The obvious message: Jews, in and by their blind(folded)ness, murdered Christ— whose authority was conferred upon the Church when he was killed.[7] By *Synagoga's* own heinous act, then, she was displaced by *Ecclesia* as God's Chosen One.

I tried tracing these women to the New Testament—my first such contact with this text!—but could find them no earlier than patristic writings, that is, those by the church fathers.[8] To my amazement, these writers identified the women as none other than Jacob's two wives, the

---

Intro. Fig. 2—Patristic Sources for Synagoga ("Synagogue") and Ecclesia ("Church")

Justin Martyr (ca. 155)	Irenaeus (ca. 180)	Cyprian (ca. 250)
The marriages of Jacob were types .... **Leah** represented your people [the Jews] and the **Synagogue**; ... **Rachel** ... our **Church**.... As the eyes of **Leah** were weak, so too ... the eyes of your souls (*Dialogue with Trypho*, 134).	[Jacob] did all for the sake of the younger, **Rachel** ... type of the **Church**.... Christ was by his Patriarchs prefiguring ... things to come (*Against Heresies* IV, 21, 3).	Jacob received two wives: the elder, **Leah**, with weak eyes, a type of the **Synagogue**; the younger, the beautiful **Rachel**, a type of the **Church** (*Treatises* XII, 1, Testimony 20).

---

daughters of Laban in Genesis 29, although now through a thoroughly Christianized interpretation (Intro. Fig. 2). Jacob's younger and beloved wife, Rachel, was said here to foreshadow the Church; her elder sister, the unwanted Leah, the Synagogue. And which one was visually impaired? Behold, it was Leah, whose "eyes were weak" (Gen 29:17). That Jacob (here, likened to "Christ") preferred the younger sister was said to foreshadow Christianity's superseding of Judaism, her elder sibling (cf. Gen 25:25).

For Modern Jews: The Haunting Irony of the "Blindfold" Image

I didn't anticipate at the time how my stumbling upon *Synagoga* would launch me toward an academic specialization in the New Testament (then singularly taboo for a Jew). I was profoundly offended by these anti-Jewish depictions, but I also realized that I had absolutely nothing substantive at my disposal with which to respond. I had always thought of Jews as being clear-sighted, yet in this instance I was simply ignorant! Never had I heard the New Testament mentioned in my home or religious school upbringing—and here I had just opened one, for the first time, when I was in college. Nor had I any Jewish friends who knew about the New Testament—how it came to be written and why it was so anti-Jewish. I resented being depicted as blindfolded, yet in this major respect had I not allowed myself to be such?

I resolved to master the materials that—given my people's sad history in Christian lands—had subverted their well-being. In my attempts, I soon began to feel increasingly empowered to deal with these texts from a position of strength instead of bewilderment, prompting me to wonder why modern Jews persist in avoiding rather than accessing this avenue for enhancing their security. Sensing that I was now *more* secure as a Jew by virtue of my *engaging* the New Testament, I was determined to show other Jews how detrimental their traditional "dodging and shunning" routine has been to them and their children.

> In effect, I interpreted *Synagoga*'s blindfold in an unconventional manner (as I will continue to do throughout this book). While Church iconographers meant the blindfold to typify *Synagoga*'s stubborn unwillingness to see Christianity's truths, to me the blindfold symbolized the willful refusal of Jews to apply to troubles caused them by the New Testament the same paradigmatic problem-solving technique that Jews have applied to every other problem in their midst: namely, knowledge.

On such a basis, I came to teach New Testament to Jewish seminary and graduate students. While initial resistance by newcomers remains the norm, so, too, is watching it dissipate once the value of this venture becomes self-evident. Because New Testament dynamics is now a required course, rabbinical candidates cannot avoid it, and those who enter the course the most resistant almost invariably leave among the most appreciative. In this respect, I have seen them recapitulate my own experience, a process I hope to repeat with my readers through this book.

An "Unheard of" Goal

This book covers an array of challenges arising for Jews from the New Testament itself and addresses them by offering scholarly analyses, manageable answers, and the practical applications that Jews require. The logical extension of this plan is an "unheard of" goal, but it is one that I wish to be seriously heard now (and Jews who are initially resistant might sample Chaps. 11 and 20 to test my proposition): if it can become solidly established that Jews will enhance their well-being by learning how to *engage* the New Testament, then it follows that Jews would benefit by setting into initial motion a radical communal change that will induce *all* Jewish seminaries, synagogues, and religious schools, as well as college students, to forgo the traditional Jewish mandate to avoid the New Testament and, instead, become knowledgeable in Gospel dynamics.*

That this is something "unheard of" does not mean it is wrong. It may well mean that it is so extraordinarily overdue as to seem anywhere from novel to unimaginable.

As for Gentile readers, this book will make amply clear why Jews have been so reticent when it comes to the New Testament. Immediately following "Notes on Terminology," Chapter 1 offers just such a recounting.

Notes on Terminology—
Keeping Our Referents Straight

Some terms used in this volume are not applied uniformly by all writers, so what follows is clarification of how I will use them. The terms are sequenced and categorized to match the entries in the accompanying figure. When words explained in these Notes appear in later chapters, they may be *signaled there* by an asterisk (*).

Term. Fig. 1—Order of Appearance of Terms within "Notes on Terminology"				
BODIES OF TEXT	**LITERARY TERMS**	**THEOLOGY**	**SOCIAL CATEGORIES**	**GEOGRAPHY**
Jewish Scripture	*Synoptic*	*Christ/Messiah*	*Christians*	*Land of Israel*
New Testament	*Synoptist*	*The Word*	*Gentiles*	*Palestine*
Tanakh	*Synoptic Problem*	*Salvation/Saved*	*Gentile-Christians*	*Diaspora*
Septuagint (LXX)	*Evangelist*	*Apocalypse*	*Jewish-Christians*	**CHRONOLOGY**
Canon/ Apocrypha	*Passion*	*Apocalyptists*	*Judaizers*	BCE/CE
Rabbinic Literature	*Passion Narrative*	*Eschatological*	*God-fearers*	**SPECIAL**
(Midrash, Mishnah, Talmud)	*Proof-texting*	*Son of Man*	*Pagans*	*Gospel Dynamics*
	Typology	*Son of God*	*Disciples/ Apostles*	
		Kerygma		

Bodies of Text

Jewish Scripture. Since "Old" (in "Old Testament") may be construed to mean obsolete, I use "Jewish scripture" (or "Jewish Bible"). Only in rare contexts will I use "Hebrew scripture," because New Testament recourse is usually to Greek translations of the Hebrew.

New Testament. While "New" (in "New Testament") may be construed to imply that this corpus supersedes the Jewish Bible, no alternative term is workable. "Christian Testament" is not understood by the general public; and "Christian *scripture*" is not suitable because Christians consider their scripture to encompass both Testaments. Moreover, since the Jewish Bible was originally the early Christians' sole scripture, the Jewish Bible itself was, in this respect, "Christians' scripture."

Tanakh. This acronym, signifying the Hebrew Bible as a whole, combines the opening Hebrew letters of the three segments: Pentateuch/*Torah* + Prophets/*Ne-vi'im* + Writings/*Khetuvim*.

Septuagint. One of the ancient Greek translations of Hebrew scripture, accomplished in stages, predominantly (if not entirely) in Alexandria, probably from the third through first centuries BCE. (The abbreviation LXX [Roman numerals equaling seventy] is due to legend ascribing its first-stage translation—the Torah—to seventy-two Jerusalem scholars, here rounded to seventy.) It differed from the Hebrew Bible (as the rabbis came to define it) in its sequencing of contents and in its additional contents (fourteen other books including Tobit, Sirach, and 1 and 2 Maccabees, among others, and known today collectively as the Apocrypha).

Canon/Canonical and **Apocrypha/Apocryphal** (as applied to the New Testament only). **"Canonical"** refers to Christian writings officially accepted as belonging to the closed authoritative list of New Testament texts. "Apocryphal" refers to Christian writings that, while resembling some in the New Testament, were not accepted for inclusion. (For Jewish Apocrypha, see **Septuagint,** above.)

Rabbinic Literature. The corpus of writings associated with the Judaism that was fashioned by the rabbis—successors to the Pharisees (see Chap. 5)—in the wake of the Temple's destruction by Rome in 70 CE. Generations of accruing oral traditions, reapplying Torah injunctions to ever-changing times, eventually became so voluminous as to require putting them down in writing in either of two organizational schemes: (1) as running commentaries on biblical texts (a format called **Midrash**); or (2) as topical groupings of materials (e.g., regarding holiday observance, family matters, jurisprudence, etc.). The earliest surviving topical collection was the **Mishnah**, finalized in the land of Israel sometime after 200 CE. Additional discussions of Torah, building upon Mishnaic sections and appended to them seriatim (paragraph by paragraph), produced the

Talmud in two distinct versions. The Jerusalem and Babylonian Talmuds—the latter is the more predominant—were finished around the fifth to sixth centuries.

Literary Terms

Synoptic (adj.) and Synoptics (noun). These refer to any or all of the three Gospels opening the New Testament (Matthew, Mark, and Luke). They lend themselves to being viewed together in parallel columns (i.e., synoptically).

Synoptist. The author of a Synoptic writing.

Synoptic Problem. How there came to pass the literary interrelationship between and among the Synoptic Gospels: their high degree of similarity in content, structure, and wording together with their substantive divergences.

Evangelist. Author of a canonical Gospel, that is, of Matthew, Mark, Luke, or John (whose respective abbreviations are Mt, Mk, Lk, and Jn, and whose adjectival forms are Matthean, Marcan, Lucan, and Johannine).

Passion. Deriving from the Latin for "suffering," this refers to Jesus' travail during his last days.

Passion Narrative. The section of each Gospel that records Jesus' Passion, found in Mark 14–15; Matthew 26–27; Luke 22–23; and John 18–19. I consider its themes to extend from the resolve to capture Jesus, continuing with the treachery ascribed to Judas, then the Last Supper, Jesus' arrest in Gethsemane, Peter's denial of Jesus, the Sanhedrin trial, Jesus' interrogation by Pilate, the Barabbas episode, and Jesus' crucifixion and expiration. (This listing relies primarily on the Synoptics.)

Proof-texting. In this volume, this expression means the Christian buttressing of a contention by citing support for it through recourse to a Jewish biblical text.

Typology. The interpretation and application from Jewish scriptures of figures (e.g., Adam), events (e.g., the Exodus), motifs (e.g., the sacrificial cult), patterns (e.g., the end of Jeremiah's ministry), objects (e.g., the Passover lamb), and so on, as symbolic prototypes of New Testament themes that are believed to fulfil them (the inference being that the same God is at work in both Testaments).

Theology

Christ. *Christos* (the Greek equivalent of the Hebrew for "Messiah") is a title, not a name, and refers to a deific being, eventually understood as Second Person of the Trinity. Since use of it ordinarily implies recognition of Jesus as divine, Jews should not employ "Jesus" and "Christ" interchangeably, or for that matter, "Jesus Christ" or "Christ" *at all*.

An exception, found frequently in this volume, occurs when, in framing or expressing authentic Christian theology, it is appropriate to use "Christ," not "Jesus."

Distinguishing **Messiah** from **Christ.** "Messiah" is the anglicized form of the Hebrew *mashiach*, meaning "anointed one" (anointment being a ritual for inaugurating figures ascending to divinely sanctioned positions, such as king, priest, or prophet[1]). In terms of its own redemption need, ancient Judaism envisioned the Messiah as a restored human king in Jerusalem, likely descended from King David, preoccupied with the entire people (not individuals), and a strong leader who will vindicate God in demonstrating the political, military, and economic freedom and strength of God's People by overthrowing Israel's foreign oppressors, fulfilling biblical prophecies[2] as *Jews* interpret them, and ushering in God's Kingdom. A more contemporary variant conceptualizes such an idealized Kingdom as a universal reign of peace that fulfils all beneficent societal hopes and ends the ills that corrupt civilization. No substitute agenda—together with any delay needed to accomplish it—is relevant for Jews in identifying the Messiah (e.g., forgiving sins or dying to atone for the sins of others, such as those of Adam, or rising from the dead as confirmation of believers' salvation).

By contrast, in terms of its own—and quite different—conception of *its* redemption need, namely redemption from ingrained Sin, Christianity came to give up for a time on such a "this worldly" demonstration, both postponing it indefinitely and yet still preaching that it would come soon. Instead, Christians imaged Jesus as the Christ, a cosmic divine entity, preexisting the world, said to have descended from heaven and become incarnate in human flesh and to have redeemed the world by his death (suffering to atone for the Sin of humanity, which began with Adam); and then to have been returned to heaven by resurrection, from which he will soon come back to earth.

Such a figure would have been incomprehensible to a first-century Hebrew, and it is *not the Messiah concept that Jews originally formulated and have maintained ever since.*

The Word. The will and mind of God made manifest in the Christ who preexisted the world, and here became incarnate.

Salvation. Understood by Christianity as deliverance, by God's grace, from the danger and penalty of Sin and its consequences in favor of a guaranteed afterlife of well-being attainable solely through faith in Jesus as the Christ, God's Son. (**"Saved,"** then, would be a person's confident state of knowing that he or she has been thus guaranteed salvation— i.e., the conviction and satisfaction that one atoning sacrifice has been offered and accepted and full forgiveness granted; it is a feeling in

someone of being safe, believing that God's Spirit rests upon him or her, and that his or her soul is immortal.) In this sense, believing both brings and is salvation.

Apocalypse. A genre of cryptic writing that purports to unveil secret wisdom about the future and visualizes a linear progress of history from a sorrowful state of life-as-it-is to a glorious coming "end of days." This will happen—perhaps imminently—by divine intervention initiated through a messianic figure who heralds or establishes the "Kingdom of God." Prominent in the arrival of this new world order will be the demise of evil (and punishment of its practitioners) along with reward of the righteous for their suffering. Additional expectations could include a general resurrection and final judgment of humanity, and even a renewed heaven and earth. Writings exemplifying this genre include parts of Daniel, in Jewish scripture, and the Revelation to John, which closes the New Testament.

Apocalyptists (or -ticists). Persons who promote or contribute to a broad range of apocalyptic expectations (see Fig. 5.3 for a sample continuum).

Eschatological. Referring to the end times (or the end of a particular age, to be followed by a radical improvement), commonly expressed or described through apocalyptic imagery.

Son of Man. A term by which the Gospels often show Jesus as referring to himself in either of two manners: (1) to reflect his humanity (e.g., Mt 8:20: "Jesus said: ... 'Foxes have holes, and birds of the air have nests; but the Son of man has nowhere to lay his head'"); or (2) to reflect his apocalyptic character (e.g., Mt 24:30: "they will see the Son of man coming on the clouds of heaven"). If Jesus used the term at all with regard to himself, he more likely did so in the former capacity only.

Son of God. Refers to "Jesus Christ" as God's Son in that he is God made manifest in human form (see Jn 1:1,14) or he was conceived by the Holy Spirit (Lk 1:35). This concept is complicated by the need to show Jesus as also being descended from King David as well as the need to designate the time by which the "Son of God" identification took hold. For example, "concerning [God's] Son ... descended from David according to the flesh and designated Son of God in power ... by his resurrection" (Rom 1:3f.).

Kerygma. The basic "proclamation" of essential religious truths of early Christian belief. In this book it refers almost exclusively to Paul's quotation (1 Cor 15:3–7) of what he says he received from earlier tradition: "that Christ died for our sins in accordance with the scriptures, that he was buried, that he was raised on the third day in accordance with the scriptures, and that he appeared to Cephas [Peter], then to the twelve. Then he appeared to.... "

Social Categories

Christians. It is unclear when the term "Christian" first came into use.[3] As a convenience, I will apply this term even to the earliest adherents of the Jesus Movement from the moment of his death onward. (The same will characterize my use of "Christianity.")

Gentiles. Non-Jews in general. Christians are Gentiles,[4] but Gentiles are not Christians unless they accept Christianity. Thus Jews should not use "Gentile" and "Christian" interchangeably. With reference to the first century CE:

- **Gentile-Christians** are Gentiles entering directly into Christian affiliation *without* first accepting Judaism.
- **Jewish-Christians** are people of Jewish extraction who accept Christianity even if they continue to consider themselves Jews. They would also include Gentiles who become Jewish as an intermediate step before becoming Christian. (Subclassifications yield greater precision.[5])

Judaizers. An often pejorative term for Christians who view Jewish ritual practice (particularly circumcision and dietary laws) as integral for a person to be considered properly observant as a Christian.

God-fearers. Gentiles who, while remaining such, nonetheless loosely attach themselves to Judaism as quasi-converts. They attend synagogue, worship the Jewish God, and observe Jewish practice to varying degrees, but they do not submit to circumcision so as fully to convert.

Pagans. Gentiles (especially followers of polytheistic religions) who are neither **God-fearers** nor Christians.

Disciples/Apostles. In consistently using the word "disciples" to refer to Jesus' inner circle of twelve, I follow the usage by Mark (his is the earliest Gospel and, I will show, the one exerting the most impact on later Jewish history). Matthew almost always follows Mark's usage, but in 10:1 he uses "apostles" to refer to the inner twelve (with "disciples" in this passage denoting a wider group). Luke follows Mark some of the time, but in 6:13 adopts "apostles" as representing the inner circle. Common parlance today follows this Lucan practice. (On the other hand, common parlance also refers to the "Apostle Paul" even though he was not one of these twelve.)

Geography

Land of Israel. Since there is no adequate English term that encompasses the regions of Judea, Samaria, and Galilee of Jesus' age, I use the Hebrew biblical paradigm *Eretz Yisrael*, translating it as "the land of Israel" (cf. 1 Sa 13:19; Ezek 47:18; 2 Chr 34:7; etc.). This is along the lines of

certain Gospel passages as well, for example, "take the child and his mother, and go to the land of Israel ... and [they] went to the land of Israel" (Mt 2:20f.); see, too, "you will not have gone through all the towns of Israel, before the Son of man comes" (Mt 10:23).

Palestine. Though often used in the above capacity, I regard "Palestine" as inappropriate because this name was placed on the land of Israel more than a century after Jesus' death by Emperor Hadrian (135 CE), who took it from the Israelites' ancient Philistine enemies—themselves occupants not of the entire land but only its southwestern coastal area. Also, "Palestine" today is a key term in Middle East political rhetoric, which further clouds its applicability to what, after all, is first-century history.

Diaspora. Greek for "spread out"; geographic areas outside the land of Israel throughout which the Jewish population is dispersed.

Chronology

BCE (Before the Common Era) and **CE** (the Common Era) are used in lieu, respectively, of B.C. and A.D.

Special

Gospel Dynamics. Those skillful techniques by which early Christians molded their traditions to address their needs decades after Jesus died. (As a central theme of this book, Gospel Dynamics are examined closely in Chaps. 8 and 23, and are mentioned throughout the chapters in between; see also the Gospel Dynamics Index.)

Part One

Renouncing Intentional Ignorance

When Advice of Sages Ceases to Be Sage Advice

Historical Overview

When, and why, did Jews first don their blindfold vis-à-vis the New Testament? During the decades when the four Gospels were being completed (70–100 CE), the early rabbis were preoccupied with creating and consolidating a viable Judaism from the ashes of the Temple's destruction by Rome in 70 CE. As time progressed, fledgling Christianity became one of their concerns, especially since Christians, who saw the Jewish Bible as their own, were interpreting it as predicting the coming of Jesus. Meanwhile, Paul, Christianity's most ardent partisan, had held and promoted ideas about the Law of Moses and the figure of "Christ-Jesus" that were unacceptable in rabbinic circles. Not only was the surfacing of the Gospels a possible factor in catalyzing the rabbis to close the Jewish Bible (an exclusionary move), but also passages in emergent rabbinic literature came to designate the Gospels as off limits for Jews.[1]

Yet it was the Gospels that contributed mightily to the way the rabbis, who themselves arose post-70, misunderstood Jesus. These leaders had never known Jesus personally, nor did they possess reliable traditions about him that had been passed down by their own forebears. Instead, the only "Jesus" they were aware of was the anti-Jewish image of him portrayed by the Gospel writers. In this way, the Evangelists mirrored their own negativity toward those contemporary Jews who rejected them and, even more so, sought to protect their community from the Empire's suspicion of all Jews in the wake of the Jewish revolt of 66–73 CE.

The rabbis had no reason to set about disengaging a real Jesus from the Gospels' portrait of him—they had no mind-set to suspect that there was such a disparity, nor, even if they had, any capacity to resolve it. Thus, the figure of Jesus—who both lived and died *a Jew*, and who

neither founded Christianity nor knew of Christian theology—instead became processed as someone "who deceived and led Israel astray,"[2] a profound misunderstanding that, spanning subsequent history, remains the norm for many, if not most, Jews today.

By holding the Jews responsible for Jesus' death, the Gospels gave rise to the epithet "Christ-killers" (see Chap. 11). During the Middle Ages especially, when the Church commanded a virtual monopoly on European learning, this identification often inflamed popular passions against Jews in Christian Europe, who lived with perpetual anxiety that Gospel accusations would become pretexts for pogroms (massacres of Jews), a fear not without good reason. In conjunction with various Crusades (beginning in 1096), Christian armies, trekking through Europe to recapture Jerusalem from the Muslim "infidel," routinely ransacked Jewish communities en route and murdered the inhabitants. They justified their actions by appealing to the Gospels' own assessments of Jews as murderers of Jesus and therefore infidels themselves.

Etched even more deeply into the modern Jewish psyche was Nazism's exploitation of New Testament supersessionist theology. This conviction—that Gentile-Christians had displaced and replaced the Jews as God's chosen people—was manipulated by Hitler's ideologues to suggest that the persistence of Jews into the twentieth century was an anomaly, a quirk or mistake of history; Jews were a fossil meant to have disappeared far earlier. Such a ploy lessened potential resistance to Hitler's "Final Solution," the plan to exterminate the entire Jewish people. Jews today who do not believe that the New Testament itself caused the Holocaust will likely yet insist that the Holocaust could not have occurred without it.

Exercise
Ask a mixed group of Christians and Jews, "What does the Cross mean to you?" Christians may say that it signals Christ's incomparable gift of his life so that they might be saved*; Jews may counter that it symbolizes unspeakable terror.

Jews no longer, then, needed to be dissuaded from examining the Gospels. Bristling, even cringing, as many still do at the mere mention of Jesus' name, the vast majority became, and remain, sufficiently averse to the New Testament entirely on their own.

Consequences of Jews' Ignorance of the New Testament
Yet avoidance of the New Testament has seriously disadvantaged the Jewish people. Anecdotal evidence will help us understand how this manifests itself today.

A Unique Crêche. On a sidewalk during December 2002, I approach a crêche (nativity) scene. Ahead of me are a Jewish mother and little boy. She averts her gaze from the crêche as if this will induce her son to do likewise. No such luck. "Say, Mama, who's that baby over there?" Without missing a beat: "Oh, that's baby Judah Maccabee!"

Jesus' Hebrew Name. In 1991, a rabbi is telling children in her classroom their Hebrew names. "Joshua, yours is Yehoshua—by the way, that's the name that Jesus had." An explosive commotion erupts from clear across the room. In the corner, covering her ears, stands a girl wincing and shrieking, "I don't ever want to hear that name; it gives me the shivers!"

Roused by the Pope. A relentless pounding on a dormitory door awakens a Jewish co-ed at Miami University (Oxford, OH). It is 3:00 a.m. in the fall of 1965. At the door is a casual acquaintance from across the hall. "TV just announced that the Pope has freed you from killing Jesus," she said. "Thought you'd want to know as soon as possible!" Mumbling "thank you," the co-ed stumbles back to bed. Years later she remains angry about the incident because she said "thank you," and because she still does not know what she should have said instead.

Bloodshed in the Classroom? In my sixth-grade homeroom, Joan asks our teacher, "My mom says Jesus was Jewish. Is she right?" Mervyn, not only skeptical but also agitated, reacts by whacking Joan across her face with his bag lunch. Blood streams down her cheek (it turns out to be Mervyn's sliced tomato). That day it dawns on me—a mere eleven-year-old—that something about Jesus' Jewishness apparently is volatile.

Mel Gibson Stymies Jewish Federations. Amid the crisis swirling around Gibson's film *The Passion of the Christ* (2003–2004), Jews implore their local Federations[3] for an Internet posting to help Christians fathom the trauma that this film is causing Jews. A common reply: "Better to post nothing." As some Federation directors later confess, they had no idea of what to say.

Talmudists to the "Rescue"? Self-appointed Talmudists* defend Gibson's film by citing *Sanhedrin* 43a to "confirm" that Jesus was condemned by the Jewish Sanhedrin. But in this instance the Talmud is actually repeating the Gospel accounts *while endeavoring to refute the charge* that the trial was unfair. Since the Talmud is itself here dependent on the Gospels, it is meaningless to enlist its testimony in this matter. Yet Gibson cites these individuals to silence Jewish critics at

large. If the latter had possessed even minimal New Testament learning, they could have silenced the "experts," but their ignorance left them bewildered.

The Infamous "Mary" Faux Pas. Will Jews be better equipped to address the next Passion film? Alas, Gibson's itself *was* the "next". The first was *Jesus Christ Superstar* (1973). When the press asked the Interreligious Affairs Department of a major Jewish organization, "Is this movie antisemitic?" the prepared response was to the effect: "Hardly, but we disapprove of depicting Jesus as being *incestuously* involved with Mary Magdalene." A public relations nightmare—Magdalene is a different Mary from Jesus' mother. These Jewish specialists in Christian–Jewish relations had never even read the Gospels! The bizarre solace is that the Talmud itself combines both of these Marys,[4] so at least the faux pas carried the weight of Jewish "tradition"!

Déjà Vu at Camp. Youngsters at Jewish summer camps repeatedly report that, in close encounters of the religious kind, they feel inept in the face of questions from Christian friends back home (most of whom are only being politely curious). The campers hesitate to ask for help from their parents, who are resistant, embarrassed, or otherwise uncomfortable replying. The distinct facial features of one camper suddenly remind me that, almost three decades earlier, it was *his* mother, then herself a camper, who had voiced the same complaints about *her* parents!

Shortening the Bible at Both Ends? At my first synagogue pulpit (before I turned to academia), a Jewish couple proudly relate how they have coped with the Hanukkah gift that their son, Danny, has just received from a Christian neighbor: a children's Bible that contains a New Testament. To "protect" Danny, they have sliced away the last hundred pages with a razor blade. "Great solution, eh Rabbi?" No, and not only because by weakening the binding they guarantee that Genesis, Exodus, Leviticus, etc., will soon likewise slither to the floor. Rather, who better to teach Danny about Jesus than his parents? Yet instead they have opted for an ostrich approach.

This returns us, of course, to our image, earlier, of *Synagoga's* blindfold.

Distilling Ten Questions

Over many years, I have distilled ten questions (from and about Christians) that Jews report as leaving them the most tongue-tied.

1.1— *Basic Questions That Jews Find the Hardest to Answer*

Theology (questions Christians ask Jews)	Holy Days (also, Christians ask Jews)	Enigma: Benefit vs. Blame (from Jews to themselves)
• Why won't you accept Jesus as the Jewish Messiah? • Isn't Jesus predicted in your own Bible? • Who *do* you think Jesus was? • Did not Jesus die for your sins? • Why not just accept Jesus and *remain* Jewish?	• *Christmas:* How do you account for Jesus' Virgin Birth? • *Maundy (Holy) Thursday:* Why won't you even attend our church Seder? • *Good Friday:* Why did you Jews kill Jesus? • *Easter:* How do you account for Jesus' empty tomb?	• If Christians say it was indispensable for humanity's salvation that Jesus die, and if Jews are said to be so vital a cog in effecting that "benefit," why are Jews *blamed* rather than *praised* for their (presumed) role in humanity's salvation?

Jews' inability to answer such basic questions seems utterly incongruous with the sophistication of a people known for the premium they place on education.

Two Studies

Since only Jewish religious professionals can drive the needed turn-around—and it is, literally, a revolution that is required—we must first get a grasp on their attitudes. Meaningful data come from perhaps only two studies, separated by exactly 100 years.

Harris Weinstock's Petition (1899)

A historic corrective to Jews' traditional New Testament avoidance was attempted with an 1899 petition[5] that was circulated by a prominent Sacramento mercantilist, Harris Weinstock. He was the long-time president of Congregation B'nai Israel, whose pulpit he frequently occupied. Circulated to Reform[6] and some Conservative Jewish leaders, it opened with these comments:

> Dear Sir: Has it ever occurred to you that ... the densest ignorance exists among even our enlightened Jews, concerning ... Jesus of Nazareth? ... There is ... much lost ... by this mistaken policy ...

because ... [when] the Jew is religiously assailed from the Christian standpoint, he is ... helpless to intelligently defend himself.... It would seem to be in the highest interest of ... Judaism that ... the rising Jew may be able to better appreciate ... the exalted place given ... to one of their teachers ... who ... taught only Jewish precepts.... It would afford me ... pleasure if ... I might receive from you an opinion on this subject....

Negativity, at one end of the spectrum of response, was acerbic, even flamboyant: "As long as I can draw my subjects from the five books of Moses," wrote M. Sessler (New Orleans), "so long shall I endeavor to keep away from my pulpit ... the name of Jesus or his history." I. Z. Huldah Frazier (Peoria, IL) felt "obliged to lend my influence to a most emphatic disapproval of such a step.... The teachings of the Nazarene neither hold nor ... reveal any new truth for the Jew." G. Taubenhaus (Brooklyn, NY) feared this proposal would "create the false impression that we are drawing nearer to Christianity." M. Elkin (Hartford, CT) averred that "to bring Christianity and its presumable founder so prominently as a subject ... would be a flagrant breach against our Jewish convictions." J. Bloch (Portland, OR) felt it "hazardous ... to confound myth ... with authenticity."

Other Jewish leaders legitimized Weinstock's endeavor provided that it was tightly circumscribed: I. Philo (Akron, OH) approved of it only if Jesus was taught "along with the other great Jewish prophets." H. Levi (Wheeling, WV) finessed: When "any thought concerning Jesus may serve to elucidate ... essentials [of Judaism], I present that thought." Surprising were those respondents who had been implementing Weinstock's proposal all along, albeit erroneously tracing Christianity to Jesus himself rather than to Paul, the Church, and the Evangelists after he died. D. Levy (New Haven, CT) never encountered objections in teaching about Jesus, "even from those who are not favorably disposed to the *founder* of Christianity." D. Philipson (Cincinnati) likewise "never hesitated" to teach about "the *founder* of Christianity." M. Jastrow (Philadelphia) taught about "the character of the *founder*." By contrast, F. de Sola Mendes (New York) gave "due notice to ... the *reputed* founder of Christianity" (cf. Elkin's "*presumable* founder," above).

Some leaders shared Weinstock's fear that Jews were at a disadvantage because of their ignorance of what G. Kohut (Dallas) termed this "chapter in Jewish history [so important that] ... we ... Jews ... cannot afford to ignore it." To D. Strouse (New Haven), "the ignorance of our people on this subject is so lamentable that any movement which will dispel this condition should be supported." A. Seasongood (Cincinnati)

declared this "one of the most important historical and religious subjects of which the majority [of Jews] are in total ignorance." S. Wise (Philadelphia) wanted Jews to know "that Jesus was a Jew of the Jews ... least understood of all among those who call themselves by his name[!]. And ... that, if he were to dwell among men today, he would find a place in the modern synagogue." K. Kohler (New York) affirmed that "while we Jews do not regard him as ... the Messiah and still less as Saviour, but see in him a son of God in the same sense all men are sons of God, we want our children to know that, in Jesus ..., Judaism produced one of the most beautiful types of humanity." (All emphases added.)

Of sixty respondents, the thirteen of greatest renown[7] endorsed Weinstock's proposal by nine to four. Although Weinstock did publish in the area,[8] no significant change came about because not one of seven required conditions was yet in place (see Chap. 23).

Roxanne Schneider-Shapiro's Survey (1999)

A second study was undertaken exactly a century later expressly to update the findings of Weinstock. Roxanne Schneider-Shapiro canvassed a far wider Jewish constituency—cantors and educators in addition to rabbis—with an interest in adult education as well as religious school training.[9] The concern was teaching not only about Jesus but also about the New Testament and Christianity.

Getting through by fax to 450 synagogues, Schneider-Shapiro received—very promptly—225 responses. A 50 percent return rate is quite remarkable for a request sent only once, suggesting that the topic aroused great interest. She sent a letter of introduction along with excerpts from Weinstock's own letter and the responses he received, as well as her own questionnaire that was more probing than Weinstock's general query (Fig. 1.2).

One respondent's assumption—this is "a totally uncontroversial issue today"—was belied by sharp rhetoric on both extremes. There was the acerbic: "Do Christians learn about Mohammed ... ? Should they? ... Our problem is assimilation. How does learning about ... Jesus meet that?"; or "kids learn more than enough about Jesus from their friends and the Christian culture of America"; "Jesus has no place in Judaism"; "it would be extremely irresponsible ... to spend precious minutes learning about the central figure of Christianity." Then there was the opposite stance: "there is little time ... to teach Jewish 'basics' but [teaching about Jesus and his role within history] is crucial to a world view for our adolescents"; "I am astounded at the ignorance of Jews [who] ... know absolutely nothing about Jesus and the New Testament.... It is incumbent

> ### 1.2—*Schneider-Shapiro's Questionnaire to Jewish Professionals*
>
> 1. Does the figure of Jesus occupy any ... part of your education program?
>
> 2. If No, why not?
>   - Opposition/Resistance from: Rabbi __, educator __, teachers __, parents __, children __ ...?
>   - Never been implemented before and hard to introduce now? __
>   - Rabbi/educator/teachers are not learned enough ... to ... implement ... such a program? __
>   - No curricular materials available? __
>   - Not enough time as is to teach about standard Jewish subjects? __ ...
>
> 3. If Yes, ...
>   a. In what educational setting...?
>   b. What is taught...?
>   c. In what context...? (... study of Christianity? Comparative religion? Jewish historical development—if so, what ... period?)
>   d. How long has this ... been in place?
>   e. What brought about ... [its] implementation? (... requests from parents or students, intermarriage, converts, ... respond to ... Missionaries, ... personal interest by rabbi/educator/teacher?)
>   f. How was the curriculum designed? ...
>   g. How did the ... teacher prepare ... for teaching this material? ...
>   h. What is the ... reaction ... [students, parents, education board, Temple board], etc.?
>
> 4. Conceptually or philosophically, why do you teach/not teach about Jesus? ...

upon Jews to correct this"; "not teaching about Jesus would be an abdication of ... responsibility"; "education can ... cure ... problems that ignorance can cause"; "ignorance breeds fear."

But would teaching such material clarify or confuse a person's Jewish identity? From a negative perspective: it "would ... transform ... [Jesus] into a Jewish hero ... problematic [when it comes to] ... maintaining a Jewish home ... [with] intermarried parents"; "increasing[ly] mixed marriages ... have committed to raising Jewish children— ... reference to Jesus would ... send a mixed message to the child and these families"; "when so many children are confused and come from intermarried families, it's best to stick to what's 'Jewish.'" The positive attitude countered: "teaching 'what we aren't'" can be helpful; it is "necessary ... [for] Identity Formation/Differentiation"; precisely because families are

intermarried, many such parents appreciate that Jewish religious education will take this on. Since even some public schools teach about Jesus, this affords an "opportunity to give a 'Jewish slant'" or "to set the record straight"; "better they should receive correct information and learn that their Temple is a place where they can be guaranteed honest and reliable answers on all ... subject matter"; "students love understanding ... how to respond to missionary encroachments."

And concerning *adult* Jewish education? "A significant number ... know nothing about the Jewish view of Jesus ... classes are offered for adults"; "adults are usually unable to answer basic questions and are pleased to have ... assistance"; "adults and confirmands are fascinated and want to know more." What, then, is taught by those so disposed? Of critical importance is "the difference in the definition of Messiah"—traditional requirements for the Messiah are laid out, and "from a Jewish perspective none ... was met by Jesus"; "many of his teachings are beautiful and meaningful"; "obviously left a rich legacy of 'hasidim' [disciples] who went on to ... build upon his lessons"; "a preacher ... whose followers made him the center of a new religion after his death and who was not followed by most Jews"; heavy emphasis must be placed on "how [Paul] caused nascent Gentile Christianity to break away from the original Jerusalem Nazarenes"; and on "what Paul did" in making over Jesus' image. There were also broader theological concerns, for example, "why Jews don't need to be saved"; "why Judaism is not [a] precursor for Christianity"; how "Judaism gave rise to Christianity."[10]

Observation

Jews need knowledge of the New Testament, but even more so they need the ability to recognize the *dynamics* of how its writings developed, along with an intelligent awareness of how to apply this recognition to enhance the well-being of Jews living in a Christian environment. With respect to these Gospel *Dynamics,** as I call them, the most interesting responses to Schneider-Shapiro's survey were: "I use ... *comparisons* of the four Gospels to ... reconstruct the Roman involvement in the ... crucifixion of Jesus ... "; "[I] *separate out* what Jesus might actually have said versus what were probably *late additions*" (i.e., misascribed to him); "[I show how] gospel writers ... *created* the story of Jesus for their ... religious purposes."[11] My view is that this is the beginning of the right way to go, and that these are the right kinds of points to make—an important avenue of discussion we will continue in Chapter 8.

Results of Ignorance
Evolving Jewish Views of Jesus[1]

That rabbis of old declared the New Testament off limits for Jews does not mean that no Jewish views of Jesus developed or changed over time. By "Jewish views," I mean perceptions about Jesus by Jews who did not associate themselves with him or with his followers, whether during his own day or later times. We will look at six such periods.

Period #1—Jesus' Ministry

Reconstructing what the Jews of Jesus' day thought about him is problematic. Several "curtains" that obscured the historical Jesus from the Gospel writers themselves also impede us from determining how Jews viewed him during his ministry.

> *Chronology.* One to two generations elapsed between Jesus' ministry (ca. 30 CE) and the completion of the four canonical Gospels (70–100 CE). So extensive a hiatus raises doubts: how accurately could these writings preserve not only the realities of Jesus' ministry but also the particulars of what Jews had then thought about him?

> *Geography.* Early Christianity spread from the land of Israel throughout the Mediterranean arena where some—possibly all four—Gospels were completed. Geographical distance impeded not only an author's knowledge of Galilee and Judea, but also his access to information about how Jews there had viewed Jesus during his ministry.

> *Demography:* By the time of the Gospels' completion (70–100 CE), most Christians were of Gentile,* not Jewish, extraction. Were Gospel re-countings of the Jews' views of Jesus formulated in any way to satisfy these Gentile interests?

Ideology. Some Gentile-Christians* were anti-Jewish. Just as Gospel depictions of Jews could reflect bias, so too could Gospel portrayals of how Jews had perceived Jesus.

Each curtain, considered in its own right, poses a substantial impediment. But the current problem—determining how Jews of Jesus' day had perceived him—demands that we visualize all four curtains superimposed, for underlying Gospel descriptions of these Jewish perceptions were traditions already obscured by the passage of time, some shaped in Gentile-Christian communities geographically removed from the land of Israel, and coalescing during years of bitter ideological invective between Christians and Jews (especially post-70). It thus becomes impossible to gauge with confidence the extent to which Jesus' Jewish contemporaries (aside from his followers) viewed him positively or negatively, or were even aware of him at all! Gospel assertions of Jesus' fame match the usual mold of Hellenistic tales of wonder-workers, and do not establish that many Jews knew of him.

Period #2—From Jesus' Death through End of the Second Century

There are few sources to help us determine how Jews of this second period viewed Jesus. The philosopher-historian Philo of Alexandria says nothing about him. While some Dead Sea Scrolls may derive from these years, none mentions Jesus. (That some believe the Scrolls refer to Jesus and John the Baptist under symbolic names "simply proves that learned fantasy knows no limits."[2])

The first-century Jewish historian Josephus, in his *Antiquities* (93 CE), makes two references to Jesus that must be approached with caution because it was the Church that preserved Josephus' writings. His long paragraph about Jesus, called the *Testimonium Flavianum*,[3] contains such particular points of Christian doctrine that most scholars dismiss it as a reworking, even outright forgery, by a later Christian hand. Here is the relevant paragraph (emphasis mine):

> About this time there lived Jesus, a wise man, *if indeed one ought to call him a man.* For he was one who wrought surprising feats and was a teacher of such people as accept the truth gladly. He won over many Jews and many of the Greeks. *He was the Messiah.* When Pilate, *upon hearing him accused by men of the highest standing amongst us,* had condemned him to be crucified, those who had in the first place come to love him did not give up their affection for him. *On the third day he appeared to them restored to life,* for *the prophets of God had prophesied these and countless other*

marvelous things about him. And the tribe of the Christians, so called after him, has still to this day not disappeared.

Later in the same work, Josephus describes the illegal execution (in 62 CE) of James, "the brother of Jesus who was called the Christ."[4] Identifying James by reference to Jesus implies that Josephus had introduced Jesus earlier—possibly where the (recast?) *Testimonium* now resides. But this does not mean that Jesus himself was well known to fellow Jews, since Josephus described many figures unfamiliar to most contemporaries.

Might Christian writings disclose what (non-Christian) Jews were then saying about Jesus? The New Testament itself appears to do so.

- Some Jews alleged that since Elijah, the Messiah's herald, had yet to appear, Jesus could not be the Messiah (Mk 9:11ff.; Mt 17:13).
- Some Jews questioned: since the Messiah was not expected from Galilee, how could Jesus of Nazareth (in Galilee) be he (cf. Jn 7:52)?
- Some Jews doubted that Jesus was descended from King David (Jn 7:40ff.)—commonly thought necessary for the Messiah.
- Jesus was crucified, but Jews claimed that the Messiah was supposed to triumph over Rome (1 Cor 1:23).
- Some Jewish skeptics denied his resurrection (Mt 28:15).

Justin Martyr's *Dialogue with Trypho* (mid-second century) purports to record a debate set in Ephesus (in today's Turkey) between Justin, a church father, and Trypho, a Jew who fled the Jews' disastrously failed Bar Kokhba revolt against Rome (132–35 CE). While the exchange was contrived—with Justin making up both sides—arguments that Justin attributed to Trypho must reflect then-current Jewish concerns: for example, that "you Christians ... formed a Christ for yourselves, for whose sake you ... throw away your lives"; it is "incredible ... almost impossible" that God descended to be born in the form of a man; Jewish scriptures "never acknowledge any other God than the ... Creator"; Christians rely on arbitrary citations from Greek scriptural translation, not the Hebrew original; aspects of Jesus' image derive from Greco-Roman mythology; and crucifixion resembles hanging, which is cursed in Deuteronomy 21:23. Indeed, Trypho appears less opposed to the idea that the Messiah had arrived than to identifying him as Jesus. Some Jews, disillusioned over Bar Kokhba, may have deemed messianic claims on behalf of the crucified Jesus preposterous.[5]

Period #3—Early Rabbinic Literature (Third through Sixth Centuries)

Allusions to Jesus in early rabbinic literature (from Babylonia as well as from the land of Israel) are sparse. We must "hunt and peck" to assemble

a portrait by combining views from different generations and academies. Moreover, some passages that were not originally about Jesus became misconstrued as such,[6] leading rabbis further astray. Above all, the Jesus to whom the rabbis reacted was not the historical man but the Gospels' reconfiguration of him.

Some rabbis thought that Jesus, in Egypt, became schooled in sorcery along with charms needed for magical feats—this is likely how they explained away Jesus' "miracles." The Gospels dated Jesus' ministry to Pontius Pilate's tenure (26–37 CE), when Jesus had been "about thirty" (Lk 3:23), yet rabbis connected Jesus with various figures spanning two centuries (and about whose dating the rabbis were also likely confused). The Talmud allotted Jesus five disciples (although the Gospels stated twelve) and, as we have noted (in Chap. 1), even confused Jesus' mother with Mary Magdalene.[7]

Elsewhere, rabbis overly accepted Gospel traditions. Anti-Jewish sentiments ascribed to Jesus they accepted as his personally rather than as retrojections (backdating) by the Evangelists. The rabbis accused Jesus of proclaiming himself divine even though the same Jesus had designated the *Shema* ("Hear, O Israel: The Lord our God, the Lord is one") his preeminent directive (Mk 12:29, citing Deut 6:4). Mindful that some Jews had been lured into Christian ranks, the rabbis denounced Jesus for attempting to "entice and lead Israel astray,"[8] and even accepted Gospel renditions of Jesus' (supposed) Sanhedrin trial—holding Jewish, not Roman, authorities responsible for his execution. Regarding Christian theology of their own day as blasphemy only strengthened their presumptions that Jesus had been a blasphemer himself. But the rabbis denied that Jesus' trial was unfair: a herald, they fancied, announced throughout the land for forty days: "He is going to be stoned because he practiced sorcery and ... led Israel astray. Let anyone who knows anything in his favor ... plead in his behalf."[9] That no one stepped forward validated his conviction.

Period #4—The Middle Ages

Jewish views of Jesus in one era most likely determined those of succeeding centuries. Misconceptions, retained and embellished, redounded to the Jews' detriment in Church-staged debates, where embarrassed Jewish disputants sometimes softened, even explained away, possible Talmudic allusions to Jesus, even to the point of occasionally proposing that some other "Jesus" was intended! Since "winning" a debate could jeopardize Jewish communal security, political considerations entered into what Jews said or refrained from saying. The Christian concern was less to attack Jews than to win converts to Christianity and to confirm

recent converts in their new faith; conquering doubt was more important than conquering Jews.[10]

Because argumentation relied on subtleties of biblical and rabbinic interpretation, philosophy, and mysticism, disputations leave us unaware of how Jesus was perceived by the wider Jewish populace. We get more information from a medieval Jewish tract called *(Sefer) Toledot Yeshu* ("[The Book of] the History of Jesus"), first mentioned by two ninth-century French archbishops but likely circulating for some time before surfacing to their attention. The text echoed and extended traditions culled from rabbinic sources, interweaving with them Gospel motifs and even mimicking Gospel style.

This parody began by introducing a chaste woman, Miriam (Mary), in Bethlehem, betrothed to a righteous man of the house of David. Nearby lived the disreputable Joseph Pandera (a Roman soldier?), a name variantly mentioned by rabbinic tradition.[11] One night, while pretending to be Miriam's betrothed husband, he forced himself on her. In due course, Miriam gave birth to Yehoshua, shortened to Yeshu. Later, with his origins known, he fled to Galilee.

He eventually returned to Judea bent on entering Jerusalem's Temple, whose foundation stone bore letters of God's Ineffable Name (YHWH), and whose possession would enable Yeshu to perform magic (miracles). Knowledge of these letters was impossible to retain because they were guarded by lions of brass whose roaring induced forgetfulness. Smuggling a small parchment into the Temple, concealed in a cut on his thigh, Yeshu inscribed on it the letters, which he forgot when the lions roared but retrieved later, upon finding and removing the parchment.

Managing to arrest him, Jewish leaders charged him with practicing sorcery and attempting to lead Jews astray. After his execution, his followers told Queen Helene that his tomb was empty—he had been resurrected! Upset, Rabbi Tanhuma (who lived centuries later!) found a gardener who explained that, fearful of Yeshu's disciples stealing the body and proclaiming it resurrected, he himself had reburied it in his garden. (Cf. Jn 20:15: Mary Magdalene mistook Jesus, resurrected, for a gardener who had removed the body; *Toledot Yeshu* accepted Mary's surmise!)

While hardly a historical source about Jesus, *Toledot Yeshu* reflected the climate of Christian Europe where Jews were relentlessly pressured to convert. Such a counter-narrative impugning Gospel claims could diminish the effectiveness of proselytizers. But at the same time, this formulation also misdirected the Jewish mind-set about Jesus even into the twentieth century, when some Jews were still recounting to their children Yiddish folklore about *Yoshke Pandera* (Yeshu [son of] Pandera)!

Period #5—Early Modern Times (Beginning with the Mid-1800s)

When ghetto walls opened in the nineteenth century, Jews exiting into Christian Europe were confronted by claims about Jesus. Stimulating discussion was a sobering undertaking by Christian scholars that is today termed the "Old [or First] Quest for the Historical Jesus." Realizing the importance of reconstructing Jesus' life in light of his specifically Jewish context, these scholars invited erudite Jews to assist them with Hebrew and Aramaic literature that Christians could not easily access, read, and evaluate. As a by-product, Jewish historians[12] began to incorporate discussion about Christian origins in relation to their Jewish context. Collectively, they posed three broad contrasts with their predecessors:

1. While earlier Jews had commonly caricatured Jesus as a sorcerer attempting to beguile Jews, Jewish reassessment stripped away misconceptions, restored respectability to Jesus' image, and reclaimed him as a Jew—and not someone who established a new religion; Christianity's breakaway arose only after Jesus' death.

2. Reconsidering what could have led to Jesus' death by crucifixion, they concluded that the Roman authorities, rather than a proper Jewish court, must have been responsible, with Jesus condemned not for blasphemy, apostasy, sorcery, or enticement, but for *sedition*.

3. The radical cleavage between Judaism and Christianity was shifted from Jesus to *Paul*.

Period #6—Today's Two Tiers: Those Who Know and Those Who Do Not

This new Jewish orientation produced a split among Jews that remains in place today. Even most well-educated Jews still do not expose themselves to this subject, justifying anew Weinstock's 1899 complaint that "the densest ignorance exists among even our enlightened Jews" (Chap. 1). Others, however, who have sensed what is at stake, initiated the progress that this book seeks to accelerate. These Jews are a tributary breaking away from what has been the wary mainstream for almost two millennia. It is time for Jews to widen the tributary into a general course, leaving the old channel to dry up entirely.

Presenting the New Testament
Order and Dis-orders

This book is not intended as a survey or standard introduction to the New Testament but as a motivation to readers, particularly Jews, to *engage* it. Accordingly, we will highlight only some of the New Testament's twenty-seven[1] writings—and only certain aspects of those so selected. Figure 3.1 maps out the New Testament in five segments, with a key that indicates our areas of concentration.

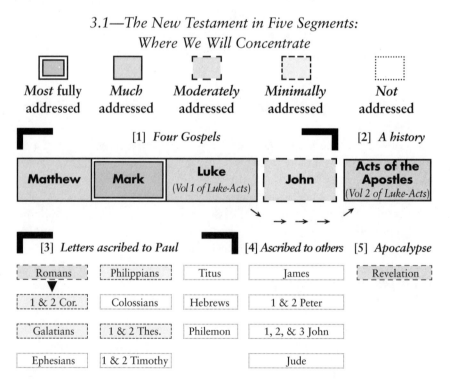

3.1—The New Testament in Five Segments:
Where We Will Concentrate

| Most fully addressed | Much addressed | Moderately addressed | Minimally addressed | Not addressed |

[1] *Four Gospels*   **[2] *A history***

| **Matthew** | **Mark** | **Luke** (Vol 1 of Luke-Acts) | **John** | **Acts of the Apostles** (Vol 2 of Luke-Acts) |

[3] *Letters ascribed to Paul*   **[4] *Ascribed to others***   **[5] *Apocalypse***

Romans	Philippians	Titus	James	Revelation
1 & 2 Cor.	Colossians	Hebrews	1 & 2 Peter	
Galatians	1 & 2 Thes.	Philemon	1, 2, & 3 John	
Ephesians	1 & 2 Timothy		Jude	

The New Testament's arrangement appears orderly: (1) It opens with four Gospels (Matthew, Mark, Luke, and John) that recount and interpret the singular importance of Jesus' life and ministry. (2) The Acts of the Apostles follows. It is a history of the early Christian movement's spread throughout the Mediterranean area. (3) Then there are fourteen Epistles (letters) commonly attributed to Paul of Tarsus. (4) Next are additional Epistles ascribed to other first-century Christian figures. (5) Last comes Revelation, which lays out an end-time scenario for a world beset by evil forces but that is ultimately redeemed.

These writings were composed from around 50 to 150,[2] but the process of collecting and authorizing the New Testament took much longer. We presume an early period of oral transmission of traditions and a considerably longer period thereafter (even into the late fourth or early fifth century) before there was agreement that these particular works would constitute a canon.*

Some Basics
Segment 1—The Four Gospels

"Gospel" is an Anglo-Saxon word growing out of "Godspell," meaning "good story" (echoed by the German *Gut Spiel*) but usually rendered "good news." In the language of composition, the Greek for Gospel is *evangelion*, which is obviously the source of "evangelical." The prefix *eu* (becoming *ev*) means "good," with *angelos* meaning "messenger" (cf. "angel"). So to "evangelize" is to be a messenger of the "good news" that the Messiah has come in the person of Jesus of Nazareth (though "Messiah"* in Christianity came to convey something quite different from its original Jewish meaning).

Reflecting their New Testament order of appearance—Matthew, Mark, Luke, John—each Gospel has an ordinal title: Matthew is the "First Gospel," Mark the "Second," Luke the "Third," and John the "Fourth." But this is problematic because scholars overwhelmingly agree that Mark (not Matthew) was the earliest Gospel and a major source upon which Matthew (as well as Luke) drew.

3.2—The "Second" Gospel Is the Earliest

"First Gospel" refers to **Matthew**—ca. 85 (drew from Mark)	"Second Gospel" refers to **Mark**—ca. 72 (the *earliest*)	"Third Gospel" refers to **Luke**—ca. 94+ (drew from Mark)	"Fourth Gospel" refers to **John**—ca. 100

Henceforth, when sequencing the Gospels, I will usually start with Mark, followed by Matthew, Luke, and John.

The Gospels relate stories about the followers whom Jesus gathered, places he visited, audiences he addressed, teachings he imparted, wonders he performed, opponents he confronted, and the Passion* he underwent. Matthew and Luke add their own versions of Jesus' genealogy and his infancy narrative (Luke also includes a boyhood story), while John moves in the direction of describing a divine figure who predated creation and later became incarnate (taking on flesh) as Jesus of Nazareth. All four Gospels close with resurrection traditions.

Why are Mark, Matthew, and Luke termed the Synoptic Gospels? "Synoptic" means conducive to being *viewed* together, much as "symphonic" means (musical themes) conducive to being *heard* together. Leaving aside for now their opening and closing matter, Figure 3.3 shows how parallel the accounts of Jesus' ministry in these three Gospels (as distinguished from John) basically are.[3]

3.3—The Synoptic Gospels' Basically Parallel Format for Jesus' Ministry

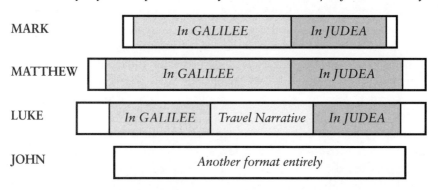

All three Synoptists* show Jesus' ministry as starting in Galilee, the northern region of the land of Israel, and as culminating in Jesus' Passion and death in Jerusalem, capital of Judea in the south (see Fig 5.1). Luke intersperses a central section—a long travel narrative on the way to Jerusalem (9:51–18:14), but his Gospel remains sufficiently parallel to Mark and Matthew for us to consider all three together.

How does John manifest another format entirely? In it Jesus' ministry lasts apparently three years (as opposed to the Synoptics' less than one) and is based more fully in Judea, with Jesus traveling among the regions. John extends to about 175 days Jesus' presence in Jerusalem before his death (compared to less than a week in the Synoptics). All in all, John's structure approximates that of the Synoptic Gospels less than 10 percent of the time (more so in its relating of the Passion than elsewhere). Is it

possible that John knew, or knew of, the Synoptics even though he presents material on Jesus so differently? I believe so, particularly in light of John's Passion material (see Chap. 21). There is also the probability that, since much time had passed, John had heard of Synoptic traditions.

The most substantial reason to view the Synoptics together is that not only are many of their traditions sequenced similarly but also much of their very wording is identical, or nearly so. (John offers few, if any, word-for-word correspondences with the Synoptic accounts.)

Segment 2—The Acts of the Apostles (Also Called "Acts")

Acts purports to be a historical account of the formation and spreading of the Church outward from Jerusalem and throughout the Diaspora. It begins with Jesus' ascension to heaven and the Holy Spirit's outpouring on the faithful, and continues with ministries to Jews, especially by Peter, and to Gentiles, especially by Paul. The book's last three-quarters emphasize Paul's several journeys in planting and sustaining young churches.

Segment 3—Paul's Epistles

Only half of the fourteen Epistles often associated with Paul were genuinely by him. The others are pseudonymous ("falsely named"), composed by later authors who were seeking to secure authority for their words through Paul's reputation. Figure 3.4 would meet with much, though not all, scholarly acceptance.

3.4—Epistles Ascribed to Paul

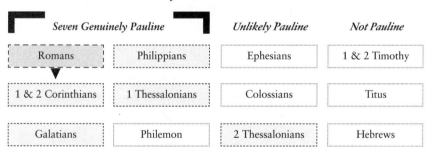

Seven Genuinely Pauline		Unlikely Pauline	Not Pauline
Romans	Philippians	Ephesians	1 & 2 Timothy
1 & 2 Corinthians	1 Thessalonians	Colossians	Titus
Galatians	Philemon	2 Thessalonians	Hebrews

Letters that actually are Pauline, constituting our earliest New Testament writings, date mainly from the 50s—predating the four Gospels. These sometimes are termed "occasional" because, being directed to particular churches that Paul founded, visited, or was yet to visit, they almost all spoke to circumstances—occasions—specific to these communities, usually imparting moral counsel and behavioral instruction.

Segment 4—Letters Ascribed to Others

Dealing with miscellaneous issues, these Epistles are called "general" (or "catholic," meaning universal) because most address Christians at large rather than specific congregations or individuals. They purport to be penned by Paul's contemporaries: one by "James" (brother of Jesus), two by "Peter" (Jesus' foremost disciple*), three by "John" (identity[ies] uncertain), and one by "Jude" (another brother of Jesus).

Segment 5—Revelation ("Apocalypse")

The sole New Testament book that is wholly apocalyptic,* this highly symbolic vision of the future judgment and consummation of all things emphasizes ultimate delivery for the Christian faithful. Written during traumatic times (persecution by Emperor Domitian, ca. 95 CE), its message is cast as delivered by an angel to a "John"[4] on Patmos, an Aegean island southwest of Ephesus (in today's Turkey), where it seems he was imprisoned or exiled.

Some Problem Areas

Difficulties for Readers of the Gospels (Segment 1)

Christian tradition identifies Matthew as among Jesus' inner circle of twelve followers; Mark, outside that circle, as secretary to Jesus' main disciple, Peter; Luke as Paul's physician and travel companion (neither of whom knew Jesus during his ministry); and John as either within Jesus' inner circle or, instead, a later "elder" in Asia Minor (some identify the two as one). Understood this way, these writers appear to offer independent testimonies that more or less corroborate each other.

But this assumption foundered once scholars discovered that Matthew and Luke relied on Mark. Independence was compromised if one Synoptist's testimony constituted a basis for the two others. As an analogy, consider a traffic accident with three ostensibly independent witnesses agreeing on what occurred—that is, until discovery that only *one* clearly saw what transpired, while the other two are only repeating what they heard from *him*!

Eventually it became further evident that all four Gospels were compiled and/or composed anonymously—that the current names ("Mark," "Matthew," etc.) were only second-century "guesses" prefaced as titles to these works. Accordingly, if the authors were not actually the persons whose names they bore, there was no longer any guarantee that they were contemporaneous with Jesus.

By "losing" their identities, we forgo also any certainty as to the authors' extraction—were they born Jewish or Gentile?—and to the church communities for whom they wrote. Moreover, now we are even

unsure that any of these writings was produced wholly by one person rather than, for example, by a compiler, then an author, and then still later an editor. For all we know, a given compilation could have belonged to a particular church and undergone revisions over time, so that what we eventually received was an *accrual*.

Compounding matters, we now know that dozens of other gospels were written. While rejected by the Church—hence now termed "apocryphal"*—might any of these (even if second-century or later) preserve pre-70 material rivaling in reliability what the canonical Gospels present?[5]

Difficulties for Readers of Acts and Paul's Epistles (Segments 2 and 3)

It commonly goes unnoticed that Luke conforms his images of Jesus (in the Gospel of Luke) and Paul (in Acts) to each other (see Chap. 17). Placement of the Gospel of John between Luke and Acts (Fig. 3.1) obscures not only that the latter two are a two-volume set but also that they share a particular theology in common. Meanwhile, we are confronted with special problems when processing Acts' presentation of Paul. Oddly, while Acts professes to know even minor details about Paul, it fails to mention his Epistles. Further, when the same subjects are addressed by Paul's Epistles and Acts, their testimonies frequently disagree in major respects.

Difficulties for Readers of the Remaining Writings (Segments 4 and 5)

While this book does not deal with the "general" Epistles, we should note that each is most likely pseudonymous. With respect to Revelation, it is an arduous undertaking to decipher its apocalyptic imagery, into or out of which each generation since its composition (ca. 95) has read its own near future. (Chap. 19 discusses its misapplication to our own day.)

Dis-Orders

Our initial impression that the New Testament is "orderly" can also be quickly dispelled. To begin with, interest in the phases of Jesus' life developed in reverse order: traditions about the end of Jesus' ministry coalesced first; stories about what occurred during his ministry later; and details about his origins last. With the Second Coming's unrelenting delay, preoccupation with Jesus' death and resurrection became supplemented by concerns to flesh out his ministry (the Gospels are thus endings with extended beginnings). But by that time (after 70), whatever traditions and echoes remained from the years around 30 could have been so reworked by oral transmission as to become less and less reliable. It was an age, moreover, when theological meaning was more valued than accurate historical reportage, and when there was increasing

concern to frame all messages in the light of how Roman officialdom might react.

A second "dis-order" is that Jesus' ministry is only artificially sequenced. Imagine a string of beads that scatters on the floor. The odds of restringing them in their original sequence are low, and matters are further complicated if some beads have been lost and have to be replaced by new ones. The Gospels' running accounts of Jesus' ministry are at best restringings of "beads" of tradition, many of which were passed down independently. Even if we presumed them all to be accurate, we could not feel confident that their sequence was correct. Instead, their current order reflects the aesthetic and theological taste of the editors who interspersed newly created traditions among those surviving and retained from the original mix.

A third major dis-order is that, after Jesus died, Jewish biblical motifs (of course pre-dating him) became enlisted to shape his Gospel image! That the Jewish Bible constituted early Christians' sole scripture made it inevitable that it would be combed for themes to which Jesus' image could be conformed. If we highlighted within the Jewish Bible all passages that were in any way alluded to in the New Testament, and then flipped back through the Jewish Bible's pages, we could spot "text plots," that is, those concentrated sections in which Christians evidently plumbed most heavily in fashioning Jesus' image (we would find these, for example, in certain psalms and in certain sections of Isaiah, Jeremiah, and Zechariah).

Even the New Testament's five segments appear dis-orderly, beyond the misplacement of Matthew before Mark. Paul's Epistles, from the 50s, antedate the Gospels (70–100), yet his letters are placed *after* them. Does this sequence prevent readers from considering whether the Evangelists perhaps molded Jesus' image to conform to Paul's views or to oppose them? Acts, written largely about Paul but at least three decades after Paul's Epistles, is placed before them. Does this interfere with our understanding of Paul on his own terms? Paul's letters themselves appear, for the most part, to be arranged in a roughly decreasing order of length, thereby complicating efforts to gauge development within Paul's thinking.

The most important dis-order of all is that the needs of later Christian communities determined how the image of the earlier Jesus became enlisted, molded, and presented; the Jesus we see may be less as-he-was than as later Christians needed him to be to address problems of their time. The same applies to the images of Pontius Pilate, Caiaphas, Judas, the Roman centurion, and others—all these were similarly adapted to the Evangelists' needs. *Quotations of these characters in the Gospel texts do not constitute evidence that these figures actually said these words.* It is simply not that kind of literature.

The Key to Our Knowledge—The Synoptic Problem

Were the canonical Gospels harmonized into one—and this was often attempted—we would lose our greatest opportunity to reconstruct Christianity's development. Here the Synoptic Gospels are more helpful than John because much of their wording is identical or nearly so. This allows us to more easily perceive when there are *disagreements* among them that, in turn, clue us into editorial practices and special motives of these three different Gospel authors.

Thus, in Figure 3.5, which presents the parable of the Wicked Tenants, our procedure is to: (1) read the version presented by the earliest Gospel,

---

3.5—*Parable of the Wicked Tenants*

Mark 12:1ff. (ca. 72) ▼	Matthew 21:33ff.— revises Mark	Luke 20:9ff.— revises Mark
A man planted a vineyard, ... let it out to tenants, and went into another country.	... a householder ... planted a vineyard ... let it out to tenants, and went into another country.	A man planted a vineyard, ... let it out to tenants, and went into another country ....
... he sent a servant ... to get from them some ... fruit of the vineyard .... They ... beat him .... He sent another ... and ... many others, some they beat and some they killed.	... he sent his servants ... to get his fruit; and the tenants ... beat one, killed another, and stoned another .... He sent other servants ... and they did the same to them.	... he sent a servant ... that they ... give him some of the fruit of the vineyard; but the tenants beat him .... He sent another ...; him also they beat .... And he sent yet a third ....
He had ... a beloved son; ... he sent him ..., saying, "they will respect my son." But those tenants said ..., "this is the heir; ... let us kill him, and the inheritance will be ours." And they ...	... he sent his son ..., saying, "they will respect my son." ... but ... they said ..., "this is the heir; ... let us kill him and have his inheritance." And they ...	... the owner ... said, ... "I will send my beloved son; ... they will respect him." But ... they said ..., "this is the heir; let us kill him, that the inheritance may be ours." And they ...
[1] *killed him, and* [2] *cast him out of the vineyard.*	[2] *cast him out of the vineyard, and* [1] *killed him.*	[2] *cast him out of the vineyard and* [1] *killed him.*

Mark (downward); and (2) then compare all three works horizontally, noting (3) when identical language appears among all three Synoptics or between any two; (4) when other language, not identical, is nonetheless noticeably similar; and (5) when—in spite of all this "sameness"—differences also appear, some modest, others possibly radical. The challenge in which we now engage ourselves—of accounting for this combination of factors—has been termed the "Synoptic Problem"* by scholars.

What process could result in the extraordinary correspondences among these three renditions—and yet also, in the last verse, yield a reversal of Mark's two clauses by both Matthew and Luke? It is helpful to note that nineteenth-century scholarship discovered that where Mark, Matthew, and Luke resemble each other, Matthew and Luke copied from Mark (Fig. 3.6).

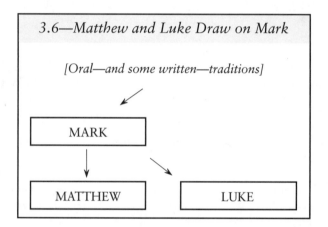

3.6—Matthew and Luke Draw on Mark

[Oral—and some written—traditions]

MARK

MATTHEW   LUKE

But this only explains those verses of the parable that are congruent. What about the last verse presented, whose two clauses are not only switched around by Matthew and Luke but are also done so by both identically? For now, it is enough simply to notice this phenomenon rather than to guess solutions (except for those readers who are curious[6]).

But how, then, can we explain, elsewhere, traditions common to Matthew and Luke yet altogether absent from Mark, meaning that Matthew and Luke could not have derived them from Mark? A familiar example would be the Lord's Prayer, presented in somewhat divergent forms by Matthew and Luke in Figure 3.7; notice that Mark has no equivalent.

3.7—*Sample of Matter Assigned to "Q"*		
Mark	**Matthew 6:9ff.** ▼	**Luke 11:2ff.**
	Pray then like this: Our Father who art in heaven, hallowed be thy name. Thy kingdom come. Thy will be done, on earth as it is in heaven.	When you pray, say: Father, hallowed be thy name. Thy kingdom come.
No Equivalent	Give us this day our daily bread; and forgive us our debts, as we also have forgiven our debtors; and lead us not into temptation, but deliver us from evil.	Give us each day our daily bread; and forgive us our sins, for we ourselves forgive every one who is indebted to us; and lead us not into temptation.

Did both Matthew and Luke have access to some source additional to Mark? As seen in Figure 3.8, most scholars solve this problem by positing a "Q" source—from *Quelle*, German for "source"—presumed to have been a collection of Jesus' teachings without much narrative content.[7]

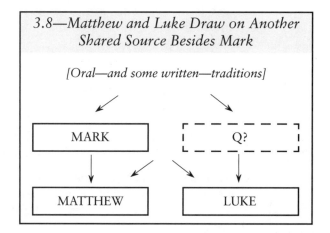

3.8—*Matthew and Luke Draw on Another Shared Source Besides Mark*

[*Oral—and some written—traditions*]

MARK   Q?

MATTHEW   LUKE

Since we do not actually have a "Q" source—it is only hypothetical—not all scholars deem it a necessity, positing instead that Matthew had his own personal source material (which they call "M," after Matthew), and that Luke drew from Matthew as well as Mark.[8] For that matter, why couldn't Luke also have had private material ("L")? What results from

those who retain "Q" in addition to positing "M" and "L" is a theory of four sources, three of them hypothetical, as shown in Figure 3.9.

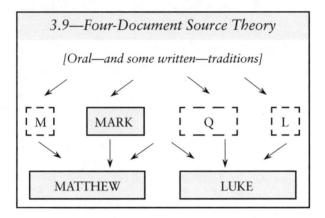

3.9—Four-Document Source Theory

[Oral—and some written—traditions]

| M | MARK | Q | L |

MATTHEW   LUKE

Also operative in Synoptic studies is a dramatically important wild card: improvisation. Sometimes Evangelists innovated their own changes with no recourse to sources! In Figure 3.10, for example, it appears that both Matthew and Luke have changed a Marcan tradition, each in his own way, with no cue to do so from sources. Matthew—where marked by [>]—increases the size of Jesus' arresting party by inserting the adjective "great," while Luke—where marked by [>]—takes it upon himself to prevent Jesus' followers from fleeing Jerusalem to Galilee (as they indeed are said to have done according to both Mark and Matthew).

3.10—Free Improvisation (i.e., Unaided by Sources)

Mark 14:43ff. ▼	Matthew 26:47ff.— revises Mark	Luke 22:47ff.— revises Mark
Judas came ... and with him a crowd with swords and clubs....	Judas came ... and with him a > *great* crowd with swords and clubs	there came a crowd, ... the man ... Judas ... leading them
And they laid hands on him and seized [Jesus]	Then they ... laid hands on Jesus and seized him	.... Then they seized [Jesus] ....
And all forsook him, and fled.	*All the disciples forsook him and fled*	*l> (CANCELS FLIGHT)*

For now it will suffice simply to notice *what* Matthew and Luke have done rather than to concern ourselves with *why* (except again for the curious[2]).

We must also ask ourselves what this might mean concerning *Mark*: did he likewise improvise with his sources? Imagine the ramifications if the Mark whom Matthew and Luke so casually changed had himself casually changed his own sources (which we do not have). Operating as they all did in a climate where historical accuracy was not valued to start with but theological accuracy was, how far have the Gospels removed us from what originally occurred, or was said to have occurred?

Conclusion

The pervasive sadness here is that devoted readers of the New Testament should be cognizant of these many problems, and yet most have no awareness of them. But for Jews to be unaware of them is doubly incomprehensible because these texts have driven so much of Jewish history. For those Christians whose theology bespeaks a sense of ongoing revelation, or those who can see no reason to suspend their thinking faculties, don't these matters call for serious attention purely as a matter of religious integrity?

We have only begun to glimpse the problems that we face with respect to the period during which the New Testament was written. What about the decades before that period: the 20s CE of Jesus' adult life and the 30s, 40s, and 50s of Paul and others? What basics do we need to know concerning the contexts of Jesus in the land of Israel and of Paul in the Diaspora?

Part Two

Basics We Should Know

Prisms for Viewing Early Christianity

The fluidity and complexity of Christianity's emergence are difficult to present, especially within relatively brief confines. Let us begin by gleaning some basic matters from Figure 4.1.

4.1—Christianity's Emergence

In the Land of ISRAEL		In the DIASPORA	
Beginning with Jewish-Christians*		**Beginning with Jewish-Christians and Gentile-Christians***	
Early 30s	Enclaves proliferate (with some elements filtering into the Diaspora)	Early 30s	After persecuting Damascus Christians, Paul joins them in accepting Jesus as the Christ; he commences missionary endeavors
		50s	Paul's **EPISTLES**
62	Execution of James	64?	Paul dies (in Rome?)
66	Jerusalem church disappears		
70	Rome destroys 2nd Temple	72?	"MARK" (written in Rome?)
		85?	"MATTHEW" (in Antioch?)
		94–125?	"LUKE"-ACTS (in Greece?)
		100?	"JOHN" (in Ephesus?)
132–135	Bar Kokhba Revolt		
?		ca. 170	New Testament is coalescing

33

On the left—the land of Israel*. After Jesus died (ca. 30 CE), some of his followers claimed that he was the Messiah* and had been raised from the dead. Among enclaves of such believers, what is often termed the mother "church" emerged in Jerusalem. On the basis of traditions early in Acts, this congregation appears initially to have been headed by Jesus' foremost disciple,* Peter, who was succeeded by Jesus' brother, James. It may be, however, that it was James, not Peter, who headed this church from its inception. As we noted in Chapter 2, Josephus reports that James was executed in 62 CE. With the year 66, when the first Jewish revolt against Rome began, this church fades from our view, but we lack solid evidence as to why—did its congregants flee the Romans, die fighting them, or join the rebels? Or had they simply already begun fading with James' death?[1] With a second, even more intense revolt beginning in 132, we lose track of these early Christians in Galilee as well as in Judea (hence the question mark at the base of that column). No doubt, along the way some of these elements filtered into the Diaspora. But theirs is not a configuration from which modern Christianity arose.

On the right—the Diaspora. Developments here did lead to a Christianity that endured (hence the extending arrow). Looming large here was the figure of Paul, who appears first to have persecuted Damascus Christians but then to have joined them before energetically disseminating his own more profound conception of what the Christian movement should be.

I place within the Diaspora not only Paul's genuine Epistles but also all four Gospels. (Some scholars would place one or more of the Gospels on the *left*—i.e., within the holy land itself.) Although proposals for communities of origin vary, mine (in Fig. 4.1) are not unusual. Nor is my dating the completed works between 72 and 100. Some would place Mark slightly earlier, even just before the Temple's fall; some move Luke-Acts into the second century (a view with which I am sympathetic). The Evangelists' names appear in quotation marks because, as noted in Chapter 3, their identities are unknowable.

One important observation from this chart is that: before the figure of Jesus (from the left) was conveyed by the Evangelists (on the right), his image was filtered through Paul's time and thought, as well as through the broader Diaspora ambience. *This is how the profile of the historical Jesus became transmuted into that of a cosmic Lord, or Christ figure*, more readily grasped by pagan* audiences than by strictly Jewish ones, who had a quite different notion of the expected Messiah. This, then, is one prism for viewing early Christian development.

A second prism refracts matters somewhat differently, although still compatibly with the first. It conceptualizes two contrasting "Configurations" of early Christianity that, throughout this book, we will continue to designate "A" and "B" (Fig. 4.2). The question mark placed between them suggests that there is a difficulty in connecting or even sequencing them.

4.2—Two Basic Configurations

"Configuration A" Christianity
(beginning as a *Jesus* Movement)

Arose in the land of Israel—an outgrowth of a small number of Jews remaining impacted by, and committed to, teachings of Jesus, to their companionship, interactions, and exchanges with him, and to their consequent belief that he was the Messiah. They admitted that he did not conform to the then political expectations for this figure, and at first were demoralized by his crucifixion. But they rebounded through faith that he rose from the dead and would imminently return to complete his mission. Some cadres of this **Jesus Movement** spread into the Diaspora, enduring longer in some areas than others. But fading, Configuration A exerted little impact on the Christianity that endured.

↘   **?**   ↖

"Configuration B" Christianity
(becoming a *Paul* Movement)

Arose primarily in the Diaspora—integrating its early beliefs with antecedent Greco-Roman religious currents that served as a matrix-in-waiting, absorbing and mutating the Jesus figure into a *cosmic Lord*. This Configuration attracted Paul. He deepened it by incorporating motifs derivative from his Judaism (especially atoning sacrifice, or atonement through sacrifice), and sacramental benefits akin to those promised by Mystery cults of dying and rising savior deities (to be detailed later in this chapter). This **Paul Movement** became the nucleus of a Christianity that endured.

Ancients living these parts were not necessarily cognizant of two Configurations, or of belonging to one more than to any other. It is from *our* vantage point that these become discernible and helpful to delineate.

The reason it becomes problematic to sequence Configurations A and B *in that order* is that dimensions of B long preceded even the emergence of A (as we will discuss shortly). Accordingly, we should conceive of them in terms of their *simultaneity*—or, better, their chronological and demographic *overlapping*.

The Rapidity of Christianity's Spread

Prominent in both foregoing prisms is Christianity's expansion. What receptivity toward Configuration B, in particular, facilitated this success?

Syncretism

First there was the syncretism stimulated by Alexander the Great's Greek Empire (beginning in the late fourth century BCE). An unprecedented intermingling of religious beliefs and practices of European, Egyptian, and Asiatic peoples reduced the Mediterranean Sea, metaphorically speaking, to a huge lake. Intensified commerce and personal travel stimulated circulation of ideas so that, eventually, there was nothing unusual about word of new religions spreading—including, in the case of our interest, from the land of Israel into the adjacent and then wider Diaspora.

Along with such news came sagas that aggrandized the fame, words, deeds, and excellences of "lords" of various cults seeking new adherents. These aretalogies—retellings of such virtues designed to inspire awe—at least loosely prepared the ground for the more developed Gospels that, later on, conformed Jesus also to conventional Hellenistic tales of wonder-workers, highlighting their divine origins and births, powers to heal, and springtime resurrections (matching agricultural renewal).

Mysteries

Mystery religions named after their mythological lords (e.g., Mithras, Bacchus, Orpheus, Osiris, Tammuz, Attis, Adonis) promised believers powerful spiritual experiences not obtainable from official public religions. Secret entry rites guaranteed initiates cleansing from personal sin, protection from worldly adversities, salvation from death, and a happy immortality—attainable by undergoing intimate, sacramental reenactments of cyclical deaths and resurrection-rebirths of cultic gods. Two early Christian sacraments so closely resemble rites from the Mysteries as to suggest that Christianity absorbed them.

1. Reminiscent of today's baptism in Christianity was the *initiatory* rite of some Mysteries that required immersion (e.g., "dying by drowning" or "being buried"; cf. Col 2:12) in water or even a deity's blood. Thus began a process by which believers could gain the same image as—and thereby genuine unification with—the cult's lord in his dying and reemergence to life anew. (Pauline Christianity, in adopting and adapting this rite, accelerated unification by adding beforehand incarnation, wherein a spiritual deity assumed human flesh.)

2. Similar to the Eucharist in Christianity was the *recurring* rite among some Mysteries that required regular partaking of a deity's sacrifice through eating and imbibing him, thereby becoming saved* along with him in his death and rising anew (literally becoming what you ate).

It is prudent not to focus solely on the parallels between religions while ignoring their differences, and not to overvalue, or misassess, the parallels to start with. Indeed, it was differences that gave Christianity its competitive edge over the Mysteries. But it was through careful fostering of similarities that Christianity gained the entré to compete with them in the first place.

As one example among many,[2] Mithraism, which came from Persia, extended westward to the area of Tarsus, Paul's native city (in what today is Turkey). Long pre-dating Christianity, it continued as a chief rival until Rome's adoption of Christianity under Emperor Constantine (fourth century). Mithras either was associated with stabbing and killing a bull or, in another strain, became identified with a bull; eating its flesh and drinking its blood were means by which initiates expected to be born again and gain assurance of the eternal life experienced by the deity. While bread and water (cf. wine?) figured in Mithraic ritual, it is debatable to what degree we have here any genuine approximation of Christianity's Eucharist. Following a last supper, so it was claimed, Mithras ascended to heaven and then returned to earth to summon the dead from their graves for last judgment. Christianity, interweaving its Jesus story with such pagan motifs, adopted the even more extraordinary changing of a sacrificial victim from an animal to that of a God-Man, and commenced his story with an incarnation whereby God became that man, and through sacraments led initiates to become one with that God. (Cf. Gal 2:20: "I have been crucified with Christ; it is no longer I who live, but Christ who lives in me.")

Without such core elements, Christianity's spark might never have caught on. In fact, early Church apologists—those who defended the faith—were embarrassed when these parallels were pointed out, and dismissed them at first as Satan's efforts to confuse the Christian faithful

and frustrate attempts to gain new adherents. Later, the Mystery religions were claimed to be God's way of preparing the Gentiles for the final form of his—"Christ's"—sacrifice.

Pre-Christian Gnosticism?

Gnosticism, a collective name for various sects that flourished after Christianity's rise, emphasized the soul's craving to escape entrapment within a material (read *evil*) body and return to its primeval source, the spiritual God of Good. Such reabsorption was achievable if predisposed souls secured proper knowledge (Greek: *gnosis*), which could only be disseminated to them by a superhuman God-sent Redeemer, the primary "aeon" emanating from the spiritual God of Good.

By the second and third centuries, Church writings derided Gnosticism as heretical. We are unsure, however, what form(s) earliest Gnosticism took or whether any of its elements, if they pre-dated Christianity, influenced Christian development.

Certainly during their coexistence, intersections of Christianity and Gnosticism proved problematic for the Church. For if matter was evil, then the spiritual Redeemer sent to this material world could not genuinely take on flesh, experience pain (including crucifixion), and thereby atone for humanity's Sin. Moreover, in Gnosticism Genesis' creator God of this material world was downgraded to some lower being (the "Demiurge"); hence, Jewish scripture was devalued along with him. Would Christianity, then, have to relinquish Jewish scriptural motifs that already punctuated Pauline and Gospel writings?

Did any Evangelists partake of incipient Gnostic schemes precisely to counter them? For example, "And the Word* became flesh and dwelt among us" (Jn 1:14) seems to echo a myth of a God-sent Redeemer descending to deliver the righteous from evil—except here, the Evangelist John insists, the Redeemer genuinely did take on flesh.

Christianity's Advantages over Judaism and over Mysteries

Christianity, still deeply bonded to Judaism, accepted and based itself on the Jewish scriptures, citing these texts to make claims for itself, with Genesis' "in the beginning" ensuring Christianity of ancient lineage and, thereby, authenticity in the Roman Empire. Christianity continued to be Jewish also in taking over completely Judaism's premium on ethical requirements as intrinsic to religion, something largely missing in paganism, and therefore perceived by some Gentiles as uniquely challenging and elevating.

Replicating Judaism's synagogue structure and its networking enabled Christianity to offer a cohesiveness that pagan religions (com-

monly organized as local enclaves) could not match. Moreover, Judaism, at this point in its history, was modeling a creative and successful missionary style that also allowed for attracting and accepting, in a kind of secondary status, Gentiles whom it styled "God-fearers."* These shared the faith, the worship, and the ethical commitments of Judaism but were not obliged to adult male circumcision or to full compliance with the dietary laws, and thus were not full converts. When Christianity emerged, however, it promised Gentiles acceptance as full members while allowing them to bypass the barriers of Jewish dietary laws and circumcision. Through this, *God-fearers became key agents in publicizing Christianity's appeal to pagans.* Christianity was cast as offering a harmonious mix of the high religion of monotheistic Judaism along with eternal life with a loving God to those who simply believed and rendered obedience to basic moral laws—all the while without insisting on conditions that very few Gentiles could accept.

The cosmic profile that Configuration B Christianity accorded to its "Lord" (Fig. 4.2) was familiar to pagans who knew that Osiris, Dionysius, Demeter, and so forth likewise promised initiates escape from worldly troubles and the securing of salvation from death (cf. Phil 3:10f.). Thus Christianity did not offer new goals as much as new ways of achieving basic goals, insisting that it alone would succeed, or certainly exceed the performance of others[3]—and without the exorbitant initiation fees that some Mysteries demanded. Further, it audaciously claimed its cult deity to be the only God, directly conflicting with polytheism but powerfully appealing to some pagans for that very reason. Whereas some cultic lords were men who became gods, Pauline Christianity added another half-cycle, claiming that, first, the deity had become man. Moreover, this "Christ" had died and been resurrected not in some remote time and unknown place but recently enough (when Paul was writing) that there were still living witnesses to him, even family members, from within the land of Israel.

In sum, then, Christianity succeeded because it concentrated on addressing religious needs raised by the competition, sometimes even employing the identical terms but framing its promises in more compelling ways. In these respects, Christianity charged "a less arduous entry-fee for the relatively similar salvation."[4]

In discussing how Christianity was refracted through the suggested prisms, have we gotten ahead of ourselves, since we have yet to even address the historical Jesus and Paul? But many of the phenomena described so far pre-dated Jesus and Paul, so we actually have been proceeding in proper chronological order. We turn now to Jesus in his setting in the land of Israel and to Paul in his context in the Diaspora.

Jesus and His Setting in the Land of Israel

We begin this chapter by identifying those basic contextual factors—places, institutions, societal groupings—that are necessary to know in any quest to define the historical Jesus. The descriptions that follow are narrowly tailored to what is most pertinent for New Testament study.

Geographical Considerations

When Herod the Great, Rome's puppet king, died in 4 BCE, his territory was parceled out among three sons. We will concern ourselves primarily with the areas of Galilee and Judea, and with Samaria, which was ruled in conjunction with Judea (see Fig. 5.1).

> *Galilee,* a northern region, which fell to the son named Herod Antipas, was site to Jesus' native town of Nazareth as well as others that he frequented (Capernaum, Bethsaida, Cana, etc.). Here lay the Sea of Galilee that he traversed, where the fishermen among his inner circle had earned their livelihood. Eleven of his twelve disciples appear to have been Galilean (Judas Iscariot was probably Judean). Near the end of Jesus' ministry, his Galilean origin likely heightened whatever suspicions Judean authorities harbored about him because Galilee was reputed to be a hotbed of dissent. *If* they chose to question him concerning whether they should pay taxes to Caesar (Mk 12:13ff. & parr), they may well have had in mind a tax revolt, in 6 CE, described in Josephus as led by a notorious "Judas of Galilee."[1] *If,* after Jesus' arrest, his disciple Peter denied knowing him, those accusing him may have detected his Galilean accent (Mk 14:70 & parr). The Gospels of Mark and Matthew present Galilee as the place to which Jesus' followers fled after his arrest in Judea and where he was expected to appear to them after his resurrection.

5.1—*The Land of Israel in the Time of Jesus*

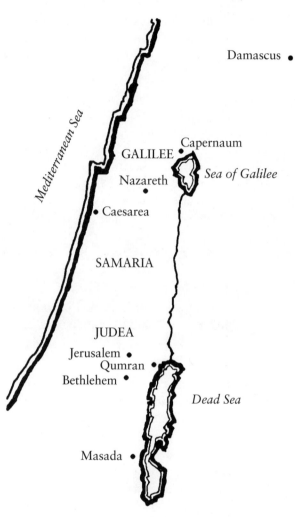

Judea, a region to the south and the location of Bethlehem, was most importantly the site of Jerusalem, with its Temple and sacrificial cult. Along with Samaria, it was ruled by Archelaus, another of Herod the Great's sons. But unlike Galilee, it came under direct Roman control in 6 CE when Archelaus was deposed in favor of Rome's own appointee as governor.[2] A series of fourteen such officials ruled Judea for most of the years from 6 CE until the Jewish revolt against Rome began in 66. The fifth of these, the prefect[3] Pontius Pilate, is mentioned in the Gospels as instrumental in Jesus' crucifixion. His rule, from 26 into 37, constitutes our basis for saying that Jesus' death occurred sometime in the early 30s (we will say 30, for convenience). Stationed at the coastal

city of Caesarea Maritima, Pilate customarily came to Jerusalem with military reinforcements for Temple pilgrimage festivals, when swellings of population might jeopardize order. One such Passover season brought Jesus' "triumphal" entry to Jerusalem (on what Christians today term "Palm Sunday"), setting the stage for his Passion.*

Samaria lay between Galilee and Judea, and along with Judea it was subject to rule first by Archelaus and then by the sequence of Roman governors. A geographical entity called "Samaria" had constituted ancient Israel's northern kingdom and was captured (722 BCE) by Assyria, which deported many natives and replaced them with Assyrian stock. This led Judeans to disparage Samaritans as not purely Jewish. As John 4:9 relates, "Jews have no dealings with Samaritans" (cf. Lk 9:53); also, in John 8:48, Jesus is asked if he is a "Samaritan" and has a "demon." Jesus' parable of the *Good* Samaritan (Lk 10:30ff.) betrays this same tension. While Samaria provided a direct route between Galilee and Judea, many avoided the area as unsafe.

The Religio-Political Context (Pre-70 CE)

In this discussion we will refer to the shaded portions, columns D and E, of Figure 5.2—"Institutions" and "Groupings."[4]

Institutions

Temple. King Solomon built the original Jerusalem Temple (tenth century BCE), which Babylonia destroyed (586 BCE). It was the Second Temple, completed around 516 BCE and subsequently enlarged, that Rome burned in 70 CE. The temple was the hub of Judea's religious observance, government, and economy, and the upper echelons of Judea's power structure (the priesthood and Sadducees) depended on it for their economic well-being and political status. It also attracted masses of Jewish pilgrims during the three festivals mandated by the Torah (first segment of the *Tanakh**)—*Pesach*/Passover (early spring); *Shavuot*/Weeks (late spring; cf. Pentecost in Acts 2:1); and *Sukkot*/Tabernacles (early fall).

Sanhedrin. Greek sources (Josephus, the Gospels, Acts) deem the kind of Sanhedrin mentioned in the New Testament an ad hoc privy council, presided over by the high priest. Despite the impression given by the New Testament, however, it was considered lawfully convened only if approved by the local Roman prefect. It dealt with political crimes, particularly sedition, and essentially rubber-stamped the convener's wishes. That Mark relates a Sanhedrin trial for Jesus does not establish that Jesus actually underwent one (see Chap. 12).

5.2—Highlights of the Period of the Second Temple in Judea

A	B	C	D	E				
Dates	Ruling Power	Local Ruler	INSTITUTIONS	GROUPINGS				
				1	2	3	4	5
586–538	Babylonian Exile							
538–333	Persian Rule		S E C O N D T E M P L E	P H A R I S E E S / S c r i b e s	P r i e s t h o o d / S A D D U C E E S	Q u m r a n / E s s e n e s	A C T I V I S T S	C H R I S T I A N S
333–142	Greek Rule							
142–63	Independence	Hasmoneans	S A N H E D R I N					
63–	Roman Rule		S Y N A G O G U E					
37–4		Herod						
4		Archelaus	▼ ▼ ▼					
- - - -	- 0 -							
6		# 1						
		# 2						
		# 3						
		# 4						
		# 5						
		# 6						
		# 7				▼		
41–44		Agrippa I			▼	▼	▼	
		# 8						
		# 9						
		# 10						
		# 11						
		# 12						
		# 13						
66		# 14						
70			▼	▼				▼
80		Gamaliel II	Sanhedrin reconstituted	Rabbis				
132–135		Bar Kokhba						

By contrast, Hebrew/Aramaic sources (rabbinic literature) apply the name "Sanhedrin" to another, later court system that differs in its leaders, members, types of cases addressed, and procedures. We must be careful not to confuse this rabbinic system with the Gospel Sanhedrin.

Synagogue. Numerous even before the Temple's destruction, synagogues were places where Jews gathered to hear scripture read and interpreted and to offer prayers. Patterns of the synagogue's calendar and liturgy became prototypical for early churches. Synagogal networks (in the Diaspora as well) played critical roles in Christianity's spread (see Chaps. 4 and 6). Practices of the synagogue that the Evangelists present in conjunction with Jesus, Paul, and their early followers may reflect, instead, practices characterizing the writers' day.

Groupings

We begin by looking at four "philosophies" as sequenced by the first-century Jewish historian, Josephus,[5] and then add other groups mentioned by the Evangelists. (Note that most of the population belonged to none of these groupings that follow.)

Pharisees. Defining "Pharisees" is daunting because writings that mention them (Josephus, Paul's Epistles, the Gospels, rabbinic literature) reflect different biases, time frames, and geographies, and "pharisee" in rabbinic literature need not always refer to this group.[6] We do best by understanding the *Gospel* Pharisees as an emerging scholar class,[7] forerunners of the rabbis, and progressive "loose constructionists"— that is, they devised oral interpretations beyond the written Torah text (what Paul, in Gal 1:14, calls "the traditions of my fathers," and Mark, in 7:5, "the tradition of the elders"). This augmenting of understandings of scripture enhanced the Torah's applicability to changing times.[8] Jesus himself shared Pharisaic traits *(italicized)*: preaching *parables* about God's coming *Kingdom*, emphasizing *repentance*, and deeming the *Shema* (Deut 6:4ff.) his fundamental teaching (Mk 12:28ff.). The Pharisees' major New Testament distinctiveness is belief in *resurrection* (Acts 23:6:ff.). The Talmud's* Pharisee-Sadducee debates so resemble Jesus' dispute with Sadducees over resurrection (Mk 12:18ff. & parr) as to suggest that Jesus here was cast in the Pharisees' role. Their active Diaspora *proselytizing* (Mt 23:15) was replicated and expanded by Christianity itself. Paul claims Pharisaic proficiency from his Diaspora training (Gal 1:14; Phil 3:5). It is most important to understand that the Evangelists' bias against the Pharisees (e.g., calling them "hypocrites") *reflects not sentiments of Jesus—most likely a Pharisee himself—but solely those of the post-70 Gospel writers themselves.*

Sadducees. Collaborative with foreign rulers, Sadducees were Hellenized Jewish aristocrats who were committed to Temple-centered Judaism and legal interpretation that enhanced the prestige and wealth of the priestly cult. Most high priests were drawn from a select few Sadducean families. As strict constructionists regarding the Torah, they rejected "new" ideas of Pharisaic oral law, especially resurrection, which they denied could be proven from the Torah.[9] With the Temple's destruction, their prominence waned.

Essenes. Not mentioned in the New Testament, the Essenes lived in urban or wilderness enclaves.[10] Presumably, their contingent at Qumran (Fig. 5.1) left us the Dead Sea Scrolls. Like Christians, Essenes viewed themselves as a Jewish eschatological* community, fulfilling scriptural predictions and harboring messianic expectations (but we should also note their substantial differences from early Christians[11]). Those at Qumran disappeared in 68 CE, probably fleeing Roman forces or dying while fighting them, or joining rebels elsewhere.

Activists. For his Greco-Roman readership, Josephus blames this "Fourth Philosophy" of patriot bandit coalitions ("Sicarii," "Zealots," etc.) for the disastrous revolt against Rome (66–73 CE). This element—professing devotion to God through violent nationalism—mushroomed from the 50s into the 60s but hearkened back to forerunners (e.g., the infamous Judas of Galilee, noted earlier). Standard Roman punishment for such subversives was crucifixion (e.g., Judas of Galilee's sons were crucified by the Roman governor Tiberius Alexander[12]). Thus we could surmise from the report that Jesus was crucified that he himself was regarded by the Roman government as such a rebel.

Chief Priests, Elders, Herodians, Scribes. These groups, in the Gospels, are mentioned amorphously. "Chief priests" and "elders" we may take generically. "Herodians" appear to have been supporters in Herod Antipas' court in Galilee and cooperative with Rome. "Scribes" are the most frequently appearing group in the earliest Gospel, Mark. What "scribe" means in other literatures (copyist, cleric, etc.) should be irrelevant to us here, because in the Gospels, in my view, we should process "scribes" as equivalent to "Pharisees" due to a Marcan error. He derived "Pharisees" from a source dealing with Galilee; but that same element was called "scribes" in two other Marcan sources, likely earlier in date, that dealt with Judea. Not realizing their equivalence, Mark misunderstood this one element as, instead, two distinct groups. Matthew and Luke, wholly dependent on Mark here, cannot discover what distinguished scribes from Pharisees because it is not evident from Mark whether *anything* did (hence, Mt 23's peculiar and repeated bracketing of "scribes, Pharisees, hypocrites!" and his occasional substitution of

Pharisees where Mark has scribes[13]). This realization by us should at the least temper the common surprise that "Pharisees" are absent from Mark's Passion Narrative, since, after all, "scribes" *are* present."

Apocalypticism: a Mind-set Rather Than a Group

"Apocalyptists,"* as used here, shared *activists'* hopes for Rome's overthrow but left the implementation of this to God. Apocalyptist sentiments cut across society—except, notably, among elements that supported the status quo (e.g., Sadducees, chief priests, and Herodians). A continuum of apocalyptist beliefs ranged from political to transcendental. It is best to envision most such adherents as falling between the extremes—that is, somewhere down the middle of Figure 5.3—with their conceptions of a Messiah varying accordingly.

5.3—A Continuum of the Apocalyptic Mind-set	
POLITICALLY Conceived	**TRANSCENDENTALLY** Conceived
Most ▼	
The **arena** conceived is *this*-worldly: God assumes rule over Rome *without* the present order dissolved ←→ ←→	The **arena** conceived is *next*-worldly: God assumes rule *with* the present order dissolved
The **scope of concerns** is *exclusivistic nationalism* aiming to secure Israel's independence and power ←→	The **scope of concerns** is *universalistic*: Gentiles also are beneficiaries of God's plan
The **world to come** betokens *material* prosperity and bliss *on earth* (at least in Israel) ←→	The **world to come** emphasizes *spiritual* ascendancy and bliss *in heaven*
The **antagonists**: *Israel vs. Rome* ←→	The **antagonists**: *God vs. supernatural powers of evil* (Satan and his hosts)
The **Messiah**: an earthly *human* temporal ruler in Israel (likely a Davidic descendant); he will annihilate Israel's enemies or proclaim God's doing so imminently ←→	The **Messiah**: a transcendent (heavenly, even preexistent) being, recalling Daniel 7:13's "Son of man"*

Most important to note is that apocalyptism and Pharisaism were compatible; both could be espoused by the same persons. Indeed, Josephus relates that, aside from their violence, the *activists* "agree in all ... things with Pharisaic notions."[14] All the more so, then, could the less radical *apocalyptists* do likewise. Jesus' preaching of an imminent coming of God's Kingdom suggests that "apocalyptic Pharisee" is the most appropriate way to designate him within the first-century landscape (see my commentary on Figure 5.5, below).

Integrating These Elements
Three Tiers of Authority in Pre-70 Judea
Josephus schematizes authority in early first-century Judea into three tiers: (I) the Roman emperor (in our case, Tiberius), even if he was never physically present; (II) the local Roman governor (in our case, Pilate); and (III) the high priest (in our case, Caiaphas). Each lower figure was directly accountable to whoever ranked directly above. Figure 5.4 diagrams these tiers from Jesus' ministry (ca. 30) until the Jewish revolt (66).

5.4—*Three Tiers of Authority in Judea (Inclusive of the Period 30–66)*		
Tier I Emperor	Tiberius / 14–37	Caligula, 37–41; Claudius, 41–54; Nero, 54–68
Tier II Roman Governor	Pilate / 26–37	9 more Governors before the Great Revolt, in 66
Tier III High Priest	Caiaphas / 18–37	15 more High Priests before the Temple's fall, in 70

Even though the governor not only outranked the high priest but could also appoint or dismiss him, *the Gospels obscure this reality*. In their portrayal, it is not Caiaphas who defers to Pilate but vice versa. Pertinent to us is the extraordinary length of Caiaphas' partnership with Pilate, whose approximately 11-year rule (26–37) compared to a meager 3.5 average for the other thirteen governors. Well preceding and also outlasting Pilate was Caiaphas' approximately 19-year tenure (18–37), compared to a scant 3.3 average for the other last twenty-seven high priests.[15] Surely, then, Caiaphas could have remained in office for so long only if he was dutifully subservient to whatever Roman governors required of him. Pilate's pejorative portrait in other sources[16] signals how the Gospels whitewash him, transferring *his* brutality to Caiaphas—a reversal that has fomented anti-Judaism ever since (particularly characterizations of Caiaphas in Passion plays and films; see Chap. 23).

Diagraming Judean Society in Jesus' Day

Figure 5.5, obviously set in symbols, is meant to illustrate the simultaneous operation of two different systems, Roman and Jewish.[17] These are shown separated by a "moat" [~ ~ ~] to symbolize Rome's safeguards against Jewish trespass.

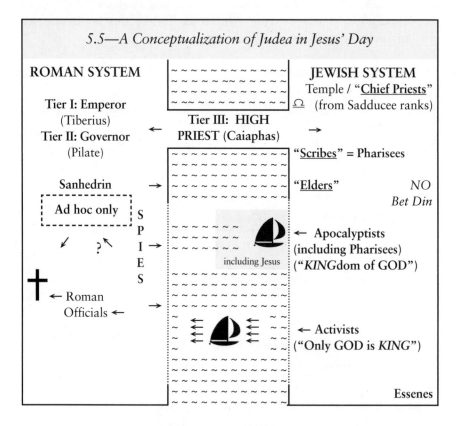

Within the Roman system, on the left, are its Tier I and II officials and their supporting spies overlooking the moat. The Sanhedrin is here ad hoc, convened rarely and only by order or consent of the governor (II) who would then assign the high priest (III) to preside over it. The Jewish system, across the moat, encompasses the Temple (with its "chief priests") along with "scribes" (i.e., Pharisees), "elders," apocalyptists, and activists (with Essenes on society's fringe). The sole bridge between the two systems, with a foot in each camp, is the high priest, leader of the Jewish system and occupying Tier III in the Roman system. He is excellently positioned (along with Rome's spies) to notice any untoward goings-on in the moat and to report them immediately to the Roman governor.

Most pertinent for our discussion are the apocalyptists, whose vessel—while always in the moat—was stationary because they saw Rome's overthrow and the coming Kingdom as God's task, not theirs. Manning the other vessel, however, and always "on the move" in trespass mode, were activists whose more assertive rallying cry (as we learn from Josephus) was essentially that "only God is King" or "we have no King but God."[18] While the respective dangers to Rome posed by these two mindsets were hardly comparable, platforms such as "*King*dom of God" and "Only God is *King*" would not seem readily distinguishable to Rome, especially when the preaching of a particularly charismatic apocalyptist, such as Jesus, would appear to reinforce aspects of the activists' cause. That persons from *both* vessels, then, could be rounded up and sent to the cross is not difficult to imagine.

There are three curiosities in the diagram: First, the question mark leading toward the ad hoc Sanhedrin in the Roman system is meant to indicate that consignment to the cross could be effected by Roman officialdom without a Sanhedrin trial; otherwise, consider the sheer volume of court sessions requiring schedule! Second, in imaging the personnel required to people this ad hoc (and essentially kangaroo) court, *Mark* imports elements from the right side (the Jewish religious system) to function under the aegis of the Roman political system for this kind of service only. Thus do "chief priests with the elders and scribes" (Mk 14:53) cross over the moat for a temporary period (see especially Fig. 12.4). Third, the reason why there is no Talmudic (see Rabbinic Literature*) "Sanhedrin" shown on the Jewish side of the diagram is that we lack proof that such an institution yet existed by Jesus' day (nor are we certain, even later on, whether and how this *bet din*—literally, "House of Justice"—originated or functioned). Hence the common exercise of heaping up discrepancies between rabbinic capital procedures detailed in the Talmud and the Gospels' reportage of Jesus' trial is (and this literally cannot be stressed enough) entirely irrelevant. Much confusion arises here because, later on, rabbinic literature uses "Sanhedrin" as synonymous with *bet din*, but only well after the position of high priest became dissolved when the Temple fell.[19]

The Significance of Post-70 Developments

Because the Gospels were produced post-70, this later period filtered and conditioned how Jesus was "remembered." It is helpful, then, to understand why the Temple's fall constituted such a watershed for Jews, Romans, and Christians.

> *For Jews.* Figure 5.6 reveals which institutions and groupings failed to survive the Temple's fall, and which ones survived as transformed, reconstituted, replaced, and so on:

5.6—The Temple's Fall as a Watershed for Jews

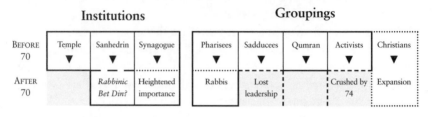

	Institutions			Groupings				
BEFORE 70	Temple ▼	Sanhedrin ▼	Synagogue ▼	Pharisees ▼	Sadducees ▼	Qumran ▼	Activists ▼	Christians ▼
AFTER 70		*Rabbinic Bet Din?*	Heightened importance	Rabbis	Lost leadership		Crushed by 74	Expansion

With the Sanhedrin (under the Roman system, in Fig. 5.5) ended, a rabbinic *bet din* began *sometime* thereafter. Synagogues, long extant, now assumed additional religious functions. Pharisees—soon, the rabbis—were the sole surviving element with whom Rome could replace priestly/Sadducean leaders who had failed to prevent rebellion. (The latter's positions, moreover—dependent on the Temple—were by now eviscerated.) Qumran was vacated (around 68). Activists at Masada were subdued (around 73). A transcending concern was that the very fabric of Jewish observance—even for Diaspora Jews—changed radically with the Temple's fall, especially because festivals for which the Torah prescribed Temple offerings now required significant reworking. (Concerning Passover, and the *post*-70 origins of the rudimentary seder, see Chap. 10.)

For Romans. The Jewish revolt continued long enough to portend danger for Rome from the Empire's inveterate enemy, Parthia (poised to invade Rome's eastern provinces in ostensible support of Jewish insurgents). Such embarrassment for Rome so lingered that, even after the rebels were subdued and their Temple destroyed, it was still necessary to stage in Rome itself pageantry marching Judean captives through the streets and displaying the Temple's captured treasures—its seven-branched lampstand, golden table of shewbread, and others—and later, in 81, sculpting images of these on Rome's Arch of Titus.

For Christians. Politically, Temple treasures, thus displayed, symbolized Judaism as a seditious cult. Because the Temple was inseparably linked to Christians' own faith, for self-protection Christians now had to distance themselves from Jews. *This is why Jesus' crucifixion became reformulated as having been driven by Jews, now cast as common enemies of Rome and Christians alike.* Theologically, the Temple's destruction signaled to some Christians that they had replaced the Jews as God's chosen, and New Testament texts, such as those in Figure 5.7, highlighted this idea.

5.7—How Christian Theology Processed the Temple's Fall

Mk 15:37ff. Jesus ... breathed his last. And the curtain of the temple was torn in two.

> [Comment: This curtain was penetrated by the high priest solely on the Day of Atonement (Yom Kippur) so he could effect expiation for the sins of the people. Now Jesus' expiration effected this atonement, for all time ending any need for the Temple, not to mention for the curtain.]

Mt 27:24f. Pilate ... washed his hands ... saying, "I am innocent of this man's blood...." And all the people answered, "His blood be on us and on our children!"

> [Comment: This is Matthew's theological justification, in the 80s, for the Temple's fall in 70.]

I Thes 2:13ff. The Jews ... killed ... the Lord Jesus.... God's wrath has come upon them at last!

> [Comment: The "wrath" refers to the Temple's fall. I consider this passage added by a post-Pauline hand—see Chap. 11.]

Heb 9:11ff. Christ ... entered once for all ... into the Holy Place, taking not ... blood of goats and calves but his own blood ... securing an eternal redemption.

> [Comment: As both perfect high priest and perfect sacrifice, Christ replaces the Temple.]

Problems in Reconstructing the Historical Jesus

Engaging the New Testament (our goal) is different from engaging Jesus. But we need to stake out some position on the Jesus figure presupposed in upcoming chapters. That I have already stated that I believe Jesus was an apocalyptic Pharisee (Fig. 5.5) does not discharge me of a more important responsibility: the need to stress that there are too many variables at play for anyone to define the historical Jesus with confidence. As a corollary, the breadth of New Testament scholarship warrants great respect, and should engender among scholars and lay readers much humility.

Several Quests

Over the past 200 years, brilliant minds have refined methods to determine who the historical Jesus was, only to see findings by one generation of scholars significantly modified, even overturned, by some succeeding enterprise. That "quests for the historical Jesus"—spurts of research extending decades at a time—are numbered (we are now ending, or in my view are now beyond, the third such quest) reveals that interim periods are essentially calls for "time-out," for giving up the venture altogether, or possibly for reversions to earlier conventional views.

Creditable (though not uniformly credible) efforts have been marshaled to show Jesus as a pacifist *or* militant, a prophet, reformer, liberator, apocalyptist, Pharisee (I combine these last two), Essene, magician, charismatic, healer/exorcist, cynic-philosopher, savior, or even pure myth. And, to an extent, there is a peculiar but true tendency for different generations of researchers to discern Jesus more as *they* are than as he was (commonly likened to peering down a well at the "person below"—who is merely our own, self-image reflected).[20]

The Gospels present a vast smorgasbord of contrasting "data." Depending on how we array whatever passages we select, different Jesus profiles may be constructed. And since the Gospels also reflect Church and editorial interests that overlay the original Jesus figure, it is as if multiple Jesuses are projected simultaneously on the same screen—rendering it impossible to discern and retrieve, with any certainty, the original. Add to these the many "problem areas" and "dis-orders" listed in Chapter 3—along with ongoing disagreements as to how best to resolve the Synoptic Problem*—and we may realize why knowledgeable New Testament readers can no longer blithely accept Gospel reportage at face value.

Formulating "Criteria"

Such frustration has spawned the creation of "criteria" for isolating sayings and acts that are authentic to Jesus. But respect even for these criteria is mixed, especially when we notice that some that were once enthusiastically touted command less favor today—meaning that the same fate may befall those criteria that are currently in vogue. Also, while some scholars view these criteria simply as potentially helpful guideposts, others accept them as a new fundamentalism of sorts. Similarly disturbing is the opposite tendency—readily dismissing a criterion when it points to some unwanted conclusion. Three well-known criteria are:

> 1. The Criterion of *Multiple Attestation*. This reasons that sayings or recountings concerning Jesus are more likely genuinely to extend back to him if we find them preserved in multiple sources that do not depend on

one another. Jesus' opposition to divorce, for instance, is found in Mark, Q, and Paul.[21] Yet the parable of the Good Samaritan, which is among those teachings most widely accepted as authentic to Jesus, appears solely in Luke (10:30ff.), thereby failing the Multiple Attestation test. (Presumably, it fares better with other criteria.)

2. The Criterion of *Embarrassment*. This reasons that New Testament materials about Jesus that are contrary to Church interests, yet still not suppressed, must be genuinely traceable to him. For example, that Jesus had siblings (Mk 6:3 & par) who are nowhere specified as *younger* "embarrasses" the virginal conception stories as later additions (unless we find some alternative way of defining "sibling," e.g., step-sibling or cousin). Or references to Jesus of Nazareth are authentic because they "embarrass" traditions that say he was born in—and should be known as "of"—Bethlehem, King David's birthplace. By this reasoning, Judas' betrayal of Jesus should also be historically true, casting as it does aspersions both on Jesus' poor judgment in selecting Judas as well as Jesus' inability later to reform him. In Chapter 15, however, I argue that Judas' betrayal of Jesus never occurred—that it fictionally arose during the 60s when Christians feared being *betrayed* to Rome by one another—so that, if I am correct, we see how the criterion of Embarrassment can lead us astray.

3. The Criterion of *Dissimilarity*. This reasons that words or acts are correctly ascribed to Jesus if they differ both from the Judaism of his day and also from early Church interests. "Love your neighbor," for example, would not be uniquely Jesus (appearing already in Lev 19:18), but "Love your enemies" could well qualify because it serves no Church interest and does not match Jewish ethics. Some ultra-skeptical scholars believe that the sole Marcan teaching that is most likely authentic to Jesus begins, "Render to Caesar the things that are Caesar's" (12:17 & parr). While there may be some basis for believing this,[22] such an apparent affirmation of loyalty to Caesar seems congruent with Church interests in warding off Roman persecution, so how, then, does this pass the criterion of Dissimilarity after all?

Upon further reflection, how can "uniqueness" be proclaimed unless we have access to the totality of first-century Jewish and Christian sources so as to assure ourselves that none of Jesus' contemporaries likewise taught what we have determined as solely *his*?[23] Yet we possess no more than a fraction of these needed materials. Further, efforts to isolate Jesus' uniqueness are questionable to begin with if they might obscure his image as an *integrated* person. It is simply not sensible to believe that persons are chiefly characterized by differences from their context and

heritage, especially when Jesus' uniqueness may very well have been conditioned by what was Jewish about him. Some scholars think that once we identify his uniqueness, we can then "add back to him" his non-unique Jewish teachings through some criterion of *Coherence*, and thereby achieve a more fully balanced figure. Such a "vexing problem [of] how we move beyond this minimum to include material that is not distinctive"[24] cannot be resolved, however, because scholars will never agree on what "coheres" with the uniqueness we may think we have established. (Of course, even agreement by scholars would not guarantee correctness concerning first-century realities.)

Which Starting Point: Sayings or Acts?

Since quests for Jesus seem destined to continue no matter what the obstacles, it becomes fundamentally important to decide whether to begin by trying to isolate his genuine sayings, and predicating thereon our selection of his genuine acts, or vice versa.

Jesus' Sayings First?

The attempt to isolate Jesus' sayings is by now a path so well-trod that, without new directions to pursue, we are stymied. This breeds a kind of desperation to devise ever more novel experiments in areas not particularly well explored before (recently, e.g., analysis of apocryphal gospels[25]; and stratifying "Q" into chronological layers[26]). But if the only new experiments possible are destined to be ever more speculative, it could very well signal that scholars are closing in on (or already have entered) their next interim "time-out."

Moreover, attempting to isolate Jesus' genuine sayings is tantamount to grabbing hold of the "wrong end of the stick." What happens if the Jesus profile we thereby distill is one that is woefully implausible for someone consigned to crucifixion? We will then have painted ourselves into a corner, with the only possible means of extrication some unconvincing reason for his arrest—was he, for example, a public nuisance, or someone who was arrested by the sheer happenstance of being caught up in the wrong crowd and at the wrong place and time? How then would the crucifixion of such an improbable candidate fit in with the placard on Jesus' cross claiming that he aspired to be "The King of the Jews," connoting sedition—or will that placard, too, be a casualty of the approach of starting with Jesus' sayings (i.e., if the Jesus we reconstruct does not match the charge on the placard, then we should jettison the placard as well)?

Would it be more advisable, then, given all these difficulties with isolating Jesus' sayings, to start instead with the act that he was crucified and then work backwards?

Jesus' Acts First?

Though I lack confidence in this option too—first, isolating Jesus' genuine acts, and then assigning to him teachings that appear consistent with them—I find it the preferable of the two options, provided that we do indeed stipulate as a first "act" that Jesus was crucified. A second act could then be the placard on his cross, alleging of him (fairly or otherwise) that he claimed that he was or that he aspired to be—or that others claimed that he was or aspired to be—"The King of the Jews." Such a placard signaled sedition. As for why Jesus might have been so designated, it could have been sufficient if he told parables of the coming of a Kingdom of God and hinted at his own possibly *royal* role within it. Meanwhile, the wording, "The King of the Jews," checks out as formulated from Rome's perspective (since Jews would use "King of Israel"[27]). Posting the accusation was a Roman deterrent lest others contemplate the same crime. Also, the Gospel declaration that the placard was posted in the public domain—where it would be witnessed—enhances likelihood of its historicity (cf. 1 Macc 14:27ff.).

A close third act could be whatever Jesus had said or done that resulted in his being consigned to the cross—most likely, some act or perceived calumny involving the Temple, since this matter surfaces far too frequently, especially in our earliest Gospel, to be peripheral let alone coincidental. In Figure 5.8 we see how the Evangelists' struggles to mitigate, deny, or at least reinterpret this Temple act or related imprecations suggest that Jesus must indeed have committed some major trespass involving the Temple. The dismissal that Jesus merely "cleansed" the Temple (of "money-changers," etc.) could be a later Church device to dilute, even camouflage, the true militance of Jesus' actual deed (see Chap. 11). This approach in effect invokes, as indispensable, some criterion of *Sufficient Alienation*—that is, given Jesus' crucifixion, what act by him was sufficiently alienating as to provoke those who had the power to execute him actually to do so?

Thereafter, additional acts can be conjectured as consistent with the first three, albeit here only with rapidly deteriorating confidence. For example, Jesus' staging and celebrating a Last Supper as his anticipation of a coming messianic banquet; or, consistent with accusations that he aspired to kingship, his entry into Jerusalem riding on an ass as if to fulfil Zechariah 9:9's "humble king" prediction—which the Church then embellished with Jewish scriptural imagery drawn from the ancient acclamation of Jehu as king.[28]

It would only be in the light of such acts that sayings (ascribed to Jesus) consistent with them might then be considered. As an example, if

	5.8—Frequent Surfacings of the Temple Accusation
Mk 11:15 & parr	He ... began to drive out those who sold and ... bought in the ***temple,*** and he overturned the tables of the money-changers....
Mk 13:1ff. & parr	As he came out of the ***temple,*** one of his disciples said..., "Look ... what wonderful ... buildings!" ... Jesus said ... " ... There will not be left ... one stone upon another ... not ... thrown down."
Mk 14:57f. & par	Some ... bore *false* witness..., "We heard him say, 'I will destroy this ***temple*** ... made with hands, and in three days ... build another, not made with hands.'"
Mk 15:29 & par	Those who passed by derided him, wagging their heads ..., "... You who would destroy the ***temple*** and build it in three days, save yourself ... come down from the cross!"
Jn 2:19ff.	"Destroy this ***temple,*** and in three days I will raise it up." ... But he spoke of the ***temple*** of his body.

Jesus meant his overturning of Temple furniture to symbolize the over-turning of the current world order,[29] it could open the way for accept-ing, as genuinely by Jesus, teachings of an imminent new "Kingdom." This would indeed make him an apocalyptic Pharisee (without necessar-ily requiring our acceptance of "Son of man"* texts as having genuinely been recited by Jesus himself[30]). Entry to this Kingdom would then de-pend on applicants accepting startling new behavioral concepts of social interrelationship, as conveyed by the underlying nucleus of certain of Jesus' parables—ideas so provocative as to rivet listeners' attention as they awaited Jesus' stinging "punch lines" that defined in radically new ways what it meant to be truly righteous.[31]

Closing

While I am not optimistic about recovering the historical Jesus, here at least are the broad contours of the Jesus whom I will presuppose throughout the rest of this book (Chap. 11 offers further embellishment).

- Jesus was a Jew, as were his followers. He did not found Christianity, a later movement that traces its origins to him.

- Jesus behaved as a Jew. Christianity's fundamental break with Jewish Law should be attributed to Paul, though Jesus may have disputed with fellow Jews on particular legal issues or on the proper emphases of legal observance (see Chap. 7).

- Jesus was a great teacher of Jewish ethics, in some ways perhaps akin to a Hebrew prophet, but with exceedingly unusual parables (presuming that we can isolate their core materials from later Church accretions).

- It may have been traditions that the historical Jesus frequented the company of "sinners" that became transmuted, eventually, into the notion that he died to atone for humanity's sins.

- Unlike impressions forthcoming from the Gospels, Jesus was influenced by his times; it was not simply his times that were influenced by him.

- Jesus may have felt a personal mission (even a messianic one) that was generated by his conviction that the end of the world order was imminent—hence his fervor to alert others to God's coming Kingdom—but Jesus did not imagine himself divine or as Daniel's supra-human "Son of man."

- He was not the Messiah because he did not bring about independence for the land of Israel from Roman oppression.

- The charges on which Jesus was arrested were political. It's possible that his preaching of God's coming Kingdom was construed as a threat to overthrow the Roman establishment along with its appointee, the high priest Caiaphas (and other pro-Roman elements within the Jewish priestly hierarchy).

- Jesus was rounded up and arrested just like other figures who were similarly perceived (Fig. 5.5), and he was executed in a process whose underlying authority derived ultimately from Rome.

Paul in His Diaspora Context

Paul was a most unconventional man who played an uncommon role in a faraway world. Thus he is a person who is very difficult to comprehend. For that reason, we hardly do him justice when our primary image of him is simply of his famous conversion on the "road to Damascus," especially when even his own testimony implicitly denies that any such occurrence transpired. (Only the book of Acts reports—invents, actually—this episode.) The treatment that Paul does warrant requires due and methodical contemplation of the complex role he played in Christianity's development and expansion. Let us begin, then, by considering how Christian missionaries before him fared—especially those whom, early on, Paul himself had persecuted!

Synagogue Receptivity to Christian Missionaries

The first Christian proselytizers must have viewed synagogues as the most natural and potentially receptive forum for their message—all the more so if the missionaries themselves once had been, or still were, synagogue members or had acquaintances who were. Here, the Pharisaic components of their preachings *(italicized)* would have required no tedious explanation: the *Messiah* has come in the person of Jesus of Nazareth, who was crucified but also *resurrected*, had now appeared to followers, and soon would return to implement his promised *Kingdom of God*. If *Jewish scriptures* could then be *expounded* to this same novel effect, so much the better. But did synagogue audiences actually prove receptive?

Late Reportage by the Evangelists

Some New Testament sources, ostensibly bearing on this question, may fail to pass muster because they primarily reflect not the earlier

times they purport to describe but, instead, only circumstances of their own later day. Acts' opening chapters, for example, emphasize Jews' early receptivity to Christianity; its middle chapters their intensifying resistance (sometimes in synagogues); and its later chapters their outright rejection of it.[1] Did matters actually progress in this fashion? Possibly, especially since, as Christianity increasingly took on the trappings of Mystery cults, Jews who may have been interested initially now became increasingly disaffected, even alienated. But more likely what we see in Acts is Luke's superimposition of his own grand theological scheme, for he is trying to account for how the ranks of a Christianity that he insists extended authentic Judaism paradoxically turned out to be overwhelmingly Gentile by his day (see Chap. 17).

Luke's Gospel, meanwhile, relates how Jesus was rejected in his hometown synagogue at Nazareth (4:16ff.). This episode would be relevant to our discussion only if Jesus' reported treatment was paradigmatic for what missionaries themselves would later undergo. However, the story does not appear reliable. Luke casts Jesus as reciting messianic texts from Isaiah, but we have no reason to believe that selections from the Prophets (the second division of the *Tanakh**) played any liturgical role already in Jesus' day (ca. 30), or even by Luke's time (the 90s). Instead, this story reflects later Christian prooftexting* (see Chaps. 7, 9, and 20), not an event that genuinely transpired during Jesus' ministry. This account shows Jesus' audience admiring him until he began to develop the more profound ramifications of what he had read—whereupon they rejected, then ejected, him. But this is, again, a reflection (here inconsistent?[2]) of Luke's need to account for Christianity's overwhelming rejection by Jews of Luke's own time, which he presents as foreshadowed by Jesus' (alleged) rejection by people of his native town.

What about the intimations by other Evangelists of synagogal rejections of Jewish-Christians? These likewise reflect the writers' own later communities rather than any realities from Jesus' day, or even soon thereafter.[3]

Late Reportage by Paul

It is now appropriate to bring in Paul's recounting of happenings that *are* early, albeit it in the Diaspora (nearby Damascus), even though his reportage also is not actually contemporary; it is during the 50s when he relates what transpired as far back as the mid- or even early 30s. However, Paul *is* giving us his personal recall and with quite an unusual bonus: testimony from two sides of the same ledger! First, apparently as

a Damascus synagogue enforcer, he persecuted Christians; but thereafter he became their persecuted proponent. We can therefore categorize his most pertinent testimonies according to whether they concern his activity before or after his "conversion."

6.1—Paul's Before-and-After Testimony Concerning Persecution

- **Concerning Paul as Persecutor (*Pre*-"Conversion")**

    Gal 1:13   You have heard of my former life in Judaism, how I *persecuted the church ... violently and tried to destroy it.*

    1 Cor 15:9   I am ... unfit to be called an apostle, because *I persecuted the church.*

    Gal 1:22f.   ... the churches ... in Judea only heard ... "He who once *persecuted* us is now preaching the faith he *once tried to destroy.*"

    Phil 3:6   As to zeal [I had been] a *persecutor of the church.*

- **Concerning Paul as Persecuted (*Post*-"Conversion")**

    2 Cor 11:23ff. Are [my rival apostles; cf. verse 5] servants of Christ? I am ... better.... *Five times I ... received at the hands of the Jews ... forty lashes less one. Three times ... beaten with rods; once ... stoned.*

    Rom 15:30f.   Pray ... that I may be *delivered from the unbelievers in Judea.*

It is noteworthy that Paul gives no hint that such persecution was illegal. Did Diaspora synagogues back then have carte blanche to impose this, and, if so, by whom was it granted? Acts 9:2 tells us of the high priest's letters of extradition to Paul to arrest Christians, but did the high priest have such Diaspora authority? Or did Roman officialdom give synagogues this right in the interest of maintaining order? Or was it that synagogues themselves felt these missionary intrusions were so intolerable that they simply responded on their own? And what, precisely, so irked them? Was the matter:

Behavioral? Something like, "Our synagogue today gave these folks leave to speak their piece. Their message was offensive; their demeanor worse. We told them to leave. They persisted so strongly that sterner measures were needed!"

Self-protective? Was it that Roman officials might get wind of synagogues that were allowing preaching about a crucified seditionist who would return now to complete his "Kingdom"? (Surely God-fearers* would quickly gossip about this with Gentiles outside!)

Sociological? Were missionaries causing rifts within synagogues? Once re-buffed by Jews, did they then take to wooing attending God-fearers?

Ritualistic? Were missionaries promising what God-fearers most wanted to hear: a full acceptance into Judaism that no longer required circum-cision or dietary observance? (Such laxities would be reprehensible to Jews.)

Theological? Were they preaching ideas that were intolerably out-landish? "But one man was resurrected!"—well, why not the right-eous of *all* Israel? "Resurrection established his Messiahship!"—but why, then, did Rome still rule? "A Second Coming is in the offing!"—but should not one suffice? "He died for others' sins!"—but how is this sensible?

As for Paul himself undergoing persecution, is what he says that he re-ceived (lashing, beating, stoning) what he himself earlier meted out?

Paul's Reversal

"Christianity" was not yet separate from Judaism in Paul's day, so his switch of affiliation was not from one religion to another but from one type of Judaism to another. Our two sources on his "conversion"—Acts (by Luke, in the 90s) and Galatians (by Paul, from the 50s)—hinder as well as help us because they disagree.

Encounter on the "Road to Damascus"? Acts—Yes; Galatians—No

According to Acts, Paul experienced the resurrected Christ while travel-ing from Jerusalem to Damascus. The supernatural features that accom-panied this encounter were sufficient to induce virtually anyone to "convert": Paul or his companions heard a voice, saw a light, fell to the ground, went blind, and so on. But doubt can be raised that any such incident occurred. Acts' own three recountings (9:1ff.; 22:6ff.; 26.12ff.) disagree in their descriptions,[4] and evidently Luke bases this episode on the Hebrew prophet Ezekiel's vision (Fig. 6.2).

6.2—Acts' "Damascus Road" Drama Echoes Ezekiel's Vision

Ezek 1:28; 2:1ff.—the brightness ... was the appearance of the likeness of the glory of the Lord....
When I saw it, I fell upon my face, and I heard the voice ... speaking ... "... I send you to the people of **Israel.**"

Acts 22:6ff.,21—As I ... drew near to Damascus ... a great light from heaven ... shone about me....
I fell to the ground and heard a voice.... "Depart; for I ... send you ... to the **Gentiles.**"

There is, moreover, no logistical correspondence between how Paul himself describes his revelation, in Galatians, and the basics shared by Acts' three recountings:

> The gospel ... preached by me ... came through *a revelation of* Jesus Christ.... When he who had set me apart before I was born, and ... called me ... was pleased to *reveal* his Son to me ... that I might preach him among the Gentiles, I did *not ... go up to Jerusalem to those who were apostles** before me but ... into Arabia [unclear where]; and again ... returned to Damascus [i.e., from Arabia].* (Gal 1:11ff.)

Here Paul describes the revelation in question as occurring while he was *within* Damascus, not on his way there; the only traveling he notes comes afterward, when he departs from Damascus for Arabia. Readers who process Paul's Epistles in light of whatever Acts has told them may understandably misassume that the revelation that Paul discusses in Galatians is what Acts relates in more vivid detail. The reality could well be, however, that Acts has deliberately altered Paul's description into the fictional story that many people today know so well.

Two Other Pauline Verses

Ironically, what may have prompted this alteration are two seemingly irrelevant Pauline verses. In one, Paul denies "go[ing] up to Jerusalem" immediately after his revelation (Gal 1:17). In the other he also insists that, until he finally did go up to Jerusalem more than three years later, he was "still not known by sight to the churches ... in Judea" (1:22f.).

Since these two passages contradict the way Luke wishes to tell Paul's biography, I submit that Luke *improvises* the account of Paul's conversion on the road *from Jerusalem*. "Road *to* Damascus" is not only our misnomer but also misses the point of what Luke means. And because this is not commonly discerned, Luke's invented history is taken literally rather than as the theological statement he intended.

With respect to these two points—(1) that Paul did *not* go up to Jerusalem directly after his revelation experienced in Damascus; and (2) that he was still *unknown by sight* to Judean churches even three years later when he did go to Jerusalem—the context we need to know is that Paul resents implications that he owes anything whatsoever to the Jerusalem mother church. Paul boasts that he is an independent operator who hears from God directly, and that it was while he was within Damascus (not on any trip there from elsewhere) that he heard from God in this fashion.

But this flies in the face of Luke's core theological principle that Christianity not only continues the heart of Judaism but that this is also reflected geographically—that is, for Luke geography *is* theology. As spelled out in greater detail in Chapter 17, to Luke, everything vital to Christianity's emergence originated in or spread outward from the fountainhead of Judaism: Jerusalem and its mother church (cf. Acts 1:8). In my view, Luke cannot tolerate Paul's two statements in Galatians, and as Paul's unauthorized biographer—and having the advantage of writing at least thirty years after Paul died—he could exercise tremendous latitude in retelling Paul's life story in the way he wishes.

So what Luke now does is reverse the thrust of Paul's description, here bending a snippet of Paul's own reportage (Gal 1:15–17) to suit Luke's own theology: he wants Paul's revelation timed and located on the road *from Jerusalem*, providing the same exaltation of Jerusalem that is consistent with the way that:

- Luke shifts Jesus' post-resurrection appearances from Galilee in the north (as per Mark and Matthew) to Judea's Jerusalem environs. (It is rather audacious of Luke to actually restrict *Jesus'* freedom of movement!)[5]
- Luke prevents Jesus' followers from fleeing to Galilee, since he needs to keep them in the vicinity of Jerusalem where he intends to have the resurrected Jesus appear.
- Luke shifts Paul's lengthy Diaspora upbringing entirely to Jerusalem.
- Luke casts Paul as Jerusalem-trained by Gamaliel.
- Luke locates Paul at Stephen's stoning just outside Jerusalem.
- Luke shows Paul securing extradition letters (to arrest Diaspora Christians) from the high priest in Jerusalem.

It is by this very last device—(I submit) *fictional* extradition letters—that Luke sets up the imagined Pauline trip to Damascus from Jerusalem. (See discussion in Chap. 21 on Luke's "governing principles.")

Luke's "Trips" as Theological Statements

It is helpful to see Luke's invented trip for Paul in the context of so many others that Luke creates: (1) Luke has Mary visit the pregnant

Elizabeth in part to give John the Baptist, still a fetus, opportunity to signal his inferiority to Jesus (Fig. 9.3). (2) Luke has Joseph and Mary—on the pretext of a census that cannot apply to Galileans—travel from Nazareth to Bethlehem so that Jesus "of Nazareth" can be born instead in King David's birthplace (Fig. 9.4). (3) Luke has the infant Jesus brought to the Temple for a redemption of the first-born ceremony so as to place him in Jerusalem at as young an age as possible (Fig. 9.5), a theme echoed (4) when Luke has Jesus' parents incomprehensibly forget their twelve-year-old in Jerusalem after his family's Passover pilgrimage—left behind so that Luke can have Jesus affirm God as his "Father" in the Temple itself. (5) Luke has Herod Antipas travel to Jerusalem (Lk 23:7ff.) so the tetrarch is available to offer a sixth attestation to Jesus' innocence all in one chapter! And (6) Luke prevents Jesus' followers from fleeing Jerusalem—a theological "non-trip" (Figs. 3.10 & 8.4)![6]

This backdrop clarifies why I claim that Paul's "road from Jerusalem" trip is likewise entirely imaginary, especially since Paul, in Galatians, implicitly denies it.

But would Luke lift a motif from Paul's own writings and then revise it to serve Lucan theology? Readers will not readily encounter this view from other scholars because, since Acts never mentions that Paul wrote Epistles, it is commonly supposed that Luke did not know of them. Yet Paul himself quotes opinions of those who declare that "his letters are weighty and strong" (2 Cor 10:10). How could the Epistles not be known by the same Luke who informs his (real or imagined) patron, Theophilus ("God-lover"), how familiar he is with "many" early Christian writings and (note well) how intent he is to *correct* them when it comes to orderliness and "truth" (Lk 1:1ff.)?

It would be "all but incredible that such a man as Luke ... should have been totally unaware that this hero of his had ever written letters" when, after all, "too many important churches owed their existence to [Paul] for his name not to have been held in reverence in many areas and his work remembered." (All the more so if Luke is himself writing in Greece—cf. Fig. 4.1—where he would be cognizant of Pauline churches that were not all that distant, such as those in Corinth, Thessalonica, Philippi, and even Galatia and Rome.) But if Luke did know of Paul's letters, why then conclude that he "quite consciously and deliberately made little or no use of them"?[7] It doesn't make sense that a biographer would forgo his only primary sources about the protagonist of three-quarters of his book (see Acts chapters 8–28).

A likely alternative is that, if Luke was so predisposed to correct Mark and others, *he would likewise do so with Paul's letters*. These also contained much "narrative [material] of the things ... accomplished among us" (Lk 1:1). If Luke wanted his own "correct" version of Paul to displace, indeed replace, that of the genuine figure, this would explain why he omitted mentioning Paul's letters: he did not want others reading them! He succeeded admirably given that the only Paul whom most Christians, and Jews, today know is Luke's made-over version of him, not the figure's actual self-testimony.

What about the second Pauline verse—that more than three years after Paul's conversion he was "still not known by sight to the churches ... in Judea" (Gal 1:22f.)? This is more trying to Luke than even the first statement because Acts had moved Paul's entire upbringing from the Diaspora into Jerusalem, capital of Judea proper—from his "youth, spent from the beginning ... at Jerusalem" (Acts 26:4). And consider the high profile Luke's Paul is given in Judea—Luke has him tutored personally by *the* chief Pharisee, Gamaliel (Acts 22:3), and not only is Paul present and assenting at Stephen's stoning (Acts 7:58ff.), but immediately thereafter (Acts 8:1) he also pursues Christians "throughout all the region of *Judea*." How, then, was he not known to them by sight?

Further, according to Acts, Paul has access to Jerusalem's high priest and the whole council of elders (Acts 22:5; cf. 9:1ff.), he personally drags Christians in the land of Israel off to prison (Acts 8:3), and much later (when he is a Christian himself) he is captured inside Jerusalem's Temple (Acts 21:27) and pulled out "when all the city was aroused" (Acts 21:30)—when "all Jerusalem was in confusion" (Acts 21:31) because of *him*. Then, as Luke has it, Paul delivers a long speech, remarkably not in Greek but in Hebrew (Acts 21:40)—Luke does not mean Aramaic, as commentators often assume, but literally Hebrew, the language that is core to Judaism—before he is subjected to a high-profile Sanhedrin trial (Acts 22:30ff.), although he should have been exempted because (according to Acts) he had (inherited?) that most rare status of being a Roman citizen (Acts 22:25ff.)!

Clearly, then, we can see how the contention by the *genuine* Paul that he was not yet known by sight to Judean Christians even three years after his conversion could topple the entire scaffolding on which Luke has constructed *his* version of Paul. So Luke writes a speech for Paul to the precise opposite effect, wherein Paul tells King Agrippa that immediately after converting (no three-year delay) he "declared first to those in Damascus, and in Jerusalem and *throughout all the region of Judea*" the fruits of his conversion (Acts 26:19–20).

Does this mean that the speeches Paul delivers in Acts are actually words that Luke invented for him? This was commonly done by Greek historians (Herodotus, Thucydides, Josephus, the author of 2 Maccabees, etc., with different gradations of invention), so it is hardly remarkable that an Evangelist would do the same. Indeed, it is a basic New Testament dynamic that whatever characters say or do may be determined by the proclamation needs of Gospel writers rather than any actual occurrence. Hence my stress (in Chap. 3) on improvisation as the wild card in resolving the Synoptic Problem, for not every recounting is grounded in sources.

The bottom line, then, is that if speeches by Paul in Acts are *Luke* speaking, then so are Paul's accounts of his conversion on the road from Jerusalem. (This is also why there are inadvertent inconsistencies in Acts' three recountings of this event—it is exactly what often happens when stories are made up.) For this reason, if we are interested in what caused Paul's reversal from persecuting Christians to joining them, we need to put Acts entirely to the side and turn our attention fully to Paul himself.

But can we believe Paul, i.e., in his epistles? More so than we can Luke, in my view.

Paul's Own Testimony

We begin, at least, with the possibility that Paul was genuinely an ecstatic visionary, and thus process his "conversion," whatever its content, as indeed suddenly transformative. Consider: "I will go on to visions and revelations of the Lord. I know a man in Christ who fourteen years ago was caught up to the third heaven" (2 Cor 12:1ff.). If Paul is here speaking of himself, is this perhaps his Galatians 1 revelation? Unfortunately, "fourteen years ago" (unless only roughly meant) does not fit.[8] But at least if we go by Paul's own testimony, he was susceptible to visionary experiences. Alternative possibilities also require consideration.

1. *Recounting His Revelation Experience Seems Secondary for Paul.* Unlike his rival apostles, Paul did not know Jesus pre-crucifixion—a disadvantage that grated on Paul. In context, then, his primary concern, when relating his revelations, was usually to stress his commission from God directly as superior to what he deems his rivals' commissions through mere human agency. That he had this agenda reminds us that the verbs with which Paul describes his claimed revelations of Christ are verbs that best enable him to maintain his credentials; his revelations must come across as directly from God or Christ-Jesus because only that is what can make Paul superior.

2. *Which Pauline Verbs?* Accordingly, let us examine the three key verbs that Paul uses here: "reveal," "see," and "appeared" (Fig. 6.3).

- *Reveal* (Gal 1) is used where Paul's primary purpose is to establish his credentials. Moreover, since Paul mentions no external phenomena to this revelation (e.g., light, blindness, a voice, falling to the ground), nothing should preclude our processing "reveal" as a strictly internal, *cognitive* breakthrough of something he had never realized before (and for which Paul can now credit God). Later, I submit, *Luke* refashioned this verb, "reveal," into a full-blown external extravaganza that had never occurred.
- *See* (1 Cor 9), used by Paul as he is racing to make a different point (his "defense"), gives us little to go on. "See," after all, is often used in a nonobjectified sense. (Consider the powerful spiritual, "Mine eyes have seen the glory of the coming of the Lord"—have they actually *seen* such a thing?)
- *Appeared* (1 Cor 15) is weaker still if the boxed matter in Figure 6.3 (vv. 3–7) was an already formalized Christian kerygma* that Paul, having "received," is now bent on "delivering." If so, Paul is locked into that word, "appeared," also respecting *himself*—for not to apply it to himself would be to concede his inferiority to his rivals!

3. *Did Paul's Revelation "From God" Come Via Those Whom He Was Persecuting?* When Paul "delivered" the kerygma that he "also received" (1 Cor 15:3), might he have "received" it from the very Damascus Christians whom he persecuted (and then joined), a channel through which he credited *God* as "pleased to *reveal* his Son to me"

6.3—The Three Key Pauline Verbs

Gal 1:15f.   When he ... was pleased to *reveal* his Son to me....

1 Cor 9:1ff.   Am I not an apostle? Have I not *seen* Jesus our Lord?... You are the seal of my apostleship in the Lord. This is my defense to those who would examine me....

1 Cor 15:3ff.   I delivered to you ... what I also received,

> that Christ died for our sins ... was buried ... was raised on the third day ... and ... *appeared* to Cephas, then to the twelve. Then ... *appeared* to more than five hundred brethren.... Then ... *appeared* to James, then ... all the apostles.

Last of all, as to one untimely born, he *appeared* also to me.

(Gal 1:16)? There are strengths to this conjecture: (a) It links Paul's persecuting of Christians with his abrupt reversal in joining the very same ones. (b) It also raises the (perhaps remote) possibility that it was with *them* that Paul went into Arabia directly after joining them, or even (c) that he lived with them for "three years" before going to Jerusalem (for the *first* time after his conversion). If we dismiss these ideas, then we still need alternative answers: if he received the kerygma from other Christians, then who were they (and from where did they get this)? And after his conversion, when rebuffed by noncomprehending Jews, with whom else then did Paul live and associate? Recall Paul's admission that he had been bent on "destroying" the church, which suggests not that he simply waited in his synagogue until Christians happened to come to him, but rather that he went after them. This kind of interaction could have facilitated his learning about their beliefs from them, first-hand, in their own setting (all the while crediting God for what he was absorbing[2]).

4. *Were the Damascus Christians Configuration B (Not A)?* This question summons the "prisms" that we discussed in Chapter 4. What should we make of the data (in Figure 6.4) that show how lopsidedly "Christ-centered" or "Lord-centered" is the Paul who, in his own genuine writings, appears averse even to mentioning Jesus' name by itself (indeed, only about 4 percent—i.e., 15 of Paul's 341 references to him—are by the single name "Jesus," alone[10]).

6.4—Paul's Rare Use of "Jesus" Alone, versus Cosmic Terms

Total uses of each term ↓

Paradigm That Paul Uses	Total #	Rom	1 Cor	2 Cor	Gal	Phil	1 Thes	Phile
"Jesus" alone	15	2	1	7	1	1	3	0
"Christ" alone	160	33	44	39	21	17	3	3
"Lord" alone	107	19	44	18	2	9	13	2
Cosmic variants (below)	59	15	13	8	3	6	11	3
Total references	341	69	102	72	27	33	30	8

"Lord"[11] and "Christ" variants are very diverse: "Christ Jesus our Lord," "Christ Jesus my Lord," "Lord Jesus Christ," "Jesus Christ our Lord," "his Son, Jesus Christ our Lord," "Lord Christ," "the Lord Jesus," "Jesus Christ as Lord," "Jesus Christ is Lord," "Jesus our Lord," and "Jesus is Lord."

That cosmic conceptualizations ("Lord," "Christ," etc.) attracted Paul to begin with is consistent with the scant attention he gives to the historical figure of Jesus throughout all his letters: relating nothing of that charismatic social reformist preacher, healer, performer of "miracles," and spinner of parables of God's coming Kingdom. Some of what little Paul does relate about this Jesus he could have picked up from the kerygma, or presupposed, or learned long after conversion when he finally visited Cephas, James, and others in Jerusalem.[12]

Which Failed Paul—Pharisaism or Judaism?

Since Paul switched not religions but one form of Judaism for another, it may be more appropriate to reflect on Paul's change in terms of "reversion" and "extension" rather than "conversion." As for reversion, are radical internal transformations genuinely as unanticipated as they may appear, or are deep-seated preparatory steps or causes evident, at least in retrospect? Paul's prowess in Pharisaism aside (Gal 1:14; Phil 3:5), was he actually dissatisfied with it, a realization jarred to the surface under his duress from persecuting Christians?

No Pauline passage jolts me, as a Jew, more than Romans 7:14ff., which lays out Paul's torment (only past, or still present?) over Sinfulness—here I capitalize the term for it denotes his state of being rather than some specific wrongdoing:

> I am carnal ... Sin ... dwells within me ... nothing good dwells within ... my flesh.... I see in my members another law ... making me captive to the law of Sin ... with my flesh I serve [it].

No matter where or when, Pharisaism saw repentance as effective, yet Paul evidently did not: "Wretched man that I am! Who will deliver me from this body of death?" (Rom 7:24). Unlike repentance—an ability within him—Paul saw that only a power sufficiently strong *outside* him could deliver him from the Sin caused him by his evil, material body, and this power Paul explicitly identified: "Thanks be to God through Jesus Christ our Lord!" (v. 25).

Moreover, what can we think about Paul's Pharisaic studies—whether this "Torah" be written or oral? Did they bring him peace or enjoyment? Evidently not, if his "Sinful passions [were] actually aroused by the law" itself (7:5):

> If it had not been for the law, I should not have known Sin ... not ... known what it is to covet if the law had not said, "You shall not covet." But Sin, finding opportunity in the commandment, wrought in me ... covetousness. (7:7f.)

What about the atonement that the Torah promised through the Temple cult? No sacrifice for "lower case" sins sufficed for Paul's Sinfulness. Only a sacrifice that Christ willingly underwent could suffice, paying the price for Sin by his death, securing reconciliation with God through rising from the dead, and thereby cleansing Paul—who, only by virtue of believing in him, became one with him, thereby securing his own reconciliation as well.

Recall here that it is only Luke, in Acts, not Paul himself, who places Paul's upbringing in Jerusalem. We must keep in mind that Paul's native city, Tarsus (in today's Turkey), was cosmopolitan, a place where Mystery cults were strong and long embedded, particularly Mithraism (see Chap. 4), and where pagans struggling to secure an afterlife by intimate participation in their deity's dying and rising continually surrounded Paul. As with his broader native environment, sacrifice for Paul was tied to remission of Sinfulness and to immortality through the God who sacrificed himself to let humans eat his body and drink his blood, thereby to become, like him, immortal. This is non-Pharisaic religion, the paganism of which Paul always had known—and whose appeal, as a Jew, he may have long suppressed—beginning with his youth. Paul's struggle may well have been to maintain his sense of being a Jew but to accommodate it within the context in which he had *always* lived.

As for *extension* (in addition now to reversion), Paul saw the channels of Christ's incarnation, death, and resurrection as extending Judaism as *he* in particular conceived it, bringing him to what he saw as a higher rung on the same ladder that his fellow Jews had always occupied with him—but one that most of them could not bring themselves to join him now in ascending further (see Chap. 14). For Paul, *that extended Judaism was the Configuration B Christianity that he came to preach.*

Why Apostle to the Gentiles?

When Paul speaks in the 50s of what transpired with him decades earlier, he likely telescopes into a transformation "of the moment" what actually played itself out in gradual stages. Yes, he may condense into but two verses (Gal 1:15–16):

a) "he who had set me apart before I was born, and ... called me ...
b) was pleased to reveal his Son to me,
c) in order that I might preach him among the Gentiles."

But what actually transpired may have been differently sequenced and spread out over time.

b) God "was pleased to reveal his Son to me."
   [*Later I came to believe that, just as with other prophets, so also must God have*]

a) "set *me* apart before I was born, and ... called me.... "
   [*Later, I deduced—or others explained to me—that my continual rebuffs by fellow Jews must mean that God had called me*]

c) "in order that I might preach [his Son] among the Gentiles."

The practical difference here, then, is that Paul's mission to the Gentiles did not come from his revelation (as he implies, in the 50s, when telescoping matters from the 30s), but rather from a second-stage rationalization and deduction: that his failure with fellow Jews must have meant that God wanted him to go to non-Jews.

But where did Gentiles enter this scheme to begin with? A chain of deductions that *might* have occurred to a Jew such as Paul could proceed as follows: First, in Judaism resurrection of just a single being would be an anomaly unless it also signaled that an end-time tidal wave of resurrections of righteous Israel was likewise imminent. (Are we meant to understand the earthquake accompanying Jesus' crucifixion, in Mt 28:2, as caused by buried bodies rumbling in their readiness to rise?) Second, if such an end time were about to commence, does not Jewish scripture itself stipulate—and frequently so[13]—that Gentiles are to participate with Jews in accepting the one true God? (This is to be *without* conversion, i.e., without circumcision and dietary laws.) Third, will not Gentiles on their own lack the capacity to realize both that this time had arrived and what it called upon them to do? Here, then, would lie the mandate for a Jew to embark on Gentile missions.

This did not mean, of course, that Paul himself should be one, or *the* one, who goes to Gentiles. But besides his deduction (from rebuffs by Jews) "that I might preach him among the Gentiles" (Gal 1:16), his talents alone could well have induced him to undertake such a career change. Who was more able than Paul to bring his God-given Jewishness, in which he was expert, and to translate it into a form that could be absorbed by Gentiles? After all, Paul saw himself as an insider to Judaism uniquely qualified to preach "Christ-Jesus" to outsiders in terms that he intuited they could comprehend and find appealing. For he himself had long known what it was to wrestle with Greek problems as a good Jew, and it was in so doing that he had shifted over to emphases that characterized the Greco-Roman context. Bringing, then, all the Jewish preparation that he could muster would enable and qualify him to answer the Greek questions—troubling him as well as pagans—*with the "Christ-Jesus" event.* And how natural it would have been for Paul then to express this deduction in familiar Jewish categories—here, after the

fashion of Isaiah and Jeremiah (Fig. 6.5; cf. Rom 1:1–2: "Paul ... called to be an apostle, set apart for the gospel of God which he promised be- forehand through his *prophets* in the holy scriptures")!

6.5—Paul Expresses His Call to Gentiles in Isaiah's and Jeremiah's Terms

Isaiah's Call	Jeremiah's Call	Paul's Call
Isa 49:1ff.—The Lord called me *from the womb*....	*Jer 1:4ff.*—The word of the Lord: ... "*Before I formed you in the womb ... and before you were born* ... I appointed you a	*Gal 1:11ff.*—When he who had *set me apart before I was born*, and ... called me ... was pleased to *reveal* his Son to me ... that *I*
" ... I ... give you as a light *to the nations* [Gentiles].... "	prophet *to the nations* [Gentiles]."	*might preach him among ... Gentiles*....

The reason we must understand "nations" in Isaiah and Jeremiah as here "Gentiles"—indeed, the Hebrew, *goyim*, can mean either—is that, if Israel is to be the light *to* them, then "nations" can only be "Gentiles."

Far-Ranging Conclusions

The Christ of Configuration B—Pauline—Christianity, which endured, eclipsed the image of the historical Jesus that was central to Configura- tion A, which dwindled away. This means that Paul played a more de- terminative role than did the historical Jesus in the emergence of the Christianity that exists today. But Paul also distanced Jesus' image from the actual historical figure so much that he thereby opened the way for Gentiles *to remove Jesus from Judaism*, both to co-opt this Jew as their own and also, eventually, to be in a position—should the need arise, as it indeed did during the 60s—to denigrate the very people from whom they had removed "Christ-Jesus" from the start.

Part Three

Reasoning Matters Through

Characteristic Jewish Perspectives on the Gospels

This is the first of two chapters that address the role of *thinking* in engaging the Gospels. Having taught New Testament to Jews in many venues, I have detected some recurring patterns of thought—a "characteristically *Jewish* mind-set" that is insightful even when uninformed. First I notice a detachment of sorts, because New Testament is not scripture for Jews. Then there is a disproportionate focus on sections, motifs, or narratives of the Gospels that cast aspersions on Jews and Judaism. And throughout there is a sadness, given the sorrows of Jewish history in which the Gospels have been so decisively influential.

Thereafter, at least five Jewish perspectives congeal. Though each is not expressly espoused by every Jewish learner, I have noticed a pronounced tendency nonetheless. These perspectives warrant a critique followed by some overall judgment of each. But the principal role of this present chapter is to serve as a transition to Chapter 8, which introduces "Gospel Dynamics."

Perspective #1: Changes in Christianity's self-perception vis-à-vis Judaism necessitated corresponding adjustments in portrayals of Jesus' stance toward Jews and Judaism, as presented in the Gospels.

Jewish readers discover apparent inconsistencies in Jesus' behavior toward fellow Jews. At times, he urges love of neighbor and turning the other cheek, yet elsewhere he himself appears vindictive. How may we reconcile the Jesus who instructs us to "love your enemies ... pray for those who persecute you" (Mt 5:44) with the Jesus who castigates even Jews believing in him as "of your father the devil ... a murderer ... a liar and ... father of lies ... " (Jn 8:31,44f.); or the Jesus who insists that "every one ... [even] angry with his brother shall be liable to judgment" (Mt 5:22) with the

Jesus who decries the Pharisees as "you serpents, you brood of vipers, how are you to escape being sentenced to hell?" (Mt 23:33)?

Inevitably, many Jewish readers infer that such conflicting images of Jesus should be viewed *developmentally*—that changes in Christianity's unfolding self-perception with respect to Judaism brought about phases of corresponding adjustments in portrayals of Jesus' stance toward Jews and Judaism. Thus—

- during a pre-Pauline phase, emergent Christianity, perceiving itself still *within* Judaism, naturally preserved or generated portrayals of Jesus as *faithful* to, and *consonant* with, Judaism;
- later, with Christianity more conscious of its own individuality and with most Jews still avoiding the Church, Jesus' figure was adjusted to reflect *regret* at Jews resisting Christian claims;
- later still, with exchanges between Christians and Jewish opponents becoming increasingly contentious, Christians' regret became supplanted by *hostility* toward Jews, with Jesus' figure, enlisted to support this accrued bitterness, now portrayed as hostile toward Jews.

What hints of Jesus' *consonance* with Judaism do Jewish learners posit for the first phase? Often, the Lord's Prayer, parables of the Kingdom, and the Great Commandment—which encompasses the *Shema* and Golden Rule. Reflecting the second phase—*regret*—are primarily echoes of Pauline sentiments such as those in Romans 9–11. *Hostility*, in the third phase, is manifested through words ascribed to Jesus (e.g., Matthew's "woes" against the Pharisees, and John's passages presenting Jesus outside the Jewish fold) and through channels other than Jesus' words (e.g., the Sanhedrin and Barabbas episodes, including especially Matthew's infamous "blood curse").[1]

Yet Perspective #1 is problematic:

- Nothing precludes the possibility that Jesus himself manifested each "stance" (fidelity, regret, hostility). Moreover, we cannot achieve consensus in distinguishing statements authentic to Jesus from those altered or even formed by the later Church. So, compartmentalizing various Jesus images seems arbitrary, even amateurish.
- Procedures of Jewish readers conveniently result in the very kind of Jesus they desire. The more they strip away what they deem traditions attributable to later Gentile churches, the more characteristically Jewish the Jesus-who-remains turns out to be. But such reasoning is circular.
- Jews' recourse to rabbinic literature—to discover presumed parallels to Jesus' teachings (and to conjecture thereby his proximity to Pharisaism)—is often methodologically flawed.[2]

- It becomes arduous to explain why Christianity ever traced its origins to a Jesus who presumably departed in no significant way from the diversified Judaism(s) of his day.

Still, these formidable objections to this approach fail to cripple it. A core assertion remains compelling: since the self-perception of some Christians vis-à-vis Judaism most likely did express itself in consecutive phases of consonance, then regret, and ultimately supplanted by anger and hostility, *some* corresponding adjustments in Jesus' image would have been forthcoming. Any imposing problems that we encounter in analyzing particular passages may not necessarily undermine the hypothesis in general since what breaks down is not the hypothesis but specific attempts to prove it. This is best seen with regard to the first and last phases. That Jesus' immediate followers remained within the synagogue—continuing to abide by Jewish practice—suggests that they identified Jesus himself as remaining consonant with Judaism. Respecting the third phase, the intensity of Gospel denunciations of Jews can still most plausibly be assigned to well after Jesus' death, which is when Christianity's attitude toward many Jews became suffused with hostility.[3] Let us then reserve judgment on Perspective #1 until we see how compatibly it fares with the plausibility of Jewish Perspectives #2 through #5. (Addressing this perspective more extensively are sections of Chaps. 8, 11–13, 15–18, and 22.)

Perspective #2: The various ways in which Paul's theology was understood influenced the Gospel portraits of Jesus.

Since Paul's Epistles (basically during the 50s) are our earliest New Testament writings, might not his thinking have influenced directions taken by differing segments of Christianity—both those who adhered to Pauline views (whether or not interpreting Paul correctly) and those who resisted Paul but were forced, nonetheless, to address his thinking (whether or not interpreting that thinking correctly)? Emphasized, then, is not what Paul said or intended but the influential role that *those interpreting Paul*—even in diverging fashions—may have played in how Jesus later became portrayed in Gospel traditions.

The conceptualization here is that Jesus' earliest images and teachings passed through the filter of Paul's interpretation concerning the meaning of the Christ (and thus as well through the lenses of others who interpreted Paul's interpretation). The consequence of this filtering process was that Jesus' image and teachings were embellished, even transformed, with at least three decisive themes generated thereby, each bearing the impress either of what Paul himself preached or of how others construed or misconstrued that preaching:

- Jesus rejected the Law of Moses;
- Christian missionaries turned from Jews to Gentiles instead; and
- Jews were superseded by Gentile-Christians as God's chosen people.[4]

Jews generally regard it as improbable that Jesus himself counseled any of these ideas. Rather, it was Pauline thought, after Jesus' lifetime, that first stimulated raising these three issues, and various churches, developing and pressing them, that belatedly ascribed them to Jesus personally. This would explain why Jesus' intimate followers vigorously opposed Paul: they perceived him as distancing himself from what *they* believed had been Jesus' own fidelity to the Law and the Jewish people. Concluding that these motifs derive more from how Paul was *interpreted* than from what Jesus personally had advanced could occasion a revolutionary reorientation of Jewish thinking about Jesus—including the inclination to reclaim him as a Jew. For only after Paul's ministry were certain Jesus-traditions fashioned in support of Pauline views (with the possibility of still other traditions then developing to counter Paul—and others still to counter any such objections to Paul).

Yet Perspective #2 is problematic:

- Do we know for certain that Paul's writings were sufficiently known by all Gospel writers who, allegedly, were influenced by them?
- Are we exaggerating Paul's uniqueness? Departures from the Law in emerging churches were not single-handedly engineered by Paul,[5] nor was he the sole missionary to Gentiles.
- It is problematic to ascribe to Paul every Christian departure from Judaism, as if Paul founded a Christianity that had no threads of connectedness with Jesus. Why not emphasize Pauline teachings that are *consonant* with those of Jesus? For example, Paul's idea of a mission to Gentiles may only have extrapolated a *latency* within Jesus who, if he expected an imminent end to the world order, did so within Jewish scriptural anticipation of Gentile involvement in that new era.

Still, certain key anomalies appear to buttress Perspective #2:[6]

Anomaly—Why did pillars of Jerusalem's church oppose Paul when he ate with Gentiles (presumably breaking Jewish dietary laws) and began bringing Gentiles directly into the Christian fold? Since some Gospel texts attest that Jesus himself had departed from the Law and counseled or predicted a turning to Gentiles, why did not James, Cephas, and John (cf. Gal 1:18–2:21) recognize Paul's consonance with Jesus? Does this not suggest that Jesus himself had never broken with the Law or counseled a turning from his own people to Gentiles?

Anomaly—If Jesus had indeed "declared all foods clean" (Mk 7:19b), why did Peter (Acts 10:14) not know this, or need a thrice-stated revelation (v. 16) concerning what clearly he should have remembered from Jesus personally? Would this not suggest that Jesus himself had never nullified dietary laws?

Anomaly—If Jesus had publicly transgressed the Sabbath or justified transgression by his disciples (cf. Mk 2:23–3:5), how could Paul's Judaizing* opponents in Galatia have insisted on Jewish calendrical observance (Gal 4:9ff.), or on general adherence to the same Law that Jesus himself had presumably disavowed? Would this not suggest that Jesus himself had never broken with the Law let alone counseled departures by others?

Anomaly—Why, when Paul debated the issue of the Law, did he not draw support from Jesus' specific *teachings* (which became embedded in Gospel traditions later on)? Since Paul argued only on general grounds that faith in Christ constitutes the sole way to salvation,* recourse to Jesus' teachings would have been useful, indeed vitally persuasive, especially because food and Sabbath issues sorely troubled Paul.[7] Would not Paul's failure to take advantage of those teachings by Jesus imply that Jesus had never been known to advance such teachings to start with?

It could appear, then, that only subsequent to Paul's break with the Law did Jesus traditions, potentially supportive of Paul's attitudes, arise in accommodation to Pauline views—that it was Pauline thought, after Jesus' ministry, that *first* stimulated the raising of precisely these issues (regarding the Law, turning to Gentiles, and supersession of Jews by Gentiles), and that only thereafter did advocates of these themes begin to press them in earnest. Jesus' intimate followers (especially his brother, James), meanwhile, vigorously opposed Paul because they perceived him as distancing himself from what *they* remembered had been Jesus' fidelity to the Law and the Jewish people.

At the same time, objections to Perspective #2 are themselves open to challenge. We deal here less with whether Paul's Epistles themselves were known than whether his *theological positions* were known. Moreover, that Paul actually produced writings that were provocative and deemed significant enough to achieve eventual canonization (or to require it as a means of controlling how they would be interpreted) is a factor that suggests Paul's fame and restores eminence to him irrespective of whatever other missionaries to Gentiles there were besides him. Paul's capacity to reinterpret Jesus' significance along lines that diverged from the earliest understandings of who Jesus was (witness Paul's elaborations concerning "crucifixion" and "resurrection") does indeed reinforce the contention that, with Paul, Christianity experienced renewal, redirection, and even transformation.

As for issues of "latency," if Galatians 2:16 ("by works of the law shall *no one* be justified") means that Jews, also, to be saved, must forgo the Law, surely this exceeds any ideas that were latent within Jesus! When Paul reverses the sequence for salvation with "the full number of the Gentiles" now *preceding* disbelieving Israel (Rom 11:25f.), this likewise exceeds any latency within Jesus toward Gentiles. Also distinctive is Paul's argument that the covenant skipped from Abraham to Christ, with membership now restricted to those in Christ regardless of whether they are Israel biologically (Rom 9:6ff.).

Jews cannot unravel why Jesus—whether as a Jewish messianic claimant himself or only thought so by others—would diverge from the Law, counsel a turning from Jews to Gentiles, or redefine chosenness in terms of Gentile-Christians superseding Jews. But Paul's significant variance from Judaism (as Jews today see it) *precisely on these issues* suggests that it was indeed *his* influence that led to a transformation of Jesus' image into what we now find incorporated within many Gospel formulations. (Sections of Chaps. 4, 6, and 14 address this perspective more extensively.)

> Perspective #3: In the process of responding to challenges by Jewish
> opponents, emerging Christianity adjusted or added to Jesus-traditions
> teachings and nuances that were not authentic to Jesus' ministry.

Conceiving that their own immediate problems (70–100 CE) had already originated back during Jesus' day (ca. 30 CE), and that the needed solutions must therefore be discoverable in *his* words and deeds, the Evangelists often recast Jesus' actual teachings to render them germane to later circumstances.

Example—Jesus' crucifixion led Jewish opponents to challenge messianic claims made for him. In turn, one Christian response was to aver that Jesus had correctly predicted his execution (cf. Mk 10:33f.). This transformed his death into a verification of his credentials (see next chapter). Other responses were to insist that Jesus could have prevented his crucifixion, but chose not to, or that, since Jewish scripture (allegedly) required the Messiah to die, Jesus' crucifixion *buttressed* his claims. Matthew 26:53f. illustrates both: "Do you think that I cannot appeal to my Father, and he will at once send me more than twelve legions of angels? But how then should the scriptures be fulfilled, that it must be so?"

Example—Jews argued that Elijah, the Messiah's herald, had yet to appear (Mk 9:11). Christian tradition, in response, conformed John the Baptist to Elijah's image, as in Mark 9:13 ("I tell you that Elijah has [already]

come"), and sharpened by Matthew 17:13 ("he was speaking to them of John the Baptist"). Additionally, Christian tradition ascribed John's death to an evil king and queen, Herod Antipas and Herodias, conforming this duo's role to their wicked counterparts, Ahab and Jezebel, who had sought Elijah's life.[8]

Example—Jews challenged Christian opponents for not keeping the dietary laws. Mark redirected Jesus' teaching, "Do you not see that whatever goes into a man from outside cannot defile him?" to mean that Jesus had "declared all foods clean" (Mk 7:19b). Jesus seemed to be saying only that what matters most is internal moral consciousness (Mk 7:15,18–19a,20), but Mark then redirected Jesus' words to address a challenge over dietary laws that first arose between Jesus' death (ca. 30) and Mark's composition (ca. 72).

Yet Perspective #3 is problematic:

- If we become preoccupied with discovering late challenges to Christianity, we may overactively imagine too many passages as "responses" of this kind when this was not their intended function.
- That Gospel traditions received their final imprimatur from later churches does not necessarily mean that all passages cohering with later church interests are inauthentic to Jesus' ministry. Some responses assigned to later churches could reaffirm, reinforce, or reformulate teachings genuinely imparted by Jesus.
- Some disagreements recorded as between Jesus' followers and "Jews" could well reflect intra-Jewish disputations (pitting Christian Jews against non-Christian Jews) or even intra-Christian disputations (not involving [non-Christian] Jews at all).

In defense of Perspective #3, it would be unreasonable to deny that new problems arose for Jesus' followers between his death and the Gospels' completion. And some of these must have involved resistance to Christians by (non-Christian) Jews, which—unsettling to Christians—would have invited the shaping of Gospel traditions to answer these challenges. The quest to disentangle such late additions from earlier materials is hardly irresponsible, provided that we avoid "discovering" what is *not* there by exercising proper discretion in searching for what may well be there. (Sections of Chaps. 8, 9, 11–13, 15–18, and 20–22 address this perspective more extensively.)

> Perspective #4: Study of the Synoptic Gospels in parallel columns
> reveals that later writers intensified the anti-Judaism of their sources.

Matthew and Luke are not only literarily dependent on Mark but they also altered his text. Some of their variations from Mark may reflect intentional adjustments—that is, any anti-Jewish remarks or posture present in Matthew or Luke but absent from parallel material in Mark could reflect the later editors' own inclinations. (An interesting corollary: anti-Judaism may decrease as we regress toward Christian origins.)

Perspective #4 appears mainly vulnerable to the objection that heightened anti-Judaism in Matthew and Luke might be only inadvertent, due to their reliance on anti-Jewish sources other than Mark. But even if these (supposed) sources were anti-Jewish, decisions to apply such touches remained the editors'. (Sections of Chaps. 16 and 22 address this perspective extensively.)

> Perspective #5: The reason that some passages in the Jewish Bible may
> seem to predict Jesus' coming is that Christian tradition conformed
> Jesus' image to match Jewish scriptural antecedents.

Missionaries cite proof-texts* from Jewish scripture that are said to demonstrate how Jesus alone fulfilled predictions of the Messiah's coming; for example, Jesus' apparent similarity with Isaiah's "Suffering Servant"[9]; or his entry to Jerusalem on a donkey, with its presumed prediction by Zechariah 9:9; or his scene on the cross with imagery from Psalm 22:1ff. (see next chapter). Reflective Jews reason that developing Gospel tradition fashioned details of Jesus' life to *match* texts alleged to foretell him.

Perspective #5 is problematic if taken to an extreme. It is better to say that, even regarding actual events in Jesus' life, scripture influenced which ones would be *remembered*. Thus, not only might narrators have created incidents "to give scriptural flavor," but from incidents that did actually occur narrators dramatized those capable of echoing the scriptures.[10] (Sections of Chaps. 8, 9, 11–13, 15, and 19–20 address this perspective extensively.)

The characteristic Jewish mind-set outlined in this chapter—whether or not achieving correct answers—demonstrates that Jews indeed do have the aptitude for our next challenge: recognizing Gospel Dynamics.

8

Mastering "Gospel Dynamics"
Avenues to Ponder

Jews may benefit from knowing the New Testament, but their even greater need is to recognize the "Gospel Dynamics" that may underlie it. Since this term is my own,[1] I define it before demonstrating its applicability:

"Gospel Dynamics" are those skillful techniques—evinced in the Gospels—by which early Christians molded their traditions to address their needs decades after Jesus died.

Some of these techniques created *those particular New Testament texts that impacted the Jewish people so deleteriously throughout history.* Whenever used in this technical sense, "Dynamic(s)" will be capitalized.

Until the early nineteenth century, the operation of (what we are terming) Gospel Dynamics went unnoticed by almost all New Testament readers. Even today, aside from those with at least some inclination or intuition along these lines, most readers have no inkling that far more may underlie (or "is going on" within) Gospel texts than they imagine, with ramifications that are potentially startling. This is especially the case for Jewish readers, for once they recognize and understand Gospel Dynamics, much of the sweep of Jewish history will stand exposed as having been driven by Christians' unhesitating acceptance of particular Gospel traditions that all along had been flashing caution signals against ready embrace. Jews need to learn how to bring such caution signals to the foreground, and to the attention of others.

What stimulated the workings of Gospel Dynamics? To begin with, early Christian communities refined their conceptualizations, especially of Jesus himself, to address problems of *their* later day, not his. Figure 8.1, while hardly exhaustive, displays a spectrum of twenty such problems.

8.1—*Twenty Sample Problems Confronting Early Christians (That Gospels Could Be Addressing)*

Problems INTERNAL to Early Christian Communities

- Discomfort over perceptions that Jesus had died a victim, not a victor
- Pressure to redefine "Messiah" in view of Jesus' crucifixion
- Impatience / frustration / doubt over delay in the Second Coming
- Urgency to stem defections from Christian ranks
- Anxiety over betrayals of Christians to Rome (by trusted companions, even relatives)
- Divisiveness generated by rifts over ritual practice

Problems EXTERNAL to Early Christian Communities—Posed by Others

Rome
- How to stem Roman persecution of Christians (commencing during the 60s)
- How to disassociate Christians (in Roman eyes) from the image of Jewish rebels (66–73)
- How to explain that Jesus' crucifixion did not mean that his later followers were seditionists
- How to shift blame for Jesus' death from Rome to another party (here, the Jews)
- How to convey that Jesus was condemned only for "blasphemy" (of no concern to Rome)

Jews
- How to demonstrate that Elijah—herald of the Messiah—already had appeared
- How to establish that Jesus was the Messiah despite his failure to fulfil Jewish expectations
- How to show that Jewish scriptures predicted Jesus' coming
- How to refine the concept of God's chosen people so as to include Gentile-Christians*
- How to justify departures from the Law of Moses by Gentile-Christians
- How to refute Jews' denials of Jesus' resurrection
- How to cope with ejections of some Jewish-Christians* from the synagogue

Rivals

The Baptist
- How to compete with the rival John the Baptist movement

Gnostics
- How to prove that the Christ genuinely took on flesh

The preference for most Christians would be to read Gospel texts in a straightforward manner—to presume that the events, persons, and teachings mentioned are accurately presented. Understandably, it can be a disconcerting notion: that some Gospel traditions, although ostensibly focusing on Jesus, were actually adjusted, or even created, to address problems that had nothing to do with his time, and that exigencies, such as those included in Figure 8.1[2], induced alterations in the way events, persons, and teachings became reported. The *processes* by which such results may have emerged are what I mean by Gospel Dynamics.

The Analogy of Moses

Did not the ancient rabbis, eager to apply statements from the Torah to their own times, reprocess Moses' image so that his teachings would "speak to" problems of a later day? Should Jews also, then, determine whether Dynamics underlie *their* scripture as well? While the nature and ramifications would differ from those pertaining to the Gospels, my personal answer is yes (see opening of Chap. 21).

Sample Gospel Dynamics

In the following examples, readers should focus less on the content—engrossing as it may seem—than on the Gospel Dynamics possibly operating behind the scenes to shape or drive that content.

> Sample Gospel Dynamic #1—Were "predictions" created as coping mechanisms?

Three middle chapters of Mark attribute to Jesus detailed predictions of what will befall him as the "Son of man"*:

Mk 8:31   And he began to teach [his disciples] that the Son of man [Jesus] must suffer many things, and be rejected by the elders and the chief priests and the scribes, and be killed, and after three days rise again.

Mk 9:31   For he was teaching his disciples..., "The Son of man [Jesus] will be delivered into the hands of men, and they will kill him; and ... after three days he will rise."

Mk 10:32ff.   He began to tell them what was to happen to him... "... the Son of man [Jesus] will be delivered to the chief priests and the scribes, and they will condemn him to death, and deliver him to the Gentiles; and they will mock him, and spit upon him, and scourge him, and kill him; and after three days he will rise."

Here is the image of a Jesus concerned about preparing his followers for what he knew might catch them unawares: his death—and resurrection to follow. Yet we may also wonder whether there is a Gospel Dynamic at work to solve a problem. These predictions correspond so precisely to the ensuing story line as to suggest their composition *after the fact* and their retrojection (backdating) to Jesus personally. Were the predictions verbalized not by Jesus to his disciples but by the Evangelist Mark to *his* later audience? Jews had expected as Messiah a victor, not a victim. Were these late "predictions" designed to counter the otherwise discouraging impression made on some by Jesus' capture and crucifixion? The Gospel Dynamic here would be: *any calamity, so long as it was said to have been prophesied first, could now corroborate Christian faith rather than undermine it.*

This kind of exercise—pondering whether certain later motives led to certain Gospel motifs—is conjectural but also necessary. The New Testament has to be *engaged*, and the search for Gospel Dynamics is one way that such engagement is accomplished. Contemplating alternative possibilities is also constructive. Perhaps, for example, these predictions were liturgical: created to be repeated and thereby to inspire worshipers affirming that Jesus knowingly and willingly underwent the worst that others could mete out to him, and yet he (quite literally) rose above it all. That he chose to go forward becomes an exhortation that worshipers do likewise, for he died—and yet he didn't, because he lives!—so that others, too, might live anew and with him, and so death might no longer have power over anyone.

Sample Gospel Dynamic #2—Were sayings that troubled the Church replaced?

The New Testament's two earliest Gospels (Mark, ca. 72 CE, and Matthew, ca. 85 CE) both render Jesus' last words on the cross as echoing Psalm 22:1: "My God, my God, why hast thou forsaken me?" Yet later writers—Luke and John—cast other "last words" in this role. See Figure 8.2 (which is a rare instance when we can display John in a fourth column).

In a moment of such physical duress, would Jesus quote Jewish scripture, or was it only the developing Christian tradition that first supplied him with such "last words"? Mark's overall depiction shows Jesus increasingly *forsaken* by a successively diminishing circle of adherents, with the progression culminating here in *God's* forsaking him as well. Does this suggest, then, that it is *Mark* who introduced Psalm 22:1? Further, when Jesus is depicted as quoting only the opening words of a psalm (here, Ps 22), are we to assume that the meaning of this psalm in

8.2—Were "Jesus' Last Words" Replaced?

Mark 15:34ff.	Matthew 27:46ff.	Luke 23:46	John 19:30
... Jesus cried with a loud voice ... *"My God, my God, why hast thou forsaken me?"* [Ps 22:1]....	... Jesus cried with a loud voice ... *"My God, my God, why hast thou forsaken me?"* [Ps 22:1]	[NO INITIAL CRY AT ALL]	he said, *"It is finished"*;
Jesus uttered a loud [WORDLESS] cry,	... Jesus cried again [WORDLESSLY] with a loud voice	Then Jesus, crying with a loud voice, said, *"Father, into thy hands I commit my spirit!"* [Ps 31:5]	[NO OTHER CRY]
and breathed his last.	and yielded up his spirit.	And ... he breathed his last.	and he ... gave up his spirit.

its entirety was intended or solely these opening words in particular? (Psalm 22 is less despondent—even triumphant—in its later verses.)

But the Dynamic that should most concern us here is that, when we turn to Luke and John, we find quite different "last words" instead. Mark and Matthew both specify that, after quoting Psalm 22:1, Jesus uttered a loud cry; did this second opportunity to speak result only in a wordless exclamation of agony, or did it also consist of words that are not related by Mark or Matthew? Luke does supply words to *this* cry, giving us thereby a *new* last utterance ("Father, into thy hands I commit my spirit," quoting Ps 31:5). But why then does Luke not also retain Mark's rendition of Jesus' first cry (" ... why hast thou forsaken me?")—surely there remains room for it in its appropriate, even if now penultimate, spot? So the question is less why Luke has additional words than why he drops out the original cry altogether. For this creates the distinct impression that Luke wishes to *replace* it. (If John knows Mark's Passion*, he could be doing the same.)

Luke's breaking of ranks demands explanation. Does he find that the original set of Jesus' last words—a lament at being forsaken—broadcasts gloom so severe as to undermine Christian faith rather than to solidify it, for it appears to show that, in Jesus' own estimation, his crucifixion

signaled rejection? Even if, by reciting Psalm 22:1, Jesus (or the early Church) intended that we examine the entirety of the psalm, such a procedure may not have been known by Luke's Gentile community, with whom only this one depressing verse might have registered. Under such circumstances, if Luke wanted Jesus' cry to be uplifting, Psalm 31:5 would have filled the bill ("Father, into thy hands I commit my spirit") even while retaining Psalm 22:1 as Jesus' now penultimate words. But Luke's omission of Mark's verse entirely shows quite a disturbing degree of license. For if Jesus' presumably last words are not sacrosanct, then what is? The very idea that an Evangelist could select his own alternative "last words"—that Jesus himself never uttered—is disconcerting.

Sample Gospel Dynamic #3—Was Jesus' image conformed to Jewish scriptural motifs?

It is one matter for Jesus (presumably) to quote Psalm 22:1, but quite another for multiple motifs of his scene on the cross to match those of this psalm, as shown in Figure 8.3. (On the mistranslation, "pierced," in Ps. 22:16, see endnote.[3])

If the Evangelists did not know sufficient details about the crucifixion scene, might they scour the Jewish Bible for motifs to which they could then *conform* that depiction? Might they import imagery, here punctuating the rest of Psalm 22, to flesh out the Jesus story? Moreover, would not this conformance constitute another means of reversing the impact

8.3—Was the Crucifixion Scene Conformed to Psalm 22?

Psalm 22 (BCE)		Mark 15 (ca. 72 CE)
1 My God, my God, why hast thou forsaken me?...	⟶	34 ... Jesus cried ... "My God, my God, why hast thou forsaken me?"
6 ... scorned by men, ... despised by the people. 7All ... mock at me ... wag their heads....	⟶	29 ... those who passed by derided him, wagging their heads....
16 ... evildoers encircle me; they have pierced my hands and feet....	⟶	24 And they crucified him,
18 they divide my garments among them, ... for my raiment they cast lots....	⟶	and divided his garments among them, casting lots for them....

of Jesus' death from ostensible defeat to stunning victory? Unlike Sample Dynamic #1, "predictions" here are *derived* from recourse to Jewish scripture itself rather than possibly invented outright (cf. Mt 26:54—"how then should the scriptures be fulfilled, that it must be so?").

Sample Gospel Dynamic #4—Could recountings of "events" be radically revamped?

In Figure 8.4 we experience differences in factual reportage regarding what the women encounter when they find Jesus' tomb empty.

8.4—*Luke Prevents Jesus' Followers from Leaving Judea*		
Mark 16:5ff.	**Matthew 28:2ff.** *—revises Mark*	**Luke 24:4ff.** *—revises Mark*
a young man ... said ..., "... Jesus ... has risen ... go, tell his disciples and Peter that	an *angel* ... said ..., "... Jesus... has risen ... go ... tell his disciples that ...	*two men* ... said ..., "Why do you seek the living among the dead?
he is going before you *to Galilee*; there you will see him, as *he* told you."	he is going before you *to Galilee*; there you will see him. Lo, *I have* told you."	Remember how *he told you, while he was still in Galilee*, that...."

Why, if Matthew and Luke both draw from Mark, do their basic facts not match? (1) The "young man" in Mark becomes an "angel" in Matthew and "two men" in Luke. (2) Is Galilee where Jesus will appear to his followers after his resurrection? Mark and Matthew say *yes*; Luke implies no. (3) Are Jesus' followers to be in Galilee to see him? Mark and Matthew say yes; Luke does not here say. (4) Did Jesus ever tell the *women* that he was going to Galilee where the *men* would see him? Mark says yes; Matthew implies no.[4] But here Luke's literary license transforms Galilee from where Jesus is predicted to appear (Mk 14:28; 16:7) into the place where Jesus once *had* revealed his impending death and resurrection, which is quite a different matter.

The Gospel Dynamic operative here is that geography to Luke carries theological implications (see Chaps. 6 and 17). Galilee is a region on the fringe of Judaism. For Luke, the resurrected Jesus must appear solely in the environs of Jerusalem itself, Judaism's geographic core. (Recall here, from Chap. 6, Luke's staging of Paul's "conversion" on the road *from* Jerusalem.) Luke, accordingly, departs from what he received as

"history" by limiting even Jesus (not only his followers) to Jerusalem. That Luke could restrict Jesus' travel leaves us to ponder how many other divergences of consequence were "improvised" in this fashion— improvisations that subsequent generations of believers unquestioningly accepted as historically true.

Sample Gospel Dynamic #5—Were traditions altered by insertions, even fictional ones?

Early Christians, in expecting Jesus' imminent return, were initially focused more on Jesus' death and belief in his resurrection than on features of his ministry per se. Hence Passion traditions were the first to coalesce. Scholars are split over whether Mark had access to a short, written version of the Passion—referred to today, albeit only theoretically, as "a pre-Marcan Passion Narrative"—that he then expanded and bequeathed to Matthew and Luke. Why is this important? In the preceding chapter, "Perspective #1" was noted to the effect that much of the anti-Jewish material in the Gospels reflects the last third of the first century. If this is correct, then a pre-Marcan Passion Narrative could have been barely anti-Jewish compared to what Mark (writing post-70) did to, and with, it. Naturally, our main concerns in such a case would lie with the Sanhedrin trial and the Barabbas episode, the two most anti-Jewish paragraphs in the New Testament. Conceptually, then, Figure 8.5 conveys the general nature of the problem we would be exploring (and will explore in Chap. 12).

A matter as conjectural as this would require if not compelling proof then at least strong circumstantial evidence even to justify discussion. At our present juncture, however, I advance this notion merely to illustrate a still different kind of *possible* Gospel Dynamic.

8.5—Did Mark Expand the Passion in Anti-Jewish Ways?

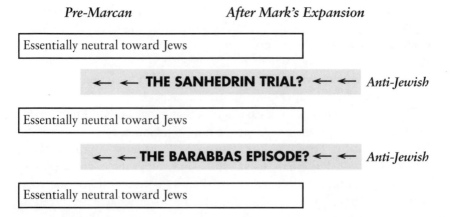

Application

For most Christians, the historical details of Jesus' ministry may not particularly matter to them as long as Gospel materials radiate existential meaning for their lives today. Jews need to understand this. In turn, Christians might consider that, for most Jews, it *does* matter what did or did not happen on the historical level if, due to the operation of Gospel Dynamics, it is *fictional* material that incited or otherwise facilitated the murder of untold numbers of Jews over later centuries.

This signals how vitally important it is for all readers to understand the extent to which Gospel Dynamics could have impacted the way in which Jesus' story came to be told: how sometimes the Evangelists borrowed from one another but also altered one another's reporting; how some late traditions may have been invented and inserted into earlier narratives; how Gospel characters sometimes may say only what the writers want them to say; how inconsistencies in a story line could be clues to editorial procedures that the Gospel writers employed; and how Gospel episodes may have been conformed to, let alone generated by, Jewish scripture.

In short, that Gospel Dynamics came into play was a normal part of the way in which texts sacred to Christianity developed. But in some cases, there were horrendous consequences for the Jewish people and, one should think, for the values of the historical Jesus himself. *There is no more productive approach to the New Testament for most Jews than to determine whether Gospel Dynamics underlie those texts that have most impacted Jewish history,* and, if so, to be able to identify and to explain these Dynamics to their fellow Jews, to their children, and to Christian friends. Facility in demonstrating Gospel Dynamics will enhance Jews' sense of well-being because it will help Christians realize that—far from being "blind"—Jews have intelligible as well as intelligent reasons for processing the New Testament in their own way.

Surely, on the issue of whether Gospel Dynamics genuinely underlie New Testament texts, Christian friends will offer Jews their own answers as befit *their* faith, so there will be here a learning experience for Jew and Christian alike. But the particular concern of this book is that gaining facility in Gospel Dynamics will give Jews confidence not to win debates but simply to feel that they have something of substance to contribute, enabling them to come across as thinking persons, instead of blindfolded ones. It is ironic, of course, that I now ask Jews to master a new technique of reading Gospel texts when in reality most Jews have never read the Gospels in any manner at all!

Part Four

Christian Holy Days

Beneficial Applications of Jewish Gospel Study

Christmas
Why the Infancy ("Virgin Birth")
Stories Arose

In moving us into a new section of this book, the current chapter examines the New Testament bases of the Christmas story, which conflates two sharply contrasting infancy narratives of Jesus—one found in Matthew, the other in Luke. Both of these relate what is often termed the "virgin birth." We will be using the more precise term "virginal conception," because it is not only the nature of Jesus' birth but more so the nature of his *conception* that is under discussion.

The backdrop of both narratives is a wider question: when in "the Christ's" existence does his divinity first become *manifest* to New Testament readers? We will term this the "moment of manifestation."[1]

Tracing the Moment of Manifestation

As we progress from Paul, to Mark, through Matthew and Luke, and then to John, the moment when Christ-Jesus' divinity becomes manifest to us regresses—that is, it shifts *earlier*. Thus:

1. Paul, our earliest writer, in the 50s, fixes the moment of manifestation later than do the Evangelists—namely, at Jesus' resurrection. This is "later" because it follows Jesus' death (cf. Rom 1:3–4: "designated Son of God in power by his resurrection from the dead").

2. Mark (ca. 72 CE), writing after Paul, shifts the moment of manifestation earlier, to Jesus' adult baptism, when the heavens open and the Holy Spirit declares: "Thou art my beloved Son" (1:11).

3. Next come Matthew and Luke (the 80s–90s)—on whom we focus in this chapter—who shift the "moment" several decades earlier still, now coincident with Jesus' conception by Mary through the Holy Spirit (Mt 1:18; Lk 1:35).

4. In the latest writer, John (ca. 100), the "moment" shifts as early as possible, to the pre-existent "Word"*: "In the beginning was the Word, and ... the Word was God" (1:1). The Christ is here pre-existent, meaning that the reader sees him manifest as divine from even before the creation of the world.

These observations are conveyed pictorially by Figure 9.1. This panoramic scheme helps us to view the infancy narratives in Matthew and Luke as representing but one stage of the four depicted.

9.1—The Regressive Shift of the "Moment of Manifestation"

AS THE FIRST CENTURY ADVANCES—*earlier* writers to *later*—
THE MOMENT WHEN CHRIST-JESUS' DIVINITY IS EVINCED REGRESSES—*later to earlier*

		(1)	(2)	(3)	(4)
At the time of	►	Paul's epistles	Mark	**Matthew and Luke**	John
datable around	►	the 50s	72	**the 80s–90s**	100
the moment when Christ-Jesus' divinity is made manifest to the reader is	►	Jesus' resurrection	Jesus' (adult) baptism	**Jesus' (virginal) conception**	Christ's pre-existence

---

Laying out matters in these terms may also clarify for us why Mark, at his relatively early date, has no birth account of Jesus at all: most likely, to his knowledge, none was yet circulating. This would be consistent with our observation in Chapter 3 that *interest in Jesus' life phases developed in reverse*: his Passion first; then his ministry (which explains why Gospels did not coalesce earlier); and his origins last. Further, the importance of Jesus' baptism (as an adult) in Mark is due to the absence of any infancy story to preempt it. John, meanwhile, latest of all the writers, also has no infancy narrative but this is likely because he was accommodating an audience who preferred, as did he, a more sophisticated pre-existent Christ figure—hardly conducive to depiction as progressing from infancy onward.

The Two Infancy Narratives—in Matthew and Luke

Matthew's and Luke's infancy stories present quite different plots, especially with respect to the geographical travels of Joseph and Mary. This suggests that, rather than working off some earlier, uniformly held tradition, these writers were independent operators exploring relatively new territory. What they contributed in common, however, is to lend to the Gospels more of a biographical cast.

Matthew's Basic Account

A lengthy genealogy purports to carry Jesus back to King David (and beyond) through the *male* line of Joseph. Unusual in genealogies, Matthew also includes four women—Tamar, Rahab, Ruth, and the wife of Uriah (i.e., Bathsheba)—who have in common checkered sexual histories.➔

9.2—*Matthew's Infancy Narrative (ca. 85)*

- Jesus' genealogy through Joseph's *male* line.
- Mary and Joseph **LIVE IN BETHLEHEM.**
- During her betrothal, Mary is found with child.
- An angel reassures a suspicious Joseph in a dream.
- Jesus is born in Bethlehem.
- Having seen a STAR, MAGI come to **JERUSALEM,**
- Then follow the STAR to **BETHLEHEM.**
- King Herod poses a danger to Jesus.
- Joseph's second dream alerts the family to flee to **EGYPT.**
- Herod dies.
- A third dream prompts the family to return from Egypt.
- A fourth dream detours them northward, to **NAZARETH.**

Matthew has Joseph and Mary, his betrothed, living in Bethlehem, of Judea (David's birthplace). Because Mary is found with child "before they came together" (1:18), Joseph suspects her of adultery.[2] But an angel reassures him, in a dream, that Mary is pregnant by the Holy Spirit (not another man).

After Jesus' birth, Magi (Gentile astrologers) from the east come to Jerusalem to inquire what location is prescribed for the birth of the "king of the Jews," whose star they had noted already two years before. (Matthew neither numbers the Magi nor identifies them as kings.[3]) The chief priests and scribes respond to Herod the Great's request by citing Micah 5:2 (5:1, in the Hebrew): the Christ was to be born "in Bethlehem of Judea" (a mere six miles to the south). Herod, alarmed at the prospect of a rival, asks the Magi to bring back word of the child's

Bethlehem whereabouts (for he intends to have him killed). The star identifies the proper house, the Magi adore Jesus, and—they themselves now directed by a dream—head back east *without* reporting to Herod.

Realizing that he has been tricked, Herod orders a slaughter of Bethlehem's male infants age two and under (the time span since the Magi first spotted the star). But Joseph, having been forewarned via his second dream, has already escaped Bethlehem, taking Mary and Jesus to Egypt. Upon Herod's death, yet a third dream directs Joseph to return the family from Egypt, but he fears Herod's son, Archelaus (Judea's new ruler). Joseph's fourth dream detours the family northward, to Nazareth, in Galilee. (This is Matthew's way of accounting for how Jesus, born in Bethlehem, became known as Jesus "of Nazareth.")

Luke's Basic Account

The angel Gabriel promises the elderly Zechariah that his barren wife, Elizabeth, will conceive John (the Baptist). Gabriel later appears in Nazareth, where Mary is betrothed to Joseph, to tell her that she, like Elizabeth, will conceive—albeit Mary through the Holy Spirit—and she will give birth to "the Son of the Most High" (1:32). When Mary visits Elizabeth in Judea, the babe in Elizabeth's womb, recognizing Mary's presence, leaps for joy.[4]

9.3—Luke's Infancy Narrative (ca. 95)

- Gabriel promises Zechariah John the Baptist's birth;
- Elizabeth conceives.
- Gabriel makes his annunciation to Mary in **NAZARETH**.
- Mary visits Elizabeth (at length); then returns to Nazareth.
- John the Baptist is born.
- Mary approaches term *in* **NAZARETH**.
- Joseph and Mary go *to* **BETHLEHEM** for a census.
- With no room in the inn, Jesus is born in a manger.
- ANGELS and SHEPHERDS appear.
- Jesus is circumcised.
- Jesus is presented in the Temple in **JERUSALEM**.
- The holy family leave Jerusalem to *return* to **NAZARETH**.

Mary returns to Nazareth. Later, she finds herself with child. When close to term, Mary accompanies Joseph from Nazareth (in Galilee) so that they can register for a census in Joseph's birthplace, Bethlehem (in Judea). While there, Mary needs to deliver. With no vacancy in the inn, a manger must suffice. Angels and shepherds rejoice. The latter inform Mary as to what this birth means. Jesus is circumcised in Bethlehem, and thereafter Luke has Joseph and Mary take Jesus to Jerusalem for a

redemption of the first-born Temple ceremony,[5] after which the holy family leave Jerusalem to return to their home in Nazareth. (This is Luke's way of accounting for how Jesus "of Nazareth" had been born in Bethlehem.)

Problems of Cohesiveness

In setting forth now a variety of problems with regard to these two narratives, our intent is not to be judgmental but simply to detect clues as to how each story developed, and what purposes each served.

Not Cohesive with One Another

Figure 9.4 highlights the major disparities between the accounts by Matthew and Luke—in their ambience, motifs, and travels. The travels

9.4—Disparities Between Infancy Narratives in Matthew and Luke

MATTHEW	⟵ ⟶	LUKE
Perilous	Ambience?	Tranquil
To Joseph	The angel announces to whom?	To Mary
In Bethlehem	Where?	In Nazareth
She resides there	Mary delivers in Bethlehem because ...	She travels there
None needed	Is an inn sought?	Yes
No	Angels and shepherds?	Yes
Yes	Magi and the Star?	No
Yes	Holy family flees to Egypt?	No
Yes	Herod massacres Bethlehem infants?	No
No	Jesus' circumcision noted?	Yes
No	Jesus' first-born redemption ceremony?	Yes
No	John the Baptist's birth story?	Yes
No	The boy Jesus (at 12) engages sages?	Yes
Yes	Is a genealogy tied to the story?	No

are especially irreconcilable: Matthew has Joseph and Mary (with the infant Jesus) begin in Bethlehem, flee to Egypt, and end up in Nazareth; Luke has Joseph and Mary begin in Nazareth, travel during her pregnancy to Bethlehem, take the infant Jesus from Bethlehem to Jerusalem, and then return to Nazareth.

These disparities proved profoundly troubling as early as the second century.[6] Some who notice them today try tracing them to a difference in informants, that is, Matthew drew on Joseph's recall, Luke on Mary's. But this must presume that Mary and Joseph did not inform one another of their separate experiences nor relate even their joint ones. For example, as concerns the latter, given that Joseph and Mary travel so extensively together, would Joseph (if Matthew's informant) fail to mention that he had taken Mary from Nazareth to Bethlehem (as per Luke), or Mary (if Luke's informant) fail to relate that she had fled to Egypt with Joseph (as per Matthew)?

To be sure, December's Christmas story so adroitly blends the two accounts that the disparities are less evident—and this is why most Christians are unaware of them. One way this blend is attempted is illustrated by the four summary paragraphs in Figure 9.5. Essentials in the first and third paragraphs are drawn from Luke, and in the second and fourth paragraphs from Matthew.

In this composite, Mary cannot have more than one "hometown" (i.e., Nazareth *and* Bethlehem). The conflation opts for Nazareth (as per Luke). This means that Bethlehem is the place where Mary is *visiting* (not residing) when giving birth. If, instead, Bethlehem is made Mary's home, then the story could no longer accommodate major motifs: for example, Joseph and Mary's trip from Nazareth to Bethlehem so as to register for the census; the inn with no vacancy (since if Mary resides in Bethlehem, no inn would be needed); and the birth in the manger.

Geographically neutral motifs could work within either format: the John the Baptist material (from Luke) and Joseph's suspicions about Mary (from Matthew). A *double* annunciation (a message delivered by an angel to a human) is also manageable in this composite: first Gabriel's Annunciation to Mary (from Luke—usually capitalized); then, once she is with child, the angel's annunciation to Joseph, during Joseph's first dream (from Matthew). Then, after Joseph's and Mary's sojourn to Bethlehem, and Jesus' delivery there by Mary the *visitor*, Jesus is circumcised and—with the business of the census (presumably) accomplished—Joseph and Mary can now transport Jesus to Jerusalem for his Temple redemption ceremony (all as per Luke).

At this juncture, however, the composite will break down without a drastic intervention. The holy family are poised to return *north*, from

9.5—The Christmas Composite

Gabriel promises Zechariah John the Baptist's birth; Elizabeth conceives. In NAZARETH, Gabriel reveals to Mary what her special role will be. After visiting Elizabeth in *Judea*, Mary returns to Nazareth in *Galilee*. John the Baptist is born.

Luke 1

During betrothal, Mary finds herself with child. Joseph is disposed to divorce her but an angel reassures him (in a dream) that Mary has conceived through the Holy Spirit, not another man.

Matthew 1

Despite Mary's advanced pregnancy, Joseph takes her to BETHLEHEM to register in a census. With no room in the inn, Jesus is born in a manger. Angels and shepherds appear. After circumcision, Jesus is brought to JERUSALEM'S Temple for a first-born's redemption ceremony.

Luke 2

☆ *Invented Segue—the Family's Return to Bethlehem from Jerusalem*

Magi, having seen a star in the east, arrive in Jerusalem. Upon learning there where Jesus has been born, they travel to BETHLEHEM, with the star guiding them. After adoring the infant, they return eastward to their home. Joseph dreams that he, Mary, and Jesus must flee to EGYPT from Herod, who soon after massacres all of Bethlehem's male infants. Once Herod dies, the holy family return from Egypt and settle in NAZARETH.

Matthew 2

Jerusalem to Nazareth (as per Luke), but Matthew's Magi and the star they follow are pressing *south*, from Jerusalem to Bethlehem! Unless the family are made to return to Bethlehem, the infant the Magi seek there will have been long gone. Hence the need for the invented segue, marked by the ☆ in Figure 9.5.

Why not, instead, simply postpone the family's Bethlehem departure to start with and allow the Magi to arrive there first—and *thereafter* the family could proceed to Jerusalem for Jesus' redemption ceremony? But

the Magi tale is intertwined with Herod's plan to kill Jesus. As a result, Joseph's second dream warns the holy family to flee from Bethlehem to Egypt. *Now* going to (the Temple in) Jerusalem, Herod's own lair, would be out of the question. The only solution, accordingly, is to have the holy family go to Jerusalem first and then *return* to Bethlehem for some (improvised) reason. This will also allow for Herod's massacre of the Bethlehem infants after the Magi have returned east and the family have fled west (to Egypt).

Not Cohesive with Succeeding Chapters

If the infancy narratives were crafted later than traditions concerning Jesus' ministry, incongruities between the opening and succeeding chapters, in both Matthew and Luke, should hardly surprise us.

At first glance, Matthew manages quite masterfully to tie in his infancy narrative with the end of his Gospel. For example, because his quotation of Isaiah 7:14→ predicts an infant named not Jesus but Emmanuel (meaning "God *with us*"), Matthew ends his Gospel with the resurrected Jesus announcing, "I am *with you* always" (28:20). Further, since Jesus *ends* his life on a cross with the placard reading "The King of the Jews" (27:37), Matthew has the Magi inquire at the *start* of his life: "Where is he who has been born *the king of the Jews*?" (2:2). Again, since in Matthew the first to pay homage to this newborn king were solely *Gentiles* (recall that the Magi do not know the scriptures),[7] so Jesus' closing "Great Commission" directs his followers to "go and make disciples of all *Gentiles*" (on this translation, see Chap. 16).

But in other respects, a lack of cohesiveness is glaring. Joseph, so central to Matthew's infancy narrative, never reappears by name. If the mission of the Magi so "troubled ... all Jerusalem" (2:3), why does there appear no public awareness of Herod's massacring all male infants in nearby Bethlehem (seemingly unknown also to Josephus, who was an expert in Herod's excesses)?

Jesus' genealogy in Luke, meanwhile, closes chapter 3. By then Jesus has begun his ministry at about age 30 (3:23). This suggests that, initially, a shorter Luke may have circulated before the two-chapter birth narrative was prefaced to it.[8]

Not Cohesive Internally

More surprising are disjunctures *within* each infancy narrative. Matthew's opening genealogy for Jesus proceeds through a male line of descendancy—Abraham through David and onward to Joseph. Its cadence leads us to expect this culmination, in 1:15–16: "Matthan the father of Jacob, and Jacob the father of Joseph, and *Joseph the father of*

Jesus." Instead, Matthew's commitment to a virginal conception forces his last-minute by passing of Joseph, who now becomes contortedly identified as "the husband of Mary, of whom Jesus was born, who is called Christ." This leaves readers to puzzle over why Matthew has presented this genealogy to start with—especially since, while establishing Davidic credentials for the now irrelevant Joseph, it provides none for Mary![9] How, then, is Jesus descended from David? (Various ancient copyists valiantly struggled to reword 1:16 but to no avail.)

In Luke, meanwhile, Mary is already "betrothed to ... Joseph, of the house of David" (1:27) when she asks Gabriel how she can conceive "since I have no husband?" (v. 34). But Gabriel has not predicted her *imminent* conception, so her skepticism is not sensible. This makes it appear that either Joseph or the virginal conception was belatedly added to this story. Further, given Gabriel's designation of Mary's child as "the Son of the Most High (1:32f.), why does Mary thereafter appear to hear from the shepherds of the special nature of her son as if for the *first* time (2:17ff.)? And why her further surprise both when Simeon characterizes Jesus as "a light for a revelation to the Gentiles" (2:32ff.) and, later (but still within Luke's "infancy" narrative), when the boy Jesus, at age twelve, terms the Temple his "Father's" house (2:48ff.)?

Also in discord are Matthew's Magi and Herod motifs. Are they interwoven from differing tales? For example, if the star leads the Magi to Bethlehem from Jerusalem, why not instead lead them from the east directly to Bethlehem? Or, if a rival to Herod's throne is born in Bethlehem,[10] why in such a serious matter does Herod depend on the Magi—strangers not subject to him—to bring him word as to the infant's whereabouts instead of directing his own police to follow the Magi (who are not particularly elusive) and in this fashion to secure the definitive information?

Did Matthew not recognize these problems? We must acknowledge that there are certain advantages to his way of conveying matters, except we cannot know for certain that he himself had them purposefully in mind.

For example, detouring the Magi to Jerusalem (rather than routing them from the east directly to Bethlehem) allows Matthew to instruct his Gentile audience that faith in pagan nature worship (i.e., dependence on a star) must yield to Christian ways of learning truth (i.e., searching the scriptures, here for Mic 5:2 [5:1, in Hebrew]). Further, since Matthew bases Jesus' birth story on that of Moses (see Chap. 16), it is actually better that Herod rely on the disobedient Magi who thereby become counterparts of the midwives who disobeyed the wicked Pharaoh (Exod 1:17ff.). Also, Matthew actually needs Herod to be tricked so that

Herod will then massacre the infants in Bethlehem to match the massacre of male Hebrew infants perpetrated by Pharaoh.

Such motifs, in turn, lead to others along these lines: Matthew needs the holy family's flight to Egypt, both so that a new Joseph the dreamer, going down to Egypt, can match the earlier Joseph the dreamer who did likewise (Gen 37), and so that Jesus as the new Moses can come out of Egypt as did his Exodus prototype. Even further, in this way Jesus (and family) can start returning home as soon as the wicked Herod dies, corresponding to how Moses (and family) could start returning home upon the wicked Pharaoh's death (Exod 2:23; 4:18ff.). Nonetheless, all these niceties are accomplished at the cost of discordance between the Magi and Herod tales running throughout the story.

The chief discordance in Luke's story line is the trek from Nazareth to Bethlehem for the Roman census, of which there was only one, in 6 CE. This means that Jesus was already at least ten, since Luke sets Jesus' birth before Herod's death in 4 BCE. (Did Luke somehow overlook Archelaus' ten-year rule, from 4 BCE through 6 CE?[11]) Further, since a ruling power's interest in a census is to determine where people are living *now* (for purposes mainly of taxation), what was the sense of Joseph's going to Bethlehem, his birthplace, when that information could simply be listed upon registering? The ancient world would have experienced "gridlock" with so many people suddenly dispersing to their birthplaces (which could require weeks of travel)! And was Mary actually to undertake so arduous a journey during her ninth month? Most startling of all, regarding local regions involved, the census of 6 CE applied only to residents of the southern territories (Judea and Samaria), not to residents of Galilee where Luke has Joseph and Mary residing.

Why, then, does this tale seem forced in so many respects? Because it is Luke's device to get primarily *Mary* (not Joseph) to Bethlehem so as to account for how Jesus "of Nazareth" came to share David's birthplace. (This is one of Luke's many created trips in service of his theology, as we discussed in Chap. 6.)

What Gave Rise to These Stories?

Since many factors may have given rise to these narratives, it was likely some confluence of two or three of these that started the process, with the others contributing secondarily. Here is a list of what may be the most important:

- *Rounding Out the Jesus Story.* If interest in phases of Jesus' life developed in reverse (first how he died, then his ministry, etc.), curiosity regarding his origins would inevitably arise—and that time had now arrived.

- *Responding to Rumors of Jesus' Origins.* Did gossip abound that Jesus was of illicit origin?[12] In a (male) genealogy for Jesus, why does Matthew include four women (along with Mary) each of whom (Tamar, Rahab, Ruth, and the wife of Uriah [i.e., Bathsheba]) was known for questionable sexual conduct?→ Does Matthew mean here to show how God intervened to preserve the messianic line even through violation of moral norms? Was a story that Mary virginally conceived intended to counter gossip, that is through an alternative explanation to adultery or rape (as by a foreign soldier) or impregnation by Joseph before marriage? This other version—virginal conception—would have been far preferable, emphasizing Mary's virtue and Jesus' purity of origins.
- *Counteracting "Adoptionism."* That Jesus' adult baptism was his "moment of manifestation" in Mark could be construed to mean that, until God "adopted" him as a Son, Jesus had been solely human. The infancy narratives advanced that moment of manifestation by about thirty years and nine months (Fig. 9.1; cf. Lk 3:23), so that Jesus could be understood as divine throughout and always.
- *Establishing Davidic Lineage.* Even at the end of the first century, Jesus was thought by some to lack Davidic ancestry and Bethlehem origins; for example, John 7:41f.: "is the Christ to come from Galilee? Has not ... scripture said that the Christ is descended from David, and comes from Bethlehem ... ?" (cf. 1:46; 7:52). Paul's earlier affirmation of Jesus' Davidic descent, in Romans 1:3, is likely natural surmise.[13] The key issue is whether, by Matthew and Luke's day, Davidic ancestry was an established sine qua non or whether *it was only now that Jews definitively made it such* as a ploy to disqualify Jesus as the Messiah. In either event, both infancy narratives appear to be devices to counter such polemic.
- *Competing with Other Cults.* While Davidic ancestry was needed for Christianity to succeed with Jews, some kind of miraculous birth account (such as virginal conception) was indispensable if Christianity was at least to match its competitors, which already possessed similar stories for their deities.

The Most Valuable Ideas in This Chapter May Be

1. We have two Gospels that lack infancy narratives (Mark and John) and two that contain them (Matthew and Luke).
2. The two that lack them do so for different reasons.
3. The two canonical infancy narratives do not share many motifs, and they contradict each other in ambience and story line.
4. Because the Christmas story appears to harmonize these contradictions so artfully, most New Testament readers remain unaware of them.

5. The two stories also lack cohesiveness internally, not to mention with later chapters of their respective Gospels.

6. It is helpful to recognize, as we progress from Paul, to Mark, through Matthew and Luke, and then to John, that the moment when Christ-Jesus' divinity becomes manifest to the reader regresses—that is, it shifts *earlier*.

7. It was likely that a confluence of many factors brought these stories into being.

8. It is unclear whether, by Matthew and Luke's day, it was already a sine qua non that the Messiah have Davidic ancestry, or whether *it was only now that Jews definitively made it such* as a ploy specifically to disqualify Jesus.

What Gospel Dynamics have We Recognized in This Chapter?

- Gospels were written to satisfy different constituencies (e.g., Greeks as well as Jews), even if this introduced discordance (e.g., virginal conception for Greeks, versus Matthew's male genealogy for Jews).

- Both Matthew and Luke devise ways to reconcile Jesus' being known as "of Nazareth" with the need to demonstrate that he was born in David's city, Bethlehem.

- That the stories in Matthew and Luke differ so greatly indicates the absence, early on, of any established infancy tradition.

- Matthew and Luke used Jewish scriptures as an extensive aid in fashioning their infancy narratives. Matthew drew especially on Moses, even Samson (for Jesus—replacing "Philistines," in Ju 13:5, with "sins," in Mt 1:21), the Joseph of Genesis (for Joseph, Mary's betrothed), and Balaam (for the Magi).[14] Luke relied on the birth story of Samuel (for facets of the Elizabeth, Mary, and Jesus depictions[15]) and the story of Abraham and Sarah (for depicting Zechariah and Elizabeth[16]).

Loose Ends Worth Tying
Making Matters More Precise

- Precision of Terminology—"Virgin Birth," "Virginal Conception," and "Immaculate Conception": Beyond preferring "virginal conception" to its ostensible synonym, "virgin birth," we should understand that "immaculate conception"—synonymous with neither—applies solely to *Mary* as a fetus, not Jesus. So as to obviate any inference that Jesus, at his conception, became tainted by Sin inherited from Mary, the notion developed post-biblically that Mary was rendered sinless simultaneously with her creation. (This became Catholic doctrine in 1854.)

- Precluding Joseph as Jesus' Father: That Joseph is shown suspicious of Mary as an adulteress is a way of excluding *him* as possibly the agent of her conception (whether before or after her betrothal to him). Even more so does insistence by Matthew 1:25 that they abstained from intercourse "until" Jesus' birth.
- Mary's "Perpetual Virginity": That the word "until" is missing from some Matthean manuscripts may result from deliberate omission in deference to the still further notion that Mary was virginal *perpetually*. Abstinence from intercourse "until" Jesus was born normally presumes commencement of intercourse thereafter, although Catholicism denies that the underlying Semitic idiom necessarily carries this implication. For some it was not appropriate to believe that Mary's womb nourished not only the Son of God but also mere mortals. Consequently, Joseph eventually became imagined as several decades older than Mary.
- Jesus' "Siblings" (Mk 6:3): That Mark has no infancy narrative or virginal conception motif, and fails to specify Jesus' siblings as *younger* than Jesus, suggests that Jesus' virginal conception narratives were late in arising. Those who insist on Mary as perpetually virginal must construe Jesus' siblings as cousins or as stemming from some previous marriage by Joseph (of which there is no canonical Gospel indication).

In What Way Did the Four Women in Matthew's Genealogy Have Checkered Sexual Histories Out of Which Came Good?

- Tamar dressed up as a harlot so as to seduce her father-in-law, Judah (Gen 38:1ff.), thereby to continue the line of Judah, which led to Jesus.
- Rahab was a prostitute who enabled the Israelites to conquer Jericho (Josh 2:1ff.) and, hence, the Promised Land thereafter.
- Ruth, a Moabitess, lay down at Boaz' feet while he was drunk (Ruth 3:6ff.,14). Their marriage produced the line that brought forth David as her great grandson (cf. also Gen 19:30ff.; Deut 23:3) and the ancestor of Jesus.
- It was through Solomon, son of Bathsheba the adulteress (2 Sa 12:24), that the Davidic line passed to Jesus.

Correcting Jews' Explanation of Isaiah 7:14

The KJV renders this text as: "Behold, a virgin shall conceive, and bear a son, and shall call his name Immanuel" (rendered "Emmanuel," by RSV, in Mt 1:23). Unfortunately, the standard Jewish response is that Isaiah used "young woman" (Hebrew: *almah*), meaning that the Greek translation, "virgin" (*parthenos*)—upon which Matthew 1:23 relies—is misleading. *Yet Isaiah's focus was not on any woman but on a measurement of time*, so Jews miss an opportunity to clarify matters.

In the context of 734 BCE, Jerusalem, capital of the southern kingdom of Judah, is under siege jointly by Syria and Israel (the northern kingdom). Isaiah informs Ahaz, King of Judah, *how long it will be* before Jerusalem emerges as saved; namely, it will be less than the span of time from the recent or imminent conception of a specific child (to be named Immanuel) until, after birth, this child "knows how to refuse the evil and choose the good" (7:16). Since the gestation period of all women is approximately the same (nine months), *the virginal status of the woman is irrelevant.* For that matter, even had Isaiah used "virgin" (which he did not), he would have meant only a woman virginal *until* intercourse but not after (something he would not ordinarily clarify given its self-evidence).

Only after establishing this basic point might Jews venture into the tangential: for example, that the woman referenced could not be Mary since any sign to be helpful for Ahaz had to materialize during *his* day (not seven centuries later); that the Hebrew tense (for "conceive") is the past or near present, not distant future; that the definite article ("the," not "a," young woman) suggests she was personally known to Isaiah or Ahaz (as a wife, e.g.); and that the child is to be named "Immanuel" (not Jesus).

Maundy (Holy) Thursday
Can We Right What's Wrong with Church "Seders"?

Passover's Attraction for Modern Christians

> Explanatory Note: "Maundy"→ (also known as "Holy") Thurs-
> day—the day before Good Friday—is understood to recall that
> evening when the Last Supper was held (as a Passover meal, accord-
> ing to the Synoptics).

Countless Christians deem the Passover Seder a splendid vehicle for experiencing, almost literally, a taste of the Jewish life led by Jesus. Each
spring, many synagogue gift shops notice brisk sales of Passover para-
phernalia to Christians. Indeed, many churches are now producing their
own Passover liturgy, punctuated by Christological passages, for example, depicting Jesus identifying matzah with his body and wine with his
blood. Some attempt to explain all facets of the Seder through the prism
of Christian theology, such that:

- The death of the firstborn foreshadows the death of Jesus (God's firstborn).
- A lamb without blemish parallels Jesus, the Lamb of God.
- Lamb's blood on wooden doorposts of Israelite homes anticipates Jesus'
  blood on the wooden cross.
- The three pieces of matzah represent the Trinity.
- The broken middle matzah constitutes the body of Jesus (middle member of the Trinity) broken on the cross.
- This matzah's stripes and holes recall Jesus' wounds (the stripes represent lashes from being whipped, and the holes represent stigmata
  from the nails through his hands and feet and the piercing of his
  side).
- The hiding and retrieval of the Afikoman (from this same piece of
  matzah) recall Jesus' burial in the tomb and resurrection therefrom.

- Passing through the Red Sea heralds the sacrament of baptism (or the Last Judgment).
- It is the *Red* Sea because of the saving blood of Jesus.

Indeed, sometimes the Jewish antecedents seem missing altogether, as shown in the following newspaper announcement:

> Shepherd's Chapel of Gravette held their annual Passover Meeting ... in Springdale, AR. Passover is a Christian religious holiday commemorating the sacrifice Jesus Christ made for the world and celebrating His resurrection.... 252 of those attending were baptized.[1]

Antecedents from Ancient Times

Certainly Passover was of focal concern even to early Christians, because the festival celebrates not only deliverance of the Hebrews from bondage in the past but also expectation of the final, messianic redemption of God's people in the future—although Christians saw Passover as signaling freedom for all humanity, achieved through the saving death and resurrection of Jesus as the Christ. As early, then, as the mid-first century CE, Paul could write of the "sacrifice" of Christ, "our paschal lamb," and urge Christians to avoid the "leaven of malice and evil" in favor of "the unleavened bread of sincerity and truth" (1 Cor 5:6ff.). The Synoptists identified Jesus' Last Supper expressly with the Passover meal itself. John set the Passover meal on the night *following* that of the Last Supper, so that Jesus' death would coincide with the sacrifice of the Passover lamb on the afternoon before the evening festival meal.➔

Despite these Christian interpretations, neither the earliest Christians nor Jesus ever practiced the kind of full-fledged Seders that many churches stage today to "reenact" the Last Supper. The mature Seder, and the Haggadah[2] to accompany it, evolved only much later than Jesus' time, and were, moreover, *rabbinic* in creation, not derived from the biblical Israelite religion that Christianity professed to co-opt and supersede. Further, since early rabbinic Judaism seems distinctly *anti-*Christian in orientation it raises the question: did the Passover Seder itself reflect, in some respect, an anti-Christian animus?

Passover Jeopardized?

We have seen (Fig. 5.6) how devastating the loss of the Jerusalem Temple was, threatening Judaism's very survival. Gamaliel II, head rabbi starting in the 80s (whose grandfather is fictionally[3] featured in Acts 5:34; 22:3), was the chief architect of new forms of Jewish observance, and he marginalized any groups that he thought inimical to Judaism's consolidation and perpetuation.

The indispensability of the Temple for Passover observance was established by the ancient editors of Deuteronomy and Kings.[4] With the Temple now in ruins, and sacrifice of paschal lambs no longer possible, what new manner of observance could be devised to allow Passover celebration to continue in a meaningful way? Within the little information that we have, Gamaliel is again central. The key rabbinic text conveys how he used to say: "Whoever does not explain these three things on Passover does not discharge one's duty ... : the Passover offering [lamb], unleavened bread, and bitter herbs" (M. Pes 10:5). The translation, "explain," is preferable to "say" or "mention" since the Passover offering, unleavened bread, and bitter herbs "obviously are prescribed by ... Gamaliel ... to be expatiated upon."[5] Given the apparent profile of Gamaliel II's interests and activities (liturgy, calendar, scripture, etc.), he certainly "fits the bill" as propounder of this dictum (to the extent that we can rely on rabbinic testimony).

Was Gamaliel's Dictum Anti-Christian?

The primary purpose of Gamaliel's formulation was to devise a framework for Passover observance in the face of the Temple's destruction. Yet it warrants our asking whether he *framed* his directive also so as to counter co-option of Passover themes by the two earliest Gospels, Mark (ca. 72 CE) and Matthew (ca. 85 CE). For when we examine their Last Supper narratives, we find no reference whatsoever to the "Passover offering" or "unleavened bread" or "bitter herbs," let alone all three—not to mention *explication* of each as Gamaliel minimally requires. Nor, for that matter, is the Exodus from Egypt recalled. Did Gamaliel know what these Last Supper narratives did *not* contain, and so frame his dictum as to invalidate designations of Jesus' Last Supper as a Passover observance?

In assessing Gamaliel's directive, note that "the oddity of having to state the meaning of [in this case Passover] symbols ... does sort of leap out at one [for] nowhere else" do we encounter an analogous kind of dictum.[6] Was Gamaliel "undoubtedly aware" of meanings Christians applied to Passover symbols, and, accordingly, was this a reason why he "ordained ... Jews everywhere ... to state [the symbols'] original Jewish significance"?[7]

There is an objection that comes from geography—Mark and Matthew may have been written for communities so far removed from the land of Israel that Gamaliel could not have been aware of them. Antioch, in *nearby* Syria, receives the most endorsements by scholars as Matthew's provenance. (If correct, this would render Mark's place

of origin irrelevant since Matthew preserves, and expands, Mark's Last Supper account.) Moreover, as a proselytizing and also networking religion, Christianity itself was eager to disseminate its ideas, especially in synagogues (see Chap. 6)! The contents of a Gospel written for one community were not geographically bound. If sections were read aloud and also passed along in paraphrase, listeners (including pagans* and non-Christian Jews) could freely relay elsewhere what they had heard. Further, since rabbis in the land of Israel (including Gamaliel) were intent on influencing Diaspora synagogues, they sent emissaries to them, and in some of these regions there were churches (even positioned close to synagogues). Whatever these rabbinic envoys witnessed, or heard, concerning church practices there they could readily report upon return.

As for Gamaliel himself, he is definitively associated (*Ber* 28b) with the *Birkat Ha-Minim* (the "benediction"—actually, malediction) against *minim*, or "heretics."[8] So if this reflected Gamaliel's general orientation, a Passover dictum directed against Christians is plausible.

Modern Jewish Enthusiasm over Church "Seders"

Over the centuries since Gamaliel's day, the Passover/Easter season has posed tension and danger and death for Jews. Medieval mythology cast them as kidnapping and killing Christian children for their blood (supposedly needed to bake Passover matzah), an accusation serving "throughout the ages to create an anti-Jewish mentality.... Hundreds of Jews [were] imprisoned, killed, ... even burnt alive.... The Papacy ... frequently denounced this charge, yet ... in numerous instances, the accusation of ritual murder was not made except with vigorous support of local church authorities,"[9] some of whom charged that Jews were thereby reenacting their murder of Jesus, or even that they had stolen the Seder from the Lord's Supper.

Is it any wonder, then, that when modern Christian interest in Seders began to emerge many Jews were intrigued that Christians were asking for invitations to local synagogues or Jewish homes where they too could experience the Seder? When, thereafter, such ceremonies began to be practiced by churches themselves, Jews noticed a disturbing trend: "Seders" suffused with Christian theology were changing Passover's meaning, not to mention its perception by the popular culture. Additionally, missionary Christians were exploiting Passover as a way to woo Jews to Christianity as well as to fund[10] their proselytizing of them, and Jews feared that this might be only the beginning of co-opting additional Jewish holidays and observances.

Why Mark's "Passover Meal" Was Not a Passover Meal

In my experience, presenting a Jewish focus on Mark's "Passover Meal Paragraph" has resulted in Christians' appreciation because they want to learn and also they want to avoid doing anything insensitive respecting the Jewish community. In presenting such a focus, concentration should be on *Mark* because his account became the basis of later renditions by Matthew and Luke.

The following analysis demonstrates that the Last Supper was originally understood by the earliest Christians themselves as an ordinary, non-Passover meal. Four categories of text warrant attention here (see Fig. 10.1):

10.1—Was the Last Supper a Passover Meal?

ORDINARY MEAL — *1 Cor 11:23 (mid-50s)*—In Paul's sole reference to the Last Supper ("the Lord Jesus, on the night when he was delivered up [to death], took bread"), the Greek word Paul uses is that for regular bread (*artos*), not the proper designation for unleavened bread (*azyma*), and Paul conveys no awareness that this meal might have been a Passover observance.

PASSOVER MEAL — *Mark (ca. 72)*—Here the entire case for identifying the Last Supper as a Passover meal rests with a single, five-verse paragraph (14:12–16).

(Ambiguous) — *Matthew (ca. 85)* and *Luke* (ca. 95)—Finding Mark's account problematic, both Matthew and Luke replicate Mark's general scheme, yet refine it in ways that, to us, may appear to undermine Mark's credibility.

ORDINARY MEAL — *John (ca. 100)*—John presents the Last Supper as occurring twenty-four hours→ *before* the Passover meal.

Since the pivotal text for identifying the Last Supper as a Passover meal is solely Mark 14:12–16, let us analyze these five verses in their context (Fig. 10.2):

10.2—Mark's Insertion of His Invented "Passover" Paragraph

1–2:   It was now two days *before* the Passover and the Feast of
        Unleavened Bread. And the chief priests and ... scribes were
        seeking how to arrest him ... and kill him; for they said, "*Not
        during the feast*, lest there be a tumult of the people." ...

10–11: Then Judas Iscariot ... went to the chief priests ... to betray him
        to them ... and he sought an opportunity....

And *on the first day of Unleavened Bread*, when they
sacrificed the Passover Lamb, his disciples said to him,
"Where will you have us ... prepare for you to eat the
Passover?" And he sent *two* of his disciples: ... "*Go   *Passover*
into the city*, and a man carrying a jar of water will   *meal*
meet you; ... wherever he enters, say to the   *created*
householder, 'The Teacher says, "Where is my guest   *and*
room, where I am to eat the Passover with my   *inserted*
disciples?"' And he will show you a large upper room   *belatedly*
furnished and ready; there prepare for us." And the
disciples ... *went to the city* and found it as he had
told them; and they prepared the Passover.

17–20: ... When it was evening he *came with the twelve*. And as they
        were at table eating, Jesus said, "... one of you will betray me,
        one ... dipping *bread* in the same dish with me...."

22–25: ... as they were eating, he took *bread*, ... blessed ... broke it, and
        gave it to them.... "Take; this is my body." ... He took a cup, and
        ... gave it to them, and they all drank.... He said..., "This is my
        blood of the covenant ... poured out for many...."

26:     And ... they went out to the Mount of Olives.

At this point I want to draw special attention to five puzzling and dis-
cordant problems to which Mark's account gives rise. I describe them as
"anomalies" because they do not sit well with the surrounding material in
which they now lie embedded. By analyzing them, we will realize that it is
simply impossible that today's church programs for Maundy Thursday
reenact Jesus' Last Supper in a historically accurate way. For all five anomalies are resolvable by this single proposal: that, *originally, in the material
Mark received, the Last Supper was understood merely as an ordinary
(i.e., non-Passover) meal.* Only later, after 70 CE, while editing this material, did Mark deliberately (but without sufficient care) transform the

occasion into a Passover observance—and, as Figure 10.2 conveys, he did this by inserting a single paragraph (14:12–16) as a lens through which he wished the story of Jesus' Last Supper now to be understood. Each anomaly was occasioned by Mark's desire to associate the death/resurrection of Jesus with the Passover experience of liberation.

Anomaly 1: Unexplained rupture of the story line

In verse 2 ("Not during the feast") the authorities intend to dispose of Jesus *before* the feast, yet in verse 12 the feast has already arrived. These two conflicting chronologies are left unreconciled. Did something go amiss with the plan to arrest Jesus before the feast? If no, and Jesus *was* arrested before the Passover meal, then clearly his Last Supper was not a Passover meal; if yes (something did go amiss), and the time for the Passover meal already arrived before his arrest, how could Mark neglect to tell us what had gone awry?

The answer is that *a single Passover Meal paragraph (14:12–16) has been inserted into an earlier story line that was resistant to it—a new time line (introducing the Passover meal) has been superimposed on an original time line (devoid of one).* Earlier tradition had held that Jesus was indeed arrested before the feast and that his Last Supper had thus preceded the time of the Passover meal. If we delete the Passover Meal paragraph (vv.12–16) we no longer have to wonder why the plan to arrest Jesus before the feast failed because, without these verses, the plan succeeded! Moreover, the story reads smoothly without these verses. (Gospel manuscripts originally lacked verse numbers, so what now appears as "verse 17" would have followed what is now designated "verse 11.")

Anomaly 2: Unnatural concentration of "Passover" material

Nothing outside verses 12–16 hints that the feast has yet arrived. Were the Last Supper a Passover meal, allusions to Passover's arrival should appear throughout the narrative rather than compressed into a short paragraph. This concentration of Passover material is another indication that the Passover Meal paragraph was folded into an earlier story line.

Anomaly 3: Telltale omissions

Note the curious absence from Mark's account of four core elements of Passover observance: matzah (missing also from 1 Cor 11:23)—it is not simply that matzah is absent but that regular bread[11] is present (cf. Mk 14:22); lamb (the main food); bitter herbs; and mention of the Exodus. *These elements are absent from material surrounding verses 12–16 because the original story line culminated in Jesus' arrest before the feast*

arrived. (Mention of Passover in verse 2 hardly counts since, in context, it argues *against* the Passover meal's arrival before the arrest.) The omission of the elements also from verses 12–16 (the Passover Meal paragraph itself) reveals how poorly Mark crafted the invented paragraph. In transforming the Last Supper into a Passover meal, he forgot, or did not know, to include the key components.

Anomaly 4: A mathematical problem?

In verses 12–16, Jesus sends two disciples from Bethany to Jerusalem to prepare the Passover meal. When Jesus himself comes thereafter, only ten remain available to accompany him (12 minus 2 leaves 10). Then verse 17 informs us that "he came with the *twelve*," but the two who went to Jerusalem do not appear to have rejoined the group.

Ordinarily we should not see this as problematic because "the twelve" could be but a formula meaning members of Jesus' circle irrespective of how many happen to be present. What catches our eye is that Matthew and Luke themselves believe that Mark has made a mistake and set about to correct it (Fig. 10.3).

10.3—*Matthew and Luke Believe Mark Has Made an Error*

Mark 14:17	Matthew 26:20	Luke 22:14
And when it was evening he came with the twelve	When it was evening, he *sat at table* with the twelve disciples	And when the *hour* came, he *sat at table*, and the apostles with him

---

If we take our cue from Matthew and Luke (for a similar problem, see Figs. 15.1 and 15.2), then we have to accord this problem due regard after all. Matthew adjusts Jesus "came with the twelve" to "*sat at table* with the twelve" (26:20).[12] Luke, meanwhile, changes "*he* came" into "*the hour* came" (22:14), leaving us to mull over how Luke matches Matthew's innovative "sat at table with" all of them. (Since this commonality in *narrative* material is not due to dependence on "Q" [see Chap. 3], did Luke have Matthew as well as Mark before him?) Suffice it to say that, if this was indeed a problem, we can easily account for how it arose: namely, in the same fashion by which we have accounted for the other anomalies. All are due to Mark's insertion of verses 12–16. Without this paragraph, there was no Passover meal to prepare, and consequently no sending of two disciples ahead to prepare it, so when Jesus arrived for his Last Supper (now, only an

ordinary meal) he could indeed have come "with the [literal] twelve," as per verse 17.

Anomaly 5: Jesus' supposed trial on a festival

It seems odd that Mark, closely followed by Matthew, insists that Jesus was tried on a Jewish festival (Nisan 15, the first day of the Feast of Unleavened Bread). Even assuming, for the sake of argument, that Jesus actually underwent a Sanhedrin trial (highly doubtful; see next two chapters), how could Jewish councilors be assembled to sit in judgment on such a holy day? The solution here proposed—that in the original tradition Jesus was arrested *before* the feast—would resolve this difficulty also.

Since all five anomalies disappear once we remove the Passover Meal paragraph, we must ask what prompted Mark to change an ordinary meal into a Passover observance? He did not fancy himself a faithful transmitter of history, nor did the context in which he functioned expect that of him. Rather, he was writing *theology*, and it was in such service that he transformed the Last Supper into a Passover meal—most likely to correlate Passover, festival of freedom for the Jews, with Jesus' death and resurrection, which brought freedom for humanity. In conveying this message, Matthew and Luke followed Mark, albeit repairing him or filling in his gaps.

Meanwhile, John's twenty-four hour disjuncture between the Last Supper and the Passover meal is likewise theologically driven. John chose to present Jesus' death as coincident with that of the paschal lamb.[13] Since the lamb had to die before the Passover meal, this required John to set the Passover meal on Friday night, *after* Jesus' death that previous afternoon. The two options (Passover meal or Passover lamb) were mutually exclusive, so only one could be incorporated by any Evangelist. That is, if Jesus were the paschal lamb, he could not be alive at the Passover meal (so the Last Supper was ordinary); if he attended a Passover meal (alive), he could not be identified with the paschal lamb (which had to have died beforehand).

This close analysis of Mark has revealed the Passover material to be *a superimposition on an underlying tradition at variance with it.* Accordingly, the entire case for the Last Supper as a Passover meal crumbles. The Matthean and Lucan chronologies lose their value because they simply replicate the chronology of Mark, their primary source. Literally countless alternative explanations and schemes have been advanced, but none has resolved the entire spectrum of problems listed here. Indeed, the very complexity of other solutions renders them that much the more suspect.[14]

Christian Reflections

Increasingly, Christian leaders are moving their communities toward a judicious reconsideration of the ramifications and consequences of what they are doing with respect to Passover. As early as the 1980s, a Roman Catholic directive stated that "when Christians celebrate this ... feast among themselves, the rites of the *haggadah* ... should be respected in all their integrity ... with sensitivity to those to whom the Seder truly belongs.... Any sense of 'restaging' the Last Supper of the Lord Jesus should be avoided," as should efforts "to 'baptize' the Seder by ending it with New Testament readings about the Last Supper or, worse, turn it into a prologue to the Eucharist."[15] Some leaders now discourage separate Christian celebrations; for example, "The Seder is a Jewish tradition that Christians should ... experience only when they are privileged to enjoy the hospitality of Jews at the Passover table. Catholic guests ... should not imagine that they are reenacting the Last Supper, which after all occurs at ... the Mass."[16]

A Lutheran guide adopts a mediating stance: "Although attendance at Seders in Jewish homes or synagogues is ... preferred, 'demonstration Seders' ... in Christian churches ... should be approached with ... awareness that this might be considered 'trampling on the other's holy ground.'"[17] (Here "demonstrate" is apt—in contrast to "conduct"— since, as a rabbinically ordained observance, the Seder may not be *conducted* by a non-Jew, only *presented* as, for instance, an educational experience.) The least problematic interfaith liturgy has been *The Passover Celebration*, edited by Leon Klenicki.[18]

The Best for Both Worlds

Mark's action here was an entirely appropriate and acceptable thing for him to do because he was not intending to write history, but *theology*. He was—as were the other Evangelists—writing to meet the needs of his community in his place and time. Yet the five anomalies laid out have shown that the Last Supper was not—and could not have been—a Passover observance of any kind, let alone a Seder.

By now, Christians may not be sure who is right, or what this should all mean in the context of the Christian–Jewish dialogue that both parties hope to nurture. Meanwhile, even Jews who feel that Mark has trespassed on Jewish sensibilities have nevertheless helped Christians to enact Seders accurately.

I feel that Jews might process matters along the following lines: In expressing their interest in the Passover Seder, some Christians are reaching out to Jews so as to honor what these Christians identify as their own Jewish roots, and by this process probably to acknowledge the genuine *Jewishness* of Jesus and his companions by depicting them celebrat-

ing a Jewish feast. What they intend to say by their celebration is essentially that this is how it all began, with the liberation of the chosen people from physical slavery and their establishment of self-sovereignty in their own land. And the Last Supper is the expanded parallel to the experience of the Exodus. This great Act is now expanded to the world—to apply to every sort of slavery or oppression, not only physical and political, but moral and spiritual.

To this, many Jews could essentially reply, Yes, that's how we see it too, as a metaphor for our continuing efforts at liberating everyone from everything that represses full human life. As great as the importance that attaches to what happened in the past—either in the distant Exodus or the early Christian era—also important is what is going to happen from now on. In the Seder, we all have the model, the metaphor, the sacred celebration, but its urgency is how we, together with each other and together with as much of the rest of the world as possible, can work to bring about the many-leveled Liberation for everyone.

The Most Valuable Ideas in This Chapter May Be

1. The Seder—fundamentally *rabbinic* in creation—was a post-70 CE response to turmoil posed by the fall of the Temple and the resulting end of the sacrificial cult.
2. Secondarily, it delegitimized the Passover veneer that Mark (and Matthew) had applied to Jesus' Last Supper.
3. Mark tried to transform an ordinary Last Supper meal into a Passover observance so that he could correlate Passover, the festival of physical and political freedom for the Jews, with Jesus' death, which brought spiritual freedom for humanity.
4. Mark accomplished this change by fashioning a single paragraph and then inserting it between (what we identify as) 14:11 and 17 (with Matthew and Luke thereafter essentially preserving what Mark had done).
5. This formulation stands at variance with earlier Christian tradition that Jesus was arrested before the evening of the Passover meal arrived.
6. At least four additional anomalies were created by Mark's insertion, all of which—like the first—vanish as soon as we remove the paragraph that he crafted.
7. Because the Seder originated after Jesus' time, and the even fuller Seder evolved over centuries later still, neither Jesus the Jew nor pre-70 Christians ever practiced a Seder of any kind, let alone celebrations like those that many churches today stage to "reenact" the Last Supper.

What Gospel Dynamics Have We Recognized in This Chapter?

- Mark attempted to adjust history—of how the Last Supper was observed—in the interests of his personal theology.
- A common literary device by Mark was the introduction of new materials into contexts where they did not originally reside.
- This Dynamic becomes obvious when the added material does not rest comfortably in its new literary surroundings. (Confirming Mark's editing in this respect is the frequency with which he uses this Dynamic elsewhere—see Figs. 8.5; 12.2–3; 12.5; 12.8; 12.10; 15.3; and 21.1; cf. Mk 15:6–15a.)

Loose Ends Worth Tying

Why John Sets Passover Twenty-Four Hours Later than Do the Synoptists

All four Gospels fix the Last Supper on Thursday night, with Jesus' death Friday afternoon, but disagree over when the Passover meal itself fell. Mark (14:12f.), upon whom Matthew (26:17f.) and Luke (22:7f.) depend, sets it Thursday night, coincident with the Last Supper; John distinguishes the two meals, setting the Passover observance the following night, Friday, directly after the Passover lamb's sacrifice that Friday afternoon (13:1–2; 18:28; 19:14,31–36). Whose chronology is correct? Theoretically, we could compute new moons astronomically to reconstruct when the Hebrew month, Nisan, began in the year Jesus died (the Passover meal occurs the evening beginning Nisan 15); on this basis, we might then be able to determine on which night of the week (Thursday or Friday) the Passover meal would have been held that year. But we do not know the year Jesus died except that it fell between 26 and 37 (when Pilate ruled Judea). The debate over competing chronologies is unproductive because, as we have seen, both options (the Synoptists' and John's) were *theologically* driven (not historically grounded).

Irony of "Maundy" Thursday

The name of the day when churches stage Seders is derived from the one Gospel (John) that overtly *precludes* the Last Supper's identification as a Passover meal! The English name, "Maundy," is derived from the Latin *mandatum* ("commandment") in John 13:34: "a new *commandment* I give to you, that you love one another; even as I have loved you."

The "Permissibility" of Christians Partaking in Jews' Seders

Exodus 12:43ff. seems to limit Passover observance to Israelites and those "converted" to Israelite observance. Jewish tradition came to read that prohibition as referring specifically to partaking of the paschal lamb *(korban pesach)* while the Temple was still standing, not to the home-based Seder of later times.[19]

Good Friday
Responding to Blame for Jesus' Death

Good Friday recalls for Christians Jesus' agony on the cross. The day has spelled agony for Jews also. Not only do the Gospels hold the Jews accountable for Jesus' death but sermons, liturgy, and scriptural readings can also compound that culpability. Thanks notably to advances initiated by the Second Vatican Council (1965),[1] educational materials (including those of some Protestant denominations as well) have substantially reduced, and even eliminated, negative presentations of the Jewish people. But even this can be problematic if the same materials fail to explain how devastatingly the Gospels impacted the sweep of *earlier* Jewish history and to caution how vulnerable recent gains are to possible setback (especially in Third World Christianity).

The chapters in each Gospel relating events from Jesus' arrest through his expiration are termed the Passion Narrative.* Those chapters in Mark warrant primary attention because his Passion became substantially the basis of renditions by Matthew and Luke (possibly even John). Its essentials are these:

Conspiracy (14:1–2,10–11). Two days before Passover and the feast of Unleavened Bread, Jewish officials seek to arrest Jesus. Judas furnishes them an opportunity to capture him.

Arrest (14:12–52). After the Last Supper, Jesus adjourns to the Garden of Gethsemane; his betrayer comes with a Jewish party who seize Jesus.

Sanhedrin Proceedings (14:53–72). Jesus undergoes a nighttime Sanhedrin trial headed by the high priest, and comprising chief priests, elders, and scribes. When Jesus affirms that he is "the Christ, the Son of the Blessed," the high priest decries this "blasphemy." The Sanhedrin condemns Jesus as deserving death. In the courtyard, Peter—identified as Jesus' follower—denies association.

Interrogation by Pilate (15:1–5). With morning, Jesus is brought before the Roman prefect who asks, "Are you the King of the Jews?" Answering "You have said so," Jesus refuses further comment.

The Prisoner Release (15:6–15). Pilate offers the Jewish crowd release of a criminal: either Jesus or Barabbas (an insurrectionist). Exhorted by their priests, the Jews opt for Barabbas and demand that Pilate crucify Jesus. Disposed to free him, but wishing to appease the crowd, Pilate consigns him to the cross.

Crucifixion (15:16–41). Jesus undergoes crucifixion between two "thieves"; the inscription of his charge reads: "The King of the Jews."

Clearly Mark blames the Jews for Jesus' death: Jesus is arrested by Jewish conspirators, condemned by a Jewish court, and charged with blasphemy—a Jewish, hardly Roman, accusation. The aroused Jewish mob elect to free not the innocent Jesus but an insurrectionist (who is also a murderer). Pilate has Jesus crucified to quell clamoring by a Jewish crowd. Later Evangelists intensify vilifications of Jews, as Mark may have done with *his* received traditions.

Most Jews have never hit upon any effective response to "Christ-killer" accusations. Notions to be countered are that: (1) the Jews were to blame for Jesus' death; (2) this involvement requires that Jews be held accountable as a people; and (3) such "corporate" accountability is transmissible to all subsequent generations.

Despite its format, the exercise that follows should not be seen as adversarial but informational. I cull here from my personal involvement[2] in the 2003–2004 controversy over the Mel Gibson film, *The Passion of the Christ*, presenting the flavor of arguments that I then heard proffered by Jews against blame of their people for Jesus' death. (It should be noted that only the smallest percentage of Jews felt well-versed enough to say anything at all; see Chap. 23.) I set these arguments forth here along with responses I heard countering them. Most Christians would not even think to offer these "rejoinders," but may yet benefit from pondering that some others have indeed proposed them. The arguments, as well as the rejoinders, are uneven in cogency and persuasiveness:

- **The "Discrepancies" Defense.** Rome did it (no Jews were involved) because there are major discrepancies between the general capital trial procedures as prescribed by the Talmud and those that the Gospels report were applied in Jesus' Sanhedrin trial. These expose the Gospel accounts as purely contrived.

  Rejoinder: The Talmud itself (Sanh 43a) explicitly tells us that Jewish officials tried and executed Jesus! And should rabbinic procedures

reflect a different court system, or stem from a later age, or be ideal-ized (i.e., these procedures were never operative to start with), then the amassing of discrepancies is irrelevant to discussing Jesus' experience anyway.

- **The "Vital Cog" Defense.** If it was vital for the world's redemption that Jesus die, and the Jews were a vital cog in effecting that death and redemption, why are they not *praised* for their role in human-ity's salvation rather than blamed?

  Rejoinder: For the same reason that Judas is vilified even though his betrayal set into motion Jesus' saving death. At the Last Supper, Jesus says that he himself "goes as it is written of him, but woe to that man by whom [he] ... is betrayed! It would have been better for that man if he not been born" (Mk 14:21 & parr). Jesus had to die but woe to heinous Judas who need not have opted to betray him! Similarly with "the Jews": Jesus had to die but woe to the heinous Jews who need not have opted to condemn him! What happened to Jesus was divinely ordained but, because the crime that Jews of their own accord chose to commit was without divine sanction, the Jews remain guilty.

- **The "Implausibilities" Defense.** Would police allow Jesus unim-peded entry to the Temple (apparently) the day after he violently "cleansed" it (Mk 11:27)? Would Judas commit treachery for merely thirty pieces of silver when, as treasurer (Jn 12:6), he could have absconded with all the disciples' money at any time? Given Rome's wariness of seditionists, would Pilate release Barabbas, an insurrectionist? Such implausibilities (among many others) under-mine claims of the Gospels' accuracy in general, not to mention their credibility in blaming the Jews in particular.

  Rejoinder: Seeming implausibilities are incidental compared to an es-sentially credible core story line about Jesus. Denial of Jewish involve-ment would be the greatest implausibility!

- **The "Unreasonability" Defense.** It is unreasonable to speak of Jews as *corporately* responsible in Jesus' death: Jews living after his day played no role; most Jewish contemporaries outside the land of Israel never knew of him, nor did most inside; and any who did were not likely present at Gospel scenes depicting Jews demanding his crucifixion.

  Rejoinder: The overwhelming majority of later Jews persisted in deny-ing Jesus' credentials, thereby associating themselves with their ances-tors who rejected Jesus and were culpable in his death.

- **The "Recourse to Scripture" Defense.** The Evangelists combed Jewish scripture for clues supposedly predictive of Jesus, enlisting these to generate "events" in Jesus' Passion—"fulfilling" the Bible with details co-opted to establish just that!

  Rejoinder: Aside from messianic passages that Jesus did fulfil, actual events of his life reminded Gospel writers of biblical texts that they enlisted as but modest embellishments.

- **The "Improvisations" Defense.** Ancient Greek writers, such as Herodotus (484–425 BCE), Thucydides (455–400 BCE), the Jewish historian, Josephus (the Evangelists' contemporary), and so forth, frequently presented audiences with invented history, even inserting their personal views into speeches they ascribed to others. The Evangelists' Greek "histories" followed similar conventions, recasting, even creating outright, events and speeches that they felt *should* have occurred.

  Rejoinder: That others may have fabricated history does not mean the same of Evangelists inspired by God. Any such recastings as they may have undertaken did not undermine their credible nucleus of reliably transmitted tradition.

Of all these Jewish defenses, the strongest may be the last two, but the rejoinders offered to any of these may leave Jews ultimately stymied. What Jews most need here is in-depth knowledge of how Passion traditions came into being (see next chapter). At the same time, the most critical factor is one Jews rarely discern: that the Jewish predilection is to address this problem only on the *historical* plane, because that is where the battle is usually waged. By the end of this chapter, we will need to engage the *theological* plane, too, in all its traumatic dimension.

The Historical Approach

Expanding on some earlier conclusions (Chap. 5), I endorse the view[3] that Jesus saw himself as God's last envoy before God's imminent intervention in history, which would purify the world of the evilness resulting from human misbehavior and achieve places of acceptance for the poor, outcast, and lowly. Jesus may even have expected to play a kind of royal role in this coming "Kingdom," whose arrival he heralded through at least one emblematic demonstration: his overturning of Temple furniture to symbolize the overturning of the current world order in favor of the coming ruling power of God.→ (His action, in other words, concerned more than money-changers.)[4]

Presumably personnel ruling this new Kingdom would differ from those governing the old, so those most acutely provoked by Jesus' portent would have been the then-current leaders: chief priestly elements. Further, threats against Rome's Jewish appointees, charged with maintaining law and order, were threats against the Empire as well—especially when framed in terms of a coming new *Kingdom*. This significant information sparked intercession by the high priest with Pilate, who then consigned Jesus to the cross.

Yet with respect to such Gospel reportage, what influenced Jewish history was not Jesus' time frame but that of the Gospel writers, which was roughly forty to seventy years after Jesus' public career. The Evangelists' ill-disposition toward those Jews who, in the writers' own day, rejected Jesus magnified any role that they presumed Jews had played in Jesus' death. Several considerations concerning this later time frame—that of the Evangelists—command attention.

Wariness of Rome

By the last third of the first century, Christians had reason to feel wary of Rome. Emperor Nero scapegoated Christians, in 64 CE, for a fire in Rome itself, inflicting upon them "grievous torments."[5] Even Christians in far reaches likely heard of this. In 66, after the Jews revolted, the inevitability of Rome's vengeance signaled danger also for Christians confused with the Jewish rebels—likely since Christians shared Jewish scripture, facets of Jewish belief and practice, and, for some, even Jewish family ties. How discomfiting it was that the founder to whom Christians traced themselves had been crucified, a *Roman* punishment for insurrectionists, and that their movement stemmed from a land associated with fanatical rebellion. Lest the stigma of their crucified Lord adhere likewise to his later followers, here was reason enough to invent, and emphasize, Pilate's endeavor to release Jesus.

Rancor Toward (Non-Christian) Jews

But if Christians claimed Jesus was innocent of sedition, why then was he crucified? This dilemma required assigning another party (beyond Rome) a role in his death. An ever-present reality for Christians during the Evangelists' age was antipathy from Jews rejecting them—an attitude *easily presumed characteristic of earlier Jews toward Jesus personally*. Consequently, we have two propositions operative: one of actual responsibility for Jesus' death by some Jewish authorities; the other of the Evangelists' predisposition toward *assigning* responsibility to Jews anyway. Even if Jews played but a minimal (or no) role in Jesus' condemnation, the Gospels may have been drawn to aggrandize (or invent)

such involvement—in order to ally Christians with Rome while present-ing Jews as enemies of both.

Christian Reliance on Jewish Scripture

Christian tradition often gathered "information" about Jesus—in the absence of real evidence—by referring to the Bible for clues presumed predictive of him as Messiah (see Chaps. 7 [end], 8, and 20). Here is a most pertinent example:

> Long ago, there lived a righteous Jew who spoke for God. Defying the religious establishment, he aroused enmity from Jewish priests. Demanding that they amend their ways, he threatened destruction of the Temple ("a den of robbers")! The priests threatened him with death. He warned that they could bring innocent blood upon them-selves. The vacillating civil authority summoned him and, pro-nouncing him innocent, expressed reluctance to heed his accusers' demands. As the just man warned, the Temple was later destroyed.

Ostensibly matching Jesus, this describes *Jeremiah*, whom Mark 11:17 actually has Jesus quote (see Fig. 11.1). The parallels between the two are simply too uncanny to be written off as coincidence. And if blaming Jesus' death on the Jews did have a basis in Jeremiah's story, then we have to reckon with the possibility that the fate of Jews, murdered as "Christ-killers," was sealed by traditions bearing no connection to Jesus at all.

The Pertinence of Blasphemy

If the placard on Jesus' cross, "The King of the Jews" (signaling sedi-tion), stigmatized later Christians as well, then defusing this accusation was imperative for their security. Useful in this regard would be Mark's account (14:53ff.)—which Matthew copied (26:57ff.)—of Jesus' San-hedrin condemnation for *blasphemy*. Christians of the Evangelists' age, hearing themselves maligned by contemporary Jews as blasphemers for exalting Jesus as more than human, would naturally suppose blasphemy likewise as the charge of which Jesus himself was accused. Portraying Jesus as condemned for blasphemy, a merely religious offense concern-ing Jews only, would assist Gospel writers in defusing notions that Jesus entertained subversive pretensions to royalty. This facilitated portraying *a Jew put to death by the Romans as a "Christian" put to death by "the Jews."* (The next chapter works this out in detail.)

11.1—Parallels Between Jeremiah and Jesus

Jeremiah		Jesus
"Has the house ... become a den of robbers ...?" (7:11)	→	"Is it not written [Jer 7:11], 'My house ... you have made ... a den of robbers'?" (Mk 11:17 & parr)
I will "do to th[is] house [temple #1] ... as I did to Shiloh [1 Sa 4–6]!" (7:14)	→	"We heard him say, 'I will destroy this temple [#2] ...'" (Mk 14:58 & par; cf. Jn 2:19)
"All the people laid hold of him, saying: 'You shall die'" (26:8)	→	"All the people" demanded his death (Mt 27:25)
An inquiry convened for Jeremiah (26:10)	→	A Sanhedrin convened for Jesus (Mk 14:53 & parr)
Priests (and others) said Jeremiah "deserves ... death" for words that "you have heard" (26:11)	→	The Sanhedrin decided that Jesus "deserves death" (Mt 26:66 [cf. Mk 14:64]) for words that "you have heard" (Mk 14:64; cf. Mt 26:65)
"you will bring innocent blood upon yourselves" (26:15)	→	"His blood be on us and on our children!" (Mt 27:25)
His captors took him for execution to the vacillating King Zedekiah, who replied: "He is in your hands ..." (38:5)	→	His captors took him for execution to the vacillating prefect Pilate, who replied: "See to it yourselves" (Mt 27:24)
Wanting a private conversation, "Zedekiah sent for Jeremiah" (38:14)	→	Wanting a private conversation, "Pilate ... called Jesus" to him (Jn 18:33)
Zedekiah was "afraid" (38:19)	→	Pilate was "the more afraid" (Jn 19:8)

Resolving the Hybrid Riddle

The "hybrid riddle" (my term) results when the following two mutually exclusive propositions are simultaneously affirmed: "benefit" and "blame" (Fig. 11.2).

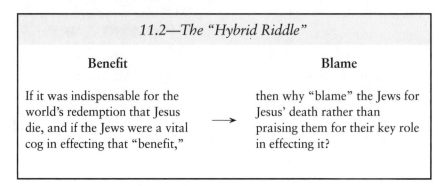

11.2—The "Hybrid Riddle"	
Benefit	**Blame**
If it was indispensable for the world's redemption that Jesus die, and if the Jews were a vital cog in effecting that "benefit," →	then why "blame" the Jews for Jesus' death rather than praising them for their key role in effecting it?

This paradox generates the most frequently asked question by Jews concerning the New Testament (cf. Fig. 1.1). So vexing is it that it appears, unresolved, even in the Second Vatican Council's landmark *Nostra Aetate* declaration![6]

But the puzzle fades when we assign each component to a different time frame. In the 30s, Configuration B Christians (review Fig. 4.2) began to understand the death of "Christ-Jesus" as *beneficial*, with their vicarious participation in his death and resurrection cleansing them from evil innate in this life, thereby enabling their salvation,* that is, rebirth unto life eternal. As Jesus' death was a necessary prelude, assignment of "blame" would have been incongruous, and this remained the case for more than two decades after his death. Moreover, given the frequency with which crucifixion was meted out, casting blame on Rome (an Empire!) would hardly be characteristic parlance.

The need to blame *the Jews* developed only when Christians became significantly more fearful of Rome beginning in the 60s and continuing throughout the period of Gospel composition—starting with Nero's scapegoating and torture of Christians, in Rome, for that city's fire (in 64 CE). Anxiety intensified with the Jewish revolt of 66 and whatever sympathetic unrest it generated among Jews elsewhere in the Empire. For Christians still to appear associated with Jewish insurgents would court danger since Christians' "founder" was a Jew known to have been crucified in a land now infamous for rebellion.

It was such cataclysmic challenges that prompted playing the "blame card" for Jesus' death against the Jews who were rejecting Christianity as well as rebelling against Rome. This ploy demonstrated that Christians,

now disassociated from Jews, did not blame *Rome* for Jesus' death. Moreover, many first-century Gentiles who rose to dominance within the Christian movement brought into Christianity their pre-existing dislike of Jews. Blaming the Jews as a "people" or "nation" was thus all the more natural for Gentile-Christian outsiders who held no visceral attachment to those now charged.

This attempted solution to the hybrid riddle, then, is that "benefit," from Jesus' death and resurrection, became accepted in Christianity during the 30s and onward. But "blame" of the Jews entered the stage only belatedly due to events in the 60s. The juxtaposition of blame to benefit generated the hybrid riddle.

The "Christ-Killer" Epithet

Perhaps no calumny unnerves Jews more than "Christ-killers." Instead of only recoiling from this canard—and reinforcing a sense of victimization—Jews would do well to master this epithet, for to know something, to understand it, affords a certain transcendence of it and freedom from it. Scholarly convention dates this expression to the fourth century,[7] but I distill six kinds of texts that root the concept within the New Testament itself. These kinds of texts combine to depict the Jews as *corporately* blameworthy in Jesus' death, with this collective blame *transmissible over time*, and with Jews characterized as *inherently murderous* and deserving *punishment* therefor:

Motifs #1 and #2 are yielded by Matthew 27:25 (see Fig. 16.3):

#1   "ALL THE PEOPLE answered, 'His blood be on us and on our children!'" Here Matthew is commonly said to expand a mere "crowd" (from Mk 15:11) into "ALL THE PEOPLE" so as to show the *entire* Jewish people as calling for Jesus' death.

#2   Here as well is the blood curse: "All the people" accept the onus for Jesus' death on "US" and foist it also "ON OUR CHILDREN"—construed to mean that the Jews' blame is transmissible over time (even in perpetuity).

Motifs #3 and #4 are yielded by the Gospel of John:

#3   Of the seventy times that John conspicuously employs the collective term "THE JEWS," almost forty are hostile (listed in Fig. 18.1).

#4   In 8:44, Jesus is said to cast "the Jews" (here even those believing in him) as *murderous* by nature (even inheritance): "You are of your father the devil, and your will is to do your father's desires. He was a MURDERER from the beginning."

Motif #5 is yielded by Acts 3:13–15:

#5   "God ... glorified his servant Jesus, WHOM YOU DELIVERED UP
        ... in the presence of Pilate, when he had decided to release
        him. But you denied the Holy and Righteous One, and asked
        for a murderer to be granted to you, and KILLED THE AUTHOR
        OF LIFE, whom God raised from the dead.

(Comment—This passage appears to reflect later tampering with the
way the text read originally.[8])

Motif #6 is taken from 1 Thessalonians 2:14ff., in possibly Paul's earliest Epistle (ca. 48 CE):

#6   "THE JEWS ... KILLED ... THE LORD JESUS and the prophets.... But
        GOD'S WRATH HAS COME UPON THEM AT LAST!" Here the Jews
        collectively not only deserve punishment but it already has
        been meted out!

(Comment—I consider this passage to be added by a post-70 hand.[9])

The groundwork for the Jews' becoming termed "Christ-killers" was
laid when Gentiles developed a proprietary interest in and came to re-
vere a *metamorphosed* Jesus figure as their divine "Christ"—thereby effectively *removing* him from Judaism. In the 60s, the Jews' revolt and
other exigencies induced especially Gentile recounters and creators of
Christian tradition to punctuate their retellings about Jesus with literary
devices that shifted responsibility (expressed as "blame") for his death
from Rome onto "the Jews." This development, later intensified especially by Rome's fourth-century adoption of Christianity, congealed into
aspersion of the Jews as *the* "Christ's" killers (or "Christ-killers"), but
aspects of this aspersion are rooted already in at least these six kinds of
New Testament texts.

Theology Eclipses History

This entire chapter has proceeded as if blaming the Jews for Jesus' death
is a historical problem only. Once word surfaced, however, early in
March 2003 about the script of the Mel Gibson film *The Passion of the
Christ*, it became obvious that whatever historians insisted *is* the point
was for most Christians *beside* the point.

Previously, standard Hollywood reenactments of Jesus' life were
heavily weighted toward historical reconstruction of the man, Jesus. Instead, the Gibson film—whose title does not even mention "Jesus"—
graphically displayed the deific Christ who underwent the cycle of
failure, rejection, suffering, bleeding, death, and thereafter resurrection

so that those "believing on him" (including today's film-goers) might achieve atonement for their evilness and triumph over death unto life everlasting. Here was the closest representation of Configuration B Christianity ever to reach the screen.

At the same time, *Jews* were astonished to see themselves depicted anew as Christ-killers—a regression to pre-Vatican II interpretations. Possibly artificial literary devices invented by Christian tradition (the blasphemy, Sanhedrin, Barabbas and blood curse motifs) were presented once again as genuinely occurring during Jesus' lifetime. It was as if the new slate was wiped clean, now rewritten with the old charges! Overflow audiences at the theaters cared nothing for meticulous historical reconstruction, and everything about "How do we rid ourselves of the evil besmirching our lives so that we may gain immortality?" What mattered was that the suffering and dying of Christ *for* them proved to each that "You *do* love me. I no longer need to say that I am unworthy. With God who loves me unconditionally, I am freed up to gain a more secure hold on my existence: I need worry no more." It was not Gibson's Christ *back then* about whom they cared but what they felt Christ was doing for them *now*.

Conclusions

This chapter sounds two wake-up calls for Jews. First, on the level of *history*, Jews must acknowledge that issues of responsibility for Jesus' death will never be successfully parried by replying simply, "Rome did it." Given the layers of complexity involved, such a response is not nuanced, sophisticated, or accurate, and it is certainly not congruent with a people priding themselves on knowledge. Jews must end this age-old cycle of visiting the ignorance of one generation upon the next.

The second wake-up call, on the level of *theology*, is that, for most Christians, no historical studies will render Gospel versions of Jesus' death any less credible. Especially with so much of Christianity's uncertain future tied up with the Third World, neither Jews nor their Christian supporters should be lulled into believing that the deicide issue is put to rest. It can and will flare up on no notice.

The Most Valuable Ideas in This Chapter May Be

1. Jews need to admit that issues of responsibility for Jesus' death will never be successfully parried by replying simply on the level of, "The Romans did it."
2. The Jewish revolt and other exigencies in the 60s induced Christian tradition to shift responsibility—in the form of "blame"—for Jesus' death from Rome onto the Jews.

3. While "benefit" from a deity's death was present from early on in Configuration B Christianity, "blame" for Jesus' death entered the stage only belatedly (escalating during the 60s), and generating thereby the paradox of the "hybrid riddle."
4. At least six roots of the aspersion, later termed "Christ-killers," are found already in New Testament texts themselves.
5. Since most religious people care primarily about the satisfaction of their existential needs, historical studies that expose Gospel polemics as not credible may exert relatively little impact.

What Gospel Dynamics Have We Recognized in This Chapter?

- The Evangelists edited their narratives of Jesus' Passion to ease problems afflicting their own post-70 Christian communities.
- Developments occurring decades *after* Jesus' death stimulated expressions of anti-Judaism that reflected the 60s and the post-70 era, not Jesus personally.
- Where information was needed to fill gaps in Jesus' story, Christian tradition drew upon, and embellished, Jewish scriptural motifs, thereby generating aspects of the Passion not rooted in fact.

Loose Ends Worth Tying

Prophetic Symbolism and Jesus' Temple Action

That Jesus' overturning of Temple furniture symbolized a coming overthrow of the current world order is in line with Hebrew prophets whose singular— even weird—demonstrations, charged with dire meaning, were deemed instrumental in bringing God's will to pass: Ahijah (1 Ki 11:29ff.) rips a garment into twelve pieces, giving ten to Jeroboam (symbolizes wresting ten Northern tribes from the South); Jeremiah (32:1ff.) purchases land in Anathoth (portends his confidence in Judah's future); Ezekiel (4:4ff.) lies 390 days on his left side (represents the years of Israel's punishment) and forty days on his right (those of Judah)—and so on.[10]

Convicted for One Crime, Blamed for Another?

We should not suppose that the priests *switched* a charge immaterial to Pilate (blasphemy) to one that would concern him (sedition), for blasphemy was likely *never* alleged of Jesus. Blasphemy is from the latest accruing layer of the Sanhedrin mosaic, and coming later still is Mark's insertion of the blasphemy *unit*: 2:5b–10 (on both, see the next chapter). Blasphemy, thus superimposed onto the earlier Jesus tradition, provides no proper basis on which to predicate any question concerning what actually happened to Jesus.

Good Friday (Extended)
Did the Sanhedrin and Barabbas Episodes Actually Occur?

The proposals in this chapter, while extending the last, are here set apart because of their *conjectural nature*. If they are correct to any substantive degree, they are most consequential. Even readers resistant to what I propose may benefit from pondering the ramifications that I have in view. Regarding what follows, readers should note that early Gospel manuscripts lacked verse numbers.

Passion Material That Mark Inherited?

What was the formative process of Mark's Passion*? Did it differ materially from what structured much in his preceding chapters, where brief units of tradition, bearing no original association with one another, were brought into sequence by the editor's artistry (recall our "string of beads" analogy from Chap. 3)? Many scholars insist that Mark constructed his Passion also in a basically similar fashion. Others contend not only that here he adopted a pre-existing skeletal account of Jesus' last days and significantly expanded it, but also that clues to such an early outline remain discernible in our canonical* text—sufficient even to allow us to reconstruct how it may have read.[1]

Generally, I am disposed to ascribe much to the Evangelists' creativity and improvisation, and less to non-extant sources that, essentially, we imagine they used. But given the overriding importance of Jesus' last days to his followers, I do find it more likely than not that some succinct Passion account arose early on (perhaps to be recited liturgically), and that Mark then appropriated this "scaffolding" and built upon it. But the attempt to *actively* reconstruct this rudimentary story is fraught with so many unknowns as to call into question whatever "results" would be forthcoming.[2]

Passion Material That Mark Added?

Approaching the matter from the opposite direction is less objection-able, that is, determining not what Mark may have inherited from a rudimentary account but what he may have *added* to one. Consider his Passion's most anti-Jewish components—the Sanhedrin and Barabbas episodes. Can we determine whether these were already integral to a pre-70 story line or, instead, whether they are Mark's own editorial ex-pansions, in all likelihood formulated to address circumstances of *his* day? (At this juncture, readers may benefit from reviewing Fig. 8.5.)

Let us examine that segment of canonical Mark's Passion that has had the greatest impact on later Jewish history: this extends from the arrest-ing party's delivery of Jesus to the high priest on Thursday night (14:53) through to the Roman prefect's consignment of him to the cross on Fri-day morning (15:15). Figure 12.1 lays out the basic clusters of material involved. Checked (√) are our two primary interests. Also, note how the Sanhedrin trial is "sandwiched" by Peter's denial of Jesus.

12.1—The Most Anti-Jewish Components
of Mark's Passion (14:53–15:15)

The SANHEDRIN Trial and Adjoining Materials					The BARABBAS Episode and Context		
14:53	14:54	14:55–65	14:66–72	15:1	15:2–5	15:6–15a	15:15b
Jesus *delivered* to HIGH PRIEST	Peter denies Jesus	√ SANHEDRIN Trial ⟶	Peter denies Jesus (cont'd)	Jesus *delivered* to PILATE	PILATE inter-rogates Jesus	√ BARABBAS Episode	PILATE consigns Jesus to cross

The SANHEDRIN Trial and Adjoining Materials (Mk 14:53–15:1)

The Two "Delivery" Texts (14:53 and 15:1)

The first and last verses of this "Sanhedrin complex" relate the two in-stances wherein Jesus is *delivered* to an authority figure. We will term these "delivery" texts. The first, 14:53, relates how, Thursday night, the party capturing Jesus in the Garden of Gethsemane delivered him to the high priest Caiaphas[3]; the second, 15:1, relates how, Friday morning, Jewish authorities delivered Jesus to the Roman prefect, Pontius Pilate. I suggest that, in their early development, these two passages were likely shorter than we find them today, and Mark's editing resulted in elongating each. The words that I propose he added are displayed in all capital letters.

Currently: 14 [53] And they led Jesus to the high priest; AND ALL THE CHIEF PRIESTS AND THE ELDERS AND THE SCRIBES WERE AS-SEMBLED.

15 [1] And as soon as it was morning the chief priests, with the elders and scribes, AND THE WHOLE COUNCIL [SAN-HEDRIN[4]] held a consultation; and they bound Jesus and led him away and delivered him to Pilate.

Initially?   14 [53] And they led Jesus to the high priest. ⸻⸻

⸻⸻

15 [1] And as soon as it was morning the chief priests, with the elders and scribes, ⸻⸻ ⸻⸻ held a consultation; and they bound Jesus and led him away and delivered him to Pilate.

I believe that Mark inserted the Sanhedrin trial *between* these two texts, and that the words in all capital letters are both by-products of that insertion and tell-tale witnesses to it. Note one such clue, for now: in 15:1, the words "AND THE WHOLE COUNCIL" constitute a mistake. Since "the chief priests, with the elders and scribes" *are* the whole council,[5] the phrase "AND THE WHOLE COUNCIL" is redundant. A verse once shorter—and error free—has been disturbed by an elongation that introduced the mistake.

If we do view these two "delivery" passages as once juxtaposed (i.e., connected), we will also notice how much of the Passion story line their relatively few words convey entirely by themselves. To repeat them, for clarity: "And they led Jesus to the high priest. And as soon as it was morning the chief priests, with the elders and scribes, held a consultation; and they bound Jesus and led him away and delivered him to Pilate." In this two-verse unit, we should also note one glaring absence and one modest presence: absent is any hint of a Sanhedrin trial of Jesus on Thursday night; but present (in 15:1) is a "consultation" on Friday morning, just prior to Jesus' delivery to Pilate. I believe that not only did the claimed Thursday night Sanhedrin trial arise as an *invention* (and was not present in any story line that Mark inherited) but also that *what sparked the idea for its creation* was this mention of Friday morning's mere "consultation"—deficient, in Christian eyes, because it did not commit the nation as such to the act of delivering Jesus to Pilate, or show proper deference due the Son of God, or even specify that Jesus was allowed to be present (let alone speak).

Thursday Night's Sanhedrin Trial (14:55–65)

Let us now examine, as a second item in Figure 12.1, the long Sanhedrin paragraph itself. This takes the form of a mosaic of five accruing layers not particularly cohesive with one another. I label them "A" through "E" (Fig. 12.2).

12.2—The Sanhedrin Mosaic of Five Accruing Layers

A   55 Now the chief priests and the whole council [Sanhedrin] sought testimony against Jesus to put him to death; but they found none. 56For many *bore false witness against him*, and *their witness did not agree*.

B   57 And some stood up and *bore false witness against him*, saying, 58"We heard him say, 'I will destroy this temple that is made with hands, and in three days I will build another, not made with hands.'" 59 Yet *not even so did their testimony agree*.

C   60 And the high priest [Caiaphas] stood up in the midst, and asked Jesus,

> [Query #1] *"Have you no answer to make? What is it that these men testify against you?"* 61 But he was *silent* and made no answer.

Again the high priest asked him,

> [Query #2] *"Are you the Christ, the Son of the Blessed?"* 62 And Jesus said, "I am; and you will see the Son of man seated at the right hand of Power, and coming with the clouds of heaven."

D   63 And the high priest tore his garments, and said, "Why do we still need witnesses? 64 You have heard his *blasphemy*. What is your decision?" And they *all* condemned him as deserving death.

E   65 And some began to spit on him, and to cover his face, and to strike him, saying to him, "Prophesy!" And the guards received him with blows.

Layer A (verses 55–56) shows the Sanhedrin as predisposed to condemn Jesus. *Layer B* (57–59) virtually repeats the previous verse (the italics show the correspondences[6]). Because verse 56 neglected to specify the *content* of the false witness, *Layer B* now provides it (which may

suggest a time-lapse[7] between the formulations of A and B). *Layer C* (60–62) seeks to supply words that were ascribed to more important persons, Jesus and Caiaphas. Here recourse is had to Jewish scripture— a standard Gospel Dynamic. Jesus appears to manifest clashing demeanors because he is harnessed to clashing proof-texts*! His silence toward Caiaphas' first query is determined by the silence of Isaiah's "Suffering Servant" (53:7: "he opened not his mouth"); and his stridency toward Caiaphas' second question is determined by the quoted "Son of man" text from Daniel 7:13 (along with Ps 110:1). *Layer D* (63–64) conveys Mark's key message: that Jesus' strident response to Caiaphas constitutes blasphemy (i.e., not sedition, which would have been Rome's chief concern). *Layer E* (65) concludes the episode.

Peter's Denial of Jesus (14:54, 66–72)

Our third and remaining item to examine in this section is Peter's denial of Jesus. This eight-verse unit is split into two segments, so that the story sandwiches the Sanhedrin trial. Its first verse (14:54), positioned *before* the trial account, shows Peter at a distance warming himself by the nighttime fire. The remaining verses (14:66–72) are positioned *after* the trial account, and show Peter vehemently denying, three times, any association with Jesus.

Why does Mark intersperse Jesus' ordeal with Peter's denial? Probably to spotlight that both figures were on trial simultaneously and to contrast how they performed. Peter is untruthful and preoccupied with *his* needs (warming himself at the fire, and preserving his welfare by denying Jesus), while Jesus is entirely truthful and preoccupied solely with fulfilling *God's* will (cf. 14:36: "not what I will, but what thou wilt").

Assessing the Sanhedrin and Adjacent Materials

As we now look over the material we have surveyed thus far, the Sanhedrin account seems to be not *reported* but *created* history, less science than art. Pieced together artificially, and with its core dialogue drawn from scriptural proof-texts, the trial paragraph appears staged by Mark to address needs of *his* constituents: replacing Rome with the Jews as the villains of the piece; replacing Pilate with the high priest as determiner of Jesus' death; and replacing a verdict of sedition (a crime of great concern to Rome) with blasphemy (a crime of no concern to Rome).

The Trial's Insertion

It is tempting to hold that the Sanhedrin paragraph was inserted into the *Peter* account (thereby explaining how Peter's story came to "sandwich" the trial).[8] My position, however, is that the Peter material—since it

manifests Mark's editorial bias against the disciples[9]—was the *latest* of
the expansions that Mark grafted onto his Passion story. Accordingly,
Peter's denial was not yet "in position" to receive the Sanhedrin trial as
an insertion.

Agreeing, however, that the trial *was* inserted, I propose a different
"candidate" as the receiving unit, namely, the two delivery passages,
14:53 and 15:1. This is easily visualized from reviewing Figure 12.1.
Imagine that we pulled out from our canonical Mark both the trial and
its embracing Peter story. Whatever materials on either side remained
would close up to fill the vacuum. Now suddenly adjacent would be the
two delivery passages—14:53 (Jesus' delivery to Caiaphas) followed immediately by 15:1 (Jesus' delivery to Pilate). Figure 12.3 depicts the insertion of the trial into what I submit was the receiving unit (the two
delivery texts—in their original *short* forms—back to back).

12.3—Mark Inserts the Sanhedrin Trial Between the "Delivery" Texts (Short Form)

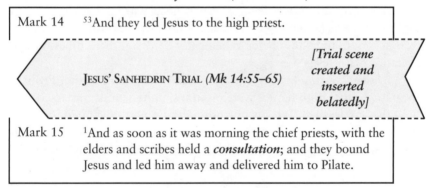

Mark 14   [53]And they led Jesus to the high priest.

JESUS' SANHEDRIN TRIAL *(Mk 14:55–65)*   *[Trial scene created and inserted belatedly]*

Mark 15   [1]And as soon as it was morning the chief priests, with the
elders and scribes held a **consultation**; and they bound
Jesus and led him away and delivered him to Pilate.

How the Delivery Texts Became Elongated

Since Figure 12.3 contains only what, I submit, was the original short
version of each delivery passage, it is time to show how and why each
verse became elongated. The words that I hold Mark added are those
appearing in all *caps* in Figure 12.4. By following the small arrows, we
can see precisely how these extra words crept into, and lengthened, the
two delivery passages.

The following problems now suddenly appear resolved:

- *Personnel Needed for Thursday Night (14:53).* Having invented Jesus'
  Sanhedrin trial, Mark needed to secure personnel to sit in judgment.
  Who should they be? In 15:1, he spotted "the chief priests, with the eld-
  ers and scribes." He borrowed these from Friday morning, extending

12.4—Mark's Editorial Fingerprints (Shaded)

Thursday Night		Friday Morning
14:53	14:55–65	15:1
And they led Jesus to the high priest;	← ← ←	And as soon as it was morning *the chief priests, with the elders and scribes*

	Sanhedrin	
✓		
AND ALL THE CHIEF PRIESTS AND THE ELDERS AND THE SCRIBES WERE ASSEMBLED.	[55] "...and the whole council"	→ AND THE WHOLE COUNCIL

held a *consultation*; and they bound Jesus and led him away and delivered him to Pilate.

their hours of service back into Thursday night—early enough for them to be on hand when the captive Jesus arrived for trial. This explains the elongation of 14:53 by the added words: "AND ALL [1] THE CHIEF PRIESTS AND [2] THE ELDERS AND [3] THE SCRIBES WERE ASSEMBLED." (Note that in Mark's frequent mentions of this triad, these are the only two instances where "elders" occupy the second position, strengthening my contention that here Mark *copied* their mention *into* 14:53 *from* that in 15:1.)

- *Whence the Redundancy Error (15:1)?* So as to smooth out the crease between the trial that he had just inserted and the two delivery passages between which he wedged it, Mark also added to 15:1 the phrase, "AND THE WHOLE COUNCIL." This, as Figure 12.4's remaining arrow shows, he drew (and now repeated) from the opening verse *inside* the Sanhedrin trial "box." But Mark was not sufficiently careful: for inside the Sanhedrin account, the phrase "now the chief priests and the whole council" makes good sense since the "elders" and "scribes," not yet mentioned, remain available as referents for "*and* the whole council." But in 15:1, *outside* the Sanhedrin box, all three groups ("chief priests," "elders," and "scribes") have already been mentioned and accounted for, leaving no one available to whom "and the whole council" can refer. So Mark's effort to smooth out a tell-tale crease instead has *exposed* the Sanhedrin trial as inserted!

- *Friday Morning's Mere "Consultation" (15:1).* Unlike the words in all capital letters, the "consultation" is *original* to its delivery passage, constituting the sole meeting mentioned—and the mention is only in passing at that. It was, as I have contended, this seemingly woeful inadequacy of a mere consultation that catalyzed the Christian invention of a full-fledged trial for the Son of God before the Sanhedrin, the supreme court of the land.

The Unadorned Early Tradition?

It would appear, then, that the basic tradition that Mark inherited related simply that, on Thursday night, Caiaphas received the captive Jesus; on Friday morning, he convened a (mere) "consultation" to report the matter to the *not-previously present* "chief priests, with the elders and scribes." Then Jesus was delivered to Pilate who, examining him briefly, consigned him to the cross.

The irony here is that, if the Thursday night trial was an expansion of the original Friday morning "consultation," the latter thereby lost its raison d'être. Even presuming that some matter still remained about which to "consult" after completion of a full-fledged trial (throughout?) the night before, what would warrant a renewed assembling of the full complement of the three leadership groups whose hours of service had already been so unduly extended? Mark would have done well now to have jettisoned, from 15:1, the no longer literarily needed "consultation." By retaining it, he here, also, divulged that the Sanhedrin trial was his insertion!

The BARABBAS Episode and Context (15:2–15)

The Barabbas episode tells of a Passover custom, in Jerusalem, when the Roman governor released to the Jews a prisoner of their choice. The Gospels depict the Jewish crowd as opting to save not Jesus but Barabbas, a murderous insurrectionist. Thereby all blame for Jesus' death comes to fall upon the Jews. It is into this paragraph, we should know, that Matthew adds his infamous blood curse (see Fig. 16.3).

The Barabbas Story's Many Problems

No source outside the New Testament confirms any such Passover custom of a prisoner release. Further, is it conceivable that Pilate, charged with maintaining law and order, would tolerate a process that could free known insurrectionists? Also, the story is inconsistent with the overall logic of the Passion plot. If Jesus' Palm Sunday entry to Jerusalem demonstrated his popularity, by what logic, then, would authorities plan

to arrest him just before Passover? This would only make him a prime candidate for "popular" release several days later.

This last discordance must be caused by the Barabbas story itself because the two verses that present the arrest plan (14:1–2) reflect a pre-70 formulation (see Chap. 10). Mark himself even tacitly acknowledges the discordance by requiring the chief priests to *stir up* the crowd to demand the release of Barabbas instead of Jesus (the same man they[10] had so effusively welcomed but days earlier).

The Purpose(s) the Barabbas Story Served

Why, then, given all the problems and disharmony that it introduces, did Mark include this tale? Was it to present a militant Barabbas as a foil for a pacifist Jesus? Or to demonstrate the Jews' preference for a rebel (resembling those who just revolted against Rome) to a law-abiding man benignly loyal to the Empire? Or to display Pilate (symbolic of Rome even in Mark's day) as convinced of Jesus' innocence? Or to contrast Roman benevolence (in allowing a prisoner release) with Jewish priestly malevolence in turning the crowd against Jesus (priests likely associated by Roman readers with the very functionaries running the very Temple that Rome had just burnt)?

Beyond these plausible reasons lies a key issue to Mark, revealed by the odd *double* appearance, in the Barabbas paragraph, of Pilate's accusation that Jesus was thought of as "The King of the Jews" (15:9 and 12). We cannot determine whether Mark co-opted the Barabbas story because it contained this emphasis, or if he himself added to the Barabbas story one or even both these mentions, or, for that matter, whether he even composed the parable himself with this to be his key motif. What is clear is that, for purposes of telling this story, there is no narrative need for mentioning this accusation even once, let alone twice.

This is not Pilate's fixation but Mark's, for Mark assigns Pilate his speaking parts. When we backtrack to Pilate's interrogation of Jesus, we now find Pilate again asking (this time Jesus personally): "Are you the King of the Jews?" (15:2). This makes three times within a dozen verses that Mark casts Pilate as using this expression. Then we discover the expression again, inscribed on the placard at Jesus' crucifixion (15:26)— this time, of course, it is indeed *Pilate's* dictation (cf. 15:18) since here is the actual historical reason for Jesus' crucifixion, and likely how the placard genuinely read. Mark is anxious about this allegation, and is struggling to defuse it. Evidently, he feels that Christians of *his* day remained endangered by Rome's identification of their (presumed) founder as being a subversive (which is what "King of the Jews" signifies).

On the matter of the interrogation especially, I submit that in an earlier formulation it contained no such "King of the Jews" question: Mark
himself added this query to what originally had been Pilate's *single* question for Jesus: "Have you no answer to make? See how many charges
they bring against you" (15:4). Again, noticing discordance is key: Pilate's (now) two queries are incommensurate in severity, and peculiarly
ordered. First comes his powerful salvo, tantamount to asking Jesus
point blank: are you a rebel against Rome? Thereafter comes only the
bland, anticlimactic query just noted. The words "again" in 15:4 ("Pilate *again* asked him") and "further" in 15:5 ("Jesus made no *further*
answer") are added clues that the rudimentary tradition of this interrogation consisted solely of *one* question, which must have been the bland
one—for were the severe question already present, how could its bland
counterpart ever have made it into the text?

The Unadorned Early Tradition?

Were we to omit the Barabbas tale itself (15:6–15a), all the problems
that it causes would vanish, leaving only the quite cogent: "But Jesus
made no answer, so that Pilate wondered; and having scourged Jesus,
he delivered him to be crucified" (15:5,15b). Gone would be the illogic
of arresting Jesus to start with, and the absurdity of Pilate's allowing release of an insurrectionist (Barabbas). And gone also is the problem
that we lack any independent confirmation of a prisoner-release custom. Moreover, if it was also from the Barabbas paragraph itself (or his
editing of it) that Mark drew the "King of the Jews" query for Pilate's
examination of Jesus, then the discordance produced there as well (that
the two questions are incommensurate in severity) also vanishes once
the Barabbas story is set aside. In sum, like the Sanhedrin trial, the
Barabbas tale appears an insertion of an episode that, historically, never
happened.

A Pre-Marcan Passion Narrative "Passively" Pursued?

At this juncture there is ample reason for us at least to wonder: if we
merely *subtracted* from canonical Mark those materials that appear to
be Marcan expansions, what "residue" from our selected segment of
study would remain? The shaded materials in Figure 12.5 depict those
items that warrant subtraction on the basis of our explorations thus far.
The materials with a white backdrop represent what would remain, simply by default, as the apparently "earlier" content. (The exact words
now to be subtracted are specified in the endnote.[11])

12.5—What Remains as the "Residue" from 14:53–15:15
shaded—Marcan expansions
white backdrop—"residue"

14:53	14:54	14:55–65	14:66–72	15:1	15:2–5	15:6–15a	15:15b
Jesus delivered to HIGH PRIEST	PETER denies Jesus	SANHEDRIN A B C *Query # 1* *Query # 2* D *Blasphemy* E →	PETER denies Jesus	Jesus delivered to PILATE	PILATE interrogates Jesus *Query # 1* *Query # 2*	BARABBAS "*King of the Jews*" ↵ "*King of the Jews*"	PILATE consigns Jesus to cross

In terms of the actual text we have been studying (14:53-15:15), what we are left with represents merely 11 percent of the Greek (12 percent of the English).[12] While we have no reason to expect that what remains could read smoothly or convey anything approaching a full story in its own right (in Greek or English), we have cause to be surprised in both respects:

> [The Residue:] MARK 14 [53] And they led Jesus to the high priest. 15 [1]And as soon as it was morning the chief priests, with the elders and scribes held a consultation; and they bound Jesus and led him away and delivered him to Pilate. [3]And the chief priests accused him of many things. [4]And Pilate asked him, "Have you no answer to make? See how many charges they bring against you." [5]But Jesus made no answer, so that Pilate wondered, [15b]and having scourged Jesus, he delivered him to be crucified.

I am not proposing that this reflects a pre-Marcan text, because the kinds of obstacles noted earlier remain problematic.[13] But what may be legitimately claimed on the basis of this exercise is that a pre-Marcan rudimentary Passion tradition *could* have proceeded with neither a Sanhedrin nor a Barabbas tale. And if so, when we factor in how the later Synoptists embellish Mark's anti-Jewish expansions (such as the way by which Matthew inserts the infamous "blood curse," in 27:25), can we avoid reflecting on how many Jews throughout history may have died (or were never conceived) because of the impact of these two tales regarding events that may never have occurred yet continue to be routinely

accepted as factual by so many to this day? How different might Jewish history have been *if all that had continued to be conveyed had resembled the "residue" alone?* This dramatizes how vital it is to weigh the possibility that Gospel Dynamics underlie key New Testament texts.

A Reverse Thrust to Mark's Editing?

Since Mark wrote, in part, to ease his constituents' concern with Rome, he had no choice but to begin with the disquieting *conclusion* of Jesus' earthly career. Mark could not change this ending fact: a Jesus crucified for sedition. But he *could* revamp the narrative process that had culminated in this event: that is, he could devise substitute officials who, earlier on, shared, even replaced, the role that Roman officials played; he could invent an alternative (Sanhedrin) court condemning Jesus for an alternative (blasphemy) verdict; and he could invent a scene in which Pilate, faced with a hostile Jewish mob, expressed skepticism of Jesus' guilt but acceded to the Jewish mob's will nonetheless.

Since Mark had to work *backwards* in this general or overarching sense, are there any specific clues justifying the conjecture that he edited his Passion material in a sequence reverse to the flow of the story line (Fig. 12.6)?

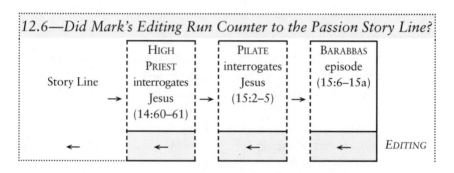

12.6—*Did Mark's Editing Run Counter to the Passion Story Line?*

	HIGH PRIEST interrogates Jesus (14:60–61)	PILATE interrogates Jesus (15:2–5)	BARABBAS episode (15:6–15a)
Story Line →	→	→	
←	←	←	← EDITING

It may appear, for example, that Pilate's added query, "Are you the King of the Jews?" surfaced first during his interrogation of Jesus and then reappeared twice later in the Barabbas episode, and finally on the placard at the cross itself. But would not the *reverse* seem more likely—that Mark started with the fact of Jesus on the cross and with the placard announcing why Jesus was there (15:26), then came his editing of the Barabbas story (15:6–15), and only thereafter did Mark draw the emphasized "King of the Jews" motif back into Pilate's interrogation of Jesus (15:2)?—review, here, from Fig. 12.5, the right-angled arrow leading toward Pilate's "Query #1."

By the same token, readers may notice that Caiaphas' two questions of Jesus in the Sanhedrin Thursday night and Pilate's two on Friday morning are parallel in structure and, in the case of the bland question, even in content. The natural inference is that Mark modeled Pilate's questions on those already assigned to Caiaphas. But why not the *reverse* (as per Fig. 12.7)?

12.7—*Mark Models Caiaphas' Questions on Pilate's*	
High Priest (Caiaphas)	**Pilate**
14 ⁶⁰... the high priest ... asked Jesus, *"Have you no answer to make? What is it that these men testify against you?"*	**SEDITION** 15 ²... Pilate asked him, *"Are you the* **King of the Jews?"**
BLASPHEMY ⁶¹... Again the high priest asked him, *"Are you the* **Christ, the Son of the Blessed?"**	... ⁴And Pilate again asked him, *"Have you no answer to make?* See how many charges they bring against you."

The reverse order is not only possible but preferable, because it means that Mark is enlisting Caiaphas to *preempt* the "King of the Jews" accusation. Mark now delves into the very Sanhedrin paragraph that *he* himself invented so as to enlist Caiaphas essentially to say: Jesus did not pretend to be "King of the Jews" (sedition) but, instead, "Christ, the Son of the Blessed"—which Caiaphas immediately clarifies to mean, "You have heard his *blasphemy*" (14:64).

Note, then, the *backward trajectory* here: Mark takes the accusation ("The King of the Jews") from the placard on the cross, makes certain that it is included not once but twice in the Barabbas episode, drags it back further into Pilate's interrogation, and then has Caiaphas preempt it in the Sanhedrin so that now the reader will understand every forthcoming accusation of "King of the Jews" to be unfounded. Further, Mark then backpedals Caiaphas' substitution—"blasphemy"—as early as Mark 2:1ff. (See the end of this chapter.)

That Mark's expansions of his inherited Passion materials reflect a backpedaling editorial style is depicted by Figure 12.8. Here the white backdrop displays the residue that, as we have already seen, is left after our subtractions. Following this, the progressively darker shadings

represent *the order in which I propose Mark introduced his expansions.* (Note how the progression from lighter shading to darker moves upwards—the lightest is at the end of the Passion story, and the darker—later insertions—enter in as we move *up* into *earlier* parts of the Passion story.)

12.8—The Sequence of Mark's Insertions into a Primitive Passion Account?

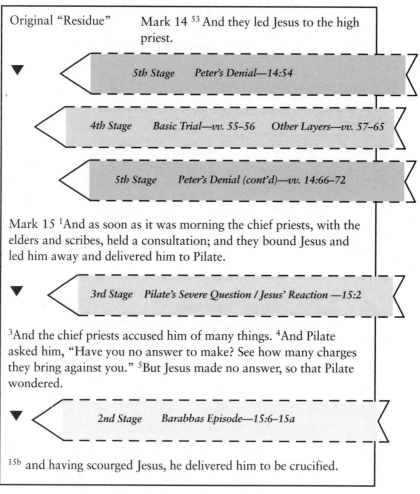

Original "Residue"   Mark 14 ⁵³ And they led Jesus to the high priest.

▼   5th Stage   Peter's Denial—14:54

4th Stage   Basic Trial—vv. 55–56   Other Layers—vv. 57–65

5th Stage   Peter's Denial (cont'd)—vv. 14:66–72

Mark 15 ¹And as soon as it was morning the chief priests, with the elders and scribes, held a consultation; and they bound Jesus and led him away and delivered him to Pilate.

▼   3rd Stage   Pilate's Severe Question / Jesus' Reaction —15:2

³And the chief priests accused him of many things. ⁴And Pilate asked him, "Have you no answer to make? See how many charges they bring against you." ⁵But Jesus made no answer, so that Pilate wondered.

▼   2nd Stage   Barabbas Episode—15:6–15a

¹⁵ᵇ and having scourged Jesus, he delivered him to be crucified.

Making Certain That We Understand Figure 12.8

- Into the "residue"—in the white background—Mark introduced as a *2nd Stage* the Barabbas episode, emphasizing "the King of the Jews."

- Then, as his *3rd Stage,* Mark doubled Pilate's questions by adding to an original bland query Mark's "King of the Jews" concern (and placing this "severe" question *first* since this was Mark's priority).
- As the *4th Stage,* Mark inserted the Sanhedrin trial between the two delivery verses, enlisting Caiaphas (in *Layer D* of Fig. 12.5—the same in 12.2) to prove to the reader that it was blasphemy, not sedition, of which Jesus was guilty—thereby diluting in advance the force of the four[14] upcoming mentions of "King of the Jews."
- The *5th* stage is Mark's introduction of Peter's denial so that it embraces the Sanhedrin proceedings, dramatizing the simultaneity of the trials of Jesus and Peter.

Reinforcement

Buttressing these contentions is that Mark's backpedaling style of Passion editing extends even beyond the confines of the Passion itself. This is best exemplified by the way that he carries Caiaphas' "blasphemy" verdict back twelve full chapters to Jesus' healing of the paralytic (opening chapter 2 of his Gospel). This is the only other Marcan text, outside the Sanhedrin scene, that shows Jesus accused of blasphemy (Fig. 12.9).

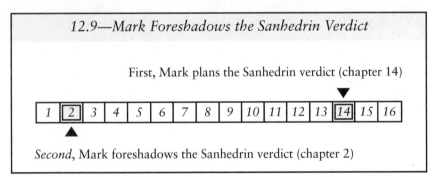

12.9—Mark Foreshadows the Sanhedrin Verdict

First, Mark plans the Sanhedrin verdict (chapter 14)

| 1 | 2 | 3 | 4 | 5 | 6 | 7 | 8 | 9 | 10 | 11 | 12 | 13 | 14 | 15 | 16 |

Second, Mark foreshadows the Sanhedrin verdict (chapter 2)

Already nearly a century ago, scholars[15] began noticing that Mark had intruded an extraneous five to six verses into the paralytic episode (hence its full dozen verses—unusually long for a tradition originally conveyed orally and also exposing that, originally, this healing story had nothing to do with blasphemy). Figure 12.10's white backdrop displays the shorter story before Mark's insertion, represented by the shaded arrow.

Note the still-evident splice marks: first, the interruption of Jesus' speaking part (at the end of verse 10); second, the awkward switching there of those he addresses (from the scribes to the paralytic, instead); and, third, the double appearance of "he said to the paralytic" (which ends both verses 5 and 10). When we remove the arrow and then close

12.10—Mark's Insertion Elongates the Paralytic's Healing

2[1] ...He returned to Capernaum ... [and] was reported ... at home....
[3]... They came, bringing to him a paralytic.... [5] ... When Jesus saw
their faith, *he said to the paralytic* [originally followed by verse 11],

"... Your sins are forgiven." [6]... Some ...
scribes ... questioned ... [7] "Why does this
man speak thus? It is *blasphemy!* ..." [8]...
Jesus ... said ... [9] "Which is easier, to say
..., 'Your sins are forgiven,' or ... 'Rise,
take up your pallet and walk'? [10] But that
you may know that *the Son of man* has
authority ... to forgive sins" — *he said
to the paralytic*

*[Blasphemy
unit inserted
belatedly]*

[11] "*I say to you*, rise, take up your pallet and go home." [12]And he
... took up the pallet and went....

up what's left, the original tale reappears (i.e., read consecutively vv.
1–5a, then 11–12). The very clumsiness of the insertion underscores
Mark's determination to enter it into the record, as early as chapter 2,
that the very first time that Sanhedrin personnel ("some ... scribes") are
depicted with Jesus they condemned him for blasphemy; and also that
Jesus here spoke of himself as the "Son of man"—just as Mark would
show Jesus doing in his strident response to Caiaphas, at his trial, a
dozen chapters later.

Easter
Empty Tomb Enigmas

It was not anything new in Jesus' teachings that the earliest Church chose to centralize; rather, it was the proclamation of his resurrection and ascension to heaven (cf. Acts 2:31). This was meant not metaphorically but literally: Jesus actually rose from the dead, appearing physically thereafter to various worthies. The primary Christian affirmation of these beliefs was the early kerygma* that Paul, in the mid-50s, said he received and was now passing on (1 Cor 15:3–7):

> 3... that Christ died for our sins in accordance with the scriptures, 4that he was buried, that he was raised on the third day in accordance with the scriptures, 5and that he appeared to Cephas [Peter], then to the twelve. 6Then he appeared to more than five hundred brethren at one time, most of whom are still alive, though some have fallen asleep. 7Then he appeared to James, then to all the apostles.

To this tradition Paul then appended, as verse 8, a statement of Jesus' post-resurrection appearance also to Paul himself.

But the focus of this chapter is a second avenue of Christian affirmation respecting the resurrection: namely, the Gospel accounts of Jesus' burial by Joseph of Arimathea, on Good Friday, linked to discovery that the tomb was empty, on Easter Sunday. Since the kerygma was created as a compact formulaic statement of the essentials of early Christian belief, many New Testament readers assume that it presupposes the *earlier* burial and empty tomb occurrences—that is, without explicitly mentioning them. We will test this presumption, beginning by examining the earliest renditions of these two episodes, by Mark (Fig. 13.1).

13.1—Mark's Renditions of the Burial and Empty Tomb

FRIDAY AFTERNOON
Burial (15:42–47)

SUNDAY MORNING
Empty Tomb (16:1–8)

Joseph of Arimathea, a respected member of the council [or "an honorable councilor"], ... also himself looking for the kingdom of God, took courage and went to Pilate, and asked for the body of Jesus.
... When [Pilate] learned ... that [Jesus] was dead, he granted the body to Joseph
... [who] ... taking him down, wrapped him in the linen shroud, and laid him in a tomb ... hewn out of the rock; and ... rolled a stone against the door....
Mary Magdalene and Mary the mother of Joses saw where he was laid.

... When the sabbath was past, [on Saturday night] Mary Magdalene, and Mary the mother of James, and Salome, bought spices ... that they might go and anoint ... [Jesus' body].... They went to the tomb when the sun had risen [Sunday morning].
... They were saying to one another, "Who will roll away the stone for us from the door of the tomb?" ... Looking up, they saw that the stone was rolled back—it was very large.
... Entering the tomb, they saw a young man ... dressed in a white robe.... He said..., "... You seek Jesus of Nazareth, who was crucified. He has risen, he is not here; see the place where they laid him. But go, tell his disciples and Peter that he is going before you to Galilee; there you will see him, as he told you."
... They went out and fled ... the tomb; for trembling and astonishment had come upon them; and *they said nothing to any one*, for they were afraid.

Friday Afternoon—Jesus' Burial (Mk 15:42–47)

Joseph of Arimathea in Composite

Mark supplies several attributes for Joseph of Arimathea. Matthew, Luke, and John add others. The resulting composite glows. Respected and rich, Joseph was a good and righteous member of the council that condemned Jesus, but *he* was not consenting to its purpose and deed. Instead, himself looking for the Kingdom of God, he not only sympathized with Jesus but, secretly, was also even his disciple. Courageously, he asked Pilate for Jesus' body. Assisted by Nicodemus, Joseph bound Jesus' corpse in linen with spices, then buried it in Joseph's own new, unused tomb, which he had hewn, and rolled a stone against its entry before leaving.

Breaking Down the Composite

When we parcel out these attributes to the Evangelists who, respectively, contributed them, matters look vastly different (Fig. 13.2).

13.2—A Breakdown of Joseph of Arimathea's Attributes

MK 15:42–47; MT 27:57–61; LK 23:50–56A; JN 19:38–42

MARK says only that Joseph
• was a RESPECTED COUNCILOR
• who was LOOKING FOR the KINGDOM OF GOD
• showed COURAGE in requesting Jesus' body
• laid it in a TOMB
• and CLOSED the entrance

MATTHEW adds that Joseph
• was RICH and Jesus' DISCIPLE
• and OWNED the NEW tomb that he HAD HEWN PERSONALLY

LUKE adds that Joseph
• was GOOD and RIGHTEOUS
• NOT CONSENTING to the council's verdict
• and the tomb was NEVER BEFORE USED

JOHN adds that Joseph
• was Jesus' disciple SECRETLY,
• and was aided by NICODEMUS

From what other source(s), besides Mark, did the later Evangelists draw their special details? I believe Mark was their only source on Joseph. Additions by Matthew and Luke (even John[1]) could result primarily from deductions that they drew from Mark, some erroneously so.

Deductions

How could this come about? Mark's notice that Joseph was seeking God's kingdom led Matthew and (I believe John) to understand Joseph as Jesus' *disciple*. Luke, meanwhile, inferred that Joseph, obviously good and righteous, could not have been consenting to the council's condemnation of Jesus. The notion that Joseph had assistance (John says in the person of Nicodemus) may be assumed since more than one person would be needed to transport the body—and we also have the words by Mark's young man at the tomb: "see the place where *they* laid him" (16:6). That the "grave" of Isaiah's Suffering Servant was to be "with a *rich* man" (Isa 53:9) led Matthew to see Joseph not only as wealthy but also as owner of the tomb. Remains from any previous corpse could undermine confidence that the tomb had been empty (both before the burial and after the resurrection), so this explains Matthew's specification that the tomb was "new" and Luke's insistence that it had never been used.

Misdeductions

But some inferences could be plainly wrong if Mark's intent was to present Joseph as Jesus' *opponent*. As unexpected as this sounds, Mark expressly has *"all"* those trying Jesus (this would have to include Joseph) condemn him as deserving death (14:64)[2]—and this in a Sanhedrin scene that Mark himself invented (so we must presume Mark planned this out as a *consistent* piece). This would also explain the absence of any depicted interaction between the women and Joseph, for Mark has cast them on opposing sides. Yes, Joseph was "looking for the kingdom of God," but so were scribes/Pharisees in general, even within the Sanhedrin.[3] Yes, Joseph was "respected," but is this Mark's way of accounting for how Joseph had access to Pilate or why Pilate showed him any deference? Yes, Joseph was courageous, for he was requesting Pilate (against the prefect's wont?[4]) to accede to Jewish law: Deuteronomy 21:23 declares that leaving a corpse hanging overnight is a reproach to God and, as Josephus plainly informs us, "the Jews used to take so much care of the burial of men, that they took down those that were condemned and crucified, and buried them before the going down of the sun."[5]

The objection that Joseph would then have asked for the other bodies as well (presuming that these, too, were dead) is not compelling. Even if we assume that the crucified Jesus was indeed flanked by other victims *and* that the Joseph story is genuine history, Gospel tradition could not allow and preserve any inference that Joseph asked for more than one corpse. This would open the possibility that he then buried them all together in his tomb—which would confuse, and compromise, the *empty* tomb story. For example, if on Sunday morning one body of several was missing, skeptics could dispute that the body missing was Jesus. Bodies were already hard to distinguish from each other after sufficient scourging and loss of blood, all the more so with the onset of decay and decomposition. It was this kind of concern that likewise gave rise to notions that the tomb was "new" and never before used (Mt 27:60; Lk 23:53).

Joseph of Arimathea and Gospel Dynamics

If the later Evangelists need have had no source on Joseph other than Mark, then does not our proper universe for interpreting Joseph shrink to Mark 14–15 alone?

Joseph Among Mark's Bit Players[6]

We should not overlook that Mark serves as the sole source (or creator) of half a dozen or so[7] bit players like Joseph. This renders it reasonable to explore whether Mark is conveying a message through all of them as

a *class*: that persons who need not have done so came through for Jesus in ways in which his *designated* supporters failed him.

- 14:3–9—*The Woman Wasting Costly Ointment*. Before the Last Supper, a woman is ridiculed by Jesus' associates for "wasting" costly ointment in prematurely anointing the body of the *live* Jesus for burial. But *Mark* effusively praises her (through Jesus) for having done a "beautiful thing" (v. 6). Because the Sabbath is imminent late Friday afternoon, Jesus' body is buried without preparation.[8] By Sunday morning, then, when the women close to Jesus belatedly bring spices for his body, their chance has passed. The virtue of the ridiculed bit player is now recounted everywhere the Gospel is preached (v. 9)[9]—even though she goes nameless!—whereas those in Jesus' own circle have let him down. What is Mark telling us here, and why?
- 14:51–52—*The Young Man in Gethsemane*. Almost seized in Gethsemane, a young man escapes naked. I surmise that Mark imports him from the Hebrew Prophet Amos (2:16): "'He who is stout of heart among the mighty shall flee away naked *in that day*,' says the Lord."[10] The verb that Mark uses to introduce him is key: the young man "followed" Jesus (14:51), the exact *opposite* verb that Mark has applied to Jesus' disciples just one verse earlier: they "forsook"[11] Jesus (14:50).
- 15:21—*Simon of Cyrene*. In taking up Jesus' cross, *this* Simon fulfils Jesus' dictum (8:38): "If any man would come after me, let him deny *himself* and take up his cross, and *follow* [as opposed to *forsake*] me.... For whoever is ashamed of me ... of him will the Son of man* be ashamed.... " The contrast here is to the other Simon (Simon Peter) who has already denied not himself but *Jesus*—and three times (14:66ff.). The bit player Simon (of Cyrene) comes through; the major Simon (Simon Peter) fails.
- 15:39—*The Roman Centurion*. Never even having seen Jesus before, this *Gentile* centurion immediately declares him "the Son of God" (a recognition never achieved among Jesus' followers or family, who have been with him continually).
- 15:40–41,47—*The Women Keeping Vigil*. They are praiseworthy but, given the relatively low esteem in which women were held, I believe that Mark is using them as a foil for Jesus' *male* disciples, whose presence is most palpably felt by their absence.

Joseph's Particular Role
Indeed, the one *man* who does witness the burial is the one who performs it—another bit player, Joseph of Arimathea. Among the Sanhedrin members *unanimously* arrayed against Jesus, only he shows the

courage and decency to accord Jesus the burial that any person deserves. Other Gospel Dynamics may also be at work in Joseph's particular case. Even though set prior to the empty tomb, a burial tale was likely a later development—a segue needed to explain how the corpse came to be removed from the cross and then laid in a tomb to start with. Further, the greatest horror of crucifixion was the prospect of being left on the cross as carrion, to decay and be devoured by vultures—that is, to receive no burial at all.[12] Since this would seem intolerable for the Son of God, a hopeful story (like that of Joseph) would inexorably have arisen. A still further Dynamic is that of aggrandizement (e.g., as in our last chapter, when the "consultation" in Mk 15:1 mushroomed into a Sanhedrin trial in 14:55–65). Inevitably, a thought of a meager burial for Jesus, in a pit or trench or criminals' graveyard,[13] would move toward a more dignified burial, culminating ultimately with a tomb, which in turn became aggrandized into one that was new, that of a rich man—indeed of a respected councilor—and so forth.

But Mark's chief Dynamic became, unwittingly, underlined by Matthew and John, who misconstrued Joseph as Jesus' "disciple." And literally that *he* truly was! Mark's intent? To show how even Joseph, someone who condemned Jesus, behaved as a true disciple *should* have behaved: he was on the scene to do that for which Jesus' official designees—his runaway disciples—had made themselves unavailable. (As for why Mark would promote such a contrast, see Chap. 15→.)

Sunday Morning—The Empty Tomb (16:1–8)

Mark's recounting of the empty tomb story, in but eight verses,[14] fails to preempt a trying problem for Matthew. Skeptical Jews in Matthew's own city deemed the empty tomb story a hoax: the disciples, they charged, had stolen the body and proclaimed Jesus' resurrection, a story "spread among the Jews to this day" (Mt 28:15). "To this day" is an uncharacteristically overt disclosure of an Evangelist's own time. Also signaling that Matthew is overwrought is his sole use, here, of "the Jews" (outside the Gentile formula, "King of the Jews"). In employing this Gentile usage (see Chap. 18), Matthew reflects the perspective of his church *external* to the Jewish community in his own day (see Chap. 16).

Matthew's Anti-Theft Device

While Matthew's empty tomb narrative more than doubles Mark's in length, roughly 50 percent is consumed with countering the theft accusation.[15] And Matthew's strategy is so cumbersome and unsophisticated as to suggest that, even though writing as late as circa 85, he knew of no

role model to guide him in responding effectively, let alone efficiently, to this allegation.

The Jewish authorities, he relates, fearing a theft of Jesus' body, stationed a guard of soldiers at the tomb (27:62–66). Witnessing an angel rolling back the stone and conversing with women, the soldiers "trembled and became like dead men" (28:4). Although they were traumatized, they still were able to report accurately to the authorities that a resurrection had occurred, only then to be bribed to lie that "his disciples came by night and stole him away while we were asleep" (28:11–15).

John, writing around 100 CE, requires but 26 words to Matthew's 227 to solve this problem: he simply has the resurrected Jesus present and conversing with Mary Magdalene (Jn 20:13b–14a).[16] I surmise that the inadequacy of Matthew's attempted corrective is due to Mark, who (writing little more than a decade before Matthew) could not then gauge the potential seriousness of the theft allegation because it was first to arise *in response to him*. This would explain why Mark left Matthew bereft of any modeling for addressing the problem. We should understand that theft accusations became a standard staple of skeptics, in many variations,[17] and could surface among doubters virtually instantaneously once hearing the empty tomb story. That Mark had not experienced such automatic and routine responses must mean that the empty tomb tradition arose either with Mark himself or, at most, so shortly before him that he had not yet become schooled in how skeptics would go about countering it.

The Women Told No One What They Saw?

Mark ends his Gospel by telling us that the women, discovering the tomb empty, "said nothing to any one for they were afraid." Matthew—likely finding this preposterous—overrules Mark by showing the women running "to tell the disciples" (28:8). In my view, Matthew fails to spot the Dynamic underlying Mark's statement: Having himself introduced (created?) the empty tomb story, Mark must *account for why no one else before his day had heard it*! His answer? The women kept it secret (reminiscent of a similar Marcan motif—the "Messianic Secret"[18]).

The Empty Tomb Tradition and Paul

Paul betrays no awareness of the empty tomb story. Here, the usual fallback position by scholars will not do: namely, that Paul was not interested in the historical Jesus' experience on earth. The Christ's resurrection is *core* to Paul's preaching, as also is Paul's concept (1 Cor 15:44) that once-physical living beings will, post-mortem, experience resurrection in a *spiritual* body *(soma pneumatikon)*. This matter is

important because, Paul tells us, in whatever form of body Christ rose, believers identifying with him would achieve the same in *their* resurrection. Since "flesh and blood cannot inherit the kingdom of God" (1 Cor 15:50), the faithful instead would gain a new body that is essentially a transformation of the physical substance to a spiritual substance (if we can speak in such terms together, i.e., "spiritual" and "substance").

It is not entirely clear what Paul meant by this notion. Certainly, *we* would have questions of him, as indeed did his constituents (e.g., 1 Cor 15:35). But included in our queries would be requests to reconcile the "spiritual body" concept with the empty tomb traditions. The latter appear to presuppose Jesus' *bodily* resurrection since it was the absence of his body that startled the visitors ("see the place where they laid him"). This would invite concerns that, in "quality," may not be sophisticated but whose absence from Paul's discussion is noticeable: For example, if a resurrected body is spiritual, why was it necessary for Jesus' physical body to be missing,[19] or if Jesus' physical body was missing, how can we speak of his resurrected body as being spiritual? Paul's style in his Epistles was to answer questions, not dodge or shirk them. The point here, then, is not how he would have fielded such questions—perhaps easily and flawlessly—but that, so far as we can tell, such questions were never posed to him. This is consistent with doubts that empty tomb traditions were even known by Paul's day in the 50s.

The Kerygma
What, then, should we make of the early kerygma's use of the word "buried"? First, it is but one verb out of four: "Christ *died* ... was *buried* ... was *raised* ... he *appeared*.... " And "died" and "buried" are to be taken together (so also the second pair), emphasizing the reality and apparent finality of Jesus' death. Accordingly, because "buried" requires no disproportionate attention, we are wrong to dwell on it unduly unless the Greek for buried *(etaphe)* here requires a tomb per se. But the term is neutral—that is, compatible with burial in a grave, pit, or trench, or buried alone or alongside others or in a common grave for criminals, or in a tomb.[20]

If we insist on reading the kerygma in light of the tomb story, then it becomes incumbent upon us to resolve why the kerygma makes no mention of the women who were the first to learn that the tomb was empty—all the more so that it was to *women* that the resurrected Jesus first appeared (Mt 28:9f.; Jn 20:14ff.). Would this be because only men qualified legally as witnesses? I prefer a different explanation, which is that only when Mark himself (ca. 72 CE) *introduced* the motif that the men ran away did he thereby leave women as the only ones of Jesus'

followers still in the vicinity and to whom the resurrected Jesus could appear—an editorial matter about which those formulating the kerygma, decades earlier, would have known nothing.

The Empty Tomb and Gospel Dynamics

Indications are, then, that the empty tomb stories historicize the kerygma, and are not presupposed by it. Further, Mark's empty tomb tradition is so late in introduction that it circulated without adequate time-testing, and this is why Mark leaves Matthew so ill-equipped to address the theft allegation.

How, then, might the very notion of the empty tomb tradition have arisen? Potentially, by a quite natural deduction: if Jesus, after death, was reported sighted, then whatever the place where his corpse had lain became presumed *vacant*. And where specifically was that place? In all likelihood no one knew—especially since neither Jesus' followers nor enemies were expecting his resurrection.[21] Indeed, there was no guarantee that, as a victim of crucifixion, Jesus had been buried at all. Thereafter, progressions would have set in (by the Dynamic of aggrandizement): Yes, the Son of God did indeed receive burial. No, burial in a pit or trench or criminals' graveyard would not do—nothing less than a tomb would suffice. Then the tomb's ownership was aggrandized from no owner at all to that by a "respected member of the council," with the application of Isaiah 53:9 making him rich, and so forth.

But why, then, would so much time have lapsed before such stories arose? Because only with the years just before Mark's writing (roughly 64–71 CE) did the need for such traditions develop, when fear of persecution and especially when tensions with disbelieving Jews escalated (see Chap. 11). These left Christians vulnerable not only to doubting their faith but also to doubters of their faith, with the resurrection the core component they most needed to believe and defend.

Consider, now, the tactical advantage of Mark's floating an empty tomb story. Skeptics having never heard of such a tale, and now forty years removed from when Jesus died, were in no position to deny that Jesus was buried in a tomb or that it was discovered empty—or even to demand to see that tomb (given the devastation of Jerusalem's environs by Roman armies just before Mark wrote). Does this mean, then, that Jews in Matthew's community actually agreed to the tomb's emptiness, and then advanced "theft" to explain it? No, here Matthew likely fails to convey how Jews posed this matter: namely, hypothetically—that is, assuming that Jesus' tomb was empty, prove to us that the disciples did not steal the body.[22]

Ramifications for Modern Jews

If an empty tomb tradition developed with, or only shortly before, Mark (ca. 72), then whatever the reasons earliest Christians had for believing that Jesus was resurrected are beyond historical reconstruction.[23] But complementing what Jews should know about Christian resurrection traditions is what Jews should understand about their own traditions: namely, that there is no necessary correlation in Judaism between being resurrected and being the Messiah. What matters for Jews today is that the contemporary *agenda* of the Messiah* be accomplished—that the sign of the Messiah's coming is not resurrection but a perfected world.

The Most Valuable Ideas in This Chapter May Be

1. For Jews today, the sign of the Messiah's coming is not resurrection but a perfected world.
2. We are prone to assume that *first* developed Jesus' burial story, *second* the empty tomb account, and *third* the kerygma's formulation; but more likely *first* the kerygma was formulated, *then* the empty tomb story decades later, and *last* the burial story (as the segue to account for how Jesus' body came to rest in that tomb).

Joseph of Arimathea

1. Mark apparently presented Joseph as Jesus' *opponent* who likely buried him out of Jewish piety (recall the practice quoted from Josephus).
2. Matthew, Luke, and John had no source regarding Joseph other than Mark.
3. Attributes they add for Joseph are misdeductions that materially *alter* his Marcan profile.
4. *Their* accounts are thus improper bases for understanding the Joseph character.
5. Joseph is but one of a cast of bit players in Mark's Passion.
6. We should think of processing Joseph's meaning, then, in conjunction with the meaning of other bit players as a class.
7. Mark intended to demonstrate how bit players (including Joseph) showed Jesus the deference that his designated followers failed to accord him.

Empty Tomb

1. That Paul was not asked to reconcile his concept of a "spiritual body" with the empty tomb traditions suggests that the latter were not yet known in Paul's day.

2. That Mark does not mention, let alone cope with, any "theft allegation" suggests that the empty tomb tradition first surfaced either with Mark himself or only shortly before him.

What Gospel Dynamics Have We Recognized in This Chapter?

- Empty tomb and burial stories responded to problems in the Evangelists' day (to deflect skeptics bent on undermining Christians' confidence in the resurrection; also, to reassure the faithful that the *crucified* Jesus had not been left unburied).
- Traditions about Jesus routinely became aggrandized (here, the fact and the mode of Jesus' burial, along with the public stature of the tomb's owner).
- Gospel traditions could arise by deduction (here, if Jesus after death was reported *sighted*, then whatever the place where his corpse had lain became presumed *vacant*).
- What Gospel characters say and do reflect the editor's needs (here, this is exemplified by words/actions of the bit players in Mark's Passion).
- Gospel accounts were embellished by recourse to Jewish scriptural texts (here, Joseph of Arimathea becomes "rich" on the basis of Isaiah 53:9).

Loose Ends Worth Tying

Joseph of Arimathea

- *Circumventing Mark's Intent.* Ingenious circumventions have been devised to show how Joseph of Arimathea was kindly disposed toward Jesus even if Mark claimed that "all" Sanhedrin members condemned him. For example, Joseph only voted for conviction out of fear of alienating his colleagues (but what, then, of his vaunted "courage"?); or Joseph deliberately absented himself during the vote (but where does Mark even hint of this?); or Joseph belonged to a *different* council than the one that condemned Jesus (see next item).
- *Respected Member of* What *"Council"?* By presuming that Joseph of Arimathea belonged to a council *different* from the Sanhedrin, we could understand that he was nonconsenting to that other body's *unanimous* condemnation of Jesus. Aside from the failure of this argument on its own merits,[24] why predicate "historical" questions on a misdeduction by Luke (that Joseph was non-consenting to the court's intent)? Mark never said this, and *he* wrote the story. Further, why predicate historical questions on what is a Marcan *fiction* to start with (that Jesus even had a Sanhedrin trial—see Chap. 12)?
- *Was Joseph of Arimathea a Real Person?* The Prophet Jonah was a real person (2 Ki 14:25) but did not undergo the adventures assigned him in

the book of Jonah. Joseph of Arimathea may well have existed without playing any such role as Mark assigns him. (While not pertinent to Gospel study, even richer legends awaited Joseph as their nucleus: he brought the Holy Grail through Gaul to Britain, built an oratory at Glastonbury, and freed Ireland from snakes.[25])

Empty Tomb

- *Empty Tomb Traditions in a Pre-Marcan Passion Narrative?* Most scholars who posit that Mark inherited a rudimentary Passion account deny that it included a burial or empty tomb tradition (consistent with my contention, here, that these stories developed late).
- *Why the Singling Out of Peter in Mark 16:7 ("But go, tell his disciples and Peter that ... ")?* Was 16:7 (along with 14:28) added by a post-Marcan hand to rehabilitate Peter? On this important matter, see Chapter 15➔.

Part Five

Primary New Testament Writings

A Concern for Jews from Each

Romans 9–11
Why Paul's Anxiety for Israel?

These three chapters from Paul's letter to Christians in Rome represent his only full statement of the proper relations between Jews and Christians (both Jewish and Gentile). We may be tantalized, then, by the prospect of readily applying them to the relationship between Jews and Christians today. Can the conversation that Paul began, but that was later broken off, now finally be resumed?[1]

If this is our intent, even Paul might pronounce our venture not "kosher," for our motive in studying these chapters would differ sharply from his aim in composing them. Since Christian–Jewish relations are not a consuming interest in any other Pauline writing, and since each of his other Epistles is prompted by particular circumstances of the churches or persons involved, Paul most likely intended Romans 9–11 not as a timeless discourse for interfaith dialogue but only a response to a more limited situation, in this case in the Roman community itself.

As for identifying that situation, we can do no more than offer conjecture, and I do so on the basis of the one scenario that remains, for me, the most compelling: In the year 49 CE, Christian missionizing activity in the Jewish quarter of Rome proved disturbing to some elements of the Jewish community. Serious unrest ensued. Emperor Claudius reacted to the turbulence by turning forcefully against the entire Jewish community, banishing many (all?) of them from the city.[2] Claudius' edict may have dramatically altered Christian demographics as well, for likely expelled along with Jews were Jewish-*Christians**—or, at the least, some of their leaders. We see this, e.g., when the book of Acts reports that Paul "found [in Corinth] a Jew named Aquila ... lately come from Italy with his wife, Priscilla, because Claudius had commanded all the Jews to leave Rome" (18:2).

Any significant reduction in Jewish-Christian leadership would have allowed *Gentile*-Christians,* by default, to take greater charge within

Rome's Christian community. Claudius' decree, however, was binding only during his lifetime. It lapsed when Nero succeeded him several years later, in 54 CE, and failed to renew it. As expelled Jews and Jewish-Christians began trickling back into Rome,[3] did tensions among Jewish, Jewish-Christian, and Gentile-Christian elements escalate?[4]

- Did returning *Jews* remain resentful and wary of Christians, whose missionary incursions had sparked Claudius' expulsion of many Jews to start with?
- Were returning *Jewish-Christians* rebuffed not only by resentful Jews but by condescending Gentile-Christians who, in the interim, had displaced them as leaders of the very church they themselves had founded?
- Did the rising *Gentile-Christians*, meanwhile, interpret the banishment of Jewish-Christian leaders as God's judgment concerning who was fit to run the Roman church? Had a status reversal set in, with Jewish-Christians rather than Gentile-Christians henceforth to be the fringe elements (a view perhaps preserved when Mark disparages Jesus' disciples, the Jewish-Christians' forerunners; see next chapter ➔)?[5]

Paul composed Romans shortly after this turn of events—likely during the spring of 56, in Corinth. It was earmarked for Gentile-Christians and arrived in Rome after exiled Jewish-Christian believers and Jews per se had commenced their return there. Paul had a personal stake here; he was at a decisive juncture in his career. Having finished missionizing the eastern Mediterranean world, he intended now to embark on the West, hoping that the city of Rome itself would become his point of departure "to Spain" (Rom 15:23f.). For matters to run smoothly for him, Paul wished Roman Christians (Jewish- and Gentile-) to achieve harmony within their diversity, and for Gentile-Christians to temper their animosity toward Jewish unbelievers.

But each of these contending societal elements had cause for disaffection with Paul personally:

- Returning *Jews* may have deemed him an apostate for appearing to abandon his Jewish heritage and to question their special status as the chosen of God.
- At least some returning *Jewish-Christians* must have learned of Paul amid their exile in Europe or Asia Minor, and knew as well of the bitter opposition that he engendered there—among Christians inclining toward Jewish observance and also among Jews per se, who were alienated, rather than persuaded, by his preaching style and combative nature.
- Paul clearly believed that *Gentile-Christians* by now constituted the majority of Rome's church (1:13ff.; 11:13; 15:15f.)—especially if

Jewish-Christian elements returning to that city had yet to replenish their numbers. Some Gentile-Christians were likely wary lest this worrisome intruder now intend to take them over.[6] Paul felt that *they* were the primary cause of contentiousness among Rome's Christians and vis-à-vis the Jews. Accordingly, Gentile-Christians above all required a theological framework that would dispose them to relate more kindly both to Jews and Jewish-Christians.

The need for Paul to mend all these fences, then, may best explain why it is mainly in Romans 9–11 that he attends to the problem of relations between Jews and Christians (both Jewish and Gentile), advancing themes left relatively unaddressed by him elsewhere: his own identity as a Jew in relation to his mission to the Gentiles; Israel's lack of faith, and her future as the people of God; Paul's personal significance for Israel and her conversion; and Jews and Gentiles in relation to the final judgment and to the righteousness of God.

Paul's Argument in Five Stages

Because Paul's writings are difficult to understand, removal of certain items of relatively lesser consequence can improve comprehension—hence a certain abridgment of our texts as I now present them.

Stage One—Israel's failure to believe does not mean that God's promises to the Hebrew Patriarchs have failed.

Distilling the Essentials of the Text:

9 2 ... I have ... unceasing anguish in my heart. 3For I could wish that I myself were accursed and cut off from Christ for the sake of my ... kinsmen by race. 4They are Israelites, and to them belong the sonship, the glory, the covenants, the giving of the law, ... the promises; 5 ... the patriarchs, and of their race, according to the flesh, is the Christ.... 6But it is not as though the word of God had failed. *For not all ... descended from Israel belong to Israel,* 7and not all are children of Abraham because they are his descendants.... 8 ... It is not the children of the flesh who are the children of God, but the children of the promise are reckoned as descendants....

What Paul Means:

Even though he claims to be commissioned by the risen Christ as apostle to the Gentiles, Paul is himself a Jew. Thus he professes his anguish that the majority of Jews refuse to recognize the Christ whom he has been preaching—even his willingness to be "cut off from Christ" if that would in some fashion assist his brethren after the flesh.➔

But beyond his personal kinship, Paul is also concerned about preserving the perception of *God's trustworthiness*. It was to the Jews that God's promises of salvation were given first. Might not most Jews' rejection of Jesus signal the failure of God's assurances to ancient Hebrew Patriarchs? How profoundly mysterious. Precisely when God's pledges to Israel⁻⁾ appeared fulfilled, by virtue of the Messiah's having come, these promises remain unrealized. For by rejecting Christ, Israel undergoes rejection herself! Has God, through this new revelation, thus canceled earlier promises to the Jews? Paul cannot accept that a trustworthy God could make promises and later nullify them. Moreover, how therefore could Gentile-Christians have any confidence in God's promises to *them*?

Paul navigates this hazardous course circuitously. He begins by asserting that God's promises to Israel were never applicable to Israel as a *whole*. Commencing with Abraham, God selected only certain persons and some of their descendants in advance (Isaac but not Ishmael; Jacob but not Esau), with no prior regard to their merit. Accordingly, only those descendants promised to Abraham *through Isaac* are the chosen "children of God"—as opposed to *all* the fleshly children of Abraham. So, too, when Isaac's wife, Rebecca, became pregnant and the twins, Esau and Jacob, were not yet born, God determined that "the older [Esau] must serve the younger [Jacob]" (Gen 25:23).

As a result, not all people descended from Abraham belong to the Israel that is "chosen." Moreover, there is also nothing to prevent God from now making a further decision as to who will be recipients of God's promises. By virtue of Paul's redefining—and, thereby, his broadening—of this category, we learn that *Gentiles* as well can become heirs of God's promises to the Hebrew Patriarchs. Those to whom God made these promises, then, were not solely Israel "according to the *flesh*," but a wider configuration conceived in terms of "Israel according to the *promise*." This means that many who are ethnically descended from Israel now happen *not* to belong to the Israel of God's promise, while many others who are not ethnically descended from Abraham *do* belong. Therefore, *that most biological Jews in Paul's day happen to have rejected Christ in no way implies that God is untrustworthy, or that his promises to Israel have been frustrated. Nor is it alarming that currently the "Israel according to the promise" is overwhelmingly Gentile* since this reality is part and parcel of the plan—by a *reliable* God—that remains fully in force.

Stage Two—God's right to choose is not limited to choosing *Jews*.

Distilling the Essentials of the Text:

9 (continued) [14] ... Is there injustice on God's part? By no means! ...
[21]Has the potter no right over the clay, to make out of the same lump

one vessel for beauty and another for menial use? ^{22}What if God ...
has endured ... vessels ... made for destruction ^{23} ... to make known
the riches of his glory for the vessels of mercy ... ^{24}even us whom he
has called, not from the Jews only but also from the Gentiles? ... ^{30} ...
Gentiles who did not pursue righteousness have attained it, that is,
righteousness through faith; ^{31}but ... Israel who pursued the righteousness ... based on law did not succeed in fulfilling that law ^{32} ...
because they did not pursue it through faith, but as if it were based on
works.

What Paul Means:
Might not God's process of electing some and rejecting others appear arbitrary? If so, Paul argues, so what? God has this prerogative! Whenever, in the potter's mind, material in his hands is not taking shape, he
simply refashions it as it suits him. Analogously, God has the prerogative to refashion an inadequate or otherwise unfulfilling vessel—defec-
tive in that, currently, it is not working out—into one more suitable.

In this sense, then, what right has anyone to object if God refuses a people (here, the majority of the Jews) who have failed God in favor of a new
complexion that happens to be overwhelmingly Gentile? Challenge of
God's elective freedom is not legitimate for persons created by God. It is
hardly what we humans do, but rather what God chooses to do with us!

Stage Three—Israel is responsible for her own failure.

Distilling the Essentials of the Text:

10 ^{1}Brethren, my ... prayer to God for [unbelieving Jews] is that they
... be saved. ^{2} ... They have a zeal for God, but it is not enlightened....
^{13}For "everyone who calls upon the name of the Lord will be saved"
[Joel 2:32]. ^{14}But how are men to call upon him in whom they have
not believed ... and ... to believe in him of whom they have never
heard? ... ^{18}But ... have they not heard? Indeed they have.... ^{21} ... of
Israel [Isaiah[says, "All day long I have held out my hands to a disobedient and contrary people" [65:2].

What Paul Means:
Although arbitrariness by God is thus allowable, it happens that God's activity has *not* been capricious at all, but conditioned rather by the failure
of most of the Jewish nation to call upon God in faith. How can this failure be explained? God has sent her (Israel) many preachers, and she could
well have assimilated their message since even Gentiles, unprepared, have
readily accepted it—so plainly has God spoken. By her own unbelief,
therefore, has Israel compromised her welfare. Gentiles, meanwhile,

who by nature did not strive to follow the "way of righteousness" before God, have nevertheless obtained it on the basis of their faith in Christ Jesus.

Paul does not question the Jews' earnestness, but he does underline its defects. To commit oneself to righteousness based on the Law is to place high value on what people can do for themselves and for God, and too little value on what only God can do for *them*. While Jews have "a zeal for God ... it is not enlightened." Those relying on themselves to accomplish what only God can accomplish for them are building their life upon an illusion.

Stage Four—Yet Israel's intransigence is also providential.

Distilling the Essentials of the Text:

11 [7] ... Israel failed to obtain what it sought. The elect obtained it, but the rest were hardened.... [11] ... Have they stumbled so as to fall? By no means! But through their trespass salvation has come to the Gentiles, so as to make Israel jealous. [12]Now ... if their failure means riches for the Gentiles, how much more will their full inclusion mean!

What Paul Means:

Israel's failure is not final. Her apostasy is only a necessary stage and prelude in an overarching process that will result in potentially *all* people's knowledge of God's grace. A hardening has *temporarily* come over most of Israel so that, in the interim, the full number of Gentiles might have an opportunity to embrace the Gospel and thereby become saved. Thereafter, Israel as a whole will become so intensely jealous over the apparent loss of her privileges, and at seeing her own possession now in the hands of Gentiles, as to accept then what she rejects now, recognizing Christ-Jesus as Lord and Savior.

Stage Five—Gentiles should behave in the knowledge that, in the end, all Israel will be saved.

Distilling the Essentials of the Text:

11 (continued) [13]I am speaking to you Gentiles.... [17] ... if some ... branches [unbelieving Jews] were broken off, and you [believing Gentiles], a wild olive shoot ... grafted in their place..., [18]do not boast over the branches ... remember it is not you that support the root, but the root that supports you. [19]You will say, "Branches [unbelieving Jews] were broken off so ... I [believing Gentiles] might be grafted in." [20] ... Do not become proud.... [21]For if God did not spare the natural branches, neither will he spare you.... [23]And even the others

[unbelieving Jews], *if they do not persist in their unbelief*, will be grafted in ... again. [24]For if you [Gentiles] have been cut from what is by nature a wild olive tree, and grafted, contrary to nature, into a cultivated olive tree, how much more [easily] will these *natural* branches [currently unbelieving Jews] be grafted back into their own olive tree? [25]Lest you be wise in your own conceits, ... understand this mystery, brethren: a hardening has come upon part of Israel, until the full number of the Gentiles comes in, [26]and so all Israel will be saved.... [28]As regards the gospel they are enemies of God, for your sake; but as regards election they are beloved for the sake of their forefathers. [29]For the gifts and call of God are irrevocable.

What Paul Means:
These are developments that Gentiles should understand and welcome: what is happening with Gentiles is actually in the service of the salvation of Israel. Yes, God desires to save Gentiles through Christ, yet not in place of the Israelites but rather *in addition to* them—preceding most of Israel but not replacing them. Nevertheless, Gentiles have come to occupy this favorable position not because they won or deserved the privilege but solely because the Jews lost it, blinded as they were by self-pride and self-reliance. Gentiles falling victim to these same weaknesses will be overtaken by the same fate. Since they are "grafted" into the spiritual Israel, Gentile-Christians should not consider themselves a new race but rather the legitimate continuation of the Israel of the past. Yet, as such, Gentile-Christians would be wise neither to despise the Jews nor to boast over them, because God has not written the Jews off. In the end, indeed, it will be not merely a remnant of Jews but rather all Israel who, *as a result of faith in Christ*, will enter the Kingdom of God and be saved. Such are the ways of God's unfathomable wisdom that Israel's very rejection by God will culminate in her salvation!

Applying Romans 9–11 in Dialogue Today: Important Clarifications

Romans 9–11 Should Be Studied in Light of the Community at Rome
We are prone to overlook that Paul's purpose in writing Romans 9–11 differed from how this text is commonly applied in Christian–Jewish dialogue today. As I have stressed, these chapters were earmarked only for the occasion of Paul's impending visit to Rome. As such, in our analyses and extrapolations from Paul's argumentation here, we must not disregard the chronological, geographical, and sociopolitical contexts that Paul had in mind and that catalyzed his exposition. That no other Pauline Epistle discusses issues so germane to what *we* term "Christian–Jewish

relations" further suggests that what we confront here is a writing addressed to this one locale.

In His Poignant Concern for the Jews, What Does Paul Leave Unmentioned?

Paul's Continued Self-Identification as a Jew? Paul seems to include himself when he insists that "a real Jew ... is one inwardly, and real circumcision is a matter of the heart" (2:28f.). His religious reorientation is not a conversion—switching affiliation from one religion of the past to another of the present—but the dawning of a new awareness that deepens and extends his Judaism. An apt analogy likens Judaism to a ladder, with the sophistication of a person's commitment a function of how high a rung he or she attains.[7] Most Jews position themselves on a rung high enough to discern Mt. Sinai and the Law that Moses received there. Paul feels that he achieves a still higher rung and vantage point that enable him to discern, *beyond* the Torah at Sinai, the benefits of the more marvelous revelation of Jesus as the Christ*—the Messiah* but only as Paul reconceptualizes him!

Unbelieving Jews will be in no position to share Paul's realization until *they* venture higher on the ladder Paul *still* occupies. Since Paul anticipates their ultimately doing so, he broadly lays out how this development will unfold: Gentiles within the church, enjoying the fruits of God's promises tendered originally to Israel's own Patriarchs, will induce Jews to crave the blessings they believe are properly theirs, mobilizing them, finally, to accept Christ-Jesus after all.

Paul's Desire to Deflect Criticism from Himself? Paul's activity as apostle to the Gentiles hardly requires him to alienate Jews. Yet his abrasive style and possibly irksome message have done just that, exposing him to charges that he has done more to distance Jews from salvation than bring them closer. Is Paul seeking to deflect this criticism? Certainly, his theological scheme shifts to *God* all responsibility for the Jews' reticence—it is God's plan that the Jews' hearts be temporarily hardened to allow the full number of Gentiles to accept Christ, thereby making Israel herself jealous. Such a scenario renders it *premature* for Israel to be widely represented in the Church early on—as in Paul's day—since that degree of demographic prominence can come about only *after* the requisite number of Gentiles have entered. The Jews' underrepresentation within Christendom in Paul's time is thus in line with proper expectation, so criticism of Paul himself on this score is not legitimate.

Paul's Disaffection with the Anti-Judaism in Rome? Roman society disdained Jews for their social cohesiveness and "superstitious" practices. Has Paul's fear that nascent anti-Judaism is spreading and is perpetuated by Rome's Gentile-Christians transformed him into a defender of *Israel* against Gentile misperceptions?[8] In assigning Jews an indispensable role at the end of history, does Paul hope not only to sober Gentile-Christians but wean them from infectious anti-Judaism?

Where Paul's Theological Scheme Breaks Down

Paul's design of what will ultimately transpire with Israel may seem oddly coherent since it enables him to cover all conflicting bases. By allowing inclusion of Gentiles among intended recipients of God's promises, Paul provides a scheme whereby currently unbelieving Jews will eventually be saved: Israel's present recalcitrance will give opportunity for Gentiles to become welcomed into Christ; in turn, evangelizing Gentiles will ultimately evoke Israel's jealousy (seeing her own privileges being enjoyed by others), thereby prompting her also, belatedly, to accept Christ. Thus Paul feels that he has demonstrated the trustworthiness of God's promises to the Patriarchs, and accounted for *why the percentage of Jewish-Christians in the church of Paul's day must for now be minuscule.*

Yet, were it not for the troubling conundrum that most Jews were rejecting Christ, would Paul ever have devised so desperate a gambit? He has, after all, redefined "Israel" in non-ethnic terms[9] such that Gentiles (without conversion to Judaism) cannot only become members of Israel *but actually constitute her majority*! That not all from Israel are "Israel" is an assertion difficult enough to maneuver. To affirm that practically *all* of "Israel" are not from Israel charts a course even more taxing: "there is nothing unclear about the goal of the argument.... But the route [Paul] traces out to reach it is virtually unnavigable."[10]

It is helpful to liken Paul's scheme to a footrace:[11] If God keeps faith with Israel, why have Gentiles reached the finish line first, leaving Israel in the dust? Is Paul proposing that God has rigged the racecourse so that the runners favored (the Jews) unexpectedly falter—though only *temporarily*—and, shockingly, those with no initial interest in running at all (Gentiles never seeking salvation) become the surprise victors? Yet Jewish theology responds that Israel starts *already at* the finish line, that Jews are within the covenant to start with and remain there unless and until they apostasize. On such a basis, there is no stumbling nor, for that matter, even any race! As for apostasy, who comes more readily to the Jewish mind on this score than Paul himself, in rejecting the Law of Moses?

Paul also makes a costly admission: by arguing that salvation for Gentiles is the prime means of reaching Jews, has he not effectively confessed that his apostleship to Gentiles is *ultimately for Israel's sake*, that the definitive goal of God's work is primarily deliverance of God's original people?[12] If so, then the failure of the Jews even more so than inclusion of Gentiles is what truly powers Paul's argument,[13] and Paul is an apostle also *to the Jews* after all, even the apostle par excellence!

As for Paul's insistence that the hardening that has come over Israel is only temporary, Jews today—approximately two millennia after Paul's ministry—overwhelmingly continue to deny Jesus as the Christ. Which course, then, is the more compelling: that this already seemingly interminable wait must continue still, or that Paul's expectation must now, at long last, be dismissed as mistaken?

Nor will it do to rescue Paul by arguing that, after Gentiles in sufficient numbers accept Christ as Savior, all Israel will likewise be saved *whether they accept Jesus or not*—that, while Gentiles are saved solely by faith in Christ, Jews could be saved solely via their "traditional covenant faithfulness."[14] Such a two-covenant formulation may be "admirable in its ecumenical scope, but there is very little evidence for it."[15] (Further, often this seems at least partially an apologetic response to Nazism's perversion of New Testament traditions as aids in justifying extermination of Jewry.) For all the potential attractiveness of such two-covenant theology in the context of modern interreligious discourse, the claim that Paul himself believed that Jews could be saved without accepting Christ is neither theologically, nor textually, defensible (Rom 11:23: "even the others, *if they do not persist in their unbelief*, will be grafted in"; cf. Gal 2:15f.: "because by works of the law shall *no one* be justified"—Paul includes here that "we ourselves, who are Jews by birth," know this). Unless he believed that accepting Christ was essential for Israel herself to be saved, why was Paul so agitated by his fellow Jews' recalcitrance, and why would he seek refuge in the contorted fantasy that Israel's *jealousy* will motivate her to accept Christ?

Why Paul Sounds Anti-Jewish

Because Paul reverses the sequence for salvation, arguing now that the "full number of Gentiles" must *precede* disbelieving Israel—and because he has the covenant skip from Abraham to Christ, *with membership now restricted to those in Christ irrespective of whether they are Jewish ethnically* (Rom 9:6ff.)—Jews will always recoil from his message, hearing it (as I frame it) essentially as:

> The fulfillment that we Jews have sought has already occurred, but *you* disbelieving Jews are blind to the fulfillment of our heritage. We were chosen not because of merit. For election is not the result of anything people do to deserve it. Rather, it was accorded us by the free choice of God. But what cannot be won by merit can be forfeited by negligence, and indeed has been so forfeited by *you*. Gentiles, never pursuing righteousness, have attained it, whereas you, always pursuing it, have missed it altogether, failing to understand that righteousness is the status that God confers on those humbly receiving it through faith as God's gift, whereas—foolishly—you assume that righteousness is a kind of life you can attain based on obedience to the Law.

When heard in this fashion, Paul is chastising fellow Jews for not accepting Christ as the fulfillment of a conceptual scheme that is foreign to them to begin with! He views Christ as a type of dying and rising Greco-Roman Savior-deity, which sharply diverges from Judaism's own understanding of the messianic role and agenda, whose contours simply do not involve bringing freedom from Sin (since persons can initiate their own reconciliation with God through repentance). Not only has Paul universalized his own predicament by including Jews under an umbrella where they certainly do not feel that they belong, but he has also failed to grasp the reality that what he construes to be the Jews' blindness they consider clear-sightedness—since no evidences that *Jews* expect to herald the arrival of the Messiah* are yet manifest!

Anti-Jewish Misapplication of Paul by Others
Inappropriate as Paul's message in itself may sound to modern Jews, later Christianity made it even more discomfiting for three reasons:

1. Because Paul was a Jew, there remained in his case a measure of positive personal orientation toward fellow Jews, a common ground that later (Gentile-Christian) writers had no (ethnic) basis for sharing.

2. Even decades after Paul died, Jewish resistance to Christianity showed no signs of abating, rendering it increasingly difficult to accept Paul's contention that the Jews' hardened status was *temporary*.

3. The calamitous fall of Jerusalem and the destruction of the Temple in 70 CE served to confirm for Christianity in particular the rejection of the "old" Israel and her replacement now by Christians as the "new" Israel. Israel's acceptance of Christ, already much delayed, now appeared no longer in the offing.

Inexorably, then, the later Church distorted Paul's position. Paul alleged the existence of a divine mystery whereby "all Israel will be saved" (Rom 11:26), such that the hardening of the Jews was only temporary; yet certain Church writers presented the Jews as hopeless enemies whose rejection was permanent and chances of salvation nil. Whereas Paul asked in Romans, "Has God rejected his people?" (11:1), answering "by no means!" the later Church replied, in effect, "by all means." Whereas Paul asked, "What advantage has the Jew?" (3:1), and then spelled it out affirmatively, the answer of the later Church was, essentially, "no superiority whatsoever."

Already by the early second century, the *Epistle of Barnabas* adopted the extreme position that, though God had extended chosenness to the Jews, Israel had taken to idol worship, building the golden calf, as a result of which God immediately suspended the contemplated covenant, now to reserve it instead for later Christians.[16] Justin Martyr carried this further, contending in his *Dialogue with Trypho* (see above, Chap. 2) that God's covenant with Israel was for her condemnation: circumcision was a branding of Jews for slaying Jesus and "cursing in your synagogues those who believe on Christ" (14). Thus Paul's contention regarding Israel's temporary rejection metamorphosed into the novel accusation that God's relationship to Israel was to her damnation—that Jews were not only rejected but never even *elected*.

Concluding Problem: Is Paul Responsible for Christian Antisemitism?

The failure to differentiate between what Paul himself believed about the Jews and what the later Church redirected his message to mean has persisted over the centuries. Accordingly, Paul became misapplied in Christian–Jewish discourse, with each community hearing what it supposed was his message in selective ways, thereby heightening acrimony between Jew and Christian.

To what degree, then, was Paul personally accountable for distortions of his thought by others? Romans supports the view that he recognized anti-Judaism as a menace. Yet certainly he failed to stave off actualization of his great fear that Gentile-Christians, becoming proud, would no longer stand in awe and respect of Jews in their midst. We must ask, then, whether Paul warned of anti-Judaism also because *he had some inkling of how his own theology could be processed right in line with it?* True, he could not have imagined the intensity of the anti-Jewish cast that later Christian writers would give to his own thought. Yet Paul did supply the theoretical structure for later Christian antisemitism. This is a tragedy mainly for Jews, but also for Christians, "because the failure

to convert Jews to Christianity has not merely disappointed Christian expectations and called into question Christian claims, but has drawn [us] Christians into unspeakable violation of our own values."[17]

The Most Valuable Ideas in This Chapter May Be

1. While Paul styles himself the "apostle to the Gentiles," in Romans 9–11 he seems preoccupied with the *Jews'* destiny, insisting that only the infusion of Christian ranks by Gentiles will induce all Jews also, eventually, to come to Christ.
2. Thereby, Paul radiates the odd impression that his apostleship to Gentiles is ultimately for Israel's sake, perhaps rendering Paul an apostle to the Jews after all, even the apostle par excellence.
3. Paul sees his religious reorientation as a departure from Pharisaism but also as an extension of Judaism as he has *reconfigured* it (see Chap. 6).
4. The urgency with which Paul warns Gentiles away from anti-Judaism may reflect his apprehension over how his own thinking might be processed in line with it.
5. Later Christianity did indeed reformulate Paul's views in an anti-Jewish direction.

Loose Ends Worth Tying

Paul's Anguish

He models his language, in Romans 9:3, on Moses' anguished intercession with God on behalf of earlier Israelite unbelievers (those who built the golden calf), including even Moses' request to be blotted out of the Lord's book if that would somehow benefit them (Exod 32:32f.).

What Promises by God Does Paul Have in Mind?

When Paul refers to God's oaths setting forth Israel's destiny, the promises he has in mind likely include Genesis 18:18 ("Abraham shall become a ... mighty nation, and all the nations ... shall bless themselves by him") and others along these lines (e.g., 22:17f.; 26:3f.; Deut 1:11; cf. 1 Chr 16:15ff.; Ps 105:8ff.)

The Gospel of Mark
Destabilizing a Betrayal by "Judas" ("the Jews"?)[1]

As the disciple of Jesus who presumably betrayed him, Judas Iscariot[2] has been exploited by those stereotyping Jews as traitors, money-grubbers, and even agents of Satan.[3] Consider the assonance of "Judas" and "Jew" and their virtually identical spelling in Greek, *Ioudas* (Judas) and *Ioudaios* (Jew), as well as in Hebrew, *Yehuda* and *Yehudi*—suggesting an intentional equation of the terms.

Antisemitic appropriation of Judas' image is a subject with which Christians, not only Jews, should be made conversant as, for example, when churches invite Jewish communities to demonstrate the Passover Seder (see Chap. 10). If we accept Matthew's account of Judas' suicide, then Jesus' Last Supper was *Judas'* also; Seder presentations could thus introduce discussion of Judas as well.

Story Line

Judas appears in each Gospel (and Acts 1). His treatment in Mark, the earliest account, is sparse: Judas offers to assist Jewish authorities bent on arresting Jesus. They promise him money. During the Last Supper, Jesus predicts his betrayal by someone present and warns of the traitor's fate. All adjourn to the Garden of Gethsemane where an armed party arrives led by Judas, who kisses Jesus to identify him for the captors, as the other disciples flee. The story's lacunae are glaring. What is Judas' motive? Why identify Jesus by a kiss? Of Judas' subsequent experience we learn nothing from Mark.

The other Synoptists try to plug these gaps. Guessing greed as Judas' motive, Matthew has him ask the authorities up front for money (26:15ff.), but this surmise is problematic: So diabolical a deed for a paltry thirty pieces of silver? So greedy a man in a company so poor to start with? Such puzzlements recede once Luke (4:13; 22:3) and John (6:70;

13:2,27; cf. 17:12) have *Satan* enter Judas: a person possessed by the devil needs less by way of psychological motivation!

In Matthew, overwhelmed by remorse, Judas returns the money and hangs himself (27:3ff.), but Acts 1:18ff. has him rupture himself in a fall (or swell up) and burst asunder—a disparity that has invited desperate conflation: that the rope for Judas' hanging snapped, plummeting him to the ground where he exploded upon impact. Yet incongruity remains: a penitent's suicide (Matthew) versus an unrepentant scoundrel's heaven-imposed death (Acts).[4] Evidently Judas' deed seemed so dastardly that either mode of death appeared too good for him, leading Papias[5] to propose that Judas' flesh became:

> so swollen that where a wagon could pass with ease he was unable to ... not even ... his head.... He died on his own property, which ... remained ... deserted because of the stench, and not even to the present day can one walk by ... without holding fast his nose ... so great had been the efflux from [Judas'] flesh upon the ground.

Worse still, in Dante's *Inferno* Judas appears frozen at the very bottom, head first in Lucifer's central mouth, clawed, bitten, and chewed for eternity (34.58–63).

Determining the Betrayal's Historicity

Embellishments aside, is the story's nucleus authentic history? Anomalies challenge us. Why, for example, is Jesus relatively mute in Gethsemane as Judas approaches to kiss him (Mk 14:45 & par)? Is this the motif of the sheep dumb before the shearer (Isa 53:7; Acts 8:32)? This brings us to ponder other parallels to Jewish scripture, fueling suspicion that the *entire* episode is fabricated (i.e., derived from these texts). Many elements of it echo stories about King David—as if to suggest that whatever David experienced transpired also with Jesus, David's "son" (cf. Mk 10:47f.; 11:10; 12:35ff.):

- David's betrayal by a trusted adviser, Ahithophel, who hangs himself (2 Sa 17:23), could have engendered Judas' betrayal and supposed hanging (in Matthew), especially in conjunction with—
- (David's) Psalm 41:9, which reveals how "even *my bosom friend* [Ahithophel] in whom I trusted, who *ate of my bread*, has lifted his heel against me" (cf. Jn 13:18), as well as—
- (David's) Psalm 55:12ff.: "it is not an enemy who taunts me ... but ... you ... my *companion*, my *familiar friend*."
- Joab, about to assassinate Amasa (David's preferred general), treacherously takes hold of him as if to *kiss* him (2 Sa 20:9).

Then there is the correlation between Judas, one of the twelve, selling his master for pieces of silver, and *Judah*—also "one of twelve"—urging Joseph's sale for pieces of silver (Gen 37:26–28; in the Septuagint,* Judah is "Judas"). Additional parallels are forthcoming from Zechariah.[6]

Assessing Factors Favoring Historicity

Two arguments seem to reassure us that Judas' betrayal of Jesus was factual, but both break down under scrutiny.

1. *Paul's Last Supper Testimony.* In the mid-50s, Paul appears to introduce his sole reference to the Last Supper with words commonly translated: "the Lord Jesus on the night when he was *betrayed* took bread" (1 Cor 11:23b), suggesting that Paul accepts the betrayal story. But "betrayed" is not Paul's intent when he uses the ambiguous Greek verb, *paradidonai*. It also means "delivered up" (which can include the sense even of *to death*), and this is how Paul uses the same verb elsewhere in his writings.[7] I submit that he intends the same meaning here. Paul's Last Supper reference thus means that Jesus took bread "on the night when he was delivered up [to death]" (not delivered up by any one party to another). This is confirmed by Paul's culminating remark (verse 26): "for as often as you eat this bread and drink this cup, you proclaim the Lord's *death* until he comes." The erroneous presumption that Paul has the betrayal in mind is what *determines* the common mistranslation, but there is no indication here that Paul even knew of Judas not to mention any betrayal by him.

2. *Embarrassment for the Church.* But why would Christian tradition invent a story so damaging to Jesus' image? During the late second century, the pagan Celsus ridiculed the presumably all-knowing Lord of Christianity for selecting among his close followers someone who became a traitor.[8] The Fourth Gospel had struggled valiantly on this score to shore up presumptions of Jesus' omniscience or foreknowledge (6:64; 13:26f.), reassuring us throughout that Jesus knew "all that was to befall him" (18:4). Yet we are still left to wonder not only about Jesus' lack of insight into Judas' character but about Jesus' inability to reform Judas once he selected him.[9]

   Meanwhile, why zero in on Judas alone when the behavior of *all other* Marcan disciples also bespeaks betrayal? As we will see in detail,→ all the disciples fail and abandon Jesus in a wide spectrum of ways, so that Judas fits within this complex rather than apart from it. The primary question thus becomes not how could a foreknowing Jesus appoint Judas but how could he appoint *any* of this inept crew. If we

accept arguments of many scholars[10] that all these denigrations of the disciples are Marcan inventions—and therefore untrue to history—then why not say the same about Judas? (Here we detect a weakness of the criterion of *Embarrassment*; see Chap. 5 [11]).

Telltale Clues of Late Invention

Other factors may heighten our skepticism regarding these matters.

How Many Disciples Saw the Resurrected Jesus—Twelve, or Only Eleven?

The early kerygma* (1 Cor 15:3b–7), as quoted by Paul, affirms that the resurrected Jesus "appeared to Cephas [Peter], then to the *twelve*" disciples. Is "twelve" intended literally—meaning Judas was included? If so, a betrayal episode was not known early on, for how could Christians have imagined Judas continuing to associate with his colleagues, let alone being rewarded along with them by a manifestation of the resurrected Christ? All the more so if he committed suicide *before* Jesus' crucifixion (Mt 27:5).

Some will argue that "the twelve" could be simply formulaic, referring to whatever number of worthy disciples (here, e.g., eleven) remained to witness the resurrected Jesus. This is reasonable. But we must take serious notice that the Synoptists did not understand the matter this way. Precisely because they took "twelve" literally, the Synoptists pare the witnesses down to "eleven" in all post-resurrection settings (Fig. 15.1[12]):

15.1 — The Synoptists' Concern to Pare "Twelve" to "Eleven"

Mk	16:14	Afterward, he appeared to the *eleven*
Mt	28:16	The *eleven* disciples went to Galilee
Lk	24:9	Returning from the tomb they told all this to the *eleven*
	24:33	They found the *eleven* gathered together
Acts	1:13	They went up to the upper room ... [1] Peter and [2] John and [3] James and [4] Andrew, [5] Philip and [6] Thomas, [7] Bartholomew and [8] Matthew, [9] James ... and [10] Simon ... and [11] Judas the son of James [a Judas different from Iscariot]
	1:26	Matthias ... was enrolled with the *eleven* apostles*

This "careful insistence" that the resurrected Jesus appeared to but eleven suggests "a *contrary* tradition ... that needed to be undermined ... the earlier tradition which Paul received and handed on" that Jesus had appeared to the twelve. "To specify 'eleven' is to show an anxiety to state the right number"[13] against the previous tradition showing twelve, not eleven. (This recalls the mathematical error that Matthew and Luke *thought* that Mark committed when using "twelve" in his Last Supper narrative; see Fig. 10.3 and commentary.)

Yes, the book of Acts relates that, at Peter's initiative, Judas was immediately replaced—through election—by a certain Matthias (although no other member of the twelve, besides Judas, was replaced upon death). But we hear nothing of this Matthias until Acts 1:23ff., written during the 90s. In my view, Acts' account is an improvised fiction *to allow continued reference to Jesus' inner circle as "twelve," but with Judas no longer among them.* Moreover, since the inner circle had been appointed by Jesus himself, how did the (imagined and improvised) notion come about that one could now gain entry by mere human election (1:15ff.)? And how are we to tolerate a scenario characterized by "the traitor Peter→ arranging for a substitute for the traitor Judas ... a monstrosity beyond imagination"?[14]

Jesus' Contradictory Intentions for Judas' Future

Jesus is cast as predicting, during the Last Supper, the betrayer's dire future: "It would have been better for that man if he had not been born" (Mk 14:21; Mt 26:24). Yet, elsewhere, in Matthew, Jesus also informs *all twelve* disciples: "In the new world, when the Son of man shall sit on his glorious throne, you who have followed me will also sit on *twelve* thrones judging the *twelve* tribes of Israel" (19:28). By envisioning each of twelve disciples as such a judge over Israel (with the number of judges matching the tribes), Jesus here appears to be reserving one judgeship for Judas as well. Nor will it do to argue, on the basis of "you who have followed me," that Judas was excluded upon ceasing to "follow" Jesus. For in Luke, Jesus *first* reveals the betrayal (22:21) and *then* offers a judgeship to the twelve, including Judas, anyway (22:30). Luke, recognizing the problem, tries omitting the *number* of thrones (while still specifying twelve tribes; see Fig. 15.2). But this accomplishes nothing. Twelve tribes requires twelve thrones, which requires that each be occupied by one of Jesus' *then* current followers (hence, Judas included).

15.2—Luke's Omission of the Number of Thrones

Matthew 19:28	Luke 22:28ff.
... in the new world ... you who have followed me will ... sit on *twelve* thrones, judging the *twelve* tribes of Israel....	*You* are those who have continued with me ... I appoint for *you*, that *you* may ... in my kingdom ... sit on _____ thrones judging the *twelve* tribes of Israel.

The twelve-judgeship saying *could have become current only in an environment that was not yet aware of a betrayal story*—that is, "penned before the stultifying story of the treason of Judas" had come into being.[15] And those who argue that this saying arose later than Jesus (i.e., it was backdated to him) would not only still be supporting the idea that the betrayal is a fiction but also pushing its date of origin even later!

When Did Judas Take Leave of the Disciples?

In Mark, it appears that everyone, including the betrayer, accompanies Jesus from the Last Supper to Gethsemane. How, then, does Judas manage to arrive heading an arresting party whom he has guided *from* wherever they have been in waiting? Recognizing the problem, John alone portrays Jesus as directing Judas' departure during the Last Supper itself (13:27–30).

We could, of course, assume that during or after the meal Judas quietly slipped away to join and lead the captors to Gethsemane. I propose another option: that precisely *within the Gethsemane scene itself a betrayal story (in its entirety) was spliced into an earlier body of tradition that contained no such incident.* It was only thereafter, then—so as to lay the groundwork for what was coming—that Mark manufactured the *preparatory* episodes of Judas' conferring with the priests and of Jesus' Last Supper "prediction" of the betrayal. The telltale clue here is that the Last Supper clause, "And as they were ... eating" (14:18), is echoed almost identically, with no narrative need, four verses later ("And as they were eating"), revealing that Mark, as a prefatory touch, inserted for Jesus a prediction of the betrayal into some *already-established* supper narrative that contained nothing of the sort (Fig. 15.3). This also shores up Jesus' image by showing him in the know rather than surprised by the betrayal.

15.3—Was Jesus' Prediction of the Betrayal Spliced into Mark 14?		
EARLY Version?	**Prediction ADDED?**	**SPLICED Text?**
[17]... he came with the twelve.		[17]... he came with the twelve.
↕	[18]*And as they were at table eating*, Jesus said ... " ... one of you will betray me...." ⟶	[18]*And as they were at table eating*, Jesus said ... " ... one of you will betray me...."
[22]*And as they were eating*, he took bread.		[22]*And as they were eating*, he took bread.

This conclusion may also explain why, as "late" as Gethsemane, Mark is still identifying Judas as "one of the twelve" (verse 43). Does Mark think us forgetful? Why restate what we heard as recently as 14:10 and 20 (not to mention as early as 3:19)? "One of the twelve," admittedly, could simply be a formulaic refrain repeated to emphasize how close the perpetrator was to Jesus. But it is also possible that a newly arising betrayal story, in circulation by Mark's day, had become *first* introduced into the Gethsemane episode—hence the need here to identify Judas as "one of the twelve". If so, all anticipatory references to the felon (3:19; 14:10f.,18; 14:20f.) would be consistent with Mark's "penchant for preparing the reader"[16] for what was coming—in this case, what was going to transpire in Gethsemane—rather than anything firmly embedded in early layers of the tradition. (On Mark's fondness for preparing the reader, see the similar editing in Figs. 12.6; 12.9; 12.10.) For that matter, the entire Passion narration may have *begun* with the arrest in Gethsemane,[17] an episode once far simpler if it originally lacked a betrayal story. Note that if the Judas story had made its first appearance in Gethsemane, then the problem of when Judas departed the Last Supper disappears (since the announcement of a betrayal at the meal would only have been a late "preparatory" addition).

There is another possibility here as well—that when the betrayal story first surfaced, the traitor was an *unspecified* "one of the twelve." Thereafter, it was Mark who decided to identify that "one of the twelve" as Judas in particular (see below).

All these factors, then, undermine confidence that the betrayal derives from early Christian tradition. My judgment is that a fictional betrayal story developed within a narrow window of time: between Paul in the 50s (who mentions the Last Supper but not a betrayal, and accepts the

resurrected Jesus' appearance to the twelve) and the Synoptists after 70, who, in post-resurrection settings, overlook no chance to scale the number of witnessing disciples down to *eleven* so as to prevent us from imagining that Judas had rejoined the others. Even more telling is the twelve-judge saying, which could not have come into being if a Judas story was already current—and the later that saying arose, the later still arose the Judas tale after that.

But what, then, might have brought this story into being, and why would the traitor have become named after the disciple "Judas" in particular?

What Brought the Story into Being?
A Mere Deduction?

One catalyst for the story could be purely deductive in nature. The belated insistence of Christianity that Jesus' crucifixion was *necessary* became one way of coping with an otherwise crushing disappointment. Predictions[18] of Jesus' fate then came to be backdated to him personally, constructions after the fact that reconfigured his execution as having been anticipated rather than unexpected, belying a potentially disconcerting reality: that his Gethsemane capture was a surprise that is not only dispiriting but also incomprehensible.

Here Matthew is particularly energetic (in 26:51ff.), insisting that although Jesus could have thwarted arrest by summoning divine assistance, instead he deliberately chose not to do so for otherwise "how ... should the scriptures be fulfilled, that [Jesus' fate] must be so?" Luke displays Jesus in Gethsemane as so powerful that he could undo the effect of violence—restoring, healed and whole, the ear severed from the high priest's slave (22:50ff.). John dramatizes Jesus' power differently: the arresting party, led by Judas, actually wilts before its "captive" (18:4ff.)!

But all these attempts are late and sophisticated embellishments. What might an early, more elementary embellishment of Jesus' arrest have been like? Perhaps a simple reasoned (or at least reasonable) surmise: that if an ostensibly powerful deific being had fallen prey to mere mortals, then the captors at the least had *inside help*, even from "one of the twelve!" If matters had developed this way, then it would hardly have taken much to substantiate the mere suspicion of a traitor: only recourse to the psalms and stories of King David, and so forth (as shown earlier), on the assumption that events in the past foreshadow the Jesus who fulfils them. Indeed, the possibility yet remains that Jewish scriptural motifs themselves *initiated* the story, although more likely there was another stimulus, with Jewish scripture thereafter brought in to embellish it.

In Response to Turmoil?

A search for another stimulus prompts the question: what was tran-spiring historically during the narrow window of opportunity that I have proposed for the story's origin—after Paul (in the 50s) but prior to Mark's Gospel (ca. 72)? The first grievous persecution of Christians as a separate group began in 64 CE, when Emperor Nero scapegoated them for a major fire in Rome. Christians were set on fire atop poles at night to serve as street lamps for the city (Tacitus, *Annals* xv.44). So as to secure a larger Christian contingent, Nero ordered those cap-tured to be tortured into *betraying* their fellow Christians. Mark's Gospel, whether or not written, as I believe, in the Roman capital it-self,→ suggests a time when betrayal of Christians had been running rampant, with informants drawn from a person's erstwhile friends, even relatives—"brother will deliver up brother to death, and the fa-ther his child ... " (13:9). Here we must remember that the Greek for "deliver up" is the same as for "betray." Any inkling that a traitor might have facilitated the Christ's arrest would likewise have been fu-eled even further by this verbal ambiguity. Indeed, here was an induce-ment to incorrectly process Paul's Last Supper reference as "the night when [Jesus] was betrayed" instead of "the night when [Jesus] was de-livered up to death."

But were such betrayals still going on in Mark's day (ca. 72), about eight years after Nero's persecution? What is pertinent is that the *prece-dent* for betrayal (as for persecution) was established in the Christian mind.[19] Moreover, the betrayal story had already become entrenched in the tradition by the time Mark wrote, so additional passage of time was not a factor in Mark's including it.

Against this backdrop of being "delivered up" even by siblings or parents, a story that Jesus himself had been "delivered up"/"betrayed" by one of *his* closest companions would have proved comforting both to the victims and to their loved ones (who could themselves yet be be-trayed!). Jesus' later followers could now identify with him and feel as-sured that he empathized and would see them through their plight. Moreover, against a setting of persecution during the 60s, how natu-rally the term "delivered up" could have become retrojected into the ministry of Jesus as well, now *historicized* to mean literal acts of bod-ily delivering up of Jesus from one party to another. We can see such historicization worked through in five episodes of Jesus' Passion in Mark (Fig. 15.4).

The probability of historical authenticity of these deliveries decreases as we move *backwards* in the story line, also suggesting the process by which the events occasioning Jesus' death came to be reconstructed

15.4—The Pattern of Delivering Up in Mark				
JUDAS	ARRESTING PARTY	CHIEF PRIESTS	PONTIUS PILATE	ROMAN SOLDIERS
"delivers up" Jesus to	delivers up Jesus to	"deliver up" Jesus to	"delivers up" Jesus to	deliver up Jesus to
ARRESTING PARTY (14:18,43f.)	CHIEF PRIESTS (14:53)	PONTIUS PILATE (15:1,10)	ROMAN SOLDIERS (15:15)	DEATH (15:16ff.)

⟵ — ⟵ — ⟵ — ⟵ — Back-working? ⟵ — ⟵ — ⟵ — ⟵

Least likely   ⟵   Most likely

(recall Figs. 12.6–12.10)—with the least likely segment the opening link: the delivering up of Jesus by a traitor. This story could be usefully directed not simply toward the victims of betrayal but also toward the informants themselves. Woe to them, as to Jesus' own betrayer (cf. 14:21)! Moreover, lest loyal Christians, overly confident, imagine themselves immune from betraying tendencies, they should know that Jesus' own deceiver had himself been one of the twelve. Let all Christians, therefore, imagine themselves sitting at the Last Supper when the betrayal was announced; and let the query of Jesus' original disciples— "surely not I?" (Mk 14:19)—be a question on the lips of later Christians as well!

Delay in the Second Coming must likewise have prompted Christians in Mark's day to fall away or to deny Jesus. "Mark's portrait of Judas warns his community that as Jesus and his ... disciples could not protect themselves from the defection of Judas, neither can the church protect itself from defectors."[20] Consider how progressively alone Jesus was left by an ever diminishing circle of adherents: by the Jewish masses who had originally welcomed him on Palm Sunday; by the disciples soon to abandon him; by Judas who betrayed him; and, perhaps worst of all, by Peter, who denied him—and three times! (Indeed, in Mark the story of Peter's denial of Jesus is essentially a parallel of Judas' betrayal of Jesus.)

In general, Mark's propensity is to address serious problems by enlisting the disciples as object lessons.⁔ He dramatizes the folly of defections by having all the disciples abandon Jesus; he anticipates denials of Christianity by having Peter disavow Jesus; and he addresses betrayal by incorporating the treachery of another one of the twelve, Judas. Then, to

diminish any impression that Jesus was a victim, Mark ascribes to Jesus *predictions* of each unsavory development: the disciples' defection (14:27); Peter's denial (14:30); Judas' betrayal (14:18). In the face of all these calamities, the common exhortation throughout becomes: "He who endures to the end will be saved" (13:13)!

Why Judas in Particular?

When the betrayal story first arose, the traitor may not yet have been designated by name, but only as an unspecified "one of the twelve." How, then, would he have become identified with Judas in particular? I submit that Mark himself named him, influenced by the Genesis account in which Judah (Judas, in Greek), "one of twelve" sons of Jacob, during a *meal*, suggested *selling* Joseph (37:25–28) and eventually received from that sale *pieces of silver*.[21] In Mark's listing of the twelve disciples (3:16ff.), only the last two, Simon and Judas, correspond to names (Simeon and Judah) among the Genesis group (Fig. 15.5):

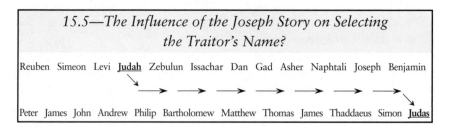

15.5—The Influence of the Joseph Story on Selecting the Traitor's Name?

Reuben Simeon Levi **Judah** Zebulun Issachar Dan Gad Asher Naphtali Joseph Benjamin

Peter James John Andrew Philip Bartholomew Matthew Thomas James Thaddaeus Simon **Judas**

And only the correlation of the one Judas with the other was suggestive—especially given the backdrop of Mark's basically anti-Jewish disposition. For Judah/Judas bore the name of that tribe of Israel from whom the name "Jew" derived. "Judas" thus echoed the Jewish people, whom Mark wished to present not only as opposing the Jesus Movement in his day (ca. 72) but also as responsible for Jesus' death.

A fictionally altered Judas would have made it easier for Mark to affix the blame for Jesus' death onto the Jewish nation whose name Judas bore, as if to say that not only Judas the Jew, but Judas *as* the *Jews*, betrayed Jesus. All the more so given the "extraordinary thematic echo between the story of individual betrayal by a close disciple and the story of communal betrayal by Jesus' blood-relatives the Jews"[22] (for the parallels in detail, see the second "Rejoinder," Chap. 11). The need to stress the *Jews* as culpable in Jesus' death would have intensified once Titus marched hundreds of Judean prisoners through the streets of Rome, probably in late 71 CE (after the Jerusalem Temple was burned and just before, as I believe, Mark wrote—and in Rome itself➔).[23]

What About the *Real* Judas?

Present in early listings of the twelve, Judas was no fiction—only the traitorous role foisted on him. Hence the early (in my view, reliable) tradition that Jesus included Judas among the twelve he destined to judge the tribes of Israel (Mt 19:28; Lk 22:30). Judas, too, would have mourned Jesus' death, and, as late as the 50s, would still have been assumed to have shared in the witnessing of the resurrected Christ by the "twelve" (1 Cor 15:5b). Only thereafter did the fiction of a traitor among the twelve gain strength, with Mark the one who, later still, designated him as "Judas" in particular to aid in transferring the blame for Jesus' death from the Romans to the Jews.

But how did Mark get away with sullying Judas' good name without protests from anyone who knew the true figure?

1. Mark saw himself as a faithful transmitter not of history but of *theology*, and we have seen how the introduction of Judas as the betrayer was consistent with Mark's other (and far more substantial) adjustments of his story line with theological purpose in mind.[24] Naming the betrayer "Judas" would appear a relatively minor adjustment, especially since I have not proposed Mark himself as responsible for the actual myth of a traitor in Jesus' midst—*that*, I believe, he inherited from its relatively recent origin. With the tale already current, it remained for Mark merely to identify the betraying disciple as Judas in particular.

2. Was anyone who had known the true figure still alive and present in Mark's vicinity? Chronology makes it likely that the real Judas was dead, and the geographical distance alone—if Mark wrote in Rome— would diminish prospects that some acquaintance of Judas was present to protest Mark's portrait of him.

3. To inquire how Mark could get away with sullying the image of Judas is to ask the larger question: how could he have tainted the reputation of *all twelve* disciples without fearing anyone's protest? This is particularly true regarding Peter's image, which, in contrast to Mark's presentation, was *positive* in the tradition. If Peter can be sullied, all the more so someone far less important, such as Judas.→

Result

The nagging conjecture remains, of course: "Had Iscariot been named Jacob ... or Jonathan instead of Judas, a name ... which too easily could become ... symbolic ... for all Jews, ... how many could have been spared a martyr's death?"[25] Jews today should defend Judas' *good* name because it is, after all, also their own. And what a fine name Judah/Judas *is!* According to Genesis this name, carrying no hint of

shame, signals to "praise the Lord" (29:35) and denotes its bearer as someone to receive "praise" (49:8). It is a name that deserves veneration by, and for, Jews who still proudly practice and maintain, literally, their Judah-ism.

The Most Valuable Ideas in This Chapter May Be

1. The fiction of Jesus' betrayal by Judas—arising during the 60s—was most likely a function of Christians' fear of being informed on to Rome, even by those whom they most trusted (Mk 13:9–13).

2. With the backdrop of the Jewish revolt in 66 CE, Christians needed to dissociate themselves from Jews. Here, the similarity (in Hebrew and Greek) of "Judas" with "Jew" suited Christian efforts to blame the Jews for Jesus' death: Jesus' betrayal by a disciple echoed the notion of a communal betrayal by Jesus' blood relatives, the Jews.

3. It also served to explain the ease by which—gauged from a later vantage point—the ostensibly powerful Christ and Son of God had fallen capture to mere mortals (the latter had inside help).

4. Inadvertently, Paul may have helped confirm, conceivably even spark, the story. In 1 Cor 11:23, the Greek of his reference to the night when Jesus "was delivered up [to death]" could also be (mis)understood as the night when Jesus "was *betrayed*."

5. The tale was likely inserted into the Gethsemane arrest scene (where, some scholars believe, the Passion narration originally *opened*).

6. Then, to lay groundwork for what was coming and to flesh out what was to follow, motifs were drawn from Jewish scripture, and Mark introduced anticipatory mentions of Judas and the betrayal into earlier chapters in or prior to the Passion.

7. Naming the traitor "Judas" was stimulated by the story in Genesis of Judah (*Judas*, in Greek), one of twelve, who decided at a meal to sell Joseph for pieces of silver (37:27f).

What Gospel Dynamics Have We Recognized in This Chapter?

- Stories—for example, here, of Judas—could be introduced into contexts where they did not originally reside. (This may be detected if aspects of an episode do not rest comfortably within their new literary surroundings, e.g., Jesus' last Supper prediction of the betrayal.)

- When spotting lacunae in an earlier narrative (here, Mark's failure to specify Judas' motive), later Evangelists often filled them even by using their imagination.

- Recourse to Jewish biblical motifs was a basic way of "substantiating" late-arising traditions (hence, recourse here to Davidic traditions, the Joseph saga, and Zechariah).

> • Any calamity—provided that it was believed prophesied by Jesus *and* that it transpired—could then serve to *corroborate* Christian faith instead of undermine it. (Here, Jesus' predictions that Peter would deny him, the disciples would abandon him, and Judas would betray him.)

Loose Ends Worth Tying

Mark's Denigration of the Disciples

In Mark, Jesus seems betrayed not merely by "*one* of the twelve" (Judas) but by "*all* of the twelve":

- By Peter, Jesus' chief disciple—already by mid-Gospel, Jesus has called him "Satan" (8:33). When Jesus predicts that Peter will deny him three times—which, inevitably, will occur—Peter has the audacity to contradict him, protests *his* unswerving loyalty, and airs doubts instead about his eleven colleagues (14:29). Indeed, so noticeably severe is Mark's critique of Peter that not only do Matthew and Luke later offer their own correctives,[26] but there may have been attempts even before them (by some post-Marcan hand) to rehabilitate Peter by altering *Mark's* Gospel itself.[27]
- By Peter, James, and John, Jesus' three innermost followers—*they* fail to discern Jesus' superiority to Moses and Elijah (in 9:5, where the booth built for Jesus should have been grander than, not equivalent to, the booths built for the others). Then these three disciples imperil Jesus (and themselves) by falling asleep, three times, in Gethsemane despite Jesus' repeated pleas to them to keep watch.
- By the disciples as a group—inept and obtuse (incapable of learning), they are accused by Jesus of hardness of heart (cf. Mk 6:52; 8:17), a phrase customarily reserved for Pharaoh (Exod 7–14, passim). Upon Jesus' arrest, ten disciples immediately flee to Galilee (cf. 14:50), leaving only Peter, Jesus' denier, and Judas, who has already betrayed him. Not one of these men shows up to comfort Jesus amid his agony on the cross. (The *women* maintaining a vigil over the tomb are a foil for the *men* whose presence is most palpably sensed by their absence.)

Why Mark's Bias Against the Disciples?

Why would Jesus wish to appoint as twelve judges over Israel such incompetents who are "hard of heart"? Why, when Paul (certainly, no "gentleman") presses his credentials against rivals—Peter chief among them—does he never reference any of Peter's, or the others', multiple *alleged* failings? These kinds of consideration suggest that Mark's characterization of the disciples (even of Judas) is fictional and of a later date. As for what could prompt such bias, my conjecture is as follows:

1. I believe that Mark wrote on behalf of the *Gentile*-Christian wing of the church at Rome. Gentile-Christians had first gained power there when, in 49 CE, Emperor Claudius expelled the *Jewish*-Christian founders/leaders from the city (see our previous chapter). Returning during the mid-50s, after Claudius' death, and expecting to resume their former status, the exiles were stymied by their Gentile-Christian replacements who now treated them with haughty condescension. (This would be the same Gentile-Christian element whom Paul criticizes in Rom 9–11.)

2. From this rivalry there arose, within the Gentile-Christian camp, traditions that demeaned the symbolic forerunners of the Jewish-Christians (namely, Jesus' *Jewish* disciples), characterizing them as hapless, disloyal, and unworthy to be leaders, distortions that undermined the status of Jewish-Christian returnees to Rome. Such sediment of traditions became second nature to Mark, himself a *Gentile*-Christian within this church during the 60s, and in this natural fashion found entry into the Gospel he wrote years later.

3. When writing around 72, in order to help his constituents cope with the ongoing legacy of the panic-stricken years beginning with Nero's persecution (in 64), Mark found it convenient to enlist these disciples—figures who for him were already of inept repute—to serve as object lessons of the failures Mark saw all about him: *defectors* from Christianity (like the runaway disciples), *deniers* of Jesus (like Peter), *betrayers* of fellow Christians (like Judas), and, more generally, the Jewish enemies of Christendom (also by name, "Judas," that is, "the Jews").

4. I date Mark circa 72, just after Titus triumphantly marched many hundreds of Judeans, captives from the Jewish revolt, through the streets of Rome. To safeguard his constituents in Rome by distancing their image from that of the rebel Jews (see Chap. 11), Mark felt it imperative to de-Judaize any impression conceivably radiated by his Gentile-led church *in Rome*—this by "Gentilizing" its image and sympathies to the fullest. Hence, he not only distanced Jesus from his disciples and even family members (through showing Jesus' disparagements of them), but he also established as *the* major foil for the *Jewish* disciples the Roman *Gentile* centurion who, presumably never even having seen Jesus before, instantly discerned what no Jew had ever realized (including not only the disciples but even Jesus' family): that Jesus "truly was the Son of God" (15:39). This must be a key verse since, with it, Mark chooses to end his Passion (directly following which comes the segue for the burial narrative).

What Suggests That Mark's Church Was at Rome?

Mark's Gospel reflects a time and locale in which Christians feared for their lives,[28] matching the time when Christians were experiencing the ongoing fall-out of the *repeatable precedent* of persecution set against them by Nero in 64, intensified by the Jewish revolt in 66, and further aggravated by Titus' triumphal return to Rome in 71 with Judean captives. Only a Gospel of Mark *distant* from the land of Israel squares with the topographical and geographical errors that this work commits,[29] and with its translations of Aramaisms that readers who lived near the holy land would not have needed. (This does not require the city of Rome in particular, but it is certainly consistent with it.) Mark explains Greek by employing Latinisms more so than other Evangelists,[30] which is consistent with a Western provenance (e.g., Rome). Matthew's more impressive Gospel was likely redacted in Syria, so only if Mark reflected an authoritative church far from Syria (e.g., Rome) could it have survived. Especially if other gospels existed (cf. Lk 1:1ff.), why did Matthew and Luke—each of whose works was so superior to Mark's—decide to copy from Mark unless it was from a most prestigious church (e.g., Rome)?[31]

"Gospel of Judas."

An apocryphal* work whose surviving elements were released to the public in 2006; written in Coptic, it *may* translate a second-century Greek original. This work conveys nothing reliable about the actual Judas.

The Gospel of Matthew
Why So "Pro-Jewish" a Flavor to So "Anti-Jewish" a Gospel?

Two dramatic passages, unique to Matthew, cast Jesus as concerned not at all with Gentiles but *solely* with the Jews. When his disciples embark on their mission, Jesus charges them: *"Go nowhere among the Gentiles, and enter no town of the Samaritans, but go rather to the lost sheep of the house of Israel" (10:5–6)*. And when implored to heal the daughter of a Canaanite woman, he intensifies this warning: *"I was sent only to the lost sheep of the house of Israel" (15:24)*. Here Jesus' concern is not simply to go to the Jews primarily but to the Jews *alone*.

Some Jews today, surprisingly conversant with these texts, quote them casually without due regard to how they originated or why such considerations would matter. Precisely because the two "lost sheep of the house of Israel" passages appear so simple to understand, they become ideal vehicles to demonstrate how complex was the process by which the Gospel According to "Matthew" developed.

Conventionally, the work we call "Matthew" is spoken of as if a single person were responsible for its entirety. The probability is not only that multiple layers of traditions became compiled in the formation of this Gospel but even that some succession of hands was responsible for revising this accumulating material. Accordingly, this chapter's references to "Matthew" as if to one person are a convenience only. Where precision is demanded, "Matthew" means the *last* editor to define and refine this Gospel's message. Another recurring matter will be whether this Christian writer was of Jewish background before accepting Christianity.

Mysteries Surrounding the "Lost Sheep of the House of Israel"

Who were these "lost sheep of the house of Israel"? Were they only a segment of Jews who strayed and now needed attentive retrieval? No, according to the final redactor, "the lost sheep" and "the house of Israel" coincide—as if with an equal sign" between them—yielding the sense of "the lost sheep *who constitute* the house of Israel." It must be the Jews as a *people* who are referenced because the other major component in each text is "Gentiles" (i.e., non-Jews)—explicit in one passage ("go nowhere among the Gentiles") and hence implicit in the parallel ("I was sent only to ... Israel").[1]

Naturally, such partiality by Jesus himself would affirm his personal commitment to fellow Jews. But if these passages arose instead from a *Jewish*-Christian wing of a church pressing its interest against some rival *Gentile*-Christian element, then these two texts might not characterize Jesus at all. Or if it was Matthew's last editor who gave rise to these statements, they could reflect *his* attitude towards the Jews but not necessarily that of Jesus. Also, possibilities can be combined—for example, this editor could advance personal views to which the historical Jesus might also have subscribed.

The "Most Jewish" Gospel?

That these two texts appear only in Matthew contributes to its popular labeling as the "most Jewish" Gospel, supported also by other factors: Papias, early second-century Bishop of Hierapolis (in today's Turkey), reports that Matthew "put together the sayings [of the Lord] in the *Hebrew* language, and each ... interpreted them as best he could."[2] Other motifs include Matthew's use of Jewish genealogy, his repeated quoting of Jewish scripture, and the way that Matthew's Jesus firmly upholds and extends Jewish law (5:17ff.):

> Think not that I have come to abolish the law and the prophets; I have come not to abolish them but to fulfil[3] them.... Whoever ... relaxes one of the least of these commandments and teaches men so, shall be called least in the kingdom of heaven....

Here, the Gospel deviates from its foremost source, Mark, which casts Jesus' disciples as straying from the law. Underscoring this divergence, Matthew conforms Jesus' life to that of Moses, Judaism's preeminent law-giver (Fig. 16.1).[4]

16.1—How Matthew Conforms Jesus to Moses the Law-Giver		
Jesus (in Matthew)	*Moses (in the Torah)*	*Commonalities*
Chaps 1 & 2	Exod 1:1–2:10	Infancy narrative
Chap 3:13–17	Exod 14:10–31	Crossing water
Chap 4:1–11	Exod 16:1–17:7	Wilderness temptation
Chaps 5, 6, & 7	Exod 19:1–23:23	Law-giving from a mountain
Chap 17:1–9	Exod 34:29–35	Transfiguration atop a mountain
Chap 28:16–20	Deut 31:7–9 (& Josh. 1:1–9)	Commissioning successor(s)

A Most "Anti-Jewish" Gospel?

Yet we can also mount rebuttals to the opposite effect—that Matthew is a most *anti*-Jewish Gospel.

First Rebuttal: Challenging Matthew's "Jewish" Traits

The litany of proofs held to establish Matthew as the most Jewish Gospel can be readily countered: Luke also employs genealogy, and Luke-Acts cites Jewish scripture even more extensively than does Matthew, yet Luke is not widely deemed Jewish on either account. Papias in this case is unavailing since our Matthew was composed not in Hebrew/Aramaic but in Greek—indeed, drawing on 92 percent of the verses in the Greek Mark, Matthew's primary source, and reproducing 51 percent of Mark's very words.[5] Matthew models Jesus on a legalistic Moses, but such typology* early on became characteristic also for *Gentile*-Christian writers. Also, did Matthew wield Moses imagery not as a Jewish motif but rather to neutralize Paul's denigration of the "law"? Coincidentally or otherwise, *Paul* is a person "who ... relaxes one of the least of these commandments and teaches men so." (It may also be coincidental that Paul calls himself "the *least* of all the apostles" in 1 Cor 15:9.)[6]

Meanwhile, the "lost sheep of ... Israel" passages need not reflect "Jewishness" because their function is unclear. Are we seriously to believe that, had Jesus *not* issued this kind of directive, his disciples would indeed have embarked upon evangelizing Gentiles? Only *after* Jesus' ministry was the notion of recruiting Gentiles introduced to Jesus' Jewish followers—and evoked consternation from the "pillars" of Jerusalem's church (cf. Gal 1:18–2:21). Further, at this stage in the story line (reflected

by Mt 10 and 15), the Jesus Movement is only fledgling. Jesus' disciples were unsophisticated.[7] Could they intelligibly articulate a message of a coming Kingdom to Gentiles in terms that could be comprehended, let alone be found appealing? During Jesus' ministry "a more unnecessary prohibition [than going to the Gentiles] can hardly be imagined."[8]

Not only, then, are the "lost sheep" statements unlikely to stem from Jesus—because they reflect a circumstance that first arose only well after his ministry—but they may not even be positively disposed toward Jews. Suppose that, by the time of the Gospel's final editor, the ranks of his church had assumed so *Gentile* a cast as to prompt him to account for what otherwise could appear anomalous: that since the Messiah concept was originated by the Jews, who then is to *blame* that Jews themselves have failed overwhelmingly to accept Jesus? The answer, this Gospel might well be telling us, lies not with Jesus who, after all, had insisted that he "was sent only to the lost sheep of ... Israel." The fault—by default—can lie solely with the Jews themselves who rebuffed, and thereby forfeited, Jesus' partiality for them. These ostensibly "pro-Jewish" passages, then, could have been devised and/or applied in an "anti-Jewish" way—to account for why Christianity's sustaining membership by Matthew's day (ca. 85) had come to depend mostly on a Gentile influx.

Second Rebuttal: Matthew's Anti-Jewish Editing of Mark

Those insisting that this Gospel is "Jewish" must explain why Matthew systematically intensifies Mark's many *negatives* toward the Jews. In Figure 16.2, Matthew profoundly alters Mark by adding but a single word:

16.2—How Matthew Makes the Sanhedrin Even More Sinister	
Mark 14:55f.	**Matthew 26:59f. —revising Mark**
The chief priests and the whole council sought _____ testimony against Jesus to put him to death; but they found none. For many bore false witness against him, and their witness did not agree.	The chief priests and the whole council sought *false* testimony against Jesus that they might put him to death, but they found none, though many false witnesses came forward.

In Mark, the Jewish leaders, presuming Jesus guilty, need to seek only true testimony against him. Matthew has them seek *false* testimony, revealing that the Jewish leaders know Jesus is *innocent*! In Figure 16.3, Matthew inserts the infamous "blood curse" (27:25) into Mark's already anti-Jewish Barabbas episode:

16.3—Matthew's Insertion of the Blood Curse

Mark 15:15	Matthew 27:24ff.—revising Mark
So Pilate, wishing to satisfy the crowd,	So when Pilate saw that ... a riot was beginning,
	he ... washed his hands before the crowd, saying, *"I am innocent of this man's blood, see to it yourselves."* And all the people answered, *"His blood be on us and on our children!"*
released ... Barabbas; and having scourged Jesus ... delivered him to be crucified.	Then he released ... Barabbas, and having scourged Jesus, delivered him to be crucified.

Figure 16.4 is Mark's sole amicable exchange between Jesus and a Jewish leader. Yet Matthew strips away all camaraderie:

16.4—How Matthew Strips Away Camaraderie Reported by Mark

Mark 12:28ff.	Matthew 22:35ff.—revising Mark
One of the scribes ... asked him, "Which commandment is the first of all?"	One of [the Pharisees], a lawyer, asked him a question, **_to test him_**. "Teacher, which is the great commandment in the law?"
Jesus answered, "The first is, *'Hear, O Israel: The Lord our God, the Lord is one; and*	And he said to him, _____ _____ _____
you shall love the Lord your God with all your heart, and with all your soul, and with all your mind, and with all your strength.' ..."	You shall love the Lord your God with all your heart, and with all your soul, and with all your mind. This is the great and first commandment....
And the scribe said..., "You are right, Teacher...." Jesus ... said to him, "You are not far from the kingdom of God."	_____ _____ _____ _____

Here, transforming conversation into confrontation, Matthew casts a Pharisee as *testing* Jesus (whereas Mark's scribe merely converses with him). Then Matthew audaciously deletes the opening sentence of the *Shema* ("Hear, O Israel ...") so that Jesus' "Great Commandment" no longer appears directed to "Israel"—which is striking, given that only Matthew reports Jesus' ostensible partiality to Israel as the "lost sheep"! Likewise telling: Matthew omits the last paragraph, Mark's single exchange of good-will between Jesus and a Jewish leader.

It is with Matthew, then, that we first detect a disturbing pattern: a Christian writer intensifies his source's negatives about Jews and omits the positive. Does Matthew's rewriting of Mark (a source that we do have) give us a clue as to what Mark himself did in rewriting his sources (which we do not have)—*that materials Mark had at his disposal may have been less anti-Jewish than Mark proceeded to make them, and that Matthew adopted this newer negativity and then intensified it further?* Was this the process by which anti-Judaism within Christian writings gradually assumed such huge dimension? Does anti-Judaism *decrease as we regress toward Christian origins* (Chap. 7)?

Third Rebuttal: Matthew's Anti-Jewish Allegorization of Key Parables

Sometimes the lesson of a Gospel parable becomes eclipsed by allegorization, a process whereby an original story's basically simple components (characters and actions) are assigned *symbolic* meanings that redirect the initially intended message. Detectable alterations may reveal the editor's (here, "Matthew's") personal biases and priorities. Let us, then, read the following (significantly abridged[9]) parable twice in Figure 16.5: first, as it stands in Matthew, and then with what (in the appended key) may be the allegorical meanings that signal Matthew's personal intentions. Keep in mind that the banquet motif may symbolize the celebration of the Messiah's coming and the establishment of God's kingdom.

If these are the allegorical meanings that Matthew intends, then his message is that, originally, the Jews were the *only* ones invited to recognize Jesus as Messiah (cf. "I was sent only to the lost sheep of the house of Israel"). But when they refused to be gathered, God used Rome to crush the rebels (Jerusalem's destruction in 70) and then invited new guests, by definition, Gentiles (since, with "those ... invited" now destroyed, only Gentiles remained). This is how the ranks of Matthew's church became predominantly Gentile-Christian.

It is not surprising if such allegorization fails to hang together because, after all, artificial meanings have been grafted onto an underlying story that is now eclipsed. *All* potential guests would decline a royal invitation and *kill* royal servants for delivering it? The king would retaliate

16.5—The Parable of the Marriage Feast (Mt 22:1–14)

First Reading: "The kingdom of heaven may be compared to a king[a] who gave a marriage feast for his son,[b] and sent his servants[c] to call those ... invited[d] ... but they would not come[e].... He sent other servants ... but they made light of it and went ... one to his farm, another to his business,[f] while the rest seized his servants ... and killed them. The king was angry, and he sent his troops[g] and destroyed those murderers and burned their city.[h] Then he said to his servants,[i] 'The wedding is ready, but those invited were not worthy. Go ... to the thoroughfares, and invite ... as many[j] as you find.' And those servants ... gathered all[j] whom they found, both bad and good; so the wedding hall[k] was filled with guests.[l]"

a God	*e Accept that Jesus is*	*j Non-Jews (Gentiles)*
b Celebrating Jesus as	* Messiah*	* — all Jews are already*
* Messiah*	*f Giving excuses for*	* killed*
c Hebrew prophets	* rejecting Jesus*	*k The Church's ranks*
* (later, apostles)*	*g Rome's Tenth Legion*	*l Assumed a Gentile-*
d The Jews	*h Jerusalem (in 70)*	* Christian complexion*
	i Apostles (Israel has	
	* killed all her prophets)*	

Second Reading: "The kingdom of heaven may be compared to God who gave a celebratory feast of recognition that his son, Jesus, is the Messiah, and sent the Hebrew prophets to call the Jews ... but they would not come (i.e., they rejected the proposition that Jesus is the Messiah).... God sent other Hebrew prophets, but some Jews still turned down the request while the rest seized the Hebrew prophets ... and killed them. God was angry, and he sent Rome's Tenth Legion and destroyed the Jews and burned Jerusalem (70 CE). Then God said to the apostles, 'The celebratory feast is ready, but the Jews were not worthy. Go ... to the thoroughfares, and invite ... as many Gentiles as you find.' And the apostles ... gathered all whom they found, both bad and good; this is how the Church's ranks assumed their current Gentile-Christian complexion."

militarily and burn the city, site of the feast itself? Food would remain servable after such delay (and destruction)? But the lesson intended is clear: the Jews themselves are accountable for Rome's burning of Jerusalem *and* for a demographic shift within Matthew's own church (see more below). Matthew allegorizes the parable to explain "why the Gospel, the invitation to the kingdom of God, passed from the Jews, the chosen people, to the gentiles," and also why this is "not God's fault."[10] The underlying parable has been conformed to the Church's own missionary situation.[11]

The next parable (Fig. 16.6) appears allegorized already in Mark 12:1–12, but Matthew further redirects it. Again, we read it once as is and then through the appended key.

16.6—The Parable of the Wicked Tenants (Mt 21:33–43)

First Reading: "A householder[a] ... planted a vineyard, ... let it out to tenants,[b] and went into another country. When the season of fruit drew near, he sent his servants[c] ... to get his fruit; ... the tenants took his servants ... beat one, killed another, ... stoned another.... He sent other servants ... they did the same to them. Afterward he sent his son[d] ... saying, 'They will respect[e] my son.' But ... the tenants ... said..., 'Let us kill him and have his inheritance' [failing another heir, they assumed the vineyard would be theirs]. And they took him and cast him out of the vineyard, and killed him. When ... the owner ... comes, what will he do to those tenants?" [The Jewish leaders whom Jesus addressed previously] said ... "He will put those wretches to a miserable death,[f] and let out the vineyard[g] to other tenants[h] who will give him ... fruits in their seasons." Jesus said..., "... Therefore ... the kingdom of God [what the "vineyard" means to Matthew] will be taken away from you[b] and given to a nation[h] producing the fruits of it."

a God	d Jesus	g the kingdom of God
b the Jews	e accept him as Messiah	h non-Israel (Gentiles)
c Hebrew prophets	f Rome crushes Jews' revolt (70)	

Second Reading: "God ... planted a vineyard, ... [and] let it out to the Jews.... When the season of fruit drew near, he sent the Hebrew prophets ... to get his fruit; ... the Jews took the Hebrew prophets ... beat one, killed another, ... stoned another.... God sent other Hebrew prophets ... the Jews did the same to them. Afterward God sent his son Jesus ... saying, 'They will accept my son Jesus as Messiah.' But ... the Jews ... said..., 'Let us kill him and have his inheritance.' And the Jews took Jesus and cast him out of the vineyard, and killed him. When ... God ... comes, what will he do to the Jews?" They said ... "God will have Rome crush their revolt (in 70 CE), and let out the kingdom of God to the Gentiles who will give him ... fruits in their seasons." Jesus said..., "... Therefore ... the kingdom of God will be taken away from you Jews and given to Gentiles producing the fruits of it [since what is specified here is another 'nation' i.e., 'non-Israel']."

If these allegorical meanings are intended, Matthew's message is that the Kingdom of God, already present among humanity in germ, requires nurturing to reach fruition. But just as a vineyard tended by wicked tillers will not deliver its fruits to a needful owner, so the Kingdom of God cannot bloom under its original tillers (the Jews). Responsibility for its nurturing must now be given over to a more faithful "nation," hence *non*-Jews (Gentiles). The key observation here, again, is that the pro-Gentile favoritism runs counter to the meaning we infer from the two "lost sheep" texts. (In this parable, too, allegorization introduces confusion.[12])

Fourth Rebuttal: How Matthew Ends His Gospel

We might imagine that how a Gospel ends provides the key to its meaning. Here, too, there is disagreement because the conventional rendering of Matthew 28:16–20 may be wrong:

> [16]Now the eleven disciples went to Galilee, to [where] ... Jesus had directed them.... [18]And Jesus ... said to them, "All authority in heaven and on earth has been given to me. [19]Go therefore and make disciples of all *nations*, baptizing them in the name of the Father and of the Son and of the Holy Spirit,[20]... lo, I am *with you* always, to the close of the age."

The problem lies with how we translate 28:19—the "Great Commission." Does Matthew's Jesus mean "make disciples of all *nations* [including the Jews] or "make disciples of all *Gentiles* [excluding the Jews]"? The plural Greek *ethne* (compare our "ethnic") can be rendered either way, but "Gentiles" would *reverse* the ostensible partiality shown Israel earlier on. (This resembles what we experience with *goyim*, the Hebrew equivalent of *ethne*, which can mean "nations" but more often means "Gentiles"—i.e., the nations *other than* the Jews.)

The usual translation offered is "nations." The reasoning is that "all nations" expands the Kingdom mission. Originally it was limited to "the lost sheep of the house of Israel," but now it expands to Gentiles also. In this fashion, "*All* authority" should point to all peoples. However, rendering the Great Commission as "make disciples of all Gentiles" would be consonant with the allegories of the Marriage Feast (22:1–14) and the Wicked Tenants (21:33–43), which close off the mission to the Jews in favor of Gentiles only. In this case, Matthew would be conveying that a *reversal* has set in: that while Jesus' hope was to limit his mission solely to "Israel," the Jews' rejection of him forces from now on a mission solely[13] to Gentiles.

The latter option appears more persuasive once we juxtapose two key passages (see Fig. 16.7):

<table>
<tr><td colspan="2">16.7—Why Ethne in Matthew's Ending May
Mean "Gentiles [Only]"</td></tr>
<tr><td>Mt 10:5–6: "Go nowhere among the <u>Gentiles</u> [ethne], and enter no town of the Samaritans, but go rather to the lost sheep of the house of Israel."</td><td>Mt 28:19: "Go and make disciples of all_____?_____[ethne]"</td></tr>
</table>

These two texts use (different cases of) the same Greek word and both passages address the same subject: namely, to whom the disciples may bring the mission. The term *ethne* in the first text must mean "Gentiles" (since there it is distinguished from "Israel"). Would it not be careless of Matthew, at the very end of his Gospel, to use the same Greek word pertaining to the same subject but now to mean something else: "nations" (inclusive of Israel) rather than "Gentiles" (exclusive of Israel)? Surely "Gentiles" must have been intended in both cases. If so, then the dramatic intent would be to show Jesus as if he is now emphatically *renouncing* his erstwhile partiality to "the lost sheep of ... Israel."[14] From going originally only to Israel—who chose to reject him—Jesus now chooses to reject *them* and to direct his followers henceforth to go only to Gentiles. The Great Commission, then, will be consistent with the allegories' message only if we translate it as: "make disciples of all Gentiles [not nations]."

There is, moreover, a progression here that reaches its culmination in "Gentiles" but not "nations." In 10:5–6, Jesus directs his followers: "Go nowhere among the Gentiles, and enter no town of the Samaritans, but go rather to the lost sheep of the house of Israel." In 15:24,28, he reaffirms his original intention: "I was sent *only* to the lost sheep of the house of Israel," yet [as a transition] also grants how "great is ... [the] faith!" of one *Gentile* woman. Six chapters later, 21:43 warns that "the kingdom of God will be taken away from you [Jews] and given to a[nother] nation [Gentiles] producing the fruits of it." Reinforcing this is 22:8 where, while "the wedding is ready ... those invited [Jews] were not worthy," so that others (Gentiles) should be invited (not in *addition* to Jews but in their *stead*). Then Jesus laments in 23:37, "O Jerusalem ... how often would I have gathered your children together as a hen gathers her brood under her wings, and you would not [accept me]!" This progression culminates in Jesus' Great Commission to his followers, in 28:19, to "go and make disciples of all Gentiles."

Some interpreters, presupposing that Matthew writes for a Jewish-Christian constituency still within the Jewish community, will insist that his vitriol is only *intra muros*, "inside the walls" (intra-family squabbling; see Chap. 21). While not denying that certain parables appear allegorized, they believe that the symbolic meanings would not be exclusionary of the Jews and hence not predictive of their displacement by Gentiles. In their sense, for example, the new invitees (in the first parable) and the new "nation" (in the second parable) symbolize new *Jewish* ethical leaders (cf. 19:28) who are more responsible than their predecessors and more likely to bear fruit (cf. 21:45).[15] The ostensible "pro-Jewishness" of the "lost sheep of ... Israel" passages is thus, in their judgment, not reversed at all but continues to set the tone for this Gospel throughout!

Since I find this a forced way to read what "Matthew" is saying, I adhere to the conventional orientation: "Matthew understands the [initially] uninvited to refer to the Gentiles" and "the punishment of the husbandmen symbolizes the ruin of Israel; the 'other people' (Matt. 21:43) are the Gentile Church" (Jeremias); "[this is the same] doctrine of the election of the Gentiles, as ... in other parts of the N.T." (Dodd); "the vineyard is taken from Israel and given to the Gentiles..., the punishment ... an allegorization of the influx of Gentiles into the church" (Crossan); "Matthew's use of 'nation' in v. [21:]43 ... understand[s] the rejection of the Jews as past and final, the result of their rejection of Jesus" (Carlston); "the transfer is from Israel to *another* people, non-Israel [i.e., Gentiles].... This radical discontinuity between Israel and her successor ... requires that we regard the rejection of Israel in Matthew as final and complete" (Hare).[16]

The major reason why the "in-house" (intra-family squabbling) scenario is not compelling is that Matthew's final editor appears to have been positioned outside of the Jewish community, meaning that, in its final redaction, Matthew is no longer an intra-family Gospel.

Matthew's Church (in Antioch)—Snapshots of Three Phases

Most often, Matthew's Gospel is linked with the church of Antioch (in Syria),[17] founded by Jewish-Christians in the late 30s and presumed still to retain this majority complexion during the time of the final editor, himself assumed to be Jewish-Christian. I accept the designation of Antioch but dispute that the final editor need be of Jewish extraction or that his church was identifiably Jewish-Christian still in his time. Events external to Antioch's Christians must be considered, and may have been determinative—although all that can be offered must be regarded as reconstruction.

Phase I—Antioch's Original Jewish-Christian Church (30s through 50s)

When Antioch's church opened itself to a Gentile mission not requiring circumcision of initiates, those Jewish-Christians favoring such a move were hobbled by outside interference from conservatives in nearby Jerusalem sent by Jesus' brother, James. This precipitated a clash between Paul and Cephas (Peter) severe enough for Paul to leave Antioch, and for Jewish-Christians to separate their table fellowship from Gentile-Christians (Gal 2:11ff.; cf. Acts 15:1ff.). We thus infer that Jewish-Christian and Gentile-Christian segments of Antioch's fledgling church had co-existed relatively harmoniously until outside interference, with Jewish-Christians clearly dominant during these early decades (see Fig. 16.8).

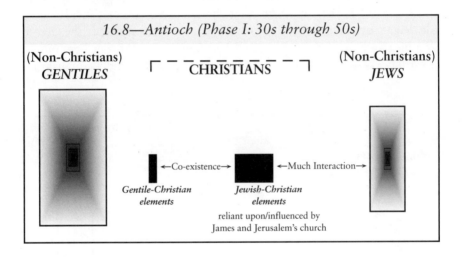

16.8—Antioch (Phase I: 30s through 50s)

(Non-Christians) **GENTILES** — CHRISTIANS — (Non-Christians) **JEWS**

←Co-existence→ ←Much Interaction→

Gentile-Christian elements *Jewish-Christian elements*

reliant upon/influenced by James and Jerusalem's church

Phase II—Trauma for Antioch's Jewish-Christians (60–70)

The mother church in nearby Jerusalem—always a bulwark for Antioch's Jewish-Christian leaders—entered decline in 62 with the execution of James. In 66, it disbanded at the onset of the Jews' revolt against Rome so "the decisive umbilical cord that had tied the Antiochene church to its Jewish identity and its Jewish past was severed"—thereby imbuing supporters of Gentile-Christians "with hope of making headway against the conservative elements" that had been obstructing them.[18] Moreover, all along the mission to bring in more Jews per se had been a relative failure while the influx of Christians from Gentile ranks had mushroomed. Then, in 70, destruction of Jerusalem's Temple prompted reflection as to whether God's covenant with the Jews was suspended, even superseded.

From 66–70, anti-Jewishness spiked within Antioch itself in the form of Gentile riots, jeopardizing security also of Jewish-Christians (associated

with Jews in Gentile eyes as well as their own). Syria's Gentile public deemed the Jewish revolt a futile gesture by upstart fanatics, and to quash it Rome recruited auxiliary forces from Syria itself. Syrian casualties fanned hatred, by Antioch's Gentiles, toward Jews in their midst.[19] Josephus informs us that "hatred of the Jews was everywhere at its height," with those in Antioch now harassed, even murdered, by Gentiles who spread rumors of Jewish plots and asked the Roman general, Titus, to expel Jews, or at least to revoke their privileges.[20]

Such tension rendered the position of Jewish-Christians precarious vis-à-vis *Gentile*-Christians, who, naturally, suspected them of harboring Jewish sympathies; and vis-à-vis *Jews*, who were wary that Jewish-Christians—sharing the Christian umbrella with Gentile fellows—harbored the same anti-Jewish animosity that characterized Antioch's wider Gentile pagan populace. With Jewish-Christians thus stymied, the demographics and balance of power within Antioch's Christian community must have begun shifting toward—if not already beyond—equalization (Fig. 16.9).

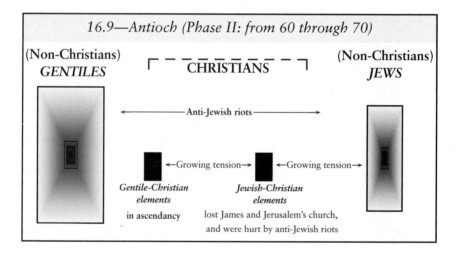

16.9—Antioch (Phase II: from 60 through 70)

| (Non-Christians) **GENTILES** | **CHRISTIANS** | (Non-Christians) **JEWS** |

←——————— Anti-Jewish riots ———————→

←Growing tension→   ←Growing tension→

Gentile-Christian elements   *Jewish-Christian elements*

in ascendancy   lost James and Jerusalem's church, and were hurt by anti-Jewish riots

Phase III—By Matthew's Day (Mid-80s)

These trends continued to reconfigure Antioch's church, so that "probably by the last third of the first century the majority among the Christians was ethnically Gentile."[21] In the years leading up to the compiling of Matthew's Gospel, then, the dwindling Jewish-Christian contingent would have had reason to feel in jeopardy. Facing possible dissolution, did they view themselves as needing to seek refuge in the Gentile-Christian wing of what once had been their own church? Or were they pushed away since, once Jews became seen as enemies of the Roman

state, it was advisable for Gentile-Christians to back away from continuing association with anyone Jewish? Whatever the specific dynamics, there was good cause for the Jewish-Christian foundation to diminish, even to fall away from Antioch's church. *It is because the shift toward a Gentile-Christian complexion became so decided that we can understand why Matthew's final editor was anti-Jewish.* After all, by that time he was writing from a vantage point external to Antioch's Jewish community, with the pervasive anti-Jewish bias from within Syria finding its way into his Gospel *via late strata* (Fig. 16.10).

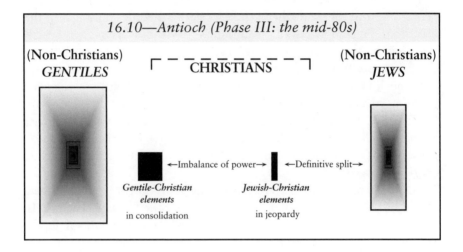

16.10—Antioch (Phase III: the mid-80s)

(Non-Christians) **GENTILES**   ┌ ─ ─ **CHRISTIANS** ─ ─ ┐   (Non-Christians) **JEWS**

←Imbalance of power→   ←Definitive split→

Gentile-Christian elements in consolidation   *Jewish-Christian elements* in jeopardy

Even Matthew's incidental texts reveal as much. While Mark 3:1 has Jesus enter *"the* synagogue," Matthew 12:9 changes this to *"their* synagogue," implying distance. Mark 6:2 has Jesus begin "to teach in *the* synagogue," but Matthew's parallel, 13:54, has him teach "in *their* synagogue." A definitive break has occurred! Matthew's Jesus addresses scribes and Pharisees in terms of *"your* synagogues" (23:34) and warns his followers (10:17) that Jews will "flog you *in their* synagogues"— quite unlike Mark's "you will be beaten *in* synagogues" (13:9). Also, Matthew laments that the allegation of a theft of Jesus' body from the tomb "has been spread among *the Jews* to this day" (28:15)—not "among our people" or "our fellow Jews" (see Chap. 13). In this, Matthew's sole independent use of "the Jews" (all others he copies from Mark), he speaks as if he and his church are disassociated from the Jewish community. How entirely unlikely it is that a church that:

> pursued a universal mission without circumcision, rejected the food laws of the Pentateuch, abandoned the "teaching of the Pharisees

and Sadducees" (Mt 16:11–12) in favor of the power to "bind and loose" invested in Peter (16:18–19) and the local church gathered around Jesus (18:18–20), could remain [still] in union with the synagogue.[22]

The Final Editor Himself

As for presumptions that "Matthew's author" was Jewish, we do not know (as noted earlier) that there was but one author or over how long a period of time the compiling of this Gospel occurred. A Jewish *sediment* of text was likely already in place—whether oral or also written—persisting from the Antiochene church's earlier decades, and it is in this light that presumptions of "Matthew's Jewishness" emerge. Strictly speaking, however, any early Jewish flavor to Antioch's Jesus traditions can carry very little weight in defining the profile of the final editor, because such facility in Jewish text and tradition as "Matthew" displays could have been easily gained in Antioch itself, even by a Gentile-Christian. With its large Jewish populace, Antioch was a seat of Jewish learning well before Matthew's day, providing its Christians with "a constant ... [Jewish] matrix out of which to grow and against which to define themselves."[23]

Further, what Jew by heritage, in editing Jesus' Great Commandment (Fig. 16.4), would expunge the first sentence of the *Shema* ("Hear, O Israel! The Lord is our God, the Lord is One"), the hallmark of Jewish monotheism as well as itself the source of the title, *Shema* ("Hear")? In effecting this omission, Matthew not only pointedly departs from Mark, whom he otherwise is carefully copying, but also tampers with *the* teaching that is the most indispensable of all Jewish verses and, according to Mark, indispensable as well to Jesus himself! On the other hand, for a *Gentile*-Christian, drawing upon Mark in the mid-80s on behalf of a church that has assumed a Gentile-Christian complexion, it would be entirely natural to omit Deuteronomy 6:4—so that Jesus' premier teaching would *not* be addressed primarily to Israel. Other individual matters likewise carry some weight here.[24] Indeed, one should think that the totality of such telltale clues makes it advisable to "start from the assumption that Mt was not a Jew"[25] rather than the other way around—at least in the case of the final editor of this Gospel.

Conclusions

Why, then, so pro-Jewish a flavor to so anti-Jewish a Gospel? Every Gospel is a patchwork of traditions that an editor has found desirable to amalgamate, even if incompatible or contradictory materials remain among them. Also, the personal orientation toward Jews by this

Gospel's final editor might have been more negative than that of his sources—especially because external happenings had so buffeted Antioch's church during the 60s and 70s, thereby setting into motion demographic trends that sharply differed from this church's existence during its earlier decades. These factors could well have induced an anti-Jewish editor to incorporate pro-Jewish material without necessarily avowing all of it—with the completed work reflecting contradictory dispositions combined. At the same time, it is possible that one person's compilation of material may have been in use in Antioch's church for some while, so a final editor could not omit what was already for them "scriptural." Instead, he could *add* to it and thus (re-)shape it. Also, if "Matthew" himself had learned about Judaism from resources within Antioch's significant Jewish milieu, did he likewise wish to enrich other Gentile converts who had entered Christianity with no grounding whatsoever in the Jewish ethical heritage, in its scriptural citation, and in its rabbinic-like exegesis?

Such options signal that any Jewish flavor of Matthew's Gospel can be explained on grounds other than simply that his is the most "Jewish" Gospel and/or that the author is Jewish by extraction or that the negativity is simply "in-house." After all, it is he who lets stand, or reshapes, the parables of the Wicked Tenants and the Marriage Feast as currently anti-Jewishly allegorized. Mindful of Christianity's predominantly Gentile ranks in the church of his own day, *the editor recasts Jesus' ministry now to conform to developments that had emerged over the decades*: "historically, the community failed with its mission to Israel; then the whole course of the story of Jesus told in the Gospel lays the foundation for this fracture."[26] Matthew's Jesus, at first presuming acceptance by Jews, had been disposed even to limit his mission to them alone. As for what had gone wrong, Matthew tells us that it was the *Jews* who had gone wrong!

Still other passages that we have not examined fit, and thereby endorse, this progression, such as the "prediction" (8:11f.) by Matthew's Jesus that "many [Gentiles] will come from east and west and sit at table with Abraham, Isaac, and Jacob in the kingdom of heaven, while the sons of the kingdom [the Jews] will be thrown into the outer darkness." The context of this prediction is the response to the *Gentile* centurion's faith, the likes of which are *not found even in Israel!* Similarly, and directly on the heels of 15:24 ("I was sent only to the lost sheep of the house of Israel"), Matthew's Jesus grants how "great is ... [the] faith!" of the *Gentile* woman who asks his aid. No wonder, also, that—following as well as prefacing Jesus' ministry—Matthew spotlights Gentiles as discerning Jesus' identity: at his birth, it is the Gentile Magi who discern that he is

"king of the Jews" (2:2); at his death, it is the Roman centurion and fellow Gentiles who identify him as "truly ... the Son of God!" (27:54).

Matthew gets these points across even though his editing leaves us with a conglomeration of traditions that do not sit well together—no doubt eliciting today's wide diversity of scholarship. As we move on now to Luke, our experience with Matthew may help to explain Luke's complaint to his patron: "inasmuch as many have undertaken to compile a narrative of the things which have been accomplished among us ... it seemed good to me also ... to write an *orderly* account for you ... " (1:3). *Some* readers[27] may wonder if Luke is criticizing *Matthew's* Gospel for not being "orderly."

The Most Valuable Ideas in This Chapter May Be

1. Although many pronounce Matthew the "most Jewish" Gospel, it can easily be read to the *opposite* effect.
2. Multiple layers of tradition were compiled in the formation of this Gospel, and probably a succession of hands was responsible for incorporating and revising this accumulating material.
3. The final editor was writing for a church that was reeling from destabilizing turbulence transpiring in Syria and the land of Israel during the 60s and 70s. This turbulence dramatically altered this church's demographics.
4. The result was that prospects for Jewish-Christians' continued dominance in Antioch's church diminished while Gentile-Christian fortunes were ascendant, with the final Matthean editor positioned outside of the Jewish community.
5. The Gospel in its finished form is concerned with explaining why its sustaining membership—originally Jewish-Christian—had come to depend mostly on a Gentile influx.

What Gospel Dynamics Have We Recognized in This Chapter?

- Post-70 anti-Jewish statements are likely a function of tensions of that era; this enables us to separate out the historical Jesus in his time from many anti-Jewish stances belatedly ascribed to him.
- The way that Matthew intensifies the anti-Judaism of Mark, his source, raises questions as to whether Mark did the same with *his* sources.
- Some parables in Matthew have undergone allegorical redirection of their meaning along lines originally unintended; detectable alterations may reveal the editor's personal priorities.

Loose Ends Worth Tying

Clues to When Traditions Are Late

If Jesus indeed uttered the "lost sheep of the house of Israel" statements (prohibiting a mission to Gentiles), why did not the "pillars" of the Jerusalem church quote them to obstruct Paul? Or, if Jesus did utter the Great Commission, how could the Jerusalem church leaders have opposed Paul at all—since by going to Gentiles Paul was only doing what Jesus had commissioned? Posing such questions helps us to realize that all three statements in Matthew (10:5–6; 15:24; 28:19) likely arose not from Jesus but only well after his day.

Trinitarian Baptismal Formula

When Matthew includes in his last verses the expression, "baptizing them in the name of the Father and of the Son and of the Holy Spirit," this does not signal that the doctrine of the Trinity was already formulated before the end of the first century. First, that doctrine may have hearkened back to these words from a later time. Second, possibly the expression was added to Matthew by a later hand (it is not missed if omitted).

The Gospel of Luke and the Book of Acts

Did Jews Flock to Christianity? Luke's Myth of the "Myriads"

The Gospel of Luke and the book of Acts are companion volumes by the same writer. The Gospel focuses on Jesus and his ministry; Acts, thereafter, is a history of the early Church. Their common themes are that Christianity embodies and continues authentic Judaism, and that Gentile-Christians now constitute the true Jews.

Christianity Embodies and Continues Authentic Judaism

Luke emphasizes how the religiosity of Jesus, his followers, and Paul models the purest form of Judaism. Luke thus improvises particulars about *Jesus* and his followers not found in other canonical* Gospels, and particulars about *Paul* not found in the Epistles. This means that, while Jesus and Paul were undeniably Jewish, the ways in which Luke chooses to display this may be *makeshift*.

Luke's Unique Portrait of Jesus and His Followers

Only in Luke's Gospel are we told that the infant Jesus was circumcised (2:21) and brought to Jerusalem's Temple for a redemption of the first-born ceremony "according to the custom of the law" (2:22,27); that the holy family journeyed to Jerusalem for Passover—one trip culminating in Jesus', at age twelve, listening, questioning, understanding, and answering the sages (2:41ff.),[1] the *central* fashioners of Judaism, in the Temple (Judaism's *central* institution); and that the adult Jesus taught daily in the Temple[2] and regularly "in their synagogues" (4:15). With respect to Jesus' followers, only Luke tells us that, before coming to Jesus' tomb, the women rested on the Sabbath "according to the *commandment*" (23:56); and that, after Jesus' post-resurrection appearances, believers were *in the Temple* blessing God (Lk 24:53; cf. Acts 2:46; 3:1; 5:42).

Luke's Unique Portrait of Paul

So as to ground Paul also in Judaism, Luke shifts his upbringing from the Diaspora to the land of Israel, and diminishes Paul's disaffection with the Law by recasting him as a proto-rabbinic Jew! This explains why only Acts (not any Epistle) reports Paul's training at the feet of the *chief* Pharisee, Gamaliel (22:3), and gives Paul a *Hebrew* name, Saul (13:9),[3] and facility in the *Hebrew* language (21:40; 22:2)—even though biblical quotations in Paul's own Epistles to Greek-speaking congregations reflect Greek translation, not the original Hebrew; Luke shows Paul willing to circumcise Timothy (16:3), in flat-out contradiction to Paul's refusal to circumcise Titus (Gal 2:3); places Paul regularly in synagogues ("as was his *custom*"; "*every* sabbath"; "for three months"[4]); and also places Paul in the Temple where he "happens to be" when he is arrested![5] This Dynamic also explains why the *Lucan* Paul, when reciting his autobiography (26:4ff.), stresses that "my manner of life from my youth ... [was] spent ... *among my own nation* and at *Jerusalem*" and "according to the *strictest* party of our religion I have lived as a *Pharisee*." Paul's Epistles, by contrast, reflect his rearing in the Diaspora and stress his break with the Law. Paul in *Acts* is anxious to allay (supposedly) false suspicions that he undermined Jewish Law (21:20ff.), although Paul's Epistles show the charge to be fully founded. Meanwhile, genuine elements of Pauline theology—justification by faith, and annulment of the Law—simply vanish in Luke's formulation that only "with respect to the hope and the resurrection of the dead" is Paul on trial (23:6; cf. 24:21).

By all such devices, then, Luke intimates that the new movement, Christianity, embodies and directly perpetuates the core of authentic Judaism—rejected not by Christianity but solely by the Jews themselves (i.e., as people, not as a faith).

The Device of Geography

We recall here from Chapter 6 that Luke also enlists geography for similar ends. Unlike Mark and Matthew, he fixes Jesus' post-resurrection appearances not in Galilee, symbolically the fringe of Judaism, but rather in Jerusalem's environs—Judaism's *core* (see Fig. 8.4; also 3.10). The genuine Paul insists that, even some years after his revelation experience, he remained "not known by sight to the churches ... in Judea" (Gal 1:22); but Acts intimates that Paul, as persecutor of the church, was early on infamous among Christians in Jerusalem[6]—where Acts also has him "brought up" and "educated" (22:3; 26:4). Similarly, while Paul experiences the risen Christ inside Damascus (Gal 1:15ff.), Luke sets this during Paul's trip commencing *from* (and commissioned by authorities of) *Jerusalem* (Acts 9:1ff.; 22:5; 26:10,12).

Downplaying Tensions with Jewish Institutions

For Luke, any friction with Jewish institutions (e.g., the Temple or Sanhedrin) by Jesus or Paul would undercut Christianity's identity as authentic Judaism. While hardly able to eradicate such tension altogether, given its deep embeddedness in Mark (and Matthew), Luke at least weakens these impressions.

Institutions Involving Jesus

Luke dilutes Jesus' Temple "Cleansing" by omitting material (Fig. 17.1).

17.1—*Luke Dilutes the Temple "Cleansing"*		
Mark 11:15ff.	**Matthew 21:12ff.**	**Luke 19:45**
He entered the temple and began to drive out those who sold and ... bought in the temple, and ...	Jesus entered the temple ... and drove out all who sold and bought in the temple, and ...	He entered the temple and began to drive out those who sold.
overturned the tables of the money-changers and ... seats of those who sold pigeons....	*overturned the tables of the money-changers and ... seats of those who sold pigeons.*	_____ _____ _____ _____

In rendering charges lodged against Jesus, Luke omits Jesus' threat regarding the Temple (Fig. 17.2):

17.2—*Luke Omits Jesus' Temple Threat*		
Mark 15:29f.	**Matthew 27:40**	**Luke 23:37**
saying, "... *You who would destroy the temple and build it in three days*, save yourself...!"	saying, "*You who would destroy the temple and build it in three days*, save yourself!"	saying, _____ _____ _____"If you are the King of the Jews, save yourself!"

Also, Luke allows no formal "decision" (cf. Mk 14:64) or "judgment" (cf. Mt 26:66) against Jesus—whether by high priest or Sanhedrin.

Institutions Involving Paul

Paul's Sanhedrin trial mirrors that of Luke's Jesus: no pronouncement of guilt. The only opinion recorded is of "some of the scribes of the Pharisees' party" that "we find nothing wrong in this man" (23:9), echoing Pilate's determination regarding Jesus in Luke 23:4,14,22. (Recall also Acts 5:33ff., where Gamaliel urges the Sanhedrin's moderation in dealing with Jesus' followers.) Later, Luke has Paul resolutely proclaim (emphasizing Jewish institutions): "They did not find me disputing ... either in the *temple* or in the *synagogue*.... They found me purified in the *temple*" (24:12,18); also, "neither against the *law* of the Jews, nor against the *temple* ... have I offended at all" (25:8). Quite extraordinarily, then, Acts portrays Paul as if he assumed essentially no position deviant from proper Judaism!

Gentile-Christians Now Constitute the True Jews

Demography is one further facet of Luke's presentation of Christianity as embodying authentic Judaism. He wishes us to believe that, initially, Christian ranks were swelled by "myriads" of Jews who confirmed Christianity as extending their own faith. Acts 21:20 summarizes "myriads," Greek for "tens of thousands," but here Luke apparently speaks of "thousands" only: "2:41 (about 3,000), 47 (others added day by day); 4:4 (about 5,000 men, possibly additional women); 5:14 (more than ever were added, multitudes); 6:1 (disciples were increasing), 7 (multiplied greatly); 21:20 (many myriads)."[7]

But the genuine Paul actually *experiences* the time frame that Luke merely describes from a vantage point of several decades later. Demographics conveyed by Paul's Epistles, in the 50s, are plainly to the opposite effect of Acts: resisting Christ, the Jews have not attained righteousness; they are "not enlightened"; they are a "disobedient and contrary people"; for the most part "hardened" and in a "stupor," they neither "see" nor "hear ... down to this very day"; they are guilty of "trespass" and "failure" and suffer "rejection"; they are "[branches] ... broken off because of ... unbelief"; the "hardening" is of *most* of Israel (Rom 9:30ff.; 10:16,21; 11:7–8,12,15,20,25).

The reality is that, by Luke's own day in the 90s, Christianity's ranks are predominantly Gentile. More so than Paul, Mark, Matthew, or John, it is incumbent upon Luke satisfactorily to explain this disparity, because it is particularly Luke who insists that Christianity's emergence vis-à-vis Judaism is not a rift but an extension of Judaism. His proposed solution is that, while Christianity's truth was no longer widely perceived by Jews in Luke's own later day, by no means was it lost on Jews of a bygone age. For when Christianity first emerged, discerning and

confirming Jews numbered even in the "myriads." Luke would have us imagine that originally "Christians [were] liked by the whole (Jewish) people ... [but we] misuse Luke's account ... when we make believe ... it offers us a documentary film of the beginnings of the Christian mission."[8] The early chapters of Acts "appear to be primitive only because the New Testament [writer] ascribed them to an earlier period"; actually, they betray both *late* and *Gentile*-Christian motives that "cannot possibly [have] come from the primitive community."[9]

Consistent with this explanation is the artistically framed reduction by stages, observable in Acts:

- from *initial, considerable* success with thousands of Jews (the opening chapters—2:41ff.; 4:4; 5:14; 6:1,7);
- to only *partial* or *mixed* success with Jews (the intermediate chapters—13:42ff.; 14:1ff.; 14:19ff.; 17:4f.; 17:10ff.);
- to *increasing resistance* encountered from Jews (the next group of chapters—18:4f.; 18:12f.; 19:8f.; 21:27f.);
- to a *culminating, final* prediction of *no* success with Jews (especially the last chapter—e.g., 28:25ff.: "this people ... shall ... *never* understand ... *never* perceive").

Note that "myriads" in Acts 21:20 summarizes conversions *before* Acts 7—that we can "arrive at the sum ... in 21:20 without the assumption of a single Jewish convert in Jerusalem after 6:7."[10]

The Role of the "God-Fearers"

The analogy of a rope is here apt. In some ropes, all strands extend the entire length, woven and interwoven. In other ropes, however, certain strands end earlier, somewhere in mid-rope, so new strands must be introduced to pick up where the initial ones leave off. The result is that many strands at rope's end are other than the natural continuation of those at its beginning.

Luke's task is, first, to demonstrate how the Christian rope, overwhelmingly Gentile at completion, was nonetheless Jewish at *inception*, and, second, to explain this transformation: how Jewish strands along the way became intermeshed, then replaced, by Gentile strands. As much as Luke needs to show Jewish strands ("myriads") at the Christian rope's beginning, he requires their noticeable *absence* by the end so as to match Gentile-Christian demography in the late first century.

As aids, Acts incorporates "God-fearers,"* quasi-converts who did attend synagogue and were vital in Christianity's spread (Chap. 6). But here they function as a literary device—the rope's *transitional* fibers—which explains why Luke restricts them to the *middle* chapters: 10:22

("God-fearing man"); 13:16 ("you that fear God"); 13:26 ("those ... that fear God"); 17:4f. ("devout Greeks"); 17:12 ("with not a few Greek[s]"); 17:17 ("devout persons"); 18:4 ("persuaded ... Greeks"). The use of God-fearers softens the transformation undergone by Christianity's ranks, preceding the incorporation of *masses* of Gentiles per se with no ostensible Jewish sympathies whatsoever. Tellingly, God-fearers abruptly vanish from Acts once they have served their transitional purpose.

The clues of Acts' intent here are discernible in Luke's Gospel as well. As early as the Nazareth episode, near the beginning of Jesus' ministry (Lk 4:16ff.), Luke reminds us how Elijah had benefited not Israel but rather the *Gentile* widow in Sidon (1 Ki 17:1,8–16), and how Elisha aided not Israel but another *Gentile*, Naaman the Syrian (2 Ki 5:1–14). Such early pointedly pro-Gentile and anti-Jewish intimations (also in Lk 20:17f.)—with no accompanying expectation of the Jews' future conversion—suggest Luke's lack of concern, all along, with salvation for Jews.[11]

Ironically, the genuine Paul finds the statistics depressing but is confident that Israel ultimately will be saved (Rom 11:26), whereas Luke, who trumpets such glorious initial statistics, *"from the outset ...* abandoned hope of converting Israel, ... [and Acts'] manifold attempts to throw a bridge between Jews and Christians no longer represent a missionary wooing of Israel [since] by Luke's time the Christian mission was directed *solely* to the Gentiles."[12]

Luke's "Paul" as Luke's Mouthpiece

Greek writers characteristically expressed personal views through speeches they attributed to important figures. Luke's sentiments are best gleaned from three verses he assigns his protagonist, (the Lucan) Paul:

> Since you [Jews] thrust [the word of God] from you, and judge yourselves unworthy of eternal life, behold, we turn to the Gentiles. (Acts 13:46)

> [Paul] shook out his garments and said to [the Jews], "Your blood be upon your heads! ... *From now on* I will go to the Gentiles." (Acts 18:5b–6)

> The Holy Spirit was right in saying ... through Isaiah the prophet [6:9f.]: "You shall indeed hear but *never* understand, and you shall indeed see but *never* perceive...." Let it be known to you then that this salvation of God has been sent to the Gentiles; *they* will listen. (Acts 28:25ff.)

This is an orientation consistent with the acerbic words Luke ascribes to Jesus in the parable of the Great Supper (Lk 14:24): "I tell you, none of those men ... invited [i.e., the Jews] shall taste my banquet." Thus, only the obstinacy of Jews in the past can account for the reality in the present that Christianity—although itself an extension of authentic Judaism—is severely un-Jewish numerically. Critical here is that readers distinguish Luke's attitude toward Judaism from that toward *Jews*:

> Because the earlier part of Acts is not overtly hostile towards Judaism, some scholars ... doubt that the ending of the book can be so definitively negative about the likelihood of Jewish conversion. But Luke is describing a progressive hardening of Christian attitudes, so that the final situation as he knows it is not what it was in the earlier days of the mission.... The future of the Christian movement lay with the Gentiles.... [Luke-Acts' final words are] a distillation of the author's controlling concept ... [that] the failed mission to the Jews is terminated in favor of the mission to the Gentiles.[13]

An Underlying Reality

Luke's presentation is an artificial device serving to explain the church of *his* time. But were there genuine metamorphoses in early Jewish attitudes toward Christianity? Some number of Jews (although not "myriads") likely *were* attracted to Jesus' program (which spawned Configuration A Christianity), initially seen by them as genuinely Jewish (see Fig. 4.2). But as Configuration B Christianity—with which Jews had less affinity—began ascending to dominance, some Jews originally drawn by the Jesus Movement now became increasingly disaffected, since Paul appeared to them to diverge from what was perceived as genuinely Jewish. Theirs, then, would not have been a changing response to the same presentation but to a *changed* presentation.

Yet Luke makes it appear instead that there was some kind of growing malfeasance among Jews themselves that caused their diminished participation in Christianity. In claiming that genuine Judaism is perpetuated by what Christianity now *is*, Luke drives a wedge between Judaism, on the one hand, and Jews who reject Jesus, on the other—thereby disinheriting those Jews. We are to understand that disbelieving Jews have orphaned themselves sociologically as well as spiritually from their own legacy! Metaphorically, were Judaism a train, then somewhere along the line Jews mistakenly got off (their mistake was rejecting Jesus) and *Gentile*-Christians embarked in their stead and remained onboard as authentic Judaism continued on. Accordingly, we readily can understand

the claim that "the anti-Jewish polemic in Acts ... [is] the most devastating and ... destructive of Judaism in all ... New Testament documents"[14]—except that I assess Luke as destructive of the *Jews*, not Judaism, because Luke-Acts insists that Judaism survives *as Christianity* while Jews have become orphaned from their own heritage.

The real Paul (of the Epistles) deeply despairs for fellow Jews (Chap. 14), who he believes are blind to the fulfillment of their own heritage, and he is apprehensive lest Gentiles no longer stand in awe and respect of Jews in their midst (Rom 11:18ff.). How ironic that the genuine Paul's apprehension of Gentile attitudes toward Jews became fulfilled in the person of Paul's unauthorized biographer, Luke, and in *his* makeover of Paul.

This chapter on Luke is shorter than on the other Evangelists because extensive attention is accorded this writer elsewhere in our volume:

- *Chapters 3 and 8 (Luke as the great "improviser").*
- *Chapter 6 (Luke's testimonies about synagogues; his presentation of Paul's conversion; his creation of fictional journeys with theological meanings; his use of Paul's Epistles; and speeches he created for Paul).*
- *Chapter 9 (Luke's infancy narrative).*
- *Chapter 21 (a summary of considerations about Luke).*

The Most Valuable Ideas in This Chapter May Be

1. Luke's two volumes—the Gospel (portraying Jesus' ministry) and Acts (a Church history)—manifest themes in common: First, Christianity embodies and continues authentic Judaism; and, second, Gentile-Christians constitute the true Jews.
2. While Jesus and Paul were Jewish, measures by which Luke displays this are makeshift (i.e., improvised).
3. Acts' claim that Christianity's ranks were initially swelled by "myriads" of Jews aims to render less incongruous the decidedly Gentile cast of Christian demography by Luke's day.
4. Luke makes it appear that some growing malfeasance among the Jews themselves diminished their ardor for Christianity, whereas actually it was Christianity that had changed—signalling not a changing response by Jews to the same presentation of Christianity but to a *changed* presentation.

What Gospel Dynamics Have We Recognized in This Chapter?

- Luke rewrites the stories of Jesus and Paul so that they conform to and remedy problems that he faces during his own day.
- The best place in Acts to gauge Luke's genuine sentiments toward the Jews is in key passages he assigns to Paul, his chief protagonist (13:46; 18:5b–6; 28:25–28).
- Luke uses geographical motifs to serve theological ends (see also Chaps. 6, 8–9).

Loose Ends Worth Tying

Do Luke's Motifs Reflect His Ethnicity?

Motifs that Luke introduces concerning Jesus' and Paul's fidelity to Judaism are not indicative that Luke himself is *Jewish*-Christian. He enlists these motifs—even creates some—solely to prove that *Gentile*-Christianity continues authentic Judaism.

Was the Boy Jesus' Presence in the Temple His Bar Mitzvah? (Lk 2:42ff.)

This custom did not exist in ancient times.

The Gospel of John
Why Are Jesus' Enemies So Conspicuously Termed "the Jews"?

Among New Testament writers, only John conspicuously uses the term "the Jews" (at least seventy[1] times). What perturbs many readers is that usually, by "the Jews," John appears to mean Jesus' *enemies*, often with the implication that Jesus and his followers were outside the Jewish people. Note how strikingly John contrasts with the Synoptists, who identify Jesus' adversaries in terms of Jewish leadership groups: chief priests, scribes, elders, Pharisees, Herodians, Sadducees. Rarely do the Synoptists use the expression "the Jews"—six times in Mark and five each in Matthew and Luke. Further, a dozen of these sixteen mentions are part of the phrase "King of the Jews" (Matthew and Luke simply lifting this formula from Mark). All told, then (Fig. 18.1), the Synoptists' independent usages of "the Jews"—that is, uses not in common by any two writers—number but four: Mark 7:3; Matthew 28:15; and Luke 7:3; 23:50f.

John has been the most popular Gospel to many Christians because of its spiritual doctrines, mysticism, and reassurances to believers (e.g., as in Jesus' farewell discourse, Jn 14–17). John's positioning of Jesus *over against* "the Jews" has so fueled Christian antisemitism that John has been labeled the "father of anti-semitism" and his Gospel one of "Christian love and Jew hatred"![2] At the least, "most Gentile readers ... do not notice the strangeness of John's having Jesus ... refer to other Jews simply as 'the Jews' ... (and often ... think of Jesus more as a Christian than as a Jew!)."[3] Even more disturbing is the way that John associates "the Jews" who, he alleges, had condemned Jesus, with Jews of John's own time, a "transfer of hostility ... creating a dangerous potential for anti-Semitism."[4] Are these characterizations of the Fourth Gospel warranted and fair?

18.1—Appearances of the Term "the Jews" (Greek: hoi Ioudaioi) in the Gospels

MARK 6	MATTHEW 5	LUKE 5	JOHN About 70
Independent	*Independent*	*Independent*	*Independent*
7:3	28:15	7:3; 23:50	**At least 39 seemingly hostile:**
			1:19; 2:18,20; 5:10,15,16,18; 6:41,52; 7:1,11,13,15,35; 8:22,48,52,57; 9:12,18,22a, 22b; 10:24,31,33; 11:8,54; 13:33; 18:12,14,31,36,38; 19:7,12,21a,31,38; 20:19
			About 25 other (some possibly hostile):
			2:6,13; 3:1,25; 4:9a,9b,22; 5:1; 6:4; 7:2; 8:31; 10:19; 11:19,31,33,36,45,55; 12:9,11; 18:20,30; 19:14,20,40,42; cf. 18:35
Formulaic "King of the Jews" 15:2,9,12, 18,26	*Formulaic* "King of the Jews" 2:2; 27:11, 29,37	*Formulaic* "King of the Jews" 23:3,37,38	*Formulaic* "King of the Jews" 18:33,39; 19:3,19,21b,21c

Important Clarifications

- Since this Gospel likely evolved in stages, with successive editors embellishing previous strata,[5] our conventional use of the "author of John" is a convenience only.
- What we read in John reflects circumstances within his particular community's locale and day and, accordingly, should not be unduly generalized.

Sample Passages in John Most Troubling to Jewish Readers

Since John's seemingly anti-Jewish texts are not limited to those explicitly mentioning "the Jews," the problem with the Fourth Gospel exceeds

what is commonly recognized. Consider the following passages from John (only a small sample) that I believe Jews would find offensive. My commentary (in brackets and italicized), while occasionally an attempt to clarify the texts, aims primarily to spell out what Jewish readers of this Gospel (in English translation) may infer these passages to mean—even if mistakenly so.

Passages Containing "the Jews" That Jewish Readers Will Likely Construe as "Anti-Jewish"

5:17f.   Jesus answered them, "My Father is working still [*God sustains life continuously—even on the sabbath*] and I am working [*just as God is (the words ascribed to Jesus suggest his equivalence with God)*]." This was why the Jews sought ... to kill him, because he not only broke the sabbath but also called God his Father, making himself equal with God.

7:1   He would not go about in Judea, because the Jews sought to kill him.

7:13   For fear of the Jews no one spoke openly of him.

8:31ff. Jesus then said to the Jews who had believed in him [*but because they could not maintain this belief, merely thirteen verses later Jesus will brand them children of the devil*]: "You seek to kill me.... I speak of what I have seen with my Father, and you do what you have heard from your father ... [*differing formulations are intended—'Father' vs. 'father'—because the Jews' father is not God but the* devil]. You are of your father the devil, and your will is to do your father's desires [*like father, like offspring*]. He was a murderer from the beginning, and has nothing to do with the truth, because there is no truth in him. When he lies, he speaks according to his own nature, for he is a liar and the father of lies.... He who is of God hears the words of God; the reason why you do not hear them is that you are not of God."

9:22   His parents [*those of the man born blind*] said that [*i.e., denied knowing how their son could now see, and denied knowing who had cured him*] because they feared the Jews, for the Jews had already agreed that, if anyone should confess [Jesus] to be Christ, he was to be put out of the synagogue [*excommunicated; in point of fact, however, this measure would not have been practiced during Jesus' lifetime*].

18:36   [*Jesus said to Pilate:*] "If my kingship were of this world, my servants would fight, that I might not be handed over to the Jews; but my kingship is not from the world."

19:38   Joseph of Arimathea ... secretly, for fear of the Jews, asked Pilate that he might take away the body of Jesus.

20:19   On the evening of that day [*the Sunday on which it was reported that Jesus had come back to life*] ... the doors being shut where the disciples were, for fear of the Jews....

Passages Not Containing "the Jews" That Jewish Readers Will Likely See as "Anti-Jewish"

1:11f.   [Jesus] came to his own home, and his own people [*the Jews*] received him not. But to all who received him ... he gave power to become children of God [*Jews there, not receiving him, were not given power to become children of God*].

1:17   The law was given through Moses; grace and truth came through Jesus Christ [*the revelation given through Moses (to the Jews) was inferior to that subsequently given through Jesus*].

3:16f.   For God so loved the world that he gave his only Son, that whoever believes in him should not perish but have eternal life [*Martin Luther termed this verse "the Gospel in miniature"*].... He who believes in him is not condemned; he who does not believe [*this includes the disbelieving* Jew] is condemned already.

3:36   He who believes in the Son has eternal life; he who does not obey [*believe in*] the Son [*here, the disobedient would include the disbelieving* Jew] shall not see life, but the wrath of God rests upon him.

14:6   "I am the way, and the truth, and the life; no one comes to the Father, but by me [*any Jew who fails to accept Jesus as the divine being, as the designated way, and so forth, will fail to gain access to God the Father*]."

Of course, excerpting John in this fashion could well skew understanding of the Gospel as a whole. Yet this is precisely how many Jews would read this work—inexorably drawn precisely to those texts that disparage Jews or Judaism, whether or not these texts name them explicitly.

Four Fundamental Questions

1. *Outside the Synoptists, is John's usage ("the Jews") unusual?* When juxtaposed to Mark, Matthew, and Luke, the Fourth Gospel's use of "the Jews" appears distinctive. But why make the Synoptists our only frame of reference? For other intertestamental writers, "Jews" or "the Jews" was standard usage, and with no denigration entailed. Particularly in the Diaspora, non-Jews customarily referred to "Jews" as such. Even Diaspora Jews sometimes adopted this non-Jewish usage when speaking of themselves *to* Gentiles.[6] Jews in the land of Israel generally referred to themselves as "Israel," but even they occasionally employed the term "Jews."[7]

   Exceptions, if any, are inconsequential as long as John's audience was at least partially Gentile. For what matters is that the way in which he uses "the Jews" does indeed conform to conventional patterns regardless of whether the speaker himself was of Jewish or Gentile extraction, or writing from within or outside the land of Israel. Accordingly, if John did apply "the Jews" in an anti-Jewish way, it is not simply his use of that term that is anti-Jewish.

2. *Could "the Jews" in John mean something other than the Jewish people?* The scope of "the Jews" in John is elastic—appearing to contract or expand in differing contexts. The range of possible understandings can be wide. Minimally, "the Jews" sometimes shrink down to a tiny subgroup of the Jewish people—for example, "the Jews who were with her in the house" (11:31); "the Jews who came with her also weeping" (11:33). Maximally, however, the term seems to inflate so as to encompass even the world at large![8]

   What results is a plethora of proposals for interpreting "the Jews" in John: the world at large; Jewry in general; descendants of the tribe of Judah, alone (contrasting to those from other tribes); residents of Judea,→ alone (contrasting, e.g., to those of Galilee); Jewish authorities, alone; the Pharisees, alone; and so forth.

   It is true, of course, that the Synoptists use group referents that also appear imprecise: "chief priests," "elders," "Herodians," "scribes." Yet each term refers to a group defined in a relatively consistent way. Why, then, in the case of John, does the meaning of "the Jews" fluctuate so? Is this a function of this Gospel's development in successive layers, each employing "the Jews" somewhat differently? Yet would the final editor be content to leave such inconsistencies unreconciled? Notwithstanding our quandary, I favor, as our wisest course, assuming that John left his audience to understand "the Jews" in the most natural sense: those members of the Jewish people "who reject the claim of Jesus to lordship, and who remain Jews because they do."[9]

3. *Is John's use of "the Jews" necessarily pejorative?* In terms of narrative
function, what role does John assign "the Jews" and what is the effect on
his readership of how he applies this term? If usage of "the Jews" by other
contemporary writers was neither unusual nor denigrating, why should
we assume that it is pejorative in John's case? Admittedly, the thirty-nine
seemingly hostile passages (Fig. 18.1) constitute a compelling starting argument—not to mention the many additional texts that exhibit, even
exude, acrimony toward Jews even without explicitly mentioning them.
These suggest that tensions between the writer's community and the synagogue were heated and that "John probably tells us as much or more
about [his] community itself than about the Jesus of history."[10]

4. *Did rabbinic authorities actually exclude or force the expulsion of Jewish-Christians from the synagogue in John's city?* Such action easily could
foment antipathy from John's constituents, and three Johannine passages
seemingly point in this direction:

9:22ff. His parents [*those of the man born blind*] said this [*denied
knowing how their son could now see, and denied knowing
who cured him*] because they feared the Jews, for the Jews had
already agreed that if any one should confess [Jesus] to be
Christ, he was to be put out of the synagogue [*excommunicated*].... They called the man who had been blind.... He answered them, " ... If this man [Jesus] were not from God, he
could do nothing." ... And they cast him out [*of the synagogue*].

12:42   But for fear of the Pharisees they [i.e., *many "even of the authorities"*] did not confess [*that they, also, believed in Jesus*],
lest they should be put out of the synagogue.

16:2   [*Jesus said:*] They will put you out of the synagogue.

Were such expulsions related to the *Birkat Ha-Minim*, the "benediction" (actually, malediction) against *minim* ("heretics")? This exclusionary curse appears to have been formulated—or reformulated from some
more primitive version—perhaps in the mid-80s by the rabbis of Yavneh
(Jamnia),[11] and came to constitute the twelfth of the so-called *Shemoneh Esreh* ("Eighteen Benedictions"), the rabbinic statutory weekday
prayer recited three times daily. Presumably no Jewish-Christian
"heretic" would be comfortable reciting a curse against himself (when
serving, e.g., as synagogue reader), or choose to belong where he heard
himself so cursed by others (BT Berakh 28b).

However suggestive this conjecture, caution is required: we cannot
be sure who was targeted by this text. Instead of Jewish-Christians

perhaps there was some other referent, for example, Jewish collaborators with Rome against fellow Jews (the prayer contained the wish that "the arrogant government be speedily uprooted in our days"). The term "heretics" itself might have been incorporated only belatedly into whatever constituted the original malediction. The version published from medieval Egyptian fragments contained the supplication: "Let the *notzrim* [presumably, Nazarenes—Christians?] and the *minim* [heretics] be destroyed in a moment." But "heretics" is imprecise—it could include Jewish-Christians but need not refer, let alone be limited, to them; and "Nazarenes" may have been added only later to an earlier text— again, at a now difficult-to-determine time.[12]

Since the history and meaning of this prayer remain disputed, how then should we process John in relation to it? And questions remain in any event: If expulsions that John mentions were experienced solely within John's city, they likely would reflect nothing of the rabbis' official malediction. And assumptions "that rabbinic enactments were immediately enforceable everywhere points to an effectiveness and power which can only be documented, and even then with difficulty, a century or two later."[13] (Regardless, readers should understand that the *Shemoneh Esreh* today contains no anti-Christian components.)

John's Use of "The Jews" Is Symbolic

The best strategy to help us solve this problem may be to determine John's definitive message. And the place most likely to reveal this is the very end of this Gospel proper: the closing verses of chapter 20 (chapter 21 is a belatedly added epilogue). John's very last words there are: "that you may *believe* that Jesus is the Christ, the Son of God, and that *believing* you may have life in his name." Statistics underscore this as John's definitive message: "believing" and related terms appear almost exactly 100 times in John. Not only is this roughly three times more than in the Synoptics combined, but when we leave out instances where Matthew and Luke simply lift material from Mark, John's personal stress on "believing" seems all the more striking.

It may be John's preoccupation with belief that solves the riddle of the role he assigns to "the Jews." Provided that "the Jews" is used in a genuinely collective sense (as opposed to referring merely to a few solitary individuals among them), "Jews" for John represent *those who stubbornly disbelieve when it is they who ought to believe*. This would account for the term's elasticity: where others besides the Jews also fail to believe, the term "the Jews" expands to include these others as well. This would resolve the enigma of why John sometimes uses the "world" and "the Jews" interchangeably, since overall he

portrays "the Jews viewed from the standpoint of Church faith, as the representatives of unbelief (and thereby ... of the unbelieving 'world' in general)."[14]

Significantly buttressing this conjecture is the discovery of what so many readers fail to discern: that John intentionally also furnishes us with counterparts of "the Jews," namely, "the disciples." This commonly goes unrecognized because, unlike "the Jews"—who actively appear throughout the Gospel—"the disciples" are relatively passive during the unfolding narrative. But at the conclusion, "when the ... [Jews] have no more role to play, the career of the disciples is just beginning...." Only now is it "time for them to become active in extension of the-things-Jesus-has-done (20:21)."[15]

John's purpose is to advance a theological proposition, which is the need for belief in the Christ. In so doing, he requires two role models: one of choosing disbelief, to be eschewed by his readers; and the second of choosing proper belief, to be emulated by his readers. Jesus' self-image could not be appropriated in either capacity, for Jesus *has to* believe in his Father. It is rather for others to exercise their choice as to what decision to reach for themselves. In sum, *"the disciples" model those who believe despite all discouragement, while "the Jews" model those who disbelieve in the face of all compelling evidence.*

The key interrelationship is thus, diagrammatically, triangular (as seen in Fig. 18.2).[16] Jesus is at the pinnacle, while at the two bases John balances "the disciples" and "the Jews" off one another, as when Jesus (the Jew) addresses "the disciples" (other Jews) with the words: "as I said to the Jews so now I say to you" (13:33).

This means that it is not Jesus whom John sets apart from the Jews but the Jews whom John wishes to distinguish not only from Jesus but also primarily *from the disciples*! Herein lies the critical error that Jewish readers especially are likely to commit. What results from their undue focus only on Jesus and the Jews is that, understandably, the element of conflict between Jesus and the Jews becomes exaggerated. *If Jewish readers divide their attention between Jesus and the Jews, they are likely to overstate the conflict motif and to see John primarily in terms of anti-Jewish polemic.*[17]

This suggests that any of "the Jews" who manages to become a believer is at least approaching discipleship, as in 8:31: "Jesus then said to the Jews who had believed in him, 'If you continue in my word, you are truly my disciples.'" That Jesus brands these same Jews as children of the devil thirteen verses later evidently establishes that these Jews have not substantially enough continued in Jesus' word, that "their simple acquiescence in his teaching was not deeply rooted in faith ... [and] quickly

---

18.2—*"The Disciples" and "the Jews" as Counterparts in John*

JESUS

"THE DISCIPLES"
(Personifying BELIEF)
Sample passages:

"THE JEWS"
(Personifying UNBELIEF)
Sample passages:

"His disciples BELIEVED in him" (2:11).

"His disciples ... BELIEVED ... the word ... Jesus had spoken" (2:22).

"We [the twelve disciples] have BELIEVED, and have come to know, that you are the Holy One of God" (6:68–69).

"[To the disciples Jesus says:] ... BELIEVE in God, BELIEVE also in me.... BELIEVE me that I am in the Father and the Father in me; or else BELIEVE me for the sake of the works themselves.... He who BELIEVES in me will also do the works that I do" (14:1–12).

"His disciples said, '... by this we BELIEVE that you came from God'" (16:29–30).

"How can you [Jews] BELIEVE? ... If you BELIEVED Moses, you would BELIEVE me, for he wrote of me. But if you do not BELIEVE his writing, how will you BELIEVE my words?" (5:44–47).

"I told you [Jews] that you would die in your sins ... unless you BELIEVE that I am he" (8:24).

"Because I tell the truth, you [Jews] do not BELIEVE me.... Why do you not BELIEVE me?" (8:45–46).

"I told you [Jews], and you do not BELIEVE" (10:25–26).

"Though he had done so many signs before [the Jewish crowd] ... they did not BELIEVE in him ... that the word [of] ... Isaiah ... be fulfilled: 'Lord, who has BELIEVED our report ...?' Therefore they could not BELIEVE" (12:37–39).

---

withered."[18] To achieve the status of a disciple means to be like the master with a steadfastness that does not waver.

The fundamental structure of John's work, accordingly, is a contrast: the disciples, imperfect as they are, slowly but surely learn to believe, while "the Jews" for the most part repeatedly fail to do so. *John's paramount concern is not anti-Judaism but rather challenging unbelievers to become believers.*

Perhaps nowhere is this clearer than in his episode of the Doubting Thomas (20:19–29). Confirming the crucial importance of this story to John is its textual location: in the very next-to-last paragraph of the Gospel's last chapter (leaving out chapter 21, the belatedly added epilogue). Followed here is the custom that the last verse of a story (20:29) conveys the narrator's chief emphasis:

> On the evening of [*resurrection Sunday*] ... the doors being shut where the disciples were, for fear of the Jews, Jesus came.... He showed them his hands and his side.... Thomas ... was not with them.... The other disciples [later] told him, "We have seen the Lord." But he said..., "Unless I see in his hands the print of the nails, and place my finger in the mark of the nails, and place my hand in his side, I will not believe." Eight days later, [Jesus'] disciples were again in the house, and Thomas ... with them. The doors were shut, but Jesus came.... He said to Thomas, "Put your finger here ... see my hands; ... put ... your hand ... in my side; do not be faithless, but believing." Thomas answered..., "My Lord and my God!" Jesus said..., "Have you believed because you have seen me? *Blessed are those who have not seen and yet believe.*"

Given the last verse, the question arises: to what degree does the story reflect John's own day, when those who can believe are limited to doing so without seeing?

The Impact of the Apparent Anti-Judaism in John

John's motive and intent are to use "the Jews" and their unbelief as a foil for "the disciples" with their belief, so that John's anti-Judaism is essentially a by-product of other concerns. Yet in terms of the inferences to which this work has given rise, anti-Judaism has become a dominant impression, and naturally has provoked much alarm among those interested in improving Christian–Jewish relations today. The true gravity of this matter is that, by literary license, the Fourth Gospel has assigned to the historical Jesus what is after all only John's own theology. Further, insofar as John presents Jesus as the Christ, and insofar as the Christ and the Father are deemed by John to be "one" (10:30; 17:11), *John has imputed his theology to God personally, thereby in effect making God appear anti-Jewish!*

When John defines the Christ as the sole way to God, he seeks to establish for Christianity a monopoly on the truth that precludes disbelieving Jews from access to the Deity. To be sure, any religion should be expected to express confidence in the truth of its own affirmations. Indeed, any religion is entitled to express its self-confidence through assertions of its

monopoly on the truth. But Judaism is assuredly entitled to object, and strongly, to John's exclusivism—and particularly to John's appropriation of Jesus the *Jew* as the critical fulcrum in an exclusionary process that bars Jews from access to God through avenues of their own determination. At the very least, Jews would wish for a deemphasizing of John 14:6, "no one comes to the Father but by me," in favor of 14:2 (but four verses earlier)—"in my Father's house are many mansions."

The Most Valuable Ideas in This Chapter May Be

1. The fundamental contrast in John is not between the Jews and Jesus but between the Jews and the disciples.
2. "The disciples" model those who believe despite all discouragement, and "the Jews" model those who disbelieve in the face of all compelling evidence.
3. John's paramount concern is thus not anti-Judaism but rather challenging unbelievers to become believers.
4. But the paramount *impression* that the Gospel may make on Jewish readers is that it is comprehensibly anti-Jewish.
5. Since, for John, the Christ and the Father are one, when John imputes his own theology to Jesus he imputes it as well to God personally, making even God appear anti-Jewish.

What Gospel Dynamics Have We Recognized in This Chapter?

- John tells us more about his community itself than about the Jesus of history.
- That John associates "the Jews"—who, he alleges, had condemned Jesus—with later Jews of John's own day constitutes a transferring of hostility that carries with it the potential for antisemitism.
- The reality is that the enmity of John's day is retrojected, not that of Jesus' day forwarded.

Loose End Worth Tying

Why "Jews" Does Not Likely Mean "Judeans." The view I adopt, cited earlier in this chapter, is that John left his audience to understand "the Jews" in the most natural sense: as members of the Jewish people who rejected the claim that Jesus was lord and remained Jews by so doing.[19] Given the contrast that I propose—not between Jesus and the Jews but between the *disciples* and the Jews—"Judeans" does not seem a plausible meaning to me.

Part Six

When Wariness Is Warranted

New Testament Knowledge for Self-Defense

The Christian Apocalypse
Jews as God's Odometer in End-Times Scenarios

"Millennium" is a technical Christian term referring to the hypothetical coming of a thousand-year kingdom of messianic peace on earth. The word derives from the Latin *mille* ("thousand") and *annus* ("year"). The concept is traceable to Revelation 20:4: "the souls of those ... who had not worshiped the beast ... came to life, and reigned with Christ a thousand years." Many persons who believe in the coming of such a kingdom ("millennialists") insist that we are living right now in the last days of history, and some even profess to tell us how its ending will unfold.

Attitudes regarding a millennium vary widely within today's American Christian culture:

- The vast majority reject any literal belief in this concept.
- A small component of those who do anticipate this thousand-year era of perfection expect Jesus to return only *after* its culmination; they thus term themselves *post*-millennialists ("post"—after).
- Most millennialists are *pre*-millennialists ("pre"—before): believing that Jesus will return *before* the millennium not only to initiate it but also personally to rule throughout its course.

Our concern will lie with pre-millennialists because their end-time scenarios cast the Jews and the State of Israel in core roles, and because most Israelis consider them their staunchest allies in America.

Because pre-millennialists hold that events on earth can go only from bad to worse until Jesus personally intervenes, they are fatalistic—indeed, from now on let us term them "catastrophists."[1] They number in the tens of millions—only a minority of America's Protestants, yet a most influential force to be reckoned with. They are best envisioned in three concentric circles:

1. Innermost are the "experts" who apply biblical prophecy—from Jewish scripture and the New Testament—to help "explain everything" currently transpiring in our world.

2. A wider circle encompasses millions of others who, while believing that the Bible offers clues about the end times, are yet less "informed" as to the particulars involved.

3. An outer circle encompasses greater millions still, who—given sufficiently alarming earthly crises—may suddenly buy into "prediction addiction," as what had been only peripheral to them now abruptly shifts to the center.[2]

Throughout this chapter, readers should remember that the vast majority of American Christians (among Roman Catholics, Episcopalians, Presbyterians, Methodists, liberal Lutherans, etc.) give catastrophic-millennialist scenarios scant attention. Moreover, even among Christians who nominally do espouse these (especially among Southern Baptists, the Assemblies of God, Seventh-Day Adventists, Pentecostals, charismatics, etc.), most are scarcely well-versed in this outlook's attendant details—some of which might strike them as simply outlandish, even repulsive.

Before delving into these details, I must highlight the following caveat.

Catastrophic-millennialists derive terms and concepts crucial to their thinking from Jewish scripture and the New Testament, but their processes of doing so are flawed. The authors of biblical books had special aims and contexts of which catastrophists appear unaware. When correctly understood, these sources invalidate the elaborate scenarios that catastrophists construct upon them. Therefore, when I identify the biblical bases that these millennialists so frequently cite, readers should understand that I *dispute* the ways by which these texts are enlisted and interpreted, and I will give examples as to why in due course.

Terms and Concepts

The Antichrist and His Mysterious Number, 666. By "Antichrist,"[3] catastrophists mean Satan's secretly groomed henchman who will rise to become the earth's final ruler by deceiving humanity into believing that he alone can solve the world's intractable problems, especially turmoil between Israel and her neighbors. Unaware of his malevolence, Israel will

sign a treaty with him guaranteeing her safety from Arab opponents and then build the Third Temple (Babylonia destroyed the First Temple in 586 BCE, Rome the Second Temple in 70 CE).

The 18 percent of American adults said to expect Jesus' return during their lifetime[4] should also wonder whether the Antichrist is already present, since his world rule commences seven years before Jesus' return. Those on the Antichrist-lookout even now rely on his profile as fleshed out by various villainous types, mostly from the book of Daniel.➔ The resulting composite: a suave, deceptive, magnetically charismatic, oratorically seductive, politically astute and cunningly manipulative leader who precipitously rises to power[5] and bears some association with the number "666"➔—the number that all persons, in loyalty to him and to be enabled to conduct normal commerce, must bear either on their right hand or forehead (Rev 13:16ff.).

Today's classic "Antichrist scenario" is of a European figure heading a ten-nation confederacy—deduced from the ten-toed statue or ten-horned beast in Daniel 2:42; 7:24 and similar imagery in Revelation 13:1ff. This supposedly signifies no less than the resurfacing, or extension, of the ancient Roman Imperial system. (Note: the groundwork for today's European Union [originally the European Economic Community] was laid in 1957's Treaty of *Rome* signed on ancient Rome's Capitoline Hill.)[6]

Tribulation. This is the name given to the Antichrist's seven-year rule when he will wreak havoc with world order.[7] At its midpoint, he will break his treaty with Israel and desecrate the Third Temple by revealing himself, therein, as the monomaniacal Beast he truly is. He will declare himself Messiah or God[8] and from now on escalate the world's miseries through: political and economic chaos; famine; plague; war; terrorism; natural disasters; even astronomical devastation—here, for example, an asteroid orbiting earth breaks apart, its debris falling with deadly effect, its gravitational pull triggering earthquakes, its remaining bulk plunging into an ocean and causing tidal waves that wipe out entire populations of coastal cities. The expression "Great Tribulation" distinguishes this even more terrible second half of the seven years. (Additionally, God's own wrath is to be unleashed during the Tribulation's fourth quarter.)

The Rapture. This means the rescue of Christian faithful via their being literally lifted off earth to rendezvous with Jesus, who descends halfway from heaven.[9] But when does the Rapture occur relative to the Tribulation?

For centuries, millennialists envisioned the Second Coming and Rapture as coinciding facets of the Tribulation's *end*. A contrary option—

"*pre*-tribulation" Rapture—was introduced in about 1830. A third option—"*mid*-tribulationist" Rapture—mediates between the two:

- *Pre*-tribulationists expect Rapture just *before* the seven-year Tribulation (let us term them "*early*-rapturists").
- *Mid*-tribulationists expect Rapture at the Tribulation's *midpoint* (let us call these "*delayed*-rapturists").
- *Post*-tribulationists expect Rapture near, or coincident with, the Tribulation's *end* (let us call these "*late*-rapturists").

Thus, early-rapturists expect to undergo none of the Tribulation since they will no longer be earthbound. Delayed-rapturists expect to undergo the Tribulation's (relatively bearable) first half, and late-rapturists its seven-year entirety. (Additional timing options also have emerged.[10])

Rapture-timing is consequential and contentious. Early-rapturism is the most popular—meaning that most who preach the slate of upcoming horrors do not expect to experience them! But delayed- and late-rapturists believe that early-rapturism is misguided and dangerous (see further below) because it seduces masses of people into being carefree and unprepared for the devastation that *is* coming for *all* persons, the misguided who preach otherwise notwithstanding.

Early-Rapturists: The Major Strain—John Nelson Darby's "Dispensationalism"

The motifs and concepts we have examined lend themselves to variant interpretations. The versions presented so far conform to those espoused by early-rapturism's dominant strain, called dispensationalism. Credited to John Nelson Darby (1800–1882), an Anglican minister in Ireland, and popularized by the *Scofield Reference Bible* (1909), it divided history into seven epochs ("dispensations") according to how God progressively deals with humanity. Our concern is with epochs #5 (from the giving of the Law by Moses up through Jesus' death); #6 (from the Church's origin through to the Rapture); and #7 (from the millennial kingdom to eternity),[11] with special focus on #6 during which we are said now to be living.

God's Two Peoples

Darby proposed that God's priorities with humanity have been separated into two discrete plans—one for an "earthly" people (the Jews), the other for a "heavenly" people (the Church). God can work with *only one group at a time* because dispensations are utterly distinct from each other. Thus, #6, dealing solely with the Church, must be utterly distinct

from #5 and #7—both of which deal solely with the Jews. In this light, we must remember that dispensation #7—"the millennial kingdom to eternity"—deals not with the Church (which by then is raptured) but with the Jews.

God's preoccupation with the Jews would have continued uninterrupted beyond #5 had they not—and unexpectedly so—rejected Jesus in the first century. That denial induced God to postpone—for a temporary but not yet readily determinable length of time (= dispensation #6)—the culmination of Jesus' redemptive work, stopping, as it were, the divine prophetic clock that all along had been operational with respect to the Jews. Here we observe that *the onus for delay in completing Jesus' work rests upon the Jews*. (This carries a potential for antisemitism—or at least for a loss of patience with the Jews—even if early-rapturists profess to love them as God's chosen people.)

With makeshift dispensation #6, then, God put together a *new* people, the Church (cf. Acts 2), which ever since has existed in a prophetic time warp, a "great parenthesis": sandwiched between God's previous preoccupation with the Jews (in #5) and God's eventual resumption of this focus (in #7). God's interim attention to the Church alone (#6)—already a long interim since it has lasted now roughly two millennia—will continue until the Rapture elevates faithful Christians into a heavenly people, bringing an end to the Church's temporary (and originally unanticipated) earthly existence.

Accordingly, complementing the Church's unusual beginning will be its abrupt end (via the Rapture) just prior to the onset of the Antichrist's seven-year Tribulation. At this juncture, God will restart the prophetic clock, and divine preoccupation will revert to the Jews. Driven by the logic that God can deal with only one group at a time—and hence that the Church (#6) and the Jews (to be #7) must be utterly separate—Darby had to insist that the Rapture would *precede* the seven-year Tribulation. Since one purpose of the Tribulation is to refine and condition a remnant of Jews to accept Jesus—in compensation for their ancestors' rejection of him—no renewed concentration on them is feasible unless the Christian faithful have already departed from the earthly scene (via the Rapture).

The Restoration of the State of Israel

From their mid-nineteenth century origins, dispensationalists had a core expectation: the reestablishment of a Jewish State.[12] Dispensationalism's credibility was thus sharply enhanced when, in 1948, Israel ceased to be merely a theological abstraction. Convinced that history has begun nearing culmination, with Israel as "ground zero"—where the end times

surely will play out—dispensationalists are now looking for signs of the Third Temple being rebuilt (during the first half of the Tribulation[13]). Ultra-orthodox Jews in Israel, also hoping for such a rebuilding, already have trained rabbis in Temple ritual sacrifice, with accouterments and officiants' robes all prepared. Incongruously, joint efforts are underway by these Jews *and* dispensationalists[14] to breed a red heifer (a biological anomaly) whose ashes are needed for ritual purification prior to embarking upon any Temple reconstruction (cf. Num 19:2ff).[15]

The Rapture Manifested

With Israel restored, anticipation of the Rapture has intensified, but how will it manifest itself? Presumably, first the deceased faithful will rise heavenward from their graves. Thereafter, the living faithful counterparts will be caught up to the clouds. As popularly understood today, faithful drivers will disappear from behind the wheel, their cars plowing on until crashing; planes will lose "select" passengers, perhaps even the pilots (and therefore possibly crash); infants (viewed as pure) will vanish from maternity wards; and so forth. (Seven years later, these "Rapture saints" will return in company with Jesus and the heavenly host to vanquish the Antichrist and other demonic forces at a terrible and climactic battle at Armageddon.)

This removal of the Christian faithful will aid the Antichrist in solidifying control over those "left behind" on earth. The latter will comprise all non-Christians and also Christians who have been such only nominally (including even some clergy). Shocked to their core, these penitents will now consult the Bible, as they ought to have done earlier. Only this will reveal how everything transpiring is a working out of God's long-scripted plan. Some now will struggle valiantly to make amends by resisting the Antichrist. This is the heroic stuff of millennialist novels[16] which falsely imagine that there exists some escape clause—allowing those left behind to earn a second chance at Rapture. (Were this only true, less distinction would be needed between those raptured and those left behind.)

End-Time Warfare and the Thereafter

Three decisive wars are now in the offing (some interpreters coalesce the first two):

- GOD SAVES ISRAEL FROM A NORTHERN CONFEDERATION ALIGNED WITH ARAB/AFRICAN NATIONS. A confederation "from the uttermost parts of the north"—inferred from "Gog, *of* the land of Magog"[17] (Ezek 38:2,14ff.)—will join with Arab/African nations in attacking Israel,

which the European-based Antichrist had promised to defend. But God, not the Antichrist, utterly annihilates Israel's enemies (Ezek 38:21ff.) during the Tribulation's first half, that is, prior to the Antichrist's self-disclosure (for by any later date he would no longer be viewable as Israel's defender).

- ARMAGEDDON, WHERE JESUS (AT HIS "SECOND COMING") OVERWHELMS THE ANTICHRIST AND ARMIES FROM VARIOUS/ALL NATIONS. "Armageddon" (cf. Rev 16:16) is anglicized from the Hebrew *har megiddo*, or *har megiddon* ("the mountain of Megiddo") overlooking a traditional battle site in northern Israel (south-southeast of Haifa). Almost two-fifths[18] of U.S. adults are said to expect the world's end in this battle, which is to occur at the close of, or directly after, the Tribulation. Yet precisely who converges here is unclear. Prominent may be a 200 million-man army (9:16) under "kings of the east" (16:12–16)—today commonly presumed China; but Revelation may have meant only peoples on the Roman Empire's "eastern" front, notably Parthia (in northern Mesopotamia and beyond). An alternative view holds that armies from *all* nations are involved, perhaps garnered by the Antichrist to attack Israel. At the height of fearful fighting, Jesus—with the heavenly host and his "Rapture saints"—descends (the Second Coming). Appearing as a warrior of frightening mien, he achieves total victory. Now the Antichrist is thrown into the lake of fire (to begin everlasting damnation), while Satan is trapped in a bottomless pit for the same 1,000 years that King Jesus will now begin to reign (Rev 20:1ff.).

- GOD'S FINAL VICTORY OVER SATAN. At millennium's end, Satan, released (20:3), straightway recruits masses from the ranks of "Gog *and* Magog" (somehow back again, after being wiped out) that either include or to which are now added multitudes born *during* the millennium period who have failed to be—or whom Satan now persuades no longer to remain—loyal to the reigning Jesus. When these encircle and besiege Jerusalem, God's fire from heaven consumes them. Now Satan also is cast into the lake of fire (joining the Antichrist) for perpetual torment (20:7ff.).

As for subsequent developments: at the Last Judgment (here history ends and eternity follows), the dead assessed before God are dealt with individually (20:11ff.); a new heaven and earth replace their antecedents (21:1ff.); and a new Jerusalem descends from heaven. Completing God's original design for creation, all who now remain live forever harmoniously and God is *with them* (fulfilling the name—as Matthew quotes it from Isaiah 7:14—"Emmanuel," which means "God with us"; cf. Mt 1:22f.; 28:20).

What Happens to the Jews?

During the Tribulation, God initiates a purging-and-refining process so as to guarantee that those Jews surviving this time around will not disappoint (by rejecting Jesus) as did their ancestors. Two-thirds of the Jews left behind at the Rapture die (Zech 13:8f.). Upon the third who do survive the Tribulation and Armageddon, God will shower those Scriptural promises reserved for the Israelites' descendants alone—for at long last the Jews reemerge as God's core concern. Priests among these survivors administer anew the sacrificial cult in the "Millennial Temple," the Fourth (modeled on Ezek 40–48), which is built to replace the "Tribulational Temple," the Third (requiring destruction because it was desecrated by the Antichrist).

Note: While some Orthodox Jews and catastrophic-millennialists *both* expect a building of one and the same new Temple (the Third), the former expect this to be permanent while the latter see this "Tribulational Temple" as short-lived, doomed because it was built as the setting for the Antichrist's self-disclosure at the Tribulation's midpoint. (Moreover, its Jewish builders were not believers in Jesus.) Now, therefore, it will be replaced—after Armageddon—by the Fourth Temple (the "Millennial Temple"), to be built by the Messiah himself (Zech 6:12f.).

Critiquing the Dispensationalist Scheme

Even leaving aside the primary concern—that dispensationalism not only misinterprets biblical texts[12] but also interrelates those bearing no connection to one another→—dispensationalism is inconsistent internally as well as vis-à-vis the New Testament itself.

Theological Anomalies

Obviously envisioning an all-powerful God, dispensationalism limits God as well. Although omniscient and foreknowing, God is caught off-guard when first-century Jews reject Jesus. Further, though omnipotent, God is *controlled* by the Jews' refusal, now for twenty centuries and counting! If the Tribulation ultimately is needed to quell Jews' stubbornness, why apply it after the Church Age (#6) rather than before and without it? (And what a trivialization of the Church—created only as a stopgap measure!) If God needed time to put Jews to the test—and created the Church only to fill the interim—then what about the horrendous fate awaiting those Christians to be "left behind" for being Christian only nominally? Darby also enfeebles God, who is allowed to

be preoccupied, at any given time, either only with the Jews or only with the Church, but not both at once.

The unbridled brutality of the Tribulation, meanwhile, obliterates what Christianity holds to be *inspired* New Testament theology. Now God personifies not Christian Love but Boundless Wrath and Inconceivable Vengeance (especially since, after having whisked the faithful to heaven, God is free to pummel the world while the remainder of humanity chooses between the Antichrist and Jesus). As for Jesus, instead of *his* Second Coming we have a First Coming of a mechanistic warrior-king on a white horse (Rev 19:15): "his eyes ... like a flame of fire ... clad in a robe dipped in blood ... a sharp sword" issuing from the mouth—the diametric opposite of the teacher of Nazareth who warned: "all who take the sword will perish by the sword" (Mt 26:52). If this is his Second Coming, then the Jesus of antiquity is a victim of his successor's success!

If dispensationalists today were to denounce societal sins and succeed, then by decelerating the world's decline would they *delay* the Second Coming, and might their efforts thus be Satan-induced? Further, if the present dispensation, the Church Age (#6), is only a "great parenthesis" to which Jewish scriptural predictions do not apply, why then do dispensationalists routinely justify their preachments by dependence on the Hebrew prophets—that the end signs they predicted are being manifested even now? By definition these predictions can only come to fruition during Dispensation #7! (Note that Darby's insistence that Jewish scriptural promises apply solely to the Jews is, of course, in flat-out contradiction to New Testament theology.)

The New Testament repeatedly prohibits trying to time the Second Coming,[20] yet Darby pinpoints this arrival exactly three and one-half years after the Antichrist's self-disclosure in the Tribulational (i.e., Third) Temple. Darby thus has substituted the Rapture for the Second Coming as the event that we should not calculate, but there is no scriptural warrant for this. Nor can dispensationalists claim that the Rapture *is* the Second Coming or that Jesus' formal return is his *Third* because Jesus never comes all the way down to earth at the Rapture (cf. 1 Thes 4:17).

Hardly Idyllic Millennial Kingdom

Meanwhile, how can it be explained that the Millennial Kingdom turns out so utterly non-idyllic? When Satan is released at the millennium's end, he finds those who hate Jesus are as numerous "as the sand of the sea" (Rev 20:8)! Yes, some have recently been so induced

by Satan's wiles, but most have despised King Jesus on their own, keeping their antipathy under wraps even for centuries (during which Satan was "tied-up," in his bottomless pit). This, then, is a disappointing "Kingdom of God," especially since many belonging to it assuredly do not meet the criteria for admission. The Kingdom is supposed to be where the Patriarchs and prophets dwell, and "the righteous ... shine like the sun"—and are penitent and wise, do God's will and sow good seed.[21] But in Darby's system Jesus does not appear to command even majority approval! And this is because, *before* the Tribulation, Darby has raptured all worthy folk "above," so they now cease to be slated for the Kingdom "below." Yes, Rapture saints may accompany Jesus back to earth at Armageddon, but then they return heavenward. They will not continue with Jesus as he reigns during the millennium down below.

So who does? Certainly not the best. Most are those who have been marred, at one time or another, by a proclivity for unbelief, namely:

1. Any surviving but only-nominal "Christians" whom the Rapture left behind, some still unfaithful and some possibly penitent (the latter are "Tribulation saints" as opposed to "Rapture saints").

2. Surviving non-Christians—by definition unbelievers—who used to constitute most of the world's populace (we cannot know how many might yet become supportive of Jesus).

3. That one-third of the Jews who, surviving the Tribulation, finally accepted Jesus after his return.

4. Any out-and-out wicked persons refusing to repent (what deeds will they do over the remaining centuries? Remember that the Last Judgment confronts them only at the millennium's *end*).

5. Any surviving persons from among those newly born *during the Tribulation* (as per Mt 24:19: "alas for those ... with child and ... those who give suck").

6. Any persons now newly born *during the millennium itself* (yet what assurance is there that these—as with the preceding group—will now opt to become faithful Christians?).

What about scripture's repeated affirmations that the Rapture saints would be blessed by being *with* Jesus always?[22] But dispensationalism holds that Jewish scriptural promises of the messianic age can be fulfilled only by and for *Jews*, so the Rapture saints can play no role in it. (This shocking realization has never occurred to many early-rapture believers.)

Distinction: Since Hebrew biblical prophecies are reserved for the Jews, dispensationalists reject *"displacement* theology," which holds that the Church supersedes the Jews and thus rightfully receives blessings originally earmarked for the Jews alone.

The coming millennial Kingdom, we need to remember, is but the delayed implementation of what had been readied for first-century *Jews* had they only accepted Jesus. Today's Rapture saints are ineligible for admission and remain a strictly "heavenly people," observing Jesus below as this *Jewish* king sits on David's *Jewish* throne in *Jewish* Jerusalem with a new *Jewish* Temple (the Fourth) nearby. Many dispensationalist Christians who are inexpert in these intricacies may routinely envision that, although raptured, *they* will help Jesus rule during the millennium; but if so, they will only be able to help from positions "heavenly," not "earthly."

The bottom-line question, then, is why would people want to experience this dismal thousand years on earth—without even the Holy Spirit, which departed with the Church at the Rapture? Because the contention that raptured saints will *not* be with Jesus is intolerable to some dispensationalists—the minority who realize this—we sometimes hear that, during the millennium, Jesus reigns only *spiritually* (i.e., long distance) *from* heaven through his saints, but this is a circumvention of dispensationalism, not its practice.

State of Israel and the Temple
If Israel's reestablishment is indispensable for the Second Coming, why, for so many centuries, were pious Christians urged to pray for Jesus' imminent return but not for return of an independent Jewish State? Further, if Jews had to accept Jesus *before* they could return to Israel (no longer "burdened by unbelief"), who waived this requirement? Where, moreover, is the expansion of Israel's borders from the Nile to the Euphrates (Gen 15:18)—is this a call to a major war well before Armageddon? And with the same concern in mind, how is the "Tribulational" Temple (the Third) to be built on the site now occupied by the eighth-century Al Aksa Mosque and the seventh-century Mosque of Omar (the Dome of the Rock, where Mohammed was said to ascend to heaven)? And why will the "Millennial" Temple (the Fourth) reactivate a Jewish sacrificial cult whose purpose was supposedly obviated by Jesus' sacrifice on Calvary[23]? Such renewed sacrifices are not *celebratory*, as dispensationalists insist, since the blueprint for the Fourth Temple, Ezekiel 40–48, explicitly states their purpose to be "making atonement" (e.g., 45:15,17f.,20).

Delayed- and Late-Rapturist Scenarios

Darby's innovation of an early Rapture has diverted tens of millions (those accepting his system) from considering how, if they had to, they might survive a Tribulation that they have been assured they will circumvent. A minority of catastrophic-millennialists—whom we have termed delayed- (i.e., *mid*-tribulationists) or late-rapturists (i.e., *post*-tribulationists)—believe that Darby is wrong and has placed his followers at unconscionable risk. Believing instead that the Rapture will not come before the Tribulation but only in its middle or at its end, they feel pressed to do the most careful preparation for the trauma that they are convinced they cannot evade.

Why Paramilitary Survivalists?

Concerning these persons, our data are skewed. This is because these elements are most noticeable to us within the ranks of antisemitic paramilitary isolationist survivalist cults (some of which may now be defunct): the Posse Comitatus; the Patriot Movement; the Covenant, Sword and Arm of the Lord; the Aryan Nation; and the National Alliance (the Alliance's *Turner Diaries* blueprinted 1995's Oklahoma City bombing). All of these accept aspects of so-called Christian Identity theology (see below), and have extremist goals that include: warding off all Federal intrusiveness into their private lives; preserving the United States as (what they contend to be) a white Christian nation; proving that "Aryans," not Jews, are the true genocidal victims; exposing the Holocaust as a hoax calculated to bring a Jewish State of Israel into being; revealing the United States as "ZOG" (Zionist Occupation Government), allegedly Israel's puppet regime; and, along these same lines, unveiling a secret international conspiracy by Jews to undermine white Christian civilization.

Delayed- or late-rapturists who are connected with paramilitary groups *may not at all resemble their counterparts on the outside* (about whom we do not know much), and it may seem puzzling to us even how they made their way into such cults to start with. Based on what has already been related, my supposition on this score goes as follows:

These persons believe that the Antichrist, bent on securing world control, will commandeer trusted agencies: international (e.g., the United Nations, the World Bank, the World Council of Churches); national (the Federal government, the Social Security Administration, the FBI and CIA, Homeland Security); and local (the press, police, municipal courts, schools), and so forth. These structures, having once contributed to a secure and stable citizenry, will now serve, instead, to jeopardize personal safety. The goal of delayed- or late-rapturists, therefore, is to remove

themselves from a society that will be controlled by these soon-to-be corrupted agencies.

In their proactive researching of techniques to evade the end-time Antichrist government, they have discovered *already extant* social bodies doing just that: isolationist paramilitary cults in private rural compounds with fallout shelters who are stockpiling food, water, energy, prescriptions and health supplies, gold, tools, and weaponry. For delayed- or late-rapturists, it is far more convenient to join these already-established enclaves than to form such communes on their own.

Lending and Blending Religious Motifs

The host militia groups, in turn, find it useful to lace their rhetoric with the tribulationist terminology of their new enrollees, which legitimizes antisocietal behavior, facilitates demonization of enemies, and rallies members' spirits. As "patriotic" white supremacists, desperate to stave off further deterioration of American hegemony, they see themselves as the Aryan Christian heritage's last defense against the *Jewish* Antichrist.

As "Seedliners," they also aver that Jesus literally meant that Jews were the seed of their "father the devil" (Jn 8:44), for Eve was seduced by the Serpent (Satan) before her sexual union with Adam, so the twins she bore had different fathers: the former union created Cain, the latter Abel. The Jews derived from Cain's later matings with non-Adamic races, making the Jews literally the spawn and pawn of Satan, as descended through Cain—with the Serpent (Satan) sometimes himself depicted as a Jewish stereotype (see Fig. 19.1). Aryans are descended through Abel.

19.1—The Seedliners' "Jewish" Serpent

The Anti-Defamation League of B'nai B'rith, with renowned expertise on such groups, elaborates on how these two "seedlines" play themselves out:

> Cain ... the product of their liaison [i.e., of Eve with the Serpent] ... was the father of the Jewish people; all Jews, therefore, are children of the devil.... The other seedline ... traces from Adam and Eve's other son, Abel, through the lost tribes to today's white European-derived believer.... Seedliners ... also believe in pre-Adamic races. That is, they contend that Adam and Eve were not the first people created by God, but were the first created in God's image. Other previous creations, not endowed with the divine likeness, were the forerunners of all the nonwhite peoples of the Earth, the "mud peoples."[24]

Adam, accordingly, was not the first man but the first *white* man, while the sub-humans arising before him were progenitors of "persons of color" (Blacks, Hispanics, and Asiatics), akin to the biblical "beasts of the field." Further, the true Israelites do not include the Jews. Rather it is the Aryan people who constitute the ten "lost tribes,"[25] and who came to America's shores after migration to western and northern Europe. The Jews, meanwhile, descended as *they* are from Cain, are demonic nonwhite[26] Israelite-imposters, and today they constitute the corporate Antichrist who already has commenced the Tribulation by unleashing the "mud peoples" currently strangling North America.

Since the Jews are but counterfeit Israelites, *no* "Old Testament" blessing is reserved for them (contrast this to dispensationalism!). Only the Aryans, as the true Israelites, are the intended and deserving recipients, the divinely empowered "Maccabees" who either will win against all odds or die in the style of Masada.[27] To avoid death, and to establish Jesus' white Christian millennial Kingdom, all depends on first destroying the Antichrist. Hitler, himself a millennialist, knew this well: his glorious 1,000-year Reich could never commence unless the Jews and their servant mud peoples were exterminated first!

This drama arising out of Eden, eternally pitting Aryan against Jew, can only be resolved by the *racial* Armageddon that is now allegedly imminent as well as inevitable—quite literally setting the forces of Light (white Aryans) against the forces of Darkness ("mud peoples" of color). Hence the need to stockpile weaponry, especially in the face of Federal gun-control initiatives that are nothing but preemptive bids by the Antichrist government to deprive white Christians of their divinely inspired Constitutional right to bear arms—and thereby to render them incapable of defending themselves against ZOG (the Zionist Occupation Government that is Washington, D.C.). This explains why some gun shows sell

copies of the *Protocols of the Learned Elders of Zion*,[28] for this secret international council of Jews is believed long ago to have seized world power via a network of camouflaged agencies that control entire governments, mold the press and public opinion, and manipulate banking and industry. It is thus held that the Jews are the Beast of Revelation, with multiple heads including any of the following: the IRS, FBI, CIA, ATF, EPA, and even the Mossad, but above all the Anti-Defamation League (alleged to be the Antichrist's foremost national watchdog).[29]

Ironically, by withdrawing from society, paramilitary groups invite the scrutiny they most seek to avoid, especially when they justify stockpiling weapons by openly predicting that the "Kingdom" can come only with violence. In tribulationist terms: if, as the persecuted elect, they refuse to accept the (666→) mark of the Antichrist, then their only alternative is to try to survive through armed self-sufficiency. For the world has fallen under primal evil, and the "Last Days" are near, so the peril of the Antichrist knocking at their door must be fiercely resisted even at the cost of death. The motivation for their survival is the prospect of rebuilding society in the originally intended purely Aryan form.

Implications for Modern Jews

The most common Jewish reaction upon learning of catastrophic-millennialist scenarios—whether pre-tribulationist (early-rapturist) or mid- or post-tribulationist (delayed- or late-rapturist)—is "Where have I been?" Other reactions include exasperation at being "the only nation on earth to have its history written in advance";[30] and depression that all major players in these scenarios have bases for despising Jews: God (because the Jews rejected and killed his son Jesus and they accepted— or themselves are—the Antichrist); Satan (because the Jews gave Jesus to the world, are God's chosen people, and refused to accept the Antichrist); the Antichrist (because Jews rejected him—especially those 144,000→ who decided to missionize for Jesus); and the nations of the world (who believe that Jews are so literally unacceptable that they must live isolated in their own land, which, nonetheless, should be obliterated). Jews, then, have no way out. Matters are aggravated when the Holocaust is trivialized as merely foreshadowing the greater torment yet in store, with Hitler—as only a prototype of the Antichrist yet to come—obscenely cast as fundamental to God's Plan.

Jews may applaud early-rapturists who love Israel as an extension of the democracy and values for which America also stands. But if this "love" is predicated, instead, on the hope that ingathering enough Jews to Israel or being able to influence Middle East politics will set into motion dispensationalism's Armageddon scenario, then how conflicting it

is for Jews to embrace those who expect them either to convert (one-third) or be killed (two-thirds) in the process culminating history as we know it. As for the one-third of Jews who do convert, by recognizing Jesus as the Christ they thereby cease to be Jews theologically—meaning that the *third* third is also lost.

In sum, then, catastrophic-millennialists appear to Jews as escapist, either vertically or horizontally. *Vertically*, they escape via "rapture," as if any effort to better the world is like rearranging the *Titanic's* deck chairs as the mighty ship is soon to go under and, more basically, a contravention of God's plan. *Horizontal* escapism, meanwhile, aptly describes those later rapturists who, withdrawing from society so as to elude the Antichrist's clutches, likewise cannot be counted on to ameliorate societal conditions; the hate and paranoia of some of these only destabilize the world further. By contrast, at the core of modern progressive Jewish messianism is the concept of "repairing the world" (*tikkun olam*)—that if we hope for a more idyllic world, *we* have to be among its creators.

The Most Valuable Ideas in This Chapter May Be

1. An unusual mechanism for coping with a deteriorating world political and social climate is the espousal that the worse things get, the better things are—that God will redress grievances of the Christian faithful only when dismay reaches the trigger point required. By this thinking, a worsening liability is transformed into a virtue.
2. Catastrophic-millennialists derive motifs crucial to their thinking from Jewish scripture and the New Testament, but their process of doing so is severely flawed.→
3. Catastrophic-millennialists appear to Jews as escapist, either vertically or horizontally: *vertical* escapism via "rapture," or *horizontal* escapism via withdrawal from society.
4. In these systems, Jews are caught in the middle, *conceived* negatively by all parties: God, Satan, the Antichrist, and the nations of the world.

What Gospel Dynamics Have We Recognized in This Chapter?

- The times producing a biblical book determine how its subject matter becomes cast.
- Yet writings that biblical authors intended solely to reflect concerns of *their* own times carry potential for being misapplied to some later day—yielding future-oriented meanings foreign to the original authors' intent.
- This is especially true when materials are ascribed to ancient worthies but framed in the (open-ended) *future* tense.

- Here it is less the Gospel writers than millennialist interpreters who practice a variant Gospel Dynamic: coalescing biblical materials from hither and yon that bear no intrinsic relation to one another, and that even individually are not understood correctly—all to construct an elaborately bizarre theological system reliant on no solid foundation whatsoever (and even seriously undermining of the New Testament's preachment itself).

Loose Ends Worth Tying

Who Is Meant by 666?

This reference is to the Emperor Nero (reigned 54–68), a suicide by a "head" (actually neck) wound. Revelation tells of the "Beast" sustaining a mortal head wound and of its "recovery" nonetheless (13:3), reflecting Christians' fear that Nero had come to life, decades later, as the persecuting Domitian (reigned 81–96)—emperor when Revelation's author wrote. By *gematria* of Hebrew transliterations, the respective numerical values for the *Greek* form, Nero*n* Caesar—and its Latin variant, Nero Caesar—are 666 and 616 (see Fig. 19.2).

19.2—Deciphering 666 (and 616) through Gematria

The *Greek* form (for Nero Caesar)—**Neron Caesar**—in Hebrew transliteration:	
Nero*n*	Caesar *(Kesar)*
nun (50) + *resh* (200) + *vav* (6) + ***nun* (50)** + *kuph* (100) + *samekh* (60) + *resh* (200) =	**666**

The *Latin* variant (for Nero Caesar)—**Nero_ Caesar**—in Hebrew transliteration:	
Nero_	Caesar *(Kesar)*
nun (50) + *resh* (200) + *vav* (6) + _____ + *kuph* (100) + *samekh* (60) + *resh* (200) =	**616**

*Note: The numerical value of Hebrew's "final nun"—present in Nero**n** but not in Nero_—is 50.*

This accounts for the differential between the two variant readings of Revelation's text (666 versus 616).

The Book of Revelation's Fundamental Flaw

In defining the Antichrist, Revelation partially relies on visions from Daniel 2 and 7, which speak in code of four empires (Babylon, Media, Persia, and Greece). But Revelation misprocesses these, instead, as Babylonia, Media-Persia, Greece, and

Rome—the last, of course, being the empire under which Jesus lived (Fig. 19.3).

19.3—How Daniel's Four Empires Were Misprocessed by Revelation

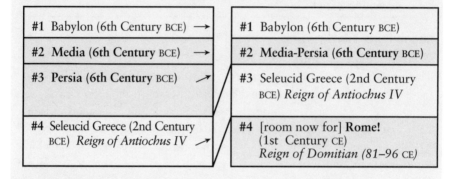

What Daniel 2 and 7 Mean	How Revelation Misprocesses Daniel
#1 Babylon (6th Century BCE) →	#1 Babylon (6th Century BCE)
#2 Media (6th Century BCE) →	#2 Media-Persia (6th Century BCE)
#3 Persia (6th Century BCE) ↗	#3 Seleucid Greece (2nd Century BCE) *Reign of Antiochus IV*
#4 Seleucid Greece (2nd Century BCE) *Reign of Antiochus IV* ↗	#4 [room now for] **Rome!** (1st Century CE) *Reign of Domitian (81–96 CE)*

Revelation purports to be about the Roman period, when Jesus lived and the author wrote. But its flawed understanding of Daniel invalidates Revelation's prescriptions for Christianity. The actual referent of the "Beast" of Revelation—on which modern millennialists base their understanding of the Antichrist—turns out to be not Nero/Domitian but Antiochus IV, villain of the Hanukkah saga, who died more than 150 years before Jesus' birth (not to mention more than 200 before Nero's reign and about 260 before the writing of Revelation itself)!

If Revelation does misunderstand Daniel, then to what seven-year period is Daniel's author referring? Not to the future tribulation predicted by dispensationalists but to a *past* seven-year period of tribulation: namely, 171–164 BCE[31] (surrounding Judah Maccabee's revolt against Antiochus IV, archtyrant of the author of Daniel's day[32]).

Who Are the 144,000 Jews?

Derived from Revelation 7:2ff. and 14:1ff. is a notion that, late during the Tribulation, 144,000 Jews from the tribes of Israel will enter special missionary service on Jesus' behalf, thereby intensifying the Antichrist's fury at *all* Jews (cf. 7:9). That Dan is missing from these contributing tribes fuels the idea that the Antichrist is from *that* tribe.[33]

Neutralizing Missionary Encroachment
Conceptual Frameworks

There will always be attempts to convince Jews to join Christian ranks. Jews who react by feeling offended should also recognize that many a Christian is simply baffled that Jews appear to forgo what they have always most wanted: salvation from the Messiah who came expressly for *them*! Were Jews to accept Jesus as the *Christian* definition of who the Messiah* was supposed to be, many Christians would not gloat but feel thrilled.

But the ordeal for Jews of losing a family member from the faith can be heartrending, with the pain intensified if proselytizers per se were involved. Christian missionaries are devising ever new ploys for luring vulnerable Jewish targets and spending hundreds of millions of dollars annually toward this end.[1] Lack of awareness by most Jews concerning the talents and tactics of these operatives only facilitates missionary advances.

Clarifying Which Christians Missionize the Jews

Most Christians have no interest in converting Jews. Some Christian theologians have even developed a "two-covenant theology"[2] holding that God, while maintaining a covenant with Christians, also sustains a separate (and antecedent) covenant with the Jews that renders efforts to convert them unwarranted. But among some of the more conservative evangelical Christians, fervor to convert Jews continues unabated— hardly surprising since, by definition, to "evangelize," meaning to bring the "good news" (of Jesus), remains integral to being an evangelical. Such persons hold that "completion" or "fulfillment" remains attainable for Jews solely through accepting Christ-Jesus and thereby ending their exclusion from God's favor. Is that not antisemitic, especially in view of the Holocaust? Not to those who contend that "failure to preach ... to the Jewish people would be a form of anti-Semitism,

depriving this ... community of its right to hear the Gospel," and that "the worst form of anti-Semitism is any sentiment that keeps a Christian from bringing the message of life to the Jewish people."[3]

Why Target Jews in Particular?

Many missionaries insist that they concentrate on Jews out of love, gratitude (for having "given" them Jesus, the apostles, the Jewish Bible), or even remorse (over centuries of persecution that Jews have endured at Christian hands). Mindful of Paul's prediction that "all Israel will be saved" (Rom 11:26), some missionaries appoint themselves agents in bringing the divine plan to fruition. But actually underlying missionaries' endeavors may instead be four theoretical conflicts of which they themselves are not aware. It is these that they seek to ease, if not resolve, by proselytizing. Each conflict is a type of cognitive dissonance, which is defined as follows in the classic (1964) sociological study, *When Prophecy Fails*, by Leon Festinger and associates[4]:

> Two ... items of knowledge ["cognition"] are *dissonant* with each other if ... they do not fit together ... or if ... one does not follow from the other.... Dissonance produces discomfort and, correspondingly, there will arise pressures to reduce ... the dissonance. *Attempts to reduce dissonance represent the observable manifestations that dissonance exists.* (Emphases added)

While the dissonance underlying Christian proselytizing of Jews is misperceived by missionaries as located within the Jews, actually it resides within those Christians' *own* faith experience.

> *Dissonance #1: The Jews originated the Messiah concept and yet have not accepted Jesus as their expected Messiah.* Logically, having given the world the Messiah concept, Jews are uniquely qualified to identify him. That Jews, instead, reject Jesus creates dissonance for some Christians, which is best eased by converting Jews.

> *Dissonance #2: The Jews have divinely inspired scriptures and yet refuse to admit that their Bible predicts Jesus' coming.* Believing that these writings embody truth, and also that Jesus was the Christ, early Christians presumed that these inspired texts were predictive of Jesus' coming. That Jews today do not understand their own scripture this way produces dissonance that can best be eased by enlightening Jews concerning the writings in which they should be the most expert.

> *Dissonance #3: Jews have survived efforts to destroy them (many presumed to be undertaken in recompense for the Jews having rejected*

Jesus) yet God has not allowed the Jews' elimination. This dissonance is reduced by concluding that God has a reason for preserving the Jews: namely, so they will remain *available* for conversion. To what end? To hasten Jesus' Second Coming (cf. dispensationalism in Chap. 19). Accordingly, converting Jews is uniquely valuable. Already during the 1980s, some pegged the "going rate" for converting but a single Jew as equal to converting 50,000 [non-Christian] Gentiles![5]

Dissonance #4: Jesus was the ultimate victor and yet Jews persist in presuming him a victim. This last type of dissonance requires more extensive explanation.

The study noted earlier, *When Prophecy Fails,* tests the thesis that, illogical as it may seem, a group's missionizing fervor may be a function of—that is, generated by—its members publicly sustaining humiliating disappointment of cherished expectations. Suppose, after taking irrevocable publicly observed actions to express confidence in the fulfillment of its prophecies, a group is confronted by undeniable evidence that its expectations had failed? Festinger and his co-authors discovered that introduction of such "disconfirmatory evidence"—creating dissonance—could result in that group's *launching overtures to convert still others* to the already discredited beliefs! Was early Christianity such an example? Festinger's study was limited to groups satisfying certain preconditions (here paraphrased):

1. Their deeply cherished expectations must be expressed through publicly observable action.

2. Such public action must be difficult to undo.

3. Expectations must be sufficiently interwoven with the external world so that events transpiring outside the group unequivocally refute the group's beliefs.

4. This "disconfirmatory" evidence must be recognized by outside persons able to deny publicly that the group's expectations had been fulfilled.

5. Now-discredited individuals within the group must be able to draw sociopsychological support from one another.

These "specify the circumstances under which increased proselyting [*sic*] would be expected to follow disconfirmation" which, paradoxically, "far from halting the movement ... gives it new life."[6]

In concentrating on movements during the sixteenth century and later, the *Prophecy* researchers discovered that often such disillusioned groups—typically lapsing into depression—soon rebounded. Reassessing what had transpired, they rationalized their alleged failures as *triumphs;* denied that their initial disappointment had been warranted;

reasserted tenaciously their former hopes; and launched missionizing endeavors to others—since "if more and more people can be persuaded that the system of belief is correct, then clearly it must ... be correct."[7]

Festinger's Failure to Apply Cognitive Dissonance to Christian Origins

I believe that, under these specifications, the early Jesus Movement should have qualified for Festinger's study:

- Jesus and his followers had indeed held deeply cherished expectations, especially that Rome's oppressive rule would be imminently replaced by a Kingdom of God.
- They undertook public actions that were difficult to undo—vocal predictions, Jesus' Temple act, and so forth.
- Jesus' crucifixion—publicly known to the external world—appeared unequivocally to refute the group's beliefs.
- This disconfirmatory evidence was recognized both by group members themselves and by outside parties (and *possibly* by Jesus himself; cf. also Fig. 8.2).
- Shaken followers drew sociopsychological support from one another.

But because "one unclarity makes the whole episode [missionizing by Jesus' followers] inconclusive with respect to our hypothesis,"[8] the Festinger group excluded early Christians from their study. Jesus had informed his followers in advance how he was soon to die, so his death *confirmed* his predictions. Accordingly, only failure to die as he had predicted would constitute disconfirmatory evidence.

Here the *Prophecy* group was deficient in scholarship, for already before 1920 many scholars had begun to claim that the "predictions" ascribed to Jesus concerning his death arose well after he died as a device (a Gospel Dynamic*) to neutralize the disconfirmatory impact of his execution (see Chap. 8). The passages that gave Festinger pause, then, not only posed no hindrance but actually and materially strengthened his thesis. If "attempts to reduce dissonance represent the observable manifestations that dissonance exists," then the predictions ascribed to Jesus reflect exactly what Festinger expected—that, rather than slinking away into oblivion, Jesus' followers, relying on word of his resurrection, launched missionary endeavors.

Here, I craft how this might be phrased within the contours of *Prophecy's* thesis: Jesus' adherents, and also observers outside them, construed his execution as *dissonant* with his preaching of God's coming Kingdom. His stunned believers lapsed into depression over his crucifixion, their cherished expectations crushed. But, unable to reconcile themselves to so ignominious an end, they reassessed their ostensible

failure in light of their treasured convictions and rallied. Driven now to rationalize Jesus' death as a triumph, they were assisted by a nurturing sense—soon conviction—that Jesus, resurrected, was with them and working for them still. Thus empowered, they shook off their depression, tenaciously reaffirmed that Jesus would yet bring the Kingdom (in a *Second* Coming), and assertively proselytized others to accept the very beliefs so recently discredited.

That the Jesus Movement could in this fashion fit the contours of *Prophecy*'s thesis does not, of course, establish that matters transpired in this fashion—only that they *could* have unfolded this way: disconfirmation strengthened early Christians' convictions and catalyzed their effort to convince others. Nor should we overlook that, while cognitive dissonance may have constituted an initiatory catalyst for missionizing, later impetus was fueled by other factors, whether joy and the impulse to share it, concern for the welfare of others who did not agree, or a sense that a delay in the Second Coming meant that missionizing had to be stepped-up. But when it comes to the *commencement* of this process, cognitive dissonance was a determinant that did match the circumstance and contours of Christianity's emergence.

Additionally, Christianity was distinctive because the cognitive dissonance that Jesus' crucifixion created was destined to recur for all time. In every successive generation, there inevitably would arise *new* "outsiders" insistent that Jesus had died a victim and that his execution had disconfirmed his credentials. Accordingly, the cyclical recurrence of such dissonance would require missionizing recurringly and perpetually—to ensure that every new generation would process Jesus' death "correctly." And, inexorably, it was the *Jews* who became seen as the greatest "disconfirmers" of all because they had generated the concept of the Messiah to begin with *and* they continued to dispute the credentials of Jesus (indeed, of Jesus in particular).

Intriguingly, Christians rather soon were able to say that Jesus did correct the world by dying, thereby making salvation available to humanity. Hence his supposed victimization was no longer dissonant but, instead, the whole point—the reason why he died, and rightly so if adherents were to rid themselves of Sin and gain immortality. There remains, then, no dissonance here. Yet every time modern Jews say that Jesus' death shows that he was not that Messiah, the dissonance returns. *So it remains the Jews above all who must be converted*!

Defusing the Proof-texting Game

Over the centuries, the second type of cognitive dissonance, highlighted here, has demanded disproportionate attention: namely, that Jews do

not recognize their own scriptures as predicting Jesus' coming. Many Christians are unaware that, for Jews, all books in today's Hebrew scriptures were complete in themselves before anyone even had projected the kind of Christ* figure that Christianity later came to propose. Jews could never imagine their Bible, standing entirely on its own, as serving any additional purpose, such as relating to Christianity. Many Jews, in turn, are themselves unaware that, by extreme contrast, some Christians view the Jewish Bible's purpose solely as a lead-up to the Gospel accounts.

A long-standing means by which some Christians demonstrate this is called "proof-texting"*—missionaries' recourse to (their interpretation of) Jewish scripture as a tactic to persuade Jews to accept Jesus. Many of those Jews who have converted to Christianity pinpoint proof-texting as having been *the* determining factor. Understandably, Jewish educators are anxious to teach Jews how to counter such an approach but, unfortunately, rely on an entirely unrealistic directive: "Master your Bible so you will know what to say." It is ill-advised to expect Jews to rattle off something like, "You missionaries mistranslate *verse A's* original Hebrew, or translate it literally instead of idiomatically; you twist *verse B* out of context; *verse C* was never fulfilled by Jesus; your use of *verse D* is arbitrary because *verse E* conveys the exact opposite meaning," and so on.

Besides the sheer impracticality of such counter-preparation, the false underlying premise is that missionaries are actually interested in hearing Jewish responses. They want conversion, not conversation, so any text sufficiently well mastered by Jews would be readily abandoned by missionaries in favor of another that Jews could not handle. Further, for Jews to spend their time learning these details only validates the missionaries' approach when what is called for is, instead, delegitimizing it.

The knowledge that Jews need involves not that about passages but, rather, mastery of *broad conceptual principles* that will invalidate proof-texting as unworthy of thinking persons, thereby calling its practitioners into intellectual disrepute. And even if Jews cannot manage to do this in the public arena, all that is called for is their ability to do this for their own satisfaction, thereby making themselves, including children, immune to missionary encroachment.

Reframing the Problem

When we look through a camera's viewfinder, if what we see is not satisfying we can make adjustments. Similarly, Jews are certainly able to reframe the proof-texting game so as to render missionaries reluctant to continue applying it.

The "Bull's-Eye" Approach

A farmer once arrayed his barn wall with bull's-eyes, with an arrow piercing the center of each. But appearances differed from reality: he had shot the arrows first and only thereafter painted a bull's-eye around each! The end result looked the same but not to someone who knew the underlying process. The Jews' task is to reveal that, often, so-called predictions from Jewish scripture are "arrows shot first," with Jesus' Gospel image a bull's-eye made to surround each one. This is a classic Gospel Dynamic (see Chap. 8; cf. 7).

Consider the bizarre lengths to which Jewish tradition has gone—out of expediency—to redefine Isaiah 53's "Suffering Servant" not as an individual but as the *collective*, "Israel." The undeniable aim has been to upstage missionary successes in identifying the Servant with (the *individual*) Jesus. The approach that Jews should have taken is that, even if the Servant meant an individual (e.g., the job description of a prophet), Jesus was modeled on the Servant, not the Servant predictive of Jesus.[9] Jesus as a sufferer was the bull's-eye that was conformed to Isaiah's text, the arrow. This is hardly to deny that Jesus suffered, but only to affirm that precisely *because* it was known that Jesus suffered recourse was had to Isaiah 53—so as to elicit from it those motifs to which the Jesus portrait could be confidently conformed. (This Dynamic is widely recognized by many Christian scholars as well.) Although missionaries are themselves unaware of this Dynamic, a large percentage of the proof-texts they select seem to point to Jesus only because Jesus was conformed to these to begin with!

The "Circumvention" Approach

All branches of modern Judaism issue less from the Hebrew Bible than from *rabbinic* interpretation of those scriptures. Today's fundamentalist Christianity, by contrast, is *biblically* based. Accordingly, when Jews give deference to proof-texting—by offering alternative explanations of Jewish scriptural texts—they are *validating* missionary contentions that biblical passages should be primary for Jewish processing of Jesus today. Therefore, Jews should *say* that, because for Jews it is the rabbis (including those today) who define what the (Jewish) Bible means, Jews are simply unmoved by, and must wholly *circumvent*, Bible proof-texting concerning Jesus as even meaningful, let alone authoritative.

The "Bibliolatry" Approach

A common denominator of Jewish biblical books is an uncompromising denunciation of idolatry. It is not commonly realized that unquestioning literalist adherence to biblical passages is a kind of idolatry called

"bibliolatry"—worship of the Bible as God, or in lieu of God (see next chapter). With reference to missionaries, it should be starkly stated that even if the Jewish Bible undeniably did identify any individual as the Messiah, modern Jews need feel no compulsion to accept that person anyway—no more so in the case of Jesus than in that of Cyrus of Persia (Isaiah 41:2f.; 44:28; 45:1f.; cf. Ezra 6:3ff.)—for in connection with neither was the world brought into conformity with the Jewish conception of the messianic age. Here, modern Jews should merely conclude that the biblical identification was *wrong*, a premise wholly destabilizing to the missionary's tactics.

The "Configurations" Approach

Jews should first establish that the "Jesus" figure whom missionaries are preaching essentially conforms to that of Configuration B, or Pauline, Christianity (review Fig. 4.2), which spawned a kind of Messiah* that Jews reject. Missionaries may refer to him in the Aramaic as "Yeshua."→ But—

- if he conforms to the incarnate supernatural dying and rising Savior-deity, Second Person of the Trinity, bringing immortality to individuals who "believe in him," and
- if adherents, presuming themselves trapped in Sin, believe they will benefit vicariously from his death and resurrection and from the sacraments that reenact those pivotal events—

then this is not the Jewish Messiah. How can someone discuss whether proof-texts from the Jewish Bible establish that Jesus is the Jewish Messiah *if there is no initial agreement on how the "Messiah" is defined*? If Jews tenaciously stand by their position, debating proof-texts will never begin.

The "Answer Sheets" Approach

What religious school educators should do, instead of focusing on passages, is to construct two sets of brief answers designed especially for *young* learners—that is, easy-to-recall potential responses, one set framed to address assertive missionaries (whom Jewish youngsters should know how to answer) and another set to share with curious Christian friends (upon whose sensibilities Jewish youngsters should be careful never to trespass).

Given that missionaries are the focus of our current chapter, what follows is a set of answers that could be developed with missionaries in mind. These answers are intended not as definitive but as illustrative of what educators could be doing as classroom projects.

Close Encounters of the Religious Kind: Brief Answers for Complex Questions[10]

This sample listing, suitable for religious school discussion, attempts to explain Jewish positions in a way that respects the views of missionaries—within the framework that reasonable people may, and often do, differ on the great themes of religion, and accepting that candor is an indispensable tool in that effort.

Christian Theology

1. *Why will you Jews not accept Jesus as the Messiah?* "Messiah" (from Hebrew) is a *Jewish* concept that, today, has come to mean God's agent who brings an end to war, famine, disease, discrimination, and suffering. Since these ills still afflict our society, Jews cannot accept *any* historical figure (including Jesus) as the Messiah. That "Christ" (Greek for "Messiah") is supposed to forgive sins or bring salvation is a *Christian*, not Jewish, idea—and it is one that *redefines* the Messiah's agenda away from what Jews intended when they originated this concept.

2. *Is not Jesus predicted in your (Jewish) Bible?* No. We would need to see his name. As for motifs that you may claim point to Jesus, Gospel writers likely conformed Jesus' image expressly to match these motifs, so your citing them would be circular reasoning. [Cf. the "'Bull's-Eye' Approach," above.] Moreover, we are not dependent solely on ancient texts but also on later revised interpretations and understandings that constantly renew our religion and keep it up to date.

3. *So who do you Jews think Jesus was?* A charismatic Jew who felt a mission to declare that God was bringing the messianic age (the "Kingdom of God") *soon*, and taught this idea. But he was mistaken.

4. *You Jews will go to hell for your sins!* Jews do not believe in a God who would use "hell" as an incentive to make them moral. Jews are moral *because that is the proper way to live.* Unlike "fear," this is a fine incentive. (Possible addition: Further, we also deny hell altogether as barbaric and contradictory to the nature of God.)

5. *Did not Jesus die for your sins?* Jews believe that people are responsible for their own actions—and so they must themselves repent to gain forgiveness. No one can accomplish this *for* them. God will accept even imperfect repentance. Any idea that people are so sinful that God personally must die for them is not Jewish. We don't hold that we've all inherited some original Sin and need to offer satisfaction for it, so none of this is of any interest to us.

Christian Holy Days

Christmas: Why won't you observe Christmas? It celebrates the Messiah's birth. Since Jews do not acknowledge that the Messiah has come, they lack a reason to celebrate it but may nonetheless appreciate the beauty of the Christmas season.

Easter: Doesn't the empty tomb prove that Jesus was resurrected? Judaism (which created the Messiah idea) professes no necessary correlation between being the Messiah and being resurrected. As for the empty tomb story, this was not the basis of early Christian belief in Jesus' resurrection but rather a deduction from reported sightings of him—meaning that wherever he had been buried thereby was left *vacated*. Moreover, evidently no empty tomb story was even written before the Gospel of Mark (ca. 72 CE [AD]), forty years after Jesus died.

Good Friday: Why did you Jews kill Jesus?
- Jews of today were not present at Jesus' death, nor were most of the 70 percent of Jews who lived outside the land of Israel in Jesus' time, nor most Jews in the land of Israel who did not know him either. Of the relatively few who *might* have seen him die, some also never knew him personally let alone bore any connection to his execution.
- Since crucifixion was a *Roman* execution method, why say that "the Jews" killed Jesus? Stating Jesus' "crime," the placard on his cross read "The King of the Jews," which was framed from *Rome's* perspective (Jews would say "our King" or "King of Israel"). This shows who was genuinely responsible.
- The issue of "blame" for Jesus' death first arose in the 60s, as Christians became increasingly fearful of Rome. This made it advantageous for Christians to protect themselves by shifting blame for Jesus' death away from Rome and onto the Jews (*rebels* against Rome). Thereby Rome and Christians would seem allied, with the Jews thought their common enemy. Thus did *a Jew put to death by Rome* become *a "Christian" put to death by Jews*.

Answering "Jewish" Messianics

Why not become an authentic Jew by accepting Jesus? Accepting Jesus makes a person not a "fulfilled" or "completed" Jew but a *Christian*. Judaism was good enough for Jesus, so it is likewise good enough for Jews today![11]

Praying for/Preying on the Jews: Coping with Jewish Messianics

The brand of missionaries last mentioned, Jews-for-Jesus and Messianic Jews, warrant special attention, especially because Jews' many confusions

about them need to be resolved. A large proportion—sometimes a majority—of messianics belonging to these groups are *Christians* who profess to have become Jews. Well-meaning members of these groups, genuinely unable to fathom the hostility directed at them by the Jewish community, resolve this cognitive dissonance as follows: "We are doing such good. Why are we so despised? This makes us like Jesus' original followers! How affirming!" Jews should distinguish between, on the one hand, the behind-the-scenes organizational apparatus that created and funds these movements, and, on the other hand, most of their rank-and-file members, who lack any vantage point from which to survey how their modern movements actually arose.

While Jews generally use the names "Jews for Jesus" and "Messianic Jews" interchangeably, it was once wrong to do so (and may still be):

- Jews for Jesus originally gave the impression of being quasi-cultic, highly aggressive, even invasive in targeting primarily *individual* Jews, with the intent of severing them not only from Judaism but also from their families of origin, and ultimately steering them toward association with evangelical Protestantism (of which Jews for Jesus considered themselves an arm). They thus appeared to pose greater danger for the welfare of individual Jews than for the Jews as a people.

- Messianic Jews appeared to pose greater danger for the welfare of the Jewish *people* by creating a copy-cat Judaism: organizing themselves congregationally; often counting their membership by family units; establishing religious schools, day-care facilities, and "counseling centers"; buying burial plots adjacent to Jewish cemeteries; seeking their own seminary; encouraging members to embrace Judaism, albeit clearly of the messianic type; presenting themselves as the ideal solution for intermarried couples and blended families who are experiencing religious problems; and essentially seeking recognition as a fifth denomination of Judaism (beside Orthodoxy, Conservative Judaism, Reform Judaism, and Reconstructionism), often by securing a listing in the Yellow Pages under "Synagogues" (rather than "Synagogues–Messianic").

These differences continue to manifest themselves, but such former distinctions have become somewhat blurred by members of these groups who themselves use the two terms ("Jews for Jesus" and "Messianic Jews") interchangeably.

Conceptual Perspectives
Philosophically, these elements misrepresent themselves as modern-day counterparts of first-century Jewish-Christian followers of Jesus who, as

it were, went underground for almost two millennia only to resurface recently as today's Jewish messianics! This is sophistry.

Theologically, these are Configuration B Christians, not A—a distinction lost on them (review Fig. 4.2). In documentation defining themselves for Christian donors, Jews for Jesus have termed themselves "evangelical fundamentalists" who "believe in affiliation with a local church" and "in the Triune God and the deity of the Lord Jesus Christ, the only begotten Son of God,"[12] even as Messianic Jews have affirmed their belief that "the nature of God is plural, consisting of the Father, Son, and the Holy Spirit, [and] that no man can obtain salvation or eternal reconciliation with God unless they [sic] repent of their sins and accept by faith the atoning work of the Blood of the Messiah Yeshua (Jesus) and believe that He died and was resurrected in triumph over sin to sit at the right hand of God forevermore...."[13] Obviously, these descriptions are not the religion *of* Jesus but the later religion *about* him, so it is absurd to present this "Yeshua" as the *Jewish* Messiah.

Ritually, these messianics are, in a minor way, "Judaizers"* of sorts (i.e., objectionable to Pauline Christianity—the issues with Paul, however, were of greater gravity: circumcision and the dietary laws). However, they actually become further *removed* from the historical Jesus by their ostensible devotion to Jewish holidays, liturgy, artifacts, and motifs whose modern manifestations originated only after Jesus died and were created by leadership of a *rabbinic* Judaism that, on arising post-70 CE, rejected Christianity. *How, then, are such manners of observance—unknown to Jesus and created by Jewish leaders who rejected Christians—supposed to make someone a more authentic Jew?*

Sociologically, it is specious to reason that, throughout history, there have always been rivulets of Jews who accept Jesus, and that today's messianics simply perpetuate these,[14] when the outside monies they now attract started burgeoning only suddenly in the 1970s, as the turn of the millennium neared, with its recurring hope for the Second Coming and even the end of the world (see previous chapter). When in previous history have rivulets of Jewish messianics received such largesse? These breeds of what used to be called Hebrew-Christians *originated* solely as a modern artifice of evangelical missionary organizations whose proselytizing efforts with Jews had always been relative failures until this new subterfuge ("You can accept Jesus and remain Jewish") was introduced. Today the mask is coming off: publications disseminated by Christian missionary groups increasingly are admitting that messianics are *their* offshoots, not derivatives from past Jewish-Christians.

Accordingly, *Jews* today who join these messianic groups are "probably the only people in the world who take on the beliefs of another religion yet deny that they have converted to that religion"! Meanwhile, *Christians* who join these groups, believing that they are going back to the original religion of, and as practiced by, Jesus, find that their theology is identical to what they had been practicing all along. Initiates may be sincere, yet "it is quite possible to be both sincere and deceitful ... [because] Jews who ... believe in Jesus as their ... Savior ... do not acknowledge that they have become Christians" and because Christians who profess to accept Judaism fail to acknowledge that, to do so, they must forgo belief in Jesus' divinity.[15]

The Most Valuable Ideas in This Chapter May Be

1. Many missionaries are not aware that fueling their activity are four types of cognitive dissonance.
2. If this were pointed out to them, they would likely perceive such dissonance as located within the Jews, when actually it resides within those Christians' *own* faith experience.
3. The claim of Jewish messianics to perpetuate Jesus' initial followers is best addressed by establishing the messianists' theology as Configuration B Christianity, which eventually branded the Christianity of Jesus' actual early followers (Configuration A) *heretical*.
4. The best index as to what these messianics believe is their self-descriptions in materials that they earmark for *Christian donors* who are supportive of their proselytizing enterprise. (Some messianics have a separate set of literature designed for Jews.)

Loose Ends Worth Tying

Five Workable Ground Rules

It is possible for those Jews and evangelicals who wish to improve relations to reach an accommodation on missionizing through five ground rules that I have proposed and that, in some settings, I have found to meet with joint approval:

1. Jews must grant that evangelicals feel it a core constituent of their faith to share with others the "good news" of Jesus.

2. Evangelical proselytism should give the impression of an equal concern to convert *all* non-Christians, not to convert Jews preeminently.

3. Once a Jew is solicited and says, "No, thank you," no missionary of that sect may again approach that Jew.

4. Even more desirable: if missionaries believe that it is God's will that Jews convert (see the previous chapter), then let them consider leaving the matter to God, and themselves bow out of the missionizing enterprise.

5. Subject to the above, Jews will reciprocate by entering into dialogue.

Is Messianics' Use of the Name "Yeshua" Legitimate?

The English name Joshua translates the Hebrew *Yehoshua*, or a later Hebrew/Aramaic form thereof, *Yeshua*—names fairly common in the first century CE. Yehoshua can mean "the Lord is salvation" or "the Lord will save/saves/has saved." The English form, Jesus, goes back to the Latin (*Iesus*), which in turn transliterates the Greek form (*Iesous*) of these Hebrew or Aramaic names. As for what Hebrew/Aramaic name(s) Jesus actually used, this cannot be definitely determined because our earliest (i.e., extant) sources mentioning him were composed in Greek.

Advice Validated by Experience

- No Jewish family should assume that any of its members is immune from enticement by these missionary groups.
- If ever a family member is lost to these groups, processing this loss in terms of "death" or even as "fault" or "guilt" usually is not helpful and can worsen matters.
- Jewish families should *not* sever relations with members who have joined these groups because improvement, even repair, of relations may still be possible, and even outright reversals by those who have thus left Judaism have been known to occur given sufficient time and patience.[16]

Part Seven

Integrating Matters

My Personal Positions
Where They May Be Distinctive

There is disagreement within New Testament scholarship on virtually every subject mentioned in this book. So that readers may better gauge why I reach my particular conclusions, I summarize here some of those ideas that have most animated my thinking in the preceding chapters of this volume.

On Engaging Sacred Texts
The Problem of Bibliolatry

Some sectors of the religious world have been accused (by other sectors) of "bibliolatry," that is, valuing their Bible itself so highly that they are almost guilty of idolatry. Paving the way for such bibliolatry is the assumption that, in the quest for truth, nothing remains incumbent upon *moderns* to perform other than to accept what we are told was fully accomplished already in the distant past. This mentality is captured by the simplistic slogan: "Jesus said it. I believe it. That settles it!" (or with some other name, such as Moses, substituted). Why, then, as Galileo asked, would we be endowed "with sense, reason, and intellect" if we were only "intended ... to forgo their use"?[1]

Further, history amply demonstrates that literal and undeviating adherence to sacred texts can fuel the passions that intensify and elongate wars, and that religious writings at war with one another can draw also their respective loyalists to war with one another. In this regard, given the religious conflicts we've seen so far, the young twenty-first century could already aptly be dubbed "the Age of Rage." The suspension of critical faculties in evaluating sacred texts undermines the potential of religion to advance civilization and to improve life. To *engage* sacred texts, then, I consider to be a

religious duty; to be *mastered by* them a forfeiture of religious responsibility.

The Problem of Trespassing

Does a volume entitled *Modern Jews Engage the New Testament* constitute trespassing beyond proper boundaries, since—in this case—it
brings along Jews willing to venture into another faith's hallowed domain? No, not if the sacred texts that are being newly explored have
themselves intruded into the Jews' own preserve by becoming *the*
prime external determinant of all of Jewish history. Jews might have
no inducement to explore the New Testament's terrain if these writings
had not irreversibly dislodged Jewish life from any of the courses that
Jews would have wished to set for themselves. Moreover, when a
younger religion co-opts the scriptures of its elder and interprets them
to the elder's detriment, the new writings that do this—later themselves canonized as sacred—at the least stand open to examination and
scrutiny.

There is the additional element that, to varying degrees among New
Testament writers, Christians are claiming to explain to Jews what the
Jews' own Bible means and even to *be* the "Jews" who the Jews themselves failed to become. Accordingly, for Jews, now on a most delayed
basis, to decide to take a deeper look at the Dynamics underlying those
texts that set forth this posture would seem a fair as well as permissible
action. Further, the Jewish people, in their effort to comprehend their
own history, need access to the New Testament because it has *directed*
so much of it.

The Problem of Timing

But why, at the current juncture, should Jews be encouraged to reflect
on Gospel Dynamics given that there has been such steady progress in
Christian–Jewish relations over recent decades? First, I interpret this
new pursuit as extending that progress. Second, I foresee a possibility
for the resurgence of regressive tendencies in Gospel interpretation—indeed, has it begun?—at the least because Christianity's future history
will be played out largely, even primarily, in the Third World.[2] It may
be questioned whether this vast arena will exhibit the capacity to comprehend the Gospels in any fashion other than literally (even if a denomination's official pronouncements prohibit anti-Jewish application
of New Testament texts). But the overriding matter, idiosyncratic
to Jews themselves, is that today is literally the first period in history
when sufficient numbers of the Jewish laity (not just their theologians,
clergy, and academicians) are psychologically primed to end their

nearly two-millennia-old avoidance strategies respecting the New Testament (see Chap. 23). We must not lose the opportunity to capitalize on this unprecedented momentum.

The Problem of Consistency

Christian readers, especially, may ask whether I personally analyze *Jewish* sacred texts (Hebrew scripture and rabbinic literature) from vantage points similar to what I bring to bear on the New Testament in this volume. Unequivocally yes. (Reflecting the influence of *all* the foregoing ideas are, especially, sections of Chaps. 1, 7–8, 11–12, 20, and 23.)

On Selected Problems of History

Galilee in Jesus' Day

Decades ago it was fashionable to compartmentalize from one another the "Hellenistic" Diaspora and the "Hebraic" land of Israel.* Then a trend toward homogenization set in as archaeological finds, particularly in Galilee, revealed varying degrees of Hellenistic impact reflected by architecture, iconography, epitaphs, and even religious conceptualization. With respect to the historical Jesus, many scholars then began a pendulum shift, some going so far as to propose that Jesus' Galilee was as thoroughly penetrated by Hellenistic culture as other parts of the Greco-Roman world; and a relative few wondering whether even Jesus himself was as Greek as he was Hebraic, if not more so.[3]

Readers will not find such a view reflected in this volume because I find this approach overdrawn. Not all data uncovered apply as early as Jesus' time. Penetrations of Hellenization, moreover, varied, with various Jews responding variously.[4] The preponderant influence that molded Jesus' message remains, in my view, natively Jewish. Moreover, in weighting factors, we must differentiate those relatively superficial in importance from those more substantive. My own weighting of such chronological, geographical, sociological, and cultural material finds no sufficient warrant to de-Judaize Jesus.[5] (Reflecting the influence of these ideas are, especially, sections of Chaps. 2 [end] and 5.)

Reconstructing the Historical Paul

Paul himself (in his genuine Epistles) and Luke (in Acts chaps. 8–28) present fundamentally contradictory portraits of who Paul was—biographically, geographically, and philosophically. I find these disparities so consequential as to *require* us to decide which writer, if either, deserves our credence, and certainly *not to steer a mediating position* that accepts as much as possible from both. Yet the latter approach is what I see commonly pursued.

I feel the wise procedure in assessing what Acts conveys about Paul is to ascertain, first, whether Luke manifests some overall outlook, or agenda, that may determine what details about Paul he provides and how he casts or molds them. In insisting that a macrocosmic view of Luke-Acts must precede a microcosmic examination of its details, I am struck by the odd failure of Acts to mention the legacy of the letters that Paul left—his own repositories of autobiographical data, not to mention of his thinking.[6]

I consider Luke's omission here deliberate. It is not that he is un-aware of Paul's letters. Rather, he is so acutely aware of them that he wants to suppress them, in favor of Luke's own portrait of Paul as a proto-rabbinic Jew brought up in Jerusalem instead of as a Greek Jew brought up in the Diaspora. To the degree, then, that scholars draw upon Acts to report on Paul, I believe that they may be perpetuating *Luke's* image of Paul, not that of the genuine figure, and thereby are *distancing* us from the real Paul rather than bringing us closer to him. This is why, in this volume, I rarely appeal to Luke's writings for accu-racy of information not only on Paul but also on Jesus and the early Church. Often, by contrast, I do rely on what Paul himself conveys in his genuine Epistles (review Fig. 3.4), qualified by my recognition of *his* self-interests.

The New Testament's positioning of Acts *before* Paul's Epistles only magnifies misunderstandings because we then become prone to process Paul's letters in light of what we have just read about him in Acts. This is one of the many "dis-orders" we addressed in Chapter 3: how this se-quencing diminishes our capacity to see Paul as he was rather than as *Luke* wanted us to see him.

I lay out in this volume ample indications that Luke has used Paul's letters for information concerning Paul (e.g., his "conversion") that Luke then altered, even contradicted, to suit his own editorial pur-poses. This raises the intriguing possibility that Luke also drew up the itineraries of Paul's travels from clues that Luke gathered from Paul's Epistles themselves. If so, then it would be circular on our part to rely—as most scholars do—on the grid that Luke furnishes. (Reflect-ing the influence of these ideas are, especially, sections of Chaps. 6–7, 14, and 17.)

Early Church History

I likewise rely on Acts far less than most scholars do for understand-ing the broad development of early Church history because I feel that Luke's governing principles *conceal* history rather than *reveal* it. I identify Luke's governing principles as these: that Christianity is not a

rift from Judaism but flows from and extends Judaism's core; that Jesus, his followers, and Paul must be understood as undeviatingly loyal to that core (even to the point that Paul himself abides by the Law of Moses!); that, accordingly, Luke also wants us to believe that "myriads" of Jews flocked to early Christian ranks; that only some kind of malfeasance among Jews themselves *eventually* caused their diminished participation in Christianity; that Christian ranks thus only *gradually* built and then tilted toward a Gentile majority; that an active role by "God-fearers" facilitated this transition (while "God-fearers" really existed, for Luke they function as a literary device); that, ultimately, the Christian mission had to become directed *solely* to Gentiles; and that Jews, by coming to reject Christianity, *orphaned* themselves, sociologically as well as spiritually, from inheriting their own due legacy.

Scholars who do not agree that these are Luke's guiding principles, or who do agree but do not believe how pervasively these principles determine the history that Luke relates, will likely accept far more of what Luke says about early Church history than do I. Paul's Epistles, in my view, afford us a more correct impression of a Christianity whose ranks became Gentile far earlier and more numerously than Acts will admit— because Luke's *theology* requires him to present the onset and growth of a Gentile-dominated Christianity on *as delayed a basis as possible*. (Reflecting the influence of these ideas are, especially, sections of Chaps. 4, 6–7, and 14–18.)

On Selected Matters of Gospel Study

Gospels Written by Jews for Jews?

In point of fact, we cannot establish with certainty the identity, locale, or extraction of a single Gospel writer, although in this volume I myself make *suggestions* along such lines. I do not comfortably resonate, then, with the common refrain that the Gospels (and Acts) were "of course" written *by Jews for Jews*. Other premises that are also too rarely scrutinized are that each Gospel reflects the writing of but a single author and achieved full completion over a relatively concentrated time frame. I side with those scholars who hold that the editorial processes involved were more complex—especially in the cases of Matthew and John—in terms both of the number of participants involved and the time required before completion. Certainly any additional hands, including one or more early compilers or late editors, would materially complicate efforts to identify whether the extraction of contributors was Jewish or Gentile, and to determine the demographics of the communities for whom they wrote.

More consideration than the usual should also be given to whether Christian communities may have preserved, from early on, treasured layers of favored traditions that, as a matter of course, *had* to be accepted by a later Gospel writer even if he was not personally enamored of them. This raises the distinct possibility that we could assess a given Evangelist on the basis of materials that he *preserves* but that may not actually *typify* him. In this volume, my approach is thus to begin by trying to grasp the overall impression and message imparted by a Gospel in its completed form, and only thereafter to examine, in that light, individual traditions that the Gospel preserves and conveys. (Reflecting the influence of these ideas are, especially, sections of Chaps. 2, 3, and 15–18.)

Sources versus Improvisation?

I believe that I am more disposed than are most scholars to ascribe some Gospel contents to the Evangelists' own creativity and improvisation rather than necessarily to sources that we do not possess. I do agree, however, that there must have existed, orally and in writing, mixtures of materials that scholars call "M" (matter accessible only to Matthew) and "L" (matter accessible only to Luke), and I am also open to ascribing to "Q" (*Quelle*, German for "source") traditions that are shared by Matthew and Luke but not by Mark (here review Figs. 3.6 through 3.10). Yet, in many such specific instances, I still appeal to "Q" less confidently, and certainly less automatically, than do most others. In particular, I look for places where Luke appears aware of how Matthew altered Mark, and had first to deduce *why* Matthew had done so and thereafter to weigh whether or not Luke himself should follow Matthew's lead (see commentary on Fig. 10.3; also 3.5). Meanwhile, efforts to divide "Q," a hypothesized document to begin with, into chronological strata that are likewise hypothetical go well beyond what I feel is justifiable.

Nonetheless, running counter to my wariness of presupposed sources, I fully endorse the theory that Mark inherited a rudimentary Passion narrative that he expanded. John, too, may have known it, although I believe it is more likely that he knew Mark's expanded Passion instead (e.g., both Evangelists intersperse Peter's denial of Jesus with the high priest's interrogation of Jesus, a placement that I am convinced Mark personally *introduced*). As for John's knowing other sections of the Synoptics (i.e., those preceding the Passion), because of the long time-lapse between the compositions of Mark (ca. 72) and John (ca. 100) I believe, more so than do many, that John *must* have been familiar with many Synoptic traditions—or at least with Marcan traditions in particular.

That the Fourth Gospel departs from the Synoptics does not necessarily mean that its editors were unaware of them (here scholarship has fluctuated[7]). The Gospel of John is generally understood to have a quite different orientation—which is why it is not "syn-optic" with the other three—quite possibly because its readership was more sophisticated and interested in more general questions, perhaps also with a view to offering an alternative to popular Gnostic sects (see Chap. 4).

I express my view of who Jesus was (an apocalyptic Pharisee) in the course of Chapters 2, 3, 5, and 11. Concerning the various scholarly "criteria" for isolating statements authentic to Jesus, I give them due regard in theory but, in practical application to specific texts, I usually find reasons to dispute their pertinence or persuasiveness. (Reflecting the influence of these ideas are sections of Chaps. 2–3, 5–13, and 15–20.)

Why I Emphasize Mark

In this volume, I accord Mark seemingly disproportionate attention because his Gospel is the most impactful on *Jewish* history. Mark's editorial techniques are those that most altered earlier Christian traditions in an anti-Jewish direction, and that bequeathed to Matthew and Luke the opportunity to embellish Mark *anti-Jewishly* as Mark himself so embellished his own sources.

In an earlier book[8] I tried to show that Mark set the pattern for how Jewish leadership groups came to punctuate the entire Synoptic tradition—the "chief priests, scribes, and elders," "Pharisees and Herodians," and "Sadducees"—and that Mark's artistry and *errors* shaped misconceptions that I believe still govern much of scholarship today. In this volume, by contrast, I emphasize Mark's literary technique of introducing new materials into contexts where they do not now rest comfortably. Figure 21.1 summarizes four important examples that we have already detailed.

Along with many other scholars—although not most—I recognize and see as significant Mark's relentless disparagement of Jesus' disciples, but I account for this bias differently than do others (see Chap. 15→). (Reflecting the influence of these ideas are, especially, sections of Chaps. 10–12, 15–16.)

21.1—Marcan Insertions That Impacted Jewish History

What Mark Does →	Why Mark Does It →	What Results →	*Reversing* the Process
Mark inserts a **"blasphemy"** unit (2:5b–10) into the healing of the paralytic	to prepare readers for "blasphemy" as Jesus' Sanhedrin verdict (Fig. 12.9).	His insertion destroys the logic of the paralytic story (Fig. 12.10).	No sooner do we subtract this unit than a cohesive story resurfaces (see Chap. 12).
Mark inserts a **"Passover"** unit (14:12–16) before the Last Supper	to alter an ordinary meal into a Passover observance.	His insertion (Fig. 10.2) creates up to five glaring incongruities.	No sooner do we subtract this unit than the incongruities vanish and a consistent storyline reappears (Chap. 10).
Mark inserts a **"Sanhedrin"** unit (that developed in layers) between 14:53 and 15:1 (Fig. 12.3) so	a "consultation" (15:1) becomes a trial, *Jewish* (not Roman) officials are blamed for Jesus' conviction, and "blasphemy" displaces sedition as the charge against him.	The layered elements are artificial and not cohesive (Fig. 12.2), and Mark's editing creates a factual error (in 15:1).	No sooner do we subtract this unit than the error vanishes and a cohesive storyline reappears (Chap. 12).
Mark inserts a **"Barabbas"** unit—with its prisoner release—between 15:5 and 15:15b	(among other reasons) to defuse the charge that Jesus was a seditionist ("The King of the Jews").	His insertion makes arresting the popular Jesus seem illogical (cf. Jesus' greeting on Palm Sunday).	No sooner do we subtract this unit than the illogic vanishes and a consistent storyline resumes (Chap. 12).

On Fashionable Contemporary Trends of Interpretation

Each of the following trends, in the post-Holocaust era, has had the not-incidental (and not coincidental) effect of aiding Jews and Christians to relate more comfortably to one another. While the trends are welcome, it does not mean that they help rather than hinder correct Gospel analysis.

In-House Squabbling?

I question the view commonly advanced that the severe anti-Jewish rhetoric in the Gospels is necessarily "intra-family squabbling"—that is, by Jewish-Christians against recalcitrant *fellow* Jews "across the street." Today, many Jews as well as Christians like this notion because it mitigates as only *apparent* the anti-Judaism in the Gospels, for how can "in-house" fighting be anti-Jewish if all contending parties themselves are Jewish? Consistent with my earlier-stated position—that the Gospels' final editors were not necessarily Jews—I am wary of any advance blanket labeling of controversy texts as "intra-family squabbling" (especially in the case of parables allegorized anti-Jewishly by Matthew and Luke). Further, what if an early stratum of tradition originated as in-house fighting but then became enlisted by a work's finalizer to criticize Jews from an *outsider's* standpoint—how, then, is the actual Gospel text to be any longer deemed in-house at all?

I do support the view that it is often *establishments* that produce divisiveness—that the rabbis as well as the Gospel editors sought to harden boundaries between Jews and Christians when relative co-existence might otherwise have maintained itself (or apparently did maintain itself anyway).[9] Yet in this book I am not myself addressing the degree and manners in which "rank-and-file Jews and Christians" continued comfortably to interact in the early centuries but, rather, what attitudes various New Testament writers—particularly the final editors of each Gospel—intended to bring to bear and that had the effect, if not also the intention, of hardening boundaries. (Reflecting the influence of these ideas are, especially, sections of Chaps. 7, 11–12, 15–18, and 22.)

Sibling Faiths?

Also more commonly heard in recent years has been the casting of rabbinic Judaism and early Christianity as "sibling faiths" that emerged from a common stream of development before undertaking diverse routes. (This counters the conventional metaphor of Judaism as the parent and Christianity its offspring.) It is difficult to assess this metaphor because it is not defined precisely or applied consistently by all of its proponents. What, for example, constitutes the Jewish sibling: pre-70 Pharisaism or post-70 yet still inchoate rabbinic Judaism—and were

these two the same? Also, was Pharisaism in the Diaspora essentially equivalent to that in the land of Israel?

Even more elusive: which "Configuration" of early Christianity is here advanced? Usually it appears to be Configuration A (review Fig. 4.2), but this Configuration was rather quickly rendered passé, in the Diaspora, by Configuration B Christianity, whose Greek components attracted more Gentiles who, in turn, came to dominate Christian ranks certainly by the late first century. Since there is no smooth development of Configuration A into Configuration B, we are left without any clear identity as to which is being proposed as the Christian sibling.

Participants in dialogue often infer the sibling metaphor to mean that the Judaism and Christianity of *today* sprang from the same parentage. Biologically speaking, genuine siblings must derive from an identical gene pool no matter how much the offspring may differ in appearance or how far, in due course, they come to diverge from one another. If Configuration A Christianity did not survive, then *it* is not the basis of modern Christianity. If for that basis we must turn to Configuration B Christianity, then from where did it derive its "genes" for a deific being who becomes "incarnate," who thereafter dies and rises, and with whom adherents acquire vicarious identification so as to be cleansed from Sin and to achieve salvation—a process whereby they rise up in consciousness of their own immortal being? Are we to believe that *these* components of Configuration B Christianity were inherited from ancient Israelite religion and Pharisaism—indeed, did not rabbinic tradition reject such concepts as utterly foreign? Since we do not, then, have here anything approaching an identical gene pool, how can we have as offspring *sibling* faiths?

Yet, for all these dissatisfactions with the "sibling faith" image, also flawed for me is the "parent-offspring" alternative. The parentage of Configuration B Christianity was largely the Greek world directly (not even through the medium of a Hellenized Judaism). So how can Christianity be seen as the daughter *solely* of an antecedent Jewish mother? Nonetheless, I do use this metaphor despite such reservations; see next chapter. (Reflecting the influence of these ideas are, especially, sections of Chaps. 4, 6, 5–18, and 22.)

Two-Covenant Theology within the New Testament?

The post-Holocaust idea (popular in some circles) that Gentiles are saved* by accepting Christ *and* that Jews can be "saved" via their traditional covenant faithfulness certainly eases problems that Jews today face respecting those proselytizing them. It also facilitates dialogue between two parties, Christians and Jews, each of whom can now see the

other as equally advantaged. But to profess that the New Testament it-self espouses a two-covenant belief in any thoroughgoing way is, I be-lieve, misleading (although this *is* commonly inferred, especially from Rom 9–11). Were this genuinely the case, why then such tortured strug-gles by Paul and each Evangelist to come up with some plausible expla-nation as to why the Jews decided to *forgo* fulfillment of their own covenant, thereby to be replaced as *chosen* by Gentile-Christians? (Re-flecting the influence of these ideas are, especially, sections of Chaps. 14–18, and the opening of 20.)

"Distortive" Readings of What Is Not There?

I appreciate an inescapable quandary of Christians of good will who struggle because their sacred scripture *appears* to generate intensely anti-Jewish sentiment. I likewise applaud those Christian denominations that have managed significantly to revise their teaching materials so as to steer their constituents away from "misunderstanding" the New Tes-tament. But to propose that what needs to be countered is only a "mis-understanding" of the New Testament is misleading. Is it not obligatory to admit that often no *distortive* misunderstanding is involved at all but, instead, a quite correctly recognized and purposefully displayed anti-Jewish thesis? Because it is a setback for Christian–Jewish relations when this vital distinction is not recognized, the next chapter is devoted to this problem alone. (Reflecting the influence of these ideas are, espe-cially, sections of Chaps. 15–16, and 22–23.)

Is the New Testament "Antisemitic"?

The Dilemma That the New Testament Poses for Concerned Jews

Given that New Testament texts have been a source of such anxiety for Jews over the centuries, it should come as no surprise that many Jews today continue to bristle, flinch, or even cringe upon hearing the name of Jesus, and they view the New Testament with varying degrees of dismay and distrust, if not dread. Jews naturally expect that Christians, in addition to looking askance, however unjustifiedly, at the Jews of *Jesus'* day, may on some level interpret (and transfer) this disapproval so it reflects on *contemporary* Jews as well. Jews fear these ten themes in particular:

1. The Jews are culpable for crucifying Jesus—as such, they are guilty of deicide.

2. The tribulations of the Jewish people throughout history constitute God's punishment of them for killing Jesus.

3. Jesus originally came to preach only to the Jews, but when they rejected him, he abandoned them for Gentiles* instead.

4. The children of Israel were God's original chosen people by virtue of an ancient covenant, but by rejecting Jesus they forfeited that chosenness— and now, by virtue of a new covenant (or "testament"), Christians have replaced the Jews as God's chosen people, the Church having become the "People of God."

5. The Jewish Bible* ("Old" Testament) repeatedly portrays the opaqueness and stubbornness of the Jewish people and their disloyalty to God.

6. The Jewish Bible ("Old" Testament) contains many predictions of the coming of Jesus as the Messiah (or "Christ"), yet the Jews are blind to the meaning of their own Bible.

7. By the time of Jesus' ministry, Judaism had ceased to be a living faith.

8. Judaism's essence is a restrictive and burdensome legalism.

9. Christianity emphasizes love, while Judaism stands for justice and a God of wrath.

10. Judaism's oppressiveness reflects the disposition of Jesus' opponents called "Pharisees" (predecessors of the "rabbis"), who in their teachings and behavior were hypocrites.

The Dilemma That the New Testament Poses for Concerned Christians

These anti-Jewish themes also pose a serious dilemma for Christians committed to improving interfaith discourse. Their quandary is inescapable: what to do when the sacred repository of their cherished teachings also seems to generate such intensely anti-Jewish sentiment? This is complicated, in turn, by Christians' paradoxical relationship to Judaism: that it was from the Jews themselves and for the sake of the Jews primarily that Jesus had come, to fulfil thereby the Jews' own scripture. Some Christians want to claim an intimate relationship and at the same time blame heavily. They want the New Testament to show clearly that "the Jews" destroyed their own redeemer, and yet they deny that the New Testament is "antisemitic." Their religion is based on an understanding that this "redemption" comes about only by the crucifixion of Jesus, and yet they blame the Jews for causing it to happen (what I have termed the "hybrid riddle"; see Chap. 11). These ideas cause much confusion. Confronted by Jewish claims that the New Testament is antisemitic, a natural tendency for some Christians is of course outright *denial*—often taking the form of impassioned defenses of the purity and positive intentionality of their tradition's holy texts. But other Christians are more open to addressing this painful issue and do so forthrightly.

"Anti-Jewish," Not "Antisemitic"

Jews who are unsure how to process all this information, and therefore how to conduct themselves in such a wide-ranging discussion, may find the guidelines offered in this chapter instructive. Our first need is to draw a distinction between antisemitism and something that appears close to it: anti-Judaism. While the New Testament may be anti-Jewish, we should not think it antisemitic. The central component of "antisemitism" is *race*. The term "antisemitism" itself was not used until the late 1800s,[1] although antisemitic practice had been in place before that. In its modern manifestation, it originated as a function of German

notions that mingled race and nationalism—particularly the idea that a nation needed to have a homogeneous population. Since homogeneity was a matter of *race*, it followed that certain peoples, for example, Jews and gypsies, needed to be excluded. Such concepts of racial homogeneity spawned, in turn, theories of racial supremacy and inferiority. Germans, by race Aryan, were to consider themselves supreme; Jews, by contrast, were of the Semitic race, and as such inferior. Antisemitism was thus "the avowed intention of racists to bar Jews from legitimate membership in the body politic in Germany or in other European states."[2]

These considerations render problematic any application of the term "antisemitism" to the New Testament, in which whatever hostility is directed against Jews is *religious*, not racial. This is evident since as soon as Jews underwent the requisite religious change—accepting Christianity—they ceased to be targets of New Testament criticism. The debate, therefore, ought to be restricted to whether the New Testament is anti-*Jewish*, not antisemitic.

The Need to Define Our Terms

Complicating the problem of whether a New Testament writing is anti-Jewish are a number of fundamental questions:

- Do we mean all of the New Testament or only certain writings, and, if the latter, is there a matter of the *degree* to which a given writing might be defined as such? Since the New Testament is a collection of documents, we should distinguish among their various writers, some of whom could be mildly anti-Jewish, others more vigorously so, and others not at all.
- If the writer or the Christian community involved acknowledges that a separation, or parting of the ways, of Christians from Jews or of Christians from Judaism has already occurred, then the categories of "anti-Jewish" or "anti-Judaism" are potentially more easily discerned. But can a New Testament author be spoken of as anti-Jewish if the writer still considers himself and/or his community within the walls (*intra muros*) of Judaism or of the Jewish people?
- There are a number of options here: (1) we can define "anti-Jewish" as being a writer's manifestation of bias, anger, and so forth toward *fellow* Jews who persist in rejecting Jesus as the Christ—such that animosity directed at these recalcitrants can be understood as what being "anti-Jewish" actually means; (2) we can reason that the belief position of the writer, or his community, is such as *to give rise to* what we later recognize to be a Christianity that is not only apart from the Judaism but also

averse to it or its practitioners; (3) we can be open to the possibility that writers assumed to be Jewish may actually, instead, have come from Gentile ranks—such that no intra-Jewish squabble is involved after all; (4) we can hypothesize that a writer of Jewish extraction could yet be a partisan of, and writing on behalf of, a predominantly Gentile-Christian community—such that, even if the writer remains Jewish, his constituency is not and possibly never was; or (5) remembering what we said in Chapter 3, we can determine that, in some cases, it is not at all conclusive which New Testament writers (if any) were of Jewish extraction or which were not. The question could even be posed with respect to Paul of Tarsus, a born Jew who may have continued to regard himself as such, but who, in the judgment of some modern readers, *could* still be considered anti-Jewish.

Another question is, what do we actually mean by "anti-Jewish"? Do we mean a bias against *Jews resistant to accepting Jesus*, or a bias against *Judaism* as distinguished from, or even taken in conjunction with, its practitioners? Suppose an author who is *Gentile* tends to see Christianity as extending authentic Judaism, a recognition that most Jews would vigorously oppose? Murkier still would be the question of whether a bias even by a *Jew* of ancient times can be considered anti-Jewish if its nature jeopardizes the welfare of Jews today.

In all these respects, the viewpoint adopted in this volume has been whether, vis-à-vis the sensibilities of Jews *today*, the views expressed by the New Testament writers of the past are disparaging toward Jews who will not accept Jesus, *and* could also bring about, or at least contribute to, bias against Jews in the modern day.

Three Categories of Christian Response

Respecting this problem as so defined, I have encountered three avenues of response by Christians today. The construction of the arguments that follow is my way of setting forth what I have culled from Christians, including some who, over time, have changed their views.

A First Avenue—Steadfast denial that the New Testament is itself anti-Jewish.

Proponents of this first avenue view the New Testament as neither a source nor a cause of Christian anti-Judaism. At least four kinds of such argument are advanced (Fig. 22.1):

22.1—Anti-Judaism in the New Testament Is Denied

I
Defensive Arguments
by Some Christians

II
My Reactions

I a) Inspired by God and reflecting divine love, the New Testament could not have been intended to encourage contempt of any people. Since Jesus spoke this language of love, preaching the turning of the other cheek, even loving one's enemies, those recording his teachings, and deeply committed to him themselves, could hardly have written works that are anti-Jewish.

II a) Since Jews do not include the New Testament among their sacred texts, any argument proceeding, as if self-evidently, from the New Testament's divine inspiration will not be persuasive. Moreover, that Jesus himself spoke the language of love hardly guarantees that those committed to him (including the Gospels' editors themselves) did so as well.

I b) The New Testament's apparently harsh language against Jews is simply prophetic rebuke out of love. Just as the Hebrew prophets, reprimanding Israelites of their day, are not to be judged anti-Jewish, neither should Jesus' criticisms of Jews be so construed. These were a kind of oratorical style or literary device not intended as final but merely to shock people into repentance before it was too late.

II b) Gospel condemnations of Jews exceed reprimands by the Hebrew prophets. The latter intended to solidify covenantal bonds between God and the Jews whereas New Testament censure of Jews warns of God's replacing them with *others*! Jesus may have scolded fellow Jews out of love, but the ferocity *ascribed* to him reflects sentiments of later Gospel editors, and is so prominently displayed that it must be judged anti-Jewish.

I c) The Gospels and book of Acts show us, approvingly, thousands of Jews accepting Jesus' message, or at least eager to hear what he had said. How, then, when the New Testament presents, with acclaim, so many Jews so positively disposed

II c) The Gospels and Acts, while not biased against all Jews, are biased against *Jews rejecting Jesus*, not opposed to Jews accepting Jesus but condemnatory of those who do not—and it is the latter with whom modern Jews identify.

toward Jesus' message and Jesus' following, can modern Jews deem the New Testament anti-Jewish?

I d) The church fathers' denunciations of Jews date from later times when the Church began forging weapons for its conflict with Judaism. Only *then* did interpreters of the sacred gospel apply their own personal biases against Jews to the non-prejudicial truths of the New Testament itself.

II d) Just as the church fathers superimposed their own later attitudes onto earlier views of the New Testament itself, so also did the four Evangelists themselves—in producing and editing these Gospels—convey and superimpose their own anti-Jewish sentiments in the very process of depicting both Jesus and his ministry.

A Second Avenue—Anti-Jewishness in the New Testament is acknowledged, but mainly in terms that minimize its importance or otherwise explain it away.

Those espousing this second approach, while acknowledging the New Testament's anti-Judaism, hope nonetheless to reduce its impact. They offer a variety of mitigating interpretations that make that bias appear of only minor consequence so that Jews will feel less offended and Christians will accord these texts less weight (Fig. 22.2)

A Third Avenue—The New Testament's anti-Jewishness is openly recognized as a serious problem that requires full confrontation.

Christians espousing this remaining approach regretfully acknowledge the New Testament as indeed anti-Jewish and then openly confront this actuality. Some believe that the New Testament may have *had* to be anti-Jewish. Developing *in part* from its mother[3]—in this case, from Judaism—and wishing to establish a viable separateness, Christianity's need to justify its existence *necessitated* expressions of negativity toward the parent. Especially because Christianity drew so heavily on Judaism in terms of its ethics, scripture, and liturgy, as well as some theological elements, the question could arise: given Judaism, why Christianity? In the process of justifying its own worth, Christianity had to show that the value Christianity recognized in Judaism must be understood as Judaism's indispensable function in God's plan in preparing the world for *Christianity*!

III	IV
Defensive Arguments by Some Christians	**My Reactions**

III a) Other ancient literatures attacked opponents. Certain New Testament polemics are even comparatively mild! That these diatribes were conventions of a bygone era frees us to dismiss them as irrelevant for modern times.

IV a) Christians today are not sufficiently conversant with conventions of ancient polemic to bring them to bear in evaluating the New Testament, which, moreover, they distinguish from most other ancient writings as the *inspired word of God*, an authority that offsets any putative mildness.

III b) Authors of New Testament writings were not conscious of contributing to a new biblical corpus. Jewish scripture was the only Bible they envisioned. Had they known the importance their writings would assume, and the possible detrimental effect their words might have on the Jews, such authors would have tempered their presentation of the Jewish people.

IV b) To suggest that such awareness would have induced them to abstain from using abusive language, or at least to tone it down, is conjectural and does not address *realities* at hand. When later Christian authorities did realize the negativity toward Jews in, e.g., the Gospels, some intensified it in their own writings!

III c) The New Testament's apparent anti-Jewish polemic was actually only "in-house" squabbling between Jews who accepted Jesus over against others who had not. Thus, even post-70, when Gospels were being composed, anti-Jewish polemics turn out only to be by *Christian* Jews against *fellow* Jews, not polemics by non-Jews against Jews.

IV c) Increasingly, after 70, churches were becoming severed from the "Synagogue," with most Christians not "in" the Jewish house at all (Chaps. 16 and 21). The "in-house squabbling" argument, while popular, convenient, and comforting, is not always soundly based and results in some unnatural readings of Gospel texts.

III d) Since Jews "gave" Christians Jesus and Paul, the twelve apostles*, and Jewish scripture, Christian expressions of negativity cannot extend deeply lest Christians cut into their own foundation in Judaism. Seemingly harsh rebuke of Jews could better be construed as exasperation *on behalf of* Jews who have not recognized the fulfillment of their own heritage. This is hardly bias!

IV d) The core issue operative here is that, since the Jews gave the world the concept of the Messiah, the Jews should also be best qualified to identify that Messiah. In failing to accept Jesus, Jews denied the core of Christian theology. Far more than mere exasperation is involved here.

At the same time, Judaism could be presented as no less than *relatively* deficient because a parent that was wholly deficient would leave questionable the value of the improvements represented by the off-spring. The ideal way for a new faith to catapult itself to supreme status was by showing itself an improvement upon what was in itself already of superlative worth, an augmentation that first had to be couched as preservation and affirmation of what it was that was being supplanted.

Moreover, since for the Greco-Roman world *antiquity* was the hall-mark of authenticity, Christianity had to identify itself as, so to speak, an "*old* new" religion (i.e., an extended or fulfilled old religion). And to achieve this, not only did it need its parent, but also *the higher the esteem in which its parent was held, the higher Christianity itself would be esteemed*—as the fulfillment of the parent religion whose scripture now carried also Christianity back to what was "in the beginning" (Gen 1:1 and Jn 1:1). The contrast, then, was between the already valuable with the now *even more* valuable. The very credibility of its newness could not come at the cost of abolition of the parent.

The notion that Christianity *fulfilled* Judaism means not that "predictions" by the Jewish Bible had been satisfied by Jesus and Christianity but that the potential of the-Judaism-that-had-come-before was only now achieving its fullest satisfaction. It is in this sense that Matthew 5:17ff. seems apt: "Think not that I have come to abolish the Law; I have come only to *fulfil* it"—which entails accepting and praising your inheritance before unveiling how you now carry it through and complete it!

It is here, then—in the context of exposing the relative inadequacy of Judaism's *best*—that Christianity emerged as anti-Jewish, holding in

tension three positions simultaneously: Judaism is good; Christianity is better; therefore Christianity emerges as anti-Jewish. But because it becomes difficult to present Christianity as extending Judaism while at the same time deprecating it, the tendency arose to bifurcate matters: first, by praising the parent religion, Judaism, as good and the daughter religion, Christianity, as better; but, second, by directing the anti-Jewishness toward *those practitioners of the parent faith who failed to recognize and then to align themselves with the new offspring.* This failure—less of Judaism than of allegedly myopic *Jews*—manifested itself as a depreciation of those Jews, berating as obtuse less the parent religion than its continued loyalists—that is, non-Christian Jews who refused to become the *offspring's* proponents.

Since such a general dynamic would have *required* Christian writers to express anti-Jewish sentiments, we must acknowledge that many New Testament passages are precisely what they appear to be: anti-Jewish. This is why denying the problem (the first avenue) or even minimizing it (the second) can only be misleading or, at the least, counterproductive.

Coping with New Testament Anti-Jewishness Today

Christians view the New Testament as sacred, but does sanctity lie only in the texts themselves or also with their *interpreters*? Some religious outlooks profess to root their sole authority in what their scriptures say; yet in practice they rely additionally on a tradition of interpretation that clarifies how these texts are to be understood in terms of relative importance. What has often resulted in the history of religions is that sacred written texts do not actually command *in practice* the degree of authority that may be laid claim to by the texts themselves. As applied to the topic at hand, the influence of New Testament passages biased against Jews could well be more a function of what modern Christian interpreters will *allow* than of the scriptural texts in and of themselves.

Second, many Christians recognize that their Bible ("Old" and "New" Testaments together) expresses some attitudes that, in the modern day, seem quite objectionable—for example, passages endorsing animal sacrifices, condoning slavery, maligning homosexuals, or demeaning women. Yet despite their genuine presence in the Bible itself, such views are often routinely ignored by many Christians who, if they are not constrained by *these* attitudes, ought to be capable of dispensing with the New Testament's anti-Judaism as well. Of course, for some Christians the categories are different because of the element of disappointment: Jews are still present but still not seeing how their whole Jewish heritage and logical situation have been brought to completion

by the "Christ Event." What many Jews, in turn, hope for is a welcoming by Christians of the Jewish religion as another option on the same footing with Christianity in bringing God's Kingdom.

Third, and posing the matter differently, what should be done when we encounter a conflict between sacred literature and religious *values*? Many interpreters of Matthew, for example, have asserted that included among the sacred values of Christianity are the mandates to turn the other cheek and to love your enemies (5:39,44). What, then, do we do with the text, found in the same Gospel, that presents Jesus assailing the Pharisees as children of hell (cf. 23:15)? A sacred image in Christianity is often said to be a "God of love"; how is this to maintain itself alongside a prophecy that a wrathful God will destroy Jerusalem to avenge the Jews' rejection of Jesus (22:7)? Is it not incumbent upon interpreters of Christian values to declare anti-Jewish passages *de*valued?

Fourth, undoubtedly the most formidable obstacle we face is unawareness on the part of the Christian laity of the role of *historical conditioning* in the formation of the New Testament's anti-Jewish passages. This is part of what I mean by "Gospel Dynamics." This laity is unaware that developments that occurred decades *after* Jesus' death were what prompted the anti-Jewishness erroneously attributed to Jesus personally. The anti-Jewish Jesus who emerges from the Gospels is thus the product of writers *who simply made the figure of Jesus in their texts the spokesperson for their own anti-Jewish orientation*, which was in turn often a function of whatever such views were current among their own constituencies. When we are told that "Jesus said" anything about the Jewish people or to the Jewish people, we should substitute: "the *Gospel writer* says that Jesus said." *Whatever the Evangelists put into the mouth of Jesus constitutes no evidence that Jesus himself said this.*

In the course of this book I have attempted to trace a process wherein religious divisiveness became sharp, even between parties who originally shared many of their essentials in common. Limited areas of theological disagreement came to be the focus of special attention and eventually emerged as the breeding ground for intense hostility—such that ultimately, whenever Christian theology mentioned Jews or Judaism, the channels of such expression came almost necessarily to be those of disparagement.

I have explained early Christianity's need not only to identify with the antiquity and divine authority of Judaism but also to justify its separateness from Judaism. And I have enumerated as well major historical factors, rooted in ancient times, that further fueled this process. But Christianity no longer has to defend its existence or justify its distinct

integrity. The underlying dynamics and attendant historical factors that originally produced and developed Christianity's anti-Judaism are themselves operative no more. Of course, this legacy is not easily relinquished today, but surely, at the least, it no longer needs to be regularly appealed to in either worship or study.

It is important for Christians to recognize as well that, while Jews today may urge changes when it comes to understanding and presenting the image of Jews and Judaism in the New Testament, Jews cannot themselves do anything by way of actual implementation other than appeal to Christians of good will. For anti-Judaism, as much as it has affected Jews, is, in one major sense, not a Jewish problem but a *Christian* problem in that only Christians can genuinely undertake the measures necessary to resolve it.

Never Again! Never Before!

This book has covered a panorama of challenges—arising from the New Testament itself—that impact and disconcert Jews living in a Christian world. It has attempted to address, in a clear, direct, and concise way, this spectrum of problems by offering historical and theological analyses and practical applications that Jews require. And it has aspired to persuade Jews of the wisdom of accelerating a radical communal change whereby their seminaries, synagogues, religious schools, and college students will forgo a traditional mandate to shun the New Testament and instead seek to secure facility in Gospel Dynamics—those skillful literary techniques by which early Christians molded their traditions to address their needs decades after Jesus died.

> This volume's thesis, accordingly, is that the ability of Jews to detect Gospel Dynamics, to explain these to themselves and their children, and ultimately to articulate them to Christian friends and to a broader Christian society, will enable Jews *to exchange their sense of victimization by the New Testament for a strong sense of confidence that they now knowledgeably control this literature and are thereby free from it*. This security will enhance their well-being in an overwhelmingly Christian environment, as promised.

This is what this book is. Also to be noted is what it is not.

A Subtlety Not to Be Glossed Over

This book's distinction between knowing New Testament and knowing Gospel Dynamics should not go overlooked. This is because Jews

who feel no incentive to read the New Testament may feel every incentive to learn about the workings of those Gospel Dynamics that continually have impacted the Jewish people so deleteriously over two millennia.

Some press coverage of this book has not captured this fuller dimension, as in the headline, "Reform Rabbi Michael J. Cook Says Jews Need to Know New Testament."[1] Naturally, since I teach this literature, I commend Jews who bring themselves to read it, and feel it vital that they do so. But I also realize that most Jews simply cannot muster any incentive to read writings that have caused their people to become "chosen" victims of the vicissitudes of Western history. Learning Gospel Dynamics, however, is an altogether different venture—one for which Jews have shown a natural aptitude (cf. Chap. 7) and that they can find to be stimulating as well as consistent with the paradigmatic means of Jewish problem-solving: namely, seeking and building knowledge. This is the incentive that can bring the hesitant to read the New Testament.

Gospel Dynamics in a Nutshell

A Gospel Dynamics approach to New Testament focuses on the degree to which the time frame producing a Gospel may have influenced how its subject matter came to be cast. Did the Evangelists impart as much or more about their own communities' needs than about the genuine Jesus of history? In particular, did the anti-Jewish sentiments attributed to certain Gospel characters reflect not those characters' historical reality but, rather, what a compiler/editor wanted his community to *see* them as professing?

I have endeavored to demonstrate how Gospel narrations were shaped by editorial improvisation in a political climate of Christians' fear of Rome, and fear of being associated in Roman eyes with the great Jewish revolt of 66 through 73 CE. The outstanding instance of this is the way the Evangelists shifted recountings of Jesus' Passion from Rome's obvious responsibility for his death (it was *Romans* who crucified) to "the Jews" instead. Because Gospel Dynamics worked to establish the Jews as an enemy-in-common of both Christians and Romans, the fate of millions of later Jews—threatened, oppressed, injured, and murdered as "Christ-killers"—was sealed by *traditions bearing no genuine connection to the historical Jesus at all!*

Indeed, it is in this regard that we have discovered fundamental distinctions between what Jesus himself may have said and what the later Church only claimed he said. A later, *vindictive* image of Jesus, disparaging of Jews and Judaism, became superimposed on an earlier,

actual figure—with this later anti-Jewishly *adjusted* image of Jesus being that to which Jews of subsequent generations inevitably responded, feeding a spiral of negative interchange within the troubled history of Christian–Jewish polemics. Since we have no reason to believe that the historical Jesus would have entertained such vitriolic sentiments toward his own people, it seems more likely that it is these Gospel processes that account for how such emphases and attitudes came to be wrongly associated with him.

Thus, reminiscent of a painting repeatedly overlaid by later retouches, what we have discovered in the Gospels are disparate Jesus images superimposed one on another, making it hard to accept that the historical Jesus and the Jesus of the Gospels were one and the same. The important practical consequence is that we must, Jews and Christians alike, stop attributing to *Jesus* the enmity toward Jews that originated mainly in the 60s and became intensified by Evangelists who wrote after the Temple's fall. Jews, in particular, must stop blaming Jesus for attitudes expressed in his name, but that were actually introduced only much later by Christian writers for reasons having to do with their local circumstances. It is *that the enmity toward Jews of the Evangelists' day (70–100) was retrojected to Jesus (ca. 30), not that any enmity toward Jews by the historical Jesus himself was forwarded.*

In the course of this kind of approach, we have found ourselves routinely posing basic questions that most Gospel readers never consider. When is Jesus' image (or that of John the Baptist, or of Judas and others) being so conformed to Jewish scriptural motifs that we may mistake the Evangelists' literary license for objective fact? When are predictions ascribed to Jesus in the Gospels actually only Church formulations *after the fact* so as to confirm Christian preaching and belief? When are words ascribed to Jesus actually responses to later Christians' impatience, frustration, skepticism, or despair over the Second Coming's seemingly incomprehensible delay, which was causing defections from the ranks? Or responses to Jewish charges that Jesus died not a victor but a victim? Or refutation of Jewish insistence that God's "chosen people" could not include Gentiles? Is a central motive of each Gospel writer (also of Paul) to rationalize Christianity's rejection by most Jews? Whenever we have good reason to suspect that a tradition is not about Jesus, but rather enlists him to deal with any of these or other matters arising decades after he died, then we are on the trail of Gospel Dynamics. (See esp. Fig. 8.1.)

We may wonder whether most Christians today are cognizant of Gospel Dynamics. Certainly we have seen that Christian scholars are

(even though they do not employ my specific term). In my experience, those Christian laypersons who *have* become thus aware have also come to grasp why Jews have found Christians' sacred scripture so threatening, and are concerned to set matters straight and to relieve this distress.

Two Incentives for Jews to Engage the New Testament

An unprecedented convergence of historical and sociological factors has positioned today's modern Jews as the first to seriously reconsider the ancient rabbinic mandate to avoid the New Testament. Driving this redirection have been two categories of modern incentive: embarrassment and opportunity.

Embarrassment: Never Again

Early in 2003 I was invited by the Bishops' Committee for Ecumenical and Interreligious Affairs (USCCB) to serve as one of seven scholars[2] who would assess the accuracy of the advance filmscript of Mel Gibson's *The Passion of the Christ*. I intend to focus here less on the movie than on an embarrassment for modern Jews that the film brought to the fore. Indeed, the film is nothing more here than an illustration of the reality that, if there is not one New Testament-based crisis for Jews, there will always be another. But given the duration of the tension and the universality of the media coverage, worldwide, that the Gibson matter attracted, let us stay with this simply as an *example* for a while.

Precipitating the invitations to the Scholar Group was concern over the persistent and central claim by the film's advance publicity that this production was *the* most historically accurate presentation of Christ's Passion ever rendered. If the claim was correct, all the better. But if not, could this movie effectively revive the canard that the Jews were corporately and in perpetuity blameworthy for Jesus' death, a contention that many Christians had come to suspect lay the most fertile soil for the Holocaust? Was there, in the offing here, a potential setback of four decades of progress since 1965's monumental revision of the deicide charge by the Second Vatican Council (see further discussion below).

Gibson's reaction to the Scholar Report (in which we did suggest many revisions) generated an international controversy that, over its most intense fifteen months (March 2003–May 2004), stimulated in response much new teaching. (I transformed one of my own such items— see Fig. 23.1—into Chap. 12 of this book.)

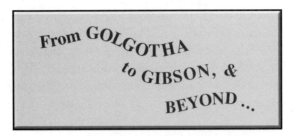

From GOLGOTHA to GIBSON, & BEYOND ...

TRUTH IN PASSION PRODUCTIONS?

"What is truth?"—Pilate (Jn 18:38)

Figure 23.1

In its released form, in my judgment, the film showed not the slightest awareness of Gospel Dynamics—especially in its acceptance as literally true the Sanhedrin and Barabbas episodes, Pilate's deference to Caiaphas, and so forth, along with countless embellishments that were not even put forth by the Gospels themselves.

Sadder still, however, was the missed opportunity for the Jewish *laity* effectively to enlighten the general populace to Jewish thinking at least on the matter of Jesus' Passion. Turning to their reservoir of knowledge, in this one area of exposure many Jews found that they had absolutely nothing upon which to draw—the people renowned for knowledge instead floundered in an abyss of bewilderment as to what to say and, even if something were found, how to say it.

Christians who were curious, concerned, or even annoyed would inquire as to what in this film was making Jews go radioactive.[3] Jews might easily have responded that, for centuries in Europe, authorities had to seal off Jewish communities whenever Passion plays were performed lest Jews be massacred by exiting theater-goers; or that Hitler classified the script of the Oberammergau Passion play (in Bavaria) as a racially important cultural document[4] for "never has the menace of Jewry been so convincingly portrayed"[5]; or that Hitler employed two performances (one at the end of 1930; the other, August 13, 1934) to indoctrinate the SS in support of his designs to exterminate the Jews. And in terms of the Gospel Dynamics that underlay all this, Jews had no understanding that many of the details that the Gospels relate about Jesus' Passion were very unlikely for any victim of Roman exemplary punishment.

That Jews were apprehensive, anxious, aggravated, and angry about the film is understandable. That they were inept is unacceptable. Centuries of assiduously avoiding training in how to respond on such matters made

it simply impossible for Jews to navigate these rough waters. Educational materials that Jewish institutions hastily churned out were of high quality, but unfortunately the general Jewish mind was not prepared for them. Had these laity known about Gospel Dynamics, they would have been ready for what their teachers were offering them in these disturbing circumstances. But a traditional, lingering ghettoization of Jewish attitudes—when it came to New Testament matters—left most of the Jewish populace bereft of any matrix-in-waiting that could assimilate what was now being readied for their benefit.

And so, as a first incentive, I offer this book—in the spirit of "never again!"—as my own suggested matrix-in-waiting for any future crises analogous in effect to this one. (In addition, the Selected Bibliography lays out an escalating educative program of recommended readings to expand what readers may have gathered from this volume itself.)

Opportunity: Never Before

History has presented Jews today with an unprecedented opening to correct what Harris Weinstock bemoaned in his 1899 petition: that fellow Jews left themselves "helpless" to respond competently to anything dealing with the New Testament because of their "dense ignorance of the origin of Christianity, the life of the Christian Savior, and the causes which led to his death" (see Chap. 1). But Weinstock was unaware of why his petition could not succeed in his day:

- He himself manifested insufficient credentials in New Testament scholarship.
- Absent were the Jewish academicians and professionals knowledgeable in New Testament who were necessary for implementing his plan.
- Even if they had existed, they would have had to be placed nation-wide.
- No major Jewish educational institution was ready to commit itself to Weinstock's plan.
- No national Jewish organizations saw the indispensability of his plan for Jews' societal security.
- Weinstock offered no way to motivate Jews to study what made them cringe, and no methodological approach that would appeal to Jewish aptitudes and excite Jewish minds.
- There was no crisis, no wake-up call, to spark Jews' awareness of the need for what he was proposing.

Today, by contrast, all of these prerequisites are not only fully in place but are also in *convergence*. This remarkable state of affairs is the result of several facts and factors.

Sociological Trends. Especially by the late twentieth century, navigating Christian America had become increasingly difficult for Jews due to the burgeoning of assimilation, intermarriage, blended families, a declining Jewish birthrate, and the continuously dwindling percentage of society constituted by Jews. Public schools were being pressed to teach courses in "Scientific Creationism" and the "New Testament as History." Millennialist end-times scenarios—especially as we approached the year 2000—were spotlighting Jews as the gauge for history's supposedly imminent culmination. Hundreds of millions of dollars annually were funding ever more assertive missionary groups. Middle East crises spawned Christian reactions so powerful and orientations so conflicting as to confound and divide the American Jewish community. Today we also see a corresponding surge in hours that Jewish professionals (rabbis, cantors, educators) must devote to counseling the intermarried; teaching conversion courses; interacting with Christian clergy; speaking in churches and sectarian colleges; and generally guiding Jewish adults and children through life in a predominantly Christian culture. This overall complexion appears to be weighing on the Jewish community far more intensely than was the case in Weinstock's generation.

Post-Holocaust Reflections and Programming. Back in 1965, as sensitive Christians were pondering the degree to which the New Testament had lent itself to Nazi exploitation, the Second Vatican Council Declaration, *Nostra Aetate* ("In Our Time"), aimed to lay to rest the deicide accusation. Together with its later attendant commentaries,[6] it dismissed the notion that Jews were corporately rejected by God for complicity in Jesus' death and for failing to recognize him as Messiah then and since. Roman Catholic teaching materials were overhauled, inducing similar changes by some Protestant denominations.

This watershed development stimulated an era of better Christian–Jewish feeling, typified by countless interfaith clergy and academic institutes on the New Testament and Judaism, and manifesting new trends of thinking, such as "two-covenant" theology, Judaism and Christianity as "sibling faiths," and the Gospels' anti-Jewish vitriol as merely "in-house squabbling." And while scholars differed on whether these positions were correct (see Chap. 21), this new parlance made for a welcoming atmosphere of conciliation, with many more Jews at least talking about the New Testament for the first time.

Academic Developments. There has also been a slow but steady increase in the number of Jewish academicians knowledgeable of, even specializing in, New Testament, paralleled by many more Jewish college students who, intentionally or inadvertently, have found themselves taking

university New Testament offerings. But remarkable above all in impact was the curriculum change by the Hebrew Union College-Jewish Institute of Religion (HUC-JIR)—urged, to start with, by alumni! This move was to accord *core course status* to what before had been offered only as electives. The change now made Cincinnati's campus in particular[7] the first Jewish seminary in history to *require* courses in the technical study of (what I have named) Gospel Dynamics for rabbinical ordination.

The best perspective from which to gauge the impact of such change is in terms of its cumulative effect. Speaking of this Cincinnati campus alone, over the past fifty-five years (beginning in 1952 with my pioneering faculty predecessor and mentor, Samuel Sandmel) we have secured job placements continent-wide for twenty to fifty graduates *annually* who, among their wider rabbinical training, are also prepared in New Testament study because they have taken our required course, various electives, or both. These graduates are now, in turn, capable of teaching adult education courses in their own synagogues on New Testament topics that bear on Jewish concerns. (This accounts in part for the huge 50 percent response—out of 450 synagogues—received by Roxanne Schneider-Shapiro in her 1999 study, especially the number reacting positively to implementation of New Testament education, as detailed in Chap. 1.) Other Jewish seminaries[8] have made, or can make, similar strides as well.

Organizational Support. We can be certain that the Union for Reform Judaism, the Anti-Defamation League, the American Jewish Committee, the Religious Action Center, the American Jewish Congress, and other national organizations would have preferred that the entire Jewish people had already been schooled in Gospel Dynamics *before* the Gibson ordeal hit, and certainly before the *next* ordeal does. (Indeed, representatives of some of these organizations wrote early endorsements of this book with at least some measure of this consideration in mind.)

Already arrayed, then, are most of the factors that Weinstock, in 1899, needed in place but lacked: nation-wide placement of Jewish professionals, and even academicians, who are knowledgeable in New Testament; a major seminary requiring in-depth knowledge of Gospel Dynamics for ordination; and national Jewish organizations (having just experienced the liabilities of Jewish ignorance) now understanding the indispensability of this new direction. In terms of the required wake-up calls, first is the cyclical recurrence (as today) of antisemitism worldwide, in whose cause the Gospels can always be exploited. Then there is the concern as to how Third World countries, where much of Christianity's future will spread and be shaped, will develop their new faith. Will there be a general return to

traditionalist, pre-Vatican II ways, especially in an age marked by a sharp retrenchment from religious progressivism? Whether it be missionizing, millennialism, or even any of the abiding ten basic questions from Figure 1.1—from why not accept Jesus as the Jewish Messiah through to the "hybrid riddle" (Chap. 11)—there is every plausible expectation that the need by Jews to become learned in this area will be ongoing in the future as it has always been in the past. The difference is that, from now on, Jews will no longer neglect this learning.

As for motivating Jews to study what deeply alienates them, a Gospel Dynamics approach is key in terms of both incentive and methodology. Of course Jews should know the New Testament itself, but in terms of Gospel Dynamics witness the motivation! Year after year rabbinical students at HUC-JIR trudge for the first time into a required core course that *forces* them to learn Gospel Dynamics. Watch their resistance melt. Wait for them to report their experimentation with teaching this very material at *their* student pulpits (often in remote communities), and the enthusiastic response of their laypeople who affirm that learning Gospel Dynamics indeed does enhance their well-being in their Christian environment.

And so I offer this book also in the spirit of "never before!" Never before has history given Jews this clear directional signal—all the factors that Weinstock lacked are now present and in convergence. So it *is* time to accelerate the revolutionary measures that this book now urges. This brings us to questions of how to implement the ideas in this volume—and others—especially with laypeople (Christians as well as Jews).

Implementing This Volume
No More "Cafeteria Approaches" for Laity

I am told that, at a conference of New Testament scholars held long ago at my alma mater, Haverford College, a Quaker institution, a venerable Christian laywoman mistakenly was permitted entry. Fascinated at hearing of Dynamics concerning the Gospels that she had never known, and impatient at her evident exclusion from the proceedings, she rose, Bible in hand, and unceremoniously interrupted astonished discussants: "I assert my prerogative [as a Friend] to speak as moved by the Spirit. I read here, in John 21:15, that Jesus said, 'Feed my *lambs*.' He never said, 'Feed my *giraffes*.' Well, brothers, when are you ever going to put the food where the lambs can get it?"

Many clergy and academicians are conditioned by what I call "benign elitism"—belief that serious scriptural text study should fall within the domain of experts only. This all but guarantees that interfaith study will operate the least among those whose participation we require the most. Laypersons will be left instead to preoccupy themselves with

the prejudices engendered by literalist comprehensions of ancient writings rather than with edifying truths that transcend them.

Has it not been within the wider *lay* social contexts (neighborhood living, business interaction, education in school and houses of worship) that suspicion and stereotyping have assumed such deep rootage—becoming virtually impervious to any shifts in attitude or policy occurring within clerical ranks? Why, then, are we sanctioning what I call a "cafeteria approach" to Gospel (and even rabbinic) traditions: allowing Jews and Christians freely to choose whatever they wish, while withholding from them *informed* opinions concerning the relative merits of what is being displayed? Thus, the average Jew selects, from the Talmud, a depiction of Jesus as an apostate from his people, while many Christians as well as Jews derive from the Gospels a Jesus image caricaturing both his fellow Jews and Judaism. By not being invited to share in the academic venture, how many Jews have we prevented from appreciating Jesus' edifying teachings, and how many Christians from discerning Jesus' own appreciation of Judaism's vitality and ongoing relationship to God?

Top-Down Administration

This is why, in the Introduction of this book, most every envisioned readership that I list contains a prominent *lay* component. But because these people need academicians and professionals to provide the programmatic means of involving them, it is also with such programs in mind that I have tailored this book—so that Jewish professionals can more easily employ it. Hence I have made chapters self-standing and on different topics, so that each can be used selectively and independently, some chapters suitable as foundations for an entire program's discussion session. Toward these ends, readers should examine both the "Suitability Index," directly following this chapter—which matches this book's contents to occasions for potential use of this volume—and, following that, the "Listing of Figures" for a convenient overview of their programming applicability.

Waters Already Charted?

For medieval iconographers, were *Synagoga* ever to appear without a blindfold, this would signal her bow to Christianity's superior claims. In my application of this image, were *Synagoga* ever to remove her blindfold, *she would be in a position to "engage" the New Testament.* This accounts for why this verb, "engage," is featured so prominently on this book's cover. For "engage" signifies eye-to-eye contact.

The time is overdue—and is *now*: *Synagoga* needs to rip off her blindfold so that she can penetrate into the New Testament's inner workings

in ways that the vast majority of Christendom has yet to do, and claim that she is clear-sighted, possessing much to say about the New Testament that *Ecclesia* herself could find illuminating. Only by so doing will the Jewish people feel returned to their element, reasserting their paradigmatic approach to problem-solving: that learning *empowers*. Societally, Jews will enhance their well-being (repeating here from Chap. 8) simply by helping Christians realize that—far from being "blind"—Jews have intelligible as well as intelligent reasons for processing the New Testament in their own way.

But for those Jews who still remain uncertain as to why any of this should be going on, *mashal le-mah ha-davar domeh*—"a parable: to what may the matter be likened?" For a thousand years, no one in Europe knew what lay beyond the cape at the tip of South Africa, for around it storms are always raging and no ship had ever managed to turn that corner. No wonder it was originally called the Cape of Storms! But in the sixteenth century, the explorer Vasco da Gama, by successfully turning that corner, discovered around that cape a great calm sea leading to India.

Of course Jews cannot but associate the New Testament as their "Cape of Storms" to be avoided, but—embedded as Jews already are within a Christian environment that produces that turbulence—I ask whether avoidance strategies in the past have proven effective? No, they have caused embarrassment and have only compounded Jews' problems. Contrast those fellow Jews, escalating rapidly in number, who *have* tried navigating a turn around this Cape of Storms, and now find themselves on the other side floundering no more. We see them at no great distance, beckoning: "Sail *this* way, these previously uncharted waters are far calmer than we once imagined. Because we have turned the cape, headway can now easily be made. We are stronger and more secure *as Jews* for doing so. We, and *you*, should have done so long ago."

It was certainly not by avoidance but solely because Vasco da Gama turned that corner that the Cape of Storms is today renamed the Cape of *Good Hope*.[9]

Suitability Index for Using This Multipurpose Book: Matching Contents to Occasion

Note: *Shaded* indicates appropriate for that audience. *Not shaded* means less appropriate.
Key: B— "Before We Proceed"; I— "Introduction"; N— "Notes on Terminology"

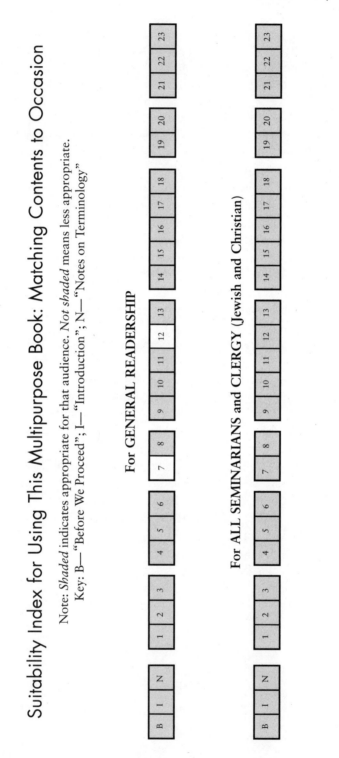

For **GENERAL READERSHIP**

For **ALL SEMINARIANS and CLERGY** (Jewish and Christian)

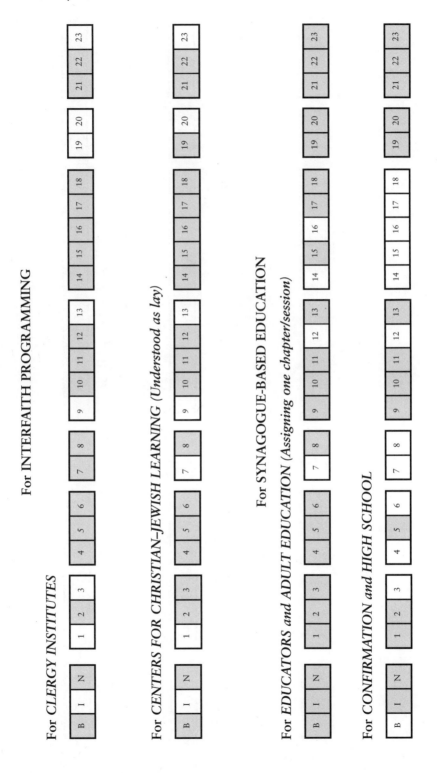

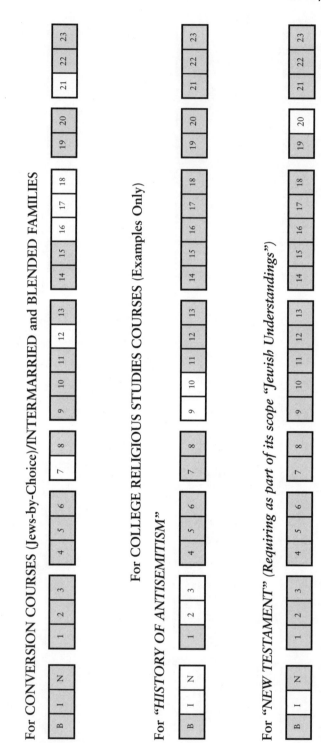

For CONVERSION COURSES (Jews-by-Choice)/INTERMARRIED and BLENDED FAMILIES

For COLLEGE RELIGIOUS STUDIES COURSES (Examples Only)

For *"HISTORY OF ANTISEMITISM"*

For *"NEW TESTAMENT" (Requiring as part of its scope "Jewish Understanding")*

Listing of Figures

Acknowledgments

I am most profoundly grateful to those who, in 2005, wrote initial endorsements for the idea of this book. Of course, they are not accountable if the finished product in any respect falls short. With their positions noted at that time: Douglas Barden (Exec. Dir., Jewish Chautauqua Society, New York); David Blewett (Dir., Ecumenical Institute for Jewish-Christian Studies, Southfield, MI); Gary M. Bretton-Granatoor (Dir., Department of Interfaith Affairs, ADL, New York); Terrance Callan (Prof. of Biblical Studies, Mount St. Mary's Seminary, Cincinnati); Philip A. Cunningham (Exec. Dir., Center for Christian-Jewish Learning, Boston College); Harry K. Danziger (President, Central Conference of American Rabbis, New York); Eugene J. Fisher (Assoc. Dir., Secretariat for Ecumenical and Interreligious Affairs, United States Conference of Catholic Bishops, Washington, DC); John T. Pawlikowski (Dir., Catholic-Jewish Studies Program, Catholic Theological Union, Chicago); Allen Podet (Prof. of Philosophy and Religious Studies, State University of New York, Buffalo); Leonard A. Schoolman (Dir., Center for Religious Inquiry, New York), and Eric H. Yoffie (President, Union for Reform Judaism, New York). Lending like-minded support were Charles Arian (Jewish Staff Scholar, Institute for Christian and Jewish Studies, Baltimore) and A. James Rudin (Senior Interreligious Advisor, the American Jewish Committee).

Although I have not known them all personally, those certain scholars present or past who have most consistently shaped my views on the material in this particular volume—in the give and take of agreement and disagreement—include Benjamin Bacon, Raymond Brown, J. Dominic Crossan, John Donahue, Morton Enslin, Ernst Haenchen, Douglas Hare, E. Elizabeth Johnson, John Meier, Heikki Räisänen, Ellis Rivkin, E. P. Sanders, Jack Sanders, Samuel Sandmel, Joseph Tyson, and Philipp Vielhauer. As for academicians who directly offered me opinions that weighed on my thinking during my writing, some are already acknowledged within the body of this volume: Philip A. Cunningham, Susan Einbinder, Eugene J. Fisher, Lawrence Hoffman, David E. Kaufman, Jonathan Sarna, Lance Sussman, Mark Washofsky, and Gary P. Zola. Also archival specialists: Fred Krome and Kevin Proffitt. Other scholars offering assistance but not thanked heretofore: David Aaron, Mary Boys, Shira Lander, Amy-Jill Levine, Richard Sarason, James

Somerville, and David Turner. Rabbis warranting my gratitude include Judy Chessin, James Cohn, Norman M. Cohen, Steven Fink, Jonathan Gerard, Micah Greenstein, David Kaufman, Leonard Schoolman, and Roxanne Schneider-Shapiro.

Helping in mustering my incentive for this controversial undertaking, in widely ranging ways, have been Henry Claman, Norman J. Cohen, Kenneth E. Ehrlich, David Ellenson, Samuel K. Joseph, Holly Robinson, Brian Romer, and Diane T. Schuster—but above all Stuart M. Matlins (publisher of Jewish Lights Publishing) who sought out my manuscript, and Mark Ogilbee (project editor for Skylight Paths Publishing) whose patient receptivity and many talents channeled this manuscript through careful revision and ultimate production. For a variety of technical assistance with producing and securing visuals, with computer processing, or trial readings, I thank Gary M. Bretton Granatoor, John Bruggeman, Brett J. Chessin, Chad M. Chessin, Marc Jennings, Marshall Marvelli, and Mary Ann Sullivan. Also, too numerous to name, are HUC-JIR alumni who campaigned to make Gospel Dynamics (as I have called them) a required core course; students of many years but especially the class of 2009; congregations where I have spoken; clergy institutes and rabbinic kallot, Union for Reform Judaism national and regional biennials, and Central Conference of American Rabbis conventions where I have taught, and, especially, the 1989 Convention of the National Association of Temple Educators (who requested this volume but, until 2004, I did not feel that the seven required factors had come into convergence; see Chap. 23).

Brevity should not eclipse the gratitude and indebtedness I feel toward Beatrice Bruteau, PhD, who painstakingly challenged literally every word of this book, in some cases repeated times, whose breadth of knowledge and depth of intelligence amaze me. How fortunate I truly am for her devotedness to this project and her perseverance in helping me to see it through.

A book on one subject, laid out in many facets, would have been less trying than a book on what seemed a score of different subjects, each begun from square one. The patience of Judy, Brett, and Chad, and the support of David, Ben and Maia, were therefore all the more comforting, and gratitude, no matter how fervently expressed, simply cannot do them justice.

Abbreviations

Expressions

& par	"and parallel" (meaning a parallel between Mark and one other Synoptist)
& parr	"and parallels" (meaning parallels of Mark with both other Synoptists)
Chap./Chaps.	"Chapter"/"Chapters"
cf.	"compare with"
Fig. x.y	Figure (Chapter number), (figure number)
n.d.	"no date"
n.s./o.s.	"new series"/"old series"
NT	"New Testament"
v./vv.	"verse"/"verses"

Publications/Organizations/Denominations

AB	*Anchor Bible*
ABD	*Anchor Bible Dictionary*
ADL	Anti-Defamation League of B'nai B'rith
ANRW	*Aufstieg und Niedergang der römischen Welt*
ATR	*Anglican Theological Review*
BAR	*Biblical Archaeological Review*
Bib	*Biblica*
BR	*Bible Review*
CBQ	*Catholic Biblical Quarterly*
CC	*Christian Century*
CCAR	Central Conference of American Rabbis
CCARJ	*Central Conference of American Rabbis Journal*
CCJL	Center for Christian Jewish Learning
ELCA	Evangelical Lutheran Church in America
ET	*Expository Times*
EV	*Evangelische Theologie*
EvTh	*Journal of Evangelical Theology*
HUC-JIR	Hebrew Union College–Jewish Institute of Religion
HUCA	*Hebrew Union College Annual*
IB	*Interpreter's Bible*

ICC	International Critical Commentary
IDB	Interpreter's Dictionary of the Bible
JAOS	Journal of the American Oriental Society
JBL	Journal of Biblical Literature
JBR	Journal of Bible and Religion
JE	Jewish Encyclopedia
JES	Journal of Ecumenical Studies
JFGM	Jewish Federation of Greater Manchester
JHC	Journal of Higher Criticism
JPS	Jewish Publication Society of America
JQR	Jewish Quarterly Review
JR	Journal of Religion
JSHJ	Journal for the Study of the Historical Jesus
JSOT	Journal for the Study of the Old Testament
JTS	Jewish Theological Seminary
KJV	King James Version
LTP	Liturgy Training Publications
LTQ	Lexington Theological Quarterly
ML	Modern Liturgy
NCCB	National Conference of Catholic Bishops
NIB	New Interpreter's Bible
NTS	New Testament Studies
NvT	Novum Testamentum
PRS	Perspectives in Religious Studies
RE	Review and Expositor
RSV	Revised Standard Version
SBL	Society of Biblical Literature
SJT	Scottish Journal of Theology
TDNT	Theological Dictionary of the New Testament
TT	Theology Today
UAHC	Union of American Hebrew Congregations
URJ	Union for Reform Judaism
USCCB	United States Conference of Catholic Bishops
VT	Vetus Testamentum
ZNW	Zeitschrift für die Neutestamentliche Wissenschaft
ZTK	Zeitschrift für Theologie und Kirche

Ancient Sources (Consult also "Notes on Terminology")

Jewish Scripture (as sequenced in Christianity)

Gen	Genesis
Exod	Exodus
Lev	Leviticus
Num	Numbers
Deut	Deuteronomy

Josh   Joshua
Ju   Judges
1 Sa   1 Samuel
2 Sa   2 Samuel
1 Ki   1 Kings
2 Ki   2 Kings
1 Chr   1 Chronicles
2 Chr   2 Chronicles
Ps   Psalms
Isa   Isaiah
Jer   Jeremiah
Ezek   Ezekiel
Dan   Daniel
Zech   Zechariah

Apocrypha (Jewish)
Tob   Tobit
1 Macc   1 Maccabees
2 Macc   2 Maccabees

Pseudepigrapha
En   Enoch

New Testament
Mt   Matthew
Mk   Mark
Lk   Luke
Jn   John
Rom   Romans
1 Cor   1 Corinthians
2 Cor   2 Corinthians
Gal   Galatians
Phil   Philippians
1 Thes   1 Thessalonians
2 Thes   2 Thessalonians
Tit   Titus
Phile   Philemon
Heb   Hebrews
Rev   Revelation

The Historian Josephus (first century CE)
Antiq   *Antiquities of the Jews*
War   *Jewish War*

Church Writings

C.Cels.   Origen of Alexandria's *Contra Celsum*
HE   Eusebius' *Ecclesiastical History*

Rabbinic Literature

(Prefatory letters indicate where text is found: M. = Mishnah; T. = Tosefta; J. = Jerusalem Talmud; no letter = Babylonian Talmud)

Berakh	Berakhoth
Shab	Shabbat
Pes	Pesahim
Yom	Yoma
Hag	Hagigah
Yeb	Yebamot
Ket	Ketubot
Sot	Sotah
Git	Gittin
Sanh	Sanhedrin
A.Z.	Avodah Zarah
Hul	Hullin
Yad	Yadayim

Notes

Epigraph

1. Letter to the Grand Duchess Christina of Tuscany (1615).

Introduction

1. Permission for use of this slide is courtesy of Mary Ann Sullivan, Bluffton University.
2. Wolfgang Seiferth, *Synagogue and Church in the Middle Ages* (New York: Frederick Ungar, 1970), plate no. 31; Gertrud Schiller, *Ikonographie der christlichen Kunst* 2 (Gütersloh: Verlaghaus Gerd Mohn, 1966+), 1: plate no. 35.
3. Seiferth, *Synagogue*, plate nos. 10, 20; Schiller, *Ikonographie* 2: plate nos. 527, 530.
4. Schiller, *Ikonographie*, 2: plate no. 527; Seiferth, *Synagogue*, plate no. 28.
5. Schiller, *Ikonographie*, 2: plate nos. 442, 451, 529, 570. Also, Seiferth, *Synagogue*, plate nos. 28, 29, 42; Ruth Mellinkoff, *Outcasts* 2 (Berkeley: Univ. of California, 1994), plate no. III.90.
6. Cf. Seiferth, *Synagogue*, 103, 120–21.
7. Seiferth, *Synagogue*, plate no. 18.
8. [Church fathers]—Influential theologians (especially during Christianity's first five centuries) who commented on New Testament theological themes.

Notes on Terminology

1. E.g., of king (1 Sa 10:1; 16:13; 2 Sa 2:4; 5:3); priest (Exod 28:41; Lev 8:12,30); and prophet (1 Ki 19:16; 1 Chr 16:22; Isa 61:1).
2. E.g., Isa 2:2–4; Jer 3:17; Joel 3:18; cf. Zech 8:23.
3. [The term: "Christian"]—Given the ease with which the Evangelists retrojected late developments, we cannot rely on the Lucan statement (Acts 11:26) that it was in Antioch (of the 30s) that the followers of Jesus "were for the first time called Christians."
4. Cf., however, Chap. 20 of this vol.
5. Raymond Brown, "Not Jewish Christianity and Gentile Christianity, But Types of Jewish/Gentile Christianity," *CBQ* 45 (1983): 74–79.

Chapter 1

1. E.g., T. Shab 13:5; cf. T. Yad 2:13.
2. Sanh 43a; cf. 107b.

3. [Federations]—Major urban Jewish communal organizations that provide charitable, recreational, and cultural services.

4. [Magdalene]—In Shab 104b and Sanh 67a: "the mother was Miriam [i.e., Mary] the dresser of women's hair ['Magdalene' resembles the Aramaic word for this profession]." Hag 4b: "bring me Miriam [again Mary] the dresser of women's hair" (the medieval Tosaphot commentary adds: "this about Miriam the dresser of women's hair took place in the second temple [era] ... she was the mother of a certain person [i.e., Jesus], as in Shab 104").

5. Entitled "Shall Jesus of Nazareth Be Taught in the Jewish Sabbath School?" (1899). The Jacob Rader Marcus Center of the American Jewish Archives (Cincinnati).

6. [Reform]—Data should be drawn widely, but substantive surveys come only from Reform Judaism.

7. [Reform]—Rabbis Kohler, Berkowitz, Philipson, Krauskopf, Hirsch, Wise, Jastrow, de Sola Mendes, Gottheil, Szold, Cohen, Felsenthal, and Heller (assessment by experts in American Jewish History: David E. Kaufman, Jonathan Sarna, Lance Sussman and Gary Zola; Fred Krome and Kevin Proffitt).

8. Harris Weinstock, *Jesus the Jew and Other Addresses* (London: Funk & Wagnalls, 1902).

9. Master's thesis by Roxanne Schneider [-Shapiro]: *Teaching Jewish Children About Jesus: Is the Advice of Our Sages Still Sage Advice?* (Cincinnati: HUC-JIR, 1999); the subtitle, which I suggested, is used also as the title for this chapter.

10. This section's quotations are from Schneider[-Shapiro], *Teaching*, 41–43, 46–47, 51–54, 56, 59–62, 65, 67, 70, 72–74, 78–81, 86, 90.

11. This section's quotations are from Schneider[-Shapiro], *Teaching*, 54, 66, 89.

Chapter 2

1. A more extensive treatment of this subject appears in my contribution, under the same title, to *Jesus through Jewish Eyes*, Beatrice Bruteau, ed. (Maryknoll: Orbis, 2001), 1–24.

2. John Meier, *A Marginal Jew* 1 (New York: Doubleday, 1991), 94.

3. [*Flavianum*]—*Antiquities of the Jews* XVIII.iii.3; 63–64. Writing in Rome at the time of Emperors Vespasian, Titus, and Domitian (69–96), comprising the *Flavian* dynasty, Josephus is termed Josephus Flavius (or the reverse).

4. *Antiq* XX.ix.1; 197–203.

5. Sequential references for this paragraph: Justin Martyr, *Dialogue with Trypho*, Introduction; §§68; 55; 27 and 68; and 67; 89.

6. Regarding "ben [son of] Stada": T. Shab 11:15; T. Sanh 10:11; Sanh 67a; Shab 104b. "Peloni" ("a certain person"): M. Yeb 4:13; T. Yeb 3:3,4; Yeb 49ab; Yom 66b. "[Ben] Netzer": Sanh 43a; Ket 51b [cf. Isa 11:1]). Possibly even "Balaam": M. Abot 5:19; M. Sanh 10:2; Sanh 106ab.

7. Jesus' miracles: Shab 104b; J. Shab 13d; cf. Mk 3:22; Mt 9:34; 12:24. Jesus' chronology: cf. Sanh 107b; Sot 47a; Shab 104b; Git 90a. Jesus' disciples: Sanh 43a; cf. M. Abot 2:8; Sanh 14a; A.Z. 8b. Magdalene: this vol., Chap. 1 n. 4.

8. Cf. Deut 13:6ff.; T. Sanh 9:7; T. Hul 2:22–24; Shab 116ab; Sanh 43a, 67a, 103a, 107b; Sot 47a; A.Z. 16b–17a.

9. Sanh 43a; cf. T. Sanh 10:11; J. Sanh 25cd; Sanh 67a.

10. I thank Susan Einbinder for this point.

11. [Pandera]—Origen of Alexandria (ca. 248) relates that the pagan philosopher Celsus (ca. 178) said he was told by a Jew that a Roman soldier, Panthera, in Judea, was Jesus' extra-marital father (*C.Cels.* 1,28,32). For variants (Pandira, Pantira, etc.): T. Hull 2:22; Shab 104b; J. Shab 14d and A.Z. 40d, 41a.

12. Notably Abraham Geiger, *Das Judenthum und seine Geschichte* (Breslau: Schletter, 1864); Heinrich Graetz, *Sinai et Golgotha* (Paris: Michael Lévy frères, 1867).

Chapter 3

1. [Twenty-seven]—Counting 1 and 2 Corinthians, 1 and 2 Thessalonians, etc., separately.

2. [50 to 150]—Likely earliest, 1 Thessalonians; latest, 2 Peter.

3. Mark encompasses approximately 11,000 Greek words; Matthew 18,300; Luke 19,400; John 16,600.

4. ["John"]—Scholars debate how many of the five works ascribed to a "John"— the Gospel of John, the Revelation (to John), the three epistles of John—shared common authorship.

5. [Apocryphal]—In 1945 more than fifty ancient Christian texts were discovered at Nag Hammadi (Egypt), confirming patristic allegations of "heretical" books.

6. [Those curious]—I trace the change to Matthew's (and Luke's) reliance on the story of righteous Naboth, who lost his "vineyard," was tried on trumped-up charges akin to blasphemy (cursing God), and was then *first* taken outside the city and *thereafter* executed (1 Ki 21:13; cf. Acts 7:58).

7. ["Q"]—Matthew and Luke present divergent forms of the Lord's Prayer (Fig. 3.7). How explain that their source in common here was "Q"? We would have to raise the problem of whose version is the more primitive: e.g., is Luke's more compact rendition closer to "Q" whereas Matthew introduced changes, or did Luke shorten the "Q" version, etc.?

8. [Luke used Matthew?]—Would this account for why Luke's change of Mark matches Matthew's—that Luke noted Matthew's change and replicated it?

9. [Again, the curious]—Matthew enlarges the arresting party so as to aggrandize Jesus' importance; Luke cancels the flight by Jesus' followers because Luke shifts Jesus' post-resurrection appearances from Galilee (as in Mark and Matthew) to Jerusalem's environs, and thus needs Jesus' followers to remain on hand there.

Chapter 4

1. See L. Michael White, *From Jesus to Christianity* (San Francisco: Harper, 2004), 229–31.

2. White, *From Jesus*, 57–66; *Religions of Antiquity*, Robert Seltzer, ed. (New York: Macmillan, 1987), 151–304.

3. Samuel Sandmel, *A Jewish Understanding of the New Testament*. Repr. (Woodstock, VT: Jewish Lights, 2005), 99ff.

4. Sandmel, *Understanding*, 102.

Chapter 5

 1. *War* II.viii.1; 117–18 / *Antiq* XVIII.i.6; 23–25 / XX.v.2; 100–04.
 2. [Archelaus replaced]—Judea (and Samaria), now incorporated into the province of Syria, became thereby part of Rome's empire.
 3. [Governors]—The earlier seven were termed "prefects," those later "procurators." (Pilate, a prefect, is often mislabeled a procurator.)
 4. [*Fig. 5.2*]—Some will date origins of the Sanhedrin, synagogue, and Pharisees before Hasmonean times. Essenes may have extended a legitimate priestly line (usurped by Hasmoneans) but, following Josephus, I present them separately from the priests. The dating of some group cut-offs in 70 (priests and Sadducees) refers only to the end of their prominence, not their existence. The reconstituted Sanhedrin lasted until the fifth century; and synagogues, rabbis, and Christians through today. New "activists" arose, and another, probably larger revolt, against Rome ensued under Bar Kokhba (132).
 5. *War* II.viii.2–14; 119–66 / *Antiq* XIII.v.9; 171–73 / XVIII.i.2–6; 11–25.
 6. [Defining Pharisees]—Rabbinic texts definitely presenting the "Pharisees" relevant to Gospel study are those that contrast *perushim* (Hebrew for "Pharisees") with *tsedduqim* (Hebrew for "Sadducees"). The same Hebrew term for "pharisees" (lower cased, so to speak) means "separatists," especially "ascetics." Factoring in those passages would hamper defining the New Testament's Pharisees; see Michael Cook, "Jesus and the Pharisees," *JES* 15 (1978): 440–61; Ellis Rivkin, "Defining the Pharisees: *The Tannaitic Sources*," *HUCA* 40,41 (1969–70): 205–49.
 7. Rivkin, *A Hidden Revolution* (Nashville: Abingdon, 1978), passim.
 8. Cf. *Antiq* XIII.x.6; 297 / XVII.ii.4; 41.
 9. *Antiq* XIII.x.6; 297 / cf. XVIII.i.4; 16 / *War* II.viii.14; 165.
10. *War* II.viii.2–13; 119–61 / *Antiq* XIII.v.9; 171–73 / XVIII.i.5; 18–22.
11. [Christian-Essene differences]—Belief in two messiahs, depreciation of women, ultra-strict legalism, and militaristic imagery (among others).
12. *Antiq* XX.v.2; 100–04. On the "Fourth Philosophy" broadly: *War* IV.iii.1–14; 121–223 / V.i.2,5; 9–14 and 33–53 / VII.x.i; 407–19.
13. [Matthew substitutes Pharisees for scribes]—Mt 12:24; 22:34,41 (cf., respectively, Mk 3:22; 12:28,35). Intricacies here involved—including passages where Mark tries to "move" the Judean scribes into Galilee (2:16; 7:1; cf. Acts 23:9)—are worked through in Michael Cook, *Mark's Treatment of the Jewish Leaders* (Leiden: Brill, 1978), 58–67.
14. [Activists shared Pharisaic orientation]—*Antiq* XVIII.i.6; 23–25.
15. [Pilate-Caiaphas' long joint-tenure]—The 14 governors from 6–66 minus Agrippa I's 3 years = 57, minus Pilate's 11 years = 46, divided by 13 other governors averages 3.5 years per governor. The 28 high priests during the Temple's last 107 years minus Caiaphas' 19 years = 88, divided by 27 other high priests averages 3.3 years per high priest. *Antiq* XX.x.1; 224–30 / cf. *Antiq* XVIII.ii.1–2; 26–35.
16. *War* II.ix.2–4; 169–77 / *Antiq* XVIII.iii.1–3, iv.1–2; 55–64, 85–89; and Lk 13:1; Philo of Alexandria, *Embassy to Gaius*, 299–305.

17. [Two-system diagram]—I credit the basic idea of this chart to Ellis Rivkin but do not wish to saddle him with my alterations. Also, I depart from him by removing the Talmudic court system from the Jewish side and by denying that Jesus had any Sanhedrin trial on the Roman side.

18. ["Only God is King"]—The Fourth Philosophy's uniqueness: "God is to be their only Ruler and Lord [*hegemona kai despoten*]" (*Antiq* XVIII.i.6; 23). The Sicarii in Egypt urged fellow Jews "to esteem God alone as their lord [*despotes*]" (*War* VII.x.1; 410); cf. resisting efforts to make them confess "Caesar as their lord [*Kaisar despoten*]" (418). John's contrasting portrayal: "Pilate said to them, 'Shall I crucify your King?' The chief priests answered, 'We have no king but *Caesar*'" (19:15).

19. ["Sanhedrin"]—The Temple's destruction, in 70, ended the position of high priest and the ad hoc Sanhedrin where he presided (when convened by authority of the Roman governor). "Sanhedrin" (Greek, *synedrion*) thereby became a free-floating, disembodied term later co-opted as an alternate title for the rabbinic *bet din*, whenever that term, applying to a *different* court system, had come into usage.

20. [Seeing Jesus as *we* are]—Thus, confident times for world improvement yielded depictions of a social-reformer Jesus; World War I an apocalyptic Son of man-type; Israel's Six Day War (1967) a militant Jesus; oppressive class struggle (e.g., Latin America) a liberator Jesus; etc.

21. Mk 10:11f.; Q 16:18 (although "Q" is hypothetical, there are ways to cite [from Matthew and Luke] reconstructions of its materials drawn); and 1 Cor 7:10f.

22. [Skeptical scholars]—Some construe the text a clever way to instruct: know the difference between claims by God and those by Caesar (it thus could be authentic to Jesus); see Robert Funk, Roy Hoover, and the Jesus Seminar, *The Five Gospels* (New York: Macmillan, 1993), 102.

23. John Meier, "The Present State of the 'Third Quest' for the Historical Jesus," *Bib* 80 (1999), 459–87.

24. Robert Miller, "The Jesus Seminar and Its Critics," §5 (paper delivered to the Historical Jesus section of the SBL, Nov. 1996).

25. [Apocryphal gospels]—I.e., pitting other gospels against those four which the Church approved (Chap. 3 n. 5). I see no compelling proofs that apocryphal works, even *if* datable early enough, offer anything that *substantially* sharpens what we know about Jesus.

26. [Stratifying "Q"]—I.e., dividing the hypothetical "Q" into chronological layers on the basis of themes or orientation, and then deciding which layer was earliest and assigning *that* as possibly helpful in reconstructing the historical Jesus (with later layers said to reflect subsequent phases of the developing Church). Absent any document to examine, I cannot see how we can confidently "stratify" it. See Bart Ehrman, *Jesus* (Oxford: Univ. Press, 1999), 132ff.

27. Mk 15:32; Mt 27:42; Jn 1:49; 12:13. See Chap. 18, below.

28. [Zechariah and Jehu]—Zech 9:9: "your king comes to you; triumphant and victorious ... humble and riding on an ass, on a colt the foal of an ass." The garments that the people threw on Jesus' colt (Mk 11:7 & parr) appear drawn from Jehu's acclamation as King, when every commander "in haste took his

garment and put it under [Jehu]" (2 Ki 9:13). My gratitude here to Beatrice Bruteau.

29. [Temple furniture]—See E. P. Sanders, upon whom I here largely draw: *Jesus and Judaism* (Philadelphia: Fortress, 1985), 63ff.; *Judaism: Practice and Belief* (Philadelphia: Trinity, 1992), 89ff.; and *The Historical Figure of Jesus* (London: Penguin, 1993), 255ff.

30. [Son of man]—I do not believe that we need to accept apocalyptic "Son of man" texts as genuine to Jesus in order to identify him as an "apocalyptic Pharisee." Even without these, Jesus could still preach the imminent coming of God's Kingdom and be crucified for so doing.

31. [Parables]—Even parables that may have originated with Jesus may be reworked extensively, or allegorized (below, Chap. 16), making them difficult to apply in identifying him. The underlying versions of those manifesting reversals and challenging ethics represent the best guess: the Prodigal Son (Lk 15:11–32); the Unmerciful Servant/Creditor (Mt 18:23–35); the Good Samaritan (Lk 10:30–35); the Talents (Mt 25:14–30) or Pounds (Lk 19:12–27); and the Laborers in the Vineyard (Mt 20:1–15).

Chapter 6

1. [Acts: Jews' increasing disaffection]—Opening: 2:41ff.; 4:4; 5:14; 6:1,7. Middle: 18:4ff.,12f.; 19:8f.; 21:27f. End: 28:25ff.

2. [Inconsistent]—Since the second volume, Acts, has multitudes of Jews early on flocking to Christianity.

3. Mk 13:9; Mt 10:17; cf. Lk 6:22; for texts in John, see below, Chap. 18.

4. Summarized by Alan Segal's *Paul the Convert* (New Haven: Yale, 1990), 7ff.

5. E.g., Lk 24:13,33,47,52; Acts 1:4,8,12.

6. [A non-trip]—By having Jesus *forbid* them to do so (Lk 24:49), against Mk 14:28 and 16:7, which explicitly direct them to meet him in Galilee.

7. This paragraph quotes John Knox, "Acts and the Pauline Letter Corpus," *Studies in Luke-Acts*, L. E. Keck and J. L. Martyn, eds. (Philadelphia: Fortress, 1980), 283; cf. Morton Enslin: "'Luke' and Paul," *JAOS* 58 (1938): 81ff.; and Enslin, "Once Again, Luke and Paul," *ZNW* 61 (1970): 253–71.

8. [Fourteen years]—Galatians was written in the 50s; "fourteen years" does not extend back far enough to reach Paul's "conversion" (likely the early 30s).

9. [Crediting God]—The thrust here is that Paul wants to claim direct revelation from God, however God saw fit to convey this (even through Paul's experience with Damascus Christians?) but in any event circumventing all dependence on the recognized Jerusalem church leaders.

10. [Mentions of Jesus alone]—Rom 3:26; 8:11; 1 Cor 12:3; 2 Cor 4:5,10 (x2),11 (x2),14; 11:4; Gal 6:17; Phil 2:10; 1 Thes 1:10; 4:14 (x2).

11. [Lord]—Not counting the appearance of "Lord" in Paul's quotations from Jewish scripture or in 1 Thes 2:15, which I see as post-Pauline (see Chap. 11, below).

12. [Paul's knowledge of Jesus]—Known primarily from the kerygma: Jesus' brother(s) (1 Cor 9:5; 15:7; Gal 1:19); his twelve disciples (1 Cor 15:5); and

that he was crucified (1 Cor 2:2) and buried (1 Cor 15:4). Presupposed: Jesus' "birth of a woman" (Gal 4:4) and Davidic descent (Rom 1:3—the latter inferable simply because he was held to be the Messiah). All that remains: Jesus' teaching on divorce (1 Cor 7:10f.) and his Last Supper (1 Cor 11:23ff.).

13. In varying degrees: Isa 2:2f.; 45:22ff.; 49:6; 51:4; 56:8; 66:19; Mic 4:1ff.; Zech 2:11; 8:20ff.; cf. Tob 14:6f.; 1 En 90:30ff.

Chapter 7

1. [Three phases]—*Consonance:* Mt 6:9ff.; parables of the Kingdom esp. in Mk 4, Mt 13 and 25, and Lk 8 and 13; Mk 12:28ff. *Regret:* Rom 9:1ff.; 10:1ff.; 11:1,11f.,25f. *Hostility:* Mt 23; Jn 5:42,45f.; 6:53; 8:23f.,37f.,44ff.; 10:34; 13:3; Mk 14:55–65 & parr; 15:6–15a & parr; Mt 27:24f.

2. Michael Cook, "Jesus and the Pharisees," *JES* 15 (1978): 441–60; Cook, "Rabbinic Judaism and Early Christianity," *RE* 84 (1987): 201–21.

3. [Hostility]—To those who believe that most Christians still perceived themselves within the Jewish people even into the 90s, tensions reported by the Gospels are *intra*-Jewish disputes. Even on such a basis, hostility (in this case toward non-Christian Jews still perceived as fellow-Jews) would remain assignable to the post-70 time frame, and the representation of Jesus as having taken up a hostile demeanor would remain a function of changes in (Jewish-)Christians' self-perception vis-à-vis non-Christian fellow Jews.

4. [Filter of Paul]—Representative passages here would be: (1) Gal 2:16; 3:10f.,23ff.; Rom 7:1ff. (2) Gal 1:15f.; 2:7; 3:11ff. (3) Gal 4:22ff.; Rom 9:6ff.,25f.,30ff., qualified by 11:23ff.

5. [Paul not unique]—Cf. Gal 2:11f., where the practice of eating with Gentiles is not expressly said to have originated at Paul's behest; and where Cephas/Peter—possibly on his own initiative—also ate with them until the arrival of James' emissaries occasioned a crisis.

6. Stimulating such reasoning is E. P. Sanders, *Jesus and Judaism* (Philadelphia: Fortress, 1985), Intro. (esp. 55ff.).

7. Gal 2:11ff.; 4:10; Rom 14:1ff.,5f.,13ff.

8. [Elijah]—Josephus, describing John the Baptist without Elijah trappings, conveys a more credible account of how John died: *Antiq* XVIII.v.2; 116–19.

9. Isa 42:1ff.; 49:1ff.; 50:4ff.; 52:13–53:12.

10. Raymond Brown, *The Death of the Messiah* (New York: Doubleday, 1994), 15.

Chapter 8

1. [The term, "Gospel Dynamics"]—E.g., Michael J. Cook, "Time To Teach Jews Gospel Dynamics," *The Forward* (Apr. 14, 2006), A7; Rachel Zoll, "Reform Rabbi Michael J. Cook Says Jews Are Handicapped by Not Knowing New Testament" (Assoc. Press: Apr. 8, 2006; 1:02 PM EDT); Cook, "My Opinion: Ending Gospel Ignorance," *Reform Judaism* (Winter 2006), 80.

2. Problems caused Christians by "Jews" here means non-Christian Jews opposing Christians.

3. [Piercing]—Absent from the Hebrew original, which reads "like a lion" or "they dig," neither clear. On the former: "a company of evildoers encircles me *like a lion*," or "biting *like a lion* my hands and my feet." On the latter, not "they dig into" my hands and feet but conceivably "my hands and feet *dig*"—surrounded, the only place to escape (poetically) begins with digging a hole.

4. [Matthew implies no]—Because he spots and corrects an error: Jesus told the *men* only, in Mk 14:28, never the women, so Matthew makes it the *angel* who tells the women.

Chapter 9

1. Raymond Brown terms this the "Christological Moment" in *The Birth of the Messiah* (Garden City: Doubleday, 1977), 30 n. 15.

2. ["Before they came together"]—Joseph and Mary are portrayed in between two steps of matrimonial procedure. During "betrothal," the bride remained at her own family home, about a year, before her formal transferral to the home of the husband—what is meant by "before they came together"—at which time a couple would first be permitted sexual relations. As a legally ratified marriage, "betrothal" was binding unlike mere engagement today, so the woman's infringement (e.g., sex with another man) was punishable as adultery.

3. [Magi as three kings]—Three gifts (Mt 2:11) do not require three Magi. But the pagan astrologer, Balaam, was traveling with *two* companions (Num 22:22) when he saw "a *star* come forth out of Jacob" (Num 24:17). Passages establishing the Magi as kings could include Ps 72:11 ("may all kings fall down before him") and Isa 60:3 ("kings [will come] to the brightness of your rising").

4. [Leaps for joy]—Beyond showing Mary hurrying to congratulate and assist Elizabeth, this story could be an effort to subordinate John to Jesus (since the sect of John's followers rivaled Christianity in Luke's day; see Acts 19:1ff.). Also, with Zechariah struck dumb (1:20ff.) and Elizabeth secluded for her initial five months (1:24), no one knows about Elizabeth's conception. That Gabriel's word concerning Elizabeth is true reassures Mary that his word to *her* is likewise.

5. [Redemption of the first-born]—Exod 13:12ff.; Num 3:44ff., 18:15ff. Actually Luke combines this with another custom: the mother's after-birth purification (Lev 12:6). The latter, not the former, could be associated with a sanctuary (Brown, *Birth*, 448). The *combination* enables Luke to bring Jesus to the Temple as early as possible (see Chap. 17, below).

6. Cf. Proto-Evangelium of James (ca. 150).

7. [First to pay homage]—Recall that shepherds are in Luke alone.

8. [Two-chapters preface]—An editor doing this could then have tried to smooth over inconsistencies between the infancy narrative and the Gospel proper: e.g., Jesus "being the son (*as was supposed*) of Joseph" (3:23); Nazareth where Jesus was "brought up" (4:16; i.e., not *born*).

9. Justin Martyr (*Dialogue* 100) is first to ascribe Davidic ancestry to Mary (second century).

10. [Birth of a rival]—See Sigmund Freud's litany of such tales, opening *Moses and Monotheism*, K. Jones, trans. (New York: Vintage, 1967).

11. [Census in 6 CE]—This census was declared in conjunction with Judea's incorporation into Syria (*Antiq* XVIII.i.1; 1–10). Given how Acts 5:37 refers to the 6 CE census with the definite article (suggesting that this was the *sole* census), Luke's dating of this census as, instead, before Herod the Great died in 4 BCE seems to make Luke roughly a decade too early (as if he overlooked the years of Archelaus' rule: 4 BCE–6 CE).

12. [Rumors concerning origins]—Mark 6:3 states: "is not this the carpenter, the son of Mary?" A Jewish male would normally be associated with his *father's* name, even after his father died. Was Jesus' father then altogether unknown? Mt 13:55 struggles to supply a "father's" presence and to weaken any opprobrium in how Mary is mentioned: he changes "the carpenter" to "the carpenter's *son*," and changes "the son of Mary" to "and is not his mother called Mary?" Cf., also, Joseph's resolve to divorce Mary (Mt 1:19), and words that John ascribes to Jesus' Jewish opponents (8:41): "We were not born of fornication" (meant to imply Jesus' illegitimacy; see Jane Schaberg, *The Illegitimacy of Jesus* [San Francisco: Harper & Row, 1987], 157ff.).

13. Paula Fredriksen, *From Jesus to Christ* (New Haven: Yale, 1988), 141.

14. [Balaam]—The Magi sighting a star seem dependent on this pagan astrologer, Balaam, sent from the *east* by the wicked king (Balak; cf. Herod) to destroy the king's perceived rivals (Israel; cf. Jesus). Balaam foils the king's designs (cf. the Magi trick Herod). Balaam sees "a star ... out of Jacob" (Num 24:17) by which he foretells Israel's ruler. The Magi "went away to their own country" (Mt 2:12), modeled on "Balaam went off to his home" (Num 24:25).

15. Elizabeth (1 Sa 1:1ff.); Mary or Elizabeth (2:1ff.); Jesus (2:26).

16. Gen 17:17ff.; 18:10ff.

Chapter 10

1. *Gravette Herald*, Apr. 23, 1997: 3.

2. [Haggadah]—Special Passover liturgy.

3. See Chap. 17, below.

4. Cf. Deut 16:2,5–6; 2 Ki 23:21–23.

5. Julius Kaplan, *The Redaction of the Babylonian Talmud* (Jerusalem: Makor, 1972), 201ff.

6. Lawrence Hoffman, in correspondence (July 15, 2004).

7. Hoffman, "Historical Introduction," *A Passover Haggadah* (New York: CCAR, 1974), 10.

8. [Heretics]—The term used may not matter: if "Nazarenes" ("Jewish-Christians") were those to be cursed, Gamaliel becomes anti-*Christian*; if *minim,* "heretics," this could still encompass Christians.

9. Jacob Marcus, *The Jew in the Medieval World* (New York: Atheneum, 1975), 121.

10. [Fund]—Through collections missionaries encouraged from churches and others for Seder demonstrations, liturgical materials, etc.

11. [Bread]—The generic, "bread," could encompass matzah. But, in discussing this festival, Hebrew scripture uses *"unleavened* bread."

12. [Sat at table]—In Matthew, Jesus sends *all* the disciples (not two) to prepare the Jerusalem meal; Luke retains Mark's sending of only two of the inner circle.

13. Cf. John 19:36 with Exod 12:46; Num 9:12; Ps 34:20(21). Paul also employed "paschal lamb" imagery with reference to Jesus (1 Cor 5:7).

14. For attempted solutions: I. H. Marshall, *Last Supper and Lord's Supper* (Grand Rapids: Eerdmans, 1980), Chap. 3; R. O'Toole, "Last Supper," *ABD* (New York: Doubleday, 1992), IV: 235ff.

15. Bishops' Committee on the Liturgy *Newsletter* (NCCB: March 1980) 12; called to my attention by Eugene Fisher.

16. Quoted from *About the NH [New Hampshire] Jewish-Catholic Seder* (CCJL, Boston College; JFGM; Roman Catholic Diocese of Manchester, 2003), 2; sent me courtesy of Philip Cunningham.

17. "Guidelines for Lutheran-Jewish Relations," ELCA (1998), extending a 1994 "Declaration to the Jewish Community."

18. *The Passover Celebration*, Leon Klenicki, ed. (Chicago: LTP, 1980; rev. 2001).

19. Regarding this I thank Mark Washofsky.

Chapter 11

1. [Second Vatican Council]—See Chap. 23.

2. See Chap. 23.

3. I am indebted here to E. P. Sanders; see above, Chap. 5 n. 29.

4. [Money-changers]—I am much indebted to E. P. Sanders also for the contents of this paragraph. Maligning the money-changers appears a literary device to camouflage genuine *militancy* by Jesus within some Temple precinct. These functionaries performed legitimate Temple services (changing pilgrims' currency into coinage acceptable on Temple premises; selling certifiedly unblemished animals for sacrifice; etc.). See *Jesus and Judaism*, 63ff., and *Judaism: Practice and Belief 63 BCE–66 CE* (Philadelphia: Trinity, 1992), 89ff.

5. Suetonius, *Life of Nero*, 16; cf. Tacitus, *Annals* xv.44.

6. ["Hybrid riddle" even in *Nostra Aetate*]—*Blame*: "... the Jewish authorities and those who followed their lead pressed for the death of Christ; still, what happened in His passion cannot be charged against all the Jews, without distinction, then alive, nor against the Jews of today...." *Benefit*: "Besides, as the Church has always held and holds now, Christ underwent His passion and death freely, because of the sins of men and out of infinite love, in order that all may reach salvation."

7. John Gager, *The Origins of Anti-Semitism* (New York: Oxford, 1983): 118ff.; Robert Wilken, *John Chrysostom and the Jews* (Berkeley: Univ. of California, 1983), passim.

8. [Acts 3:13–15 reflects tampering]—It is not that verses following (e.g., 3:17) *soften* this one but, rather, that *they* are original, with this verse's anti-Jewish phraseology *added*. Possibly the original here read: "God ... glorified his servant Jesus. But you denied the Holy and Righteous One, whom God raised from the dead." Later words were grafted in from the Barabbas tale. Another expression, from later theology, is awkward (God raises the "Author of life" from the dead?).

<u>9</u>. [1 Thes 2:14–16 by a later hand]—Supporters of this text's authenticity—who still agree that "God's wrath" must mean the Temple's destruction—have to explain how Paul, writing around 50, can use the *past* tense when referring to an event twenty years later ("God's wrath *has come* upon them at last!"). Thus it is not unusual to be told that God's wrath was—or Paul *saw* it as—*already* dangling over the Jews two decades earlier, or that it was so inevitable as to be *as good as* past! More plausible is the conjecture that someone well after 70 felt "called upon" to add this touch (drawing on Mt 23:31–24:2 and Acts 7:52). Yet we lack manuscript evidence that this was added. On the other hand, the oldest extant versions of 1 Thessalonians date from centuries later: that an insertion was accomplished early enough to be entered into surviving copies seems more persuasive than ascription of these verses to Paul himself, *especially since he saw Jesus' death as a benefit, not a cause for blame.*

<u>10</u>. [Prophetic demonstrations]—Other examples from Sanders (*Historical*, 253ff.): Ezekiel takes a sun-dried brick and draws in relief Jerusalem under siege, and uses an iron plate, a griddle, to symbolize God's role in Jerusalem's fall (4:1ff.); uses a sword (5:1ff.) to cut off hair and beard (shorn hair = the fate awaiting the people); dramatizes the gathering of whatever belongings exiles could carry (12:1ff.); joins two sticks together (37:15ff. = the reestablishment of a united Israel).

Chapter 12

1. Marion Soards surveys attempted reconstructions: "The Question of a Premarcan Passion Narrative," *The Death of the Messiah* 2, Raymond Brown, ed. (New York: Doubleday: 1994), 1492–1524. Mainly critiquing the theory is Werner Kelber, ed., *The Passion in Mark* (Philadelphia: Fortress, 1976).

2. [Unknowns]—E.g., did Mark retain the pre-Marcan text's wording verbatim, preserve *all* of it, interweave additional sources with it, etc.? Linguistic studies do not help (Soards, "Premarcan Passion," 1520).

3. [Caiaphas]—Mark does not name the high priest. We use "Caiaphas" (Mt 26:3) for convenience.

4. [Sanhedrin]—Every appearance of "council" in our Chap. 12 translates the Greek *synedrion* (Sanhedrin).

5. [The whole council]—The high priest is encompassed within "the chief priests." If we protest him separate, then, still, 15:1 should read "and the high priest," not "and the whole council."

6. [Correspondences]—Manifest in Greek as well as English (although readers should know that the RSV sometimes translates, as exactly the same, phraseology that, in Greek, is slightly variant).

7. [Time-lapse]—Otherwise v. 56 might simply have been rewritten altogether.

8. E.g., John Donahue, *Are You the Christ?* (Missoula: Scholars Press, 1973): 62.

9. [Mark's bias]—See Chap. 15➜, below.

10. [They]—Some readers, realizing the problem, argue that it was a different crowd. But why, then, Mark's statement that the chief priests had to "stir" them up?

11. [Precise verbal equivalents]—First we subtract apparent Marcan *expansions*: Peter's denial of Jesus (14:54,66–72); the Sanhedrin trial (14:55–65); Pilate's

"severe" question and Jesus' minimal answer thereto (15:2); and the Barabbas episode (15:6–15a). Then also correlative Marcan *editorial adjustments*: "and all the chief priests and the elders and the scribes were assembled" (from 14:53); "and the whole council" (from 15:1); also "again" (from 15:4), and "further" (from 15:5).

12. [Percentages]—Of 551 Greek words, subtracting 492 leaves 59; of the 691 English words, subtracting 606 leaves 85.

13. [Obstacles still in play]—See Chap. 12 n. 2, above.

14. [Four upcoming mentions of "King of the Jews"]—One in Pilate's interrogation, two in the Barabbas paragraph, one on the placard.

15. E.g., Benjamin Bacon, *The Beginnings of Gospel Story* (New Haven: Yale, 1909), 24, 26; W. Bousset, *Kyrios Christos* (Nashville: Abingdon, 1970; original 1913), 77ff.; Rudolf Bultmann, *History of the Synoptic Tradition*, J. Marsh, trans. (Oxford: Blackwell, 1963; original 1921), 15; E. Klostermann, *Das Markusevangelium* (Tübingen: Mohr, 1926), 25; B. H. Branscomb, *The Gospel of Mark* (London: Houder & Stoughton, 1937), 45; Vincent Taylor, *The Formation of the Gospel Tradition* (London: Macmillan, 1949), 66ff.

Chapter 13

1. [Even John]—Almost three decades later, would John not at least know of Mark's Joseph tradition (without direct access to Mark's text)?

2. ["All" condemned Jesus]—Preserved neither by Matthew nor Luke; nor does Matthew or John include Joseph within any council.

3. See Fig. 16.4 (Mark, only), and commentary to Figs. 5.2 and 5.3.

4. *War* II.ix.2–4; 169–77 / *Antiq* XVIII.iii.1–2; 55–62.

5. *War* IV.v.2; 317; cf. Tob 1.17; 2.4.

6. [Bit-players]—Akin to this approach is William Lyons, "On the Life and Death of Joseph of Arimathea," *JSHJ* 2 (2004): 29–53; and akin to what follows thereafter is C. Black, *The Disciples According to Mark* (Sheffield: JSOT, 1989); and J. F. Williams, *Other Followers of Jesus* (Sheffield: Sheffield Academic Press, 1994).

7. [Half-a-dozen or so]—Because the person defending Jesus (cutting off the ear of the high priest's slave) gets fleeting attention, he may not belong with the others, although *he* comes to Jesus' physical aid, which no one else does.

8. [Suitably preparing Jesus' body]—Which was to be washed and anointed with oils and spices, then wrapped in linen containing spices.

9. [Her virtue]—This story appears in other versions (Lk 7:36–50; Jn 12:1–8), but it is Mark's personal bent to connect the woman's action with Jesus' burial; see Robert Funk and the Jesus Seminar, *The Acts of Jesus* (San Francisco: Harper, 1998), 136.

10. [Amos 2:16]—Since unrolling scrolls to find Jewish scriptural texts was cumbersome, likely assembled were "testimony" collections: selected texts, copied without reference to context, especially containing phrases such as "in that day" (like Amos 2:16)—taken to reference the day of *Jesus*. Errors could thus occur (e.g., in context Amos does not present positively the man he describes).

See J. Rendel Harris, *Testimonies*, 2 vol (Cambridge: Univ. Press, 1916–20); Alessandro Falcetta, "The Testimony Research of James Rendel Harris," *NvT* 45 [2003]: 280–99.

11. ["Forsook"]—Peter "followed" Jesus but ultimately to forsake him (14:54). The Amos text is problematic because it requires also that the young man "flee."

12. J. D. Crossan, *Who Killed Jesus?* (San Francisco: HarperCollins, 1995), 160–88; Crossan and J. L. Reed, *Excavating Jesus* (San Francisco: Harper-Collins, 2001), 230–70; Martin Hengel, *Crucifixion* (Philadelphia: Fortress, 1977), 22–32.

13. Funk, *Acts*, 160.

14. [Eight verses]—16:9–20, added belatedly, usually appear printed in italics or a footnote, their content apparently drawn partially from endings of the other Gospels (Mt 28:18ff.; Lk 24:23f.; Jn 20:11ff.).

15. [50 percent]—227 words (= 27:62–66; 28:4,11–15) out of 425 comprising Matthew's empty tomb account (in Greek: 170 words out of 343).

16. [Theft in John] —"Theft" is John's concern in 20:2,13,15. Words I count as 26 (Greek: 23) are: "'Because they have taken away my Lord, and I do not know where they have laid him.' Saying this, she turned round and saw Jesus standing."

17. [Variations]—E.g., a secret admirer removed the body to his own plot; Joseph shifted the body from his tomb to another; Jewish authorities stole the body to preempt the disciples' theft.

18. [Messianic Secret]—A motif to the effect that Jesus instructed followers not to divulge his identity until he had risen (cf. 9:9). Among other possible purposes, this was useful in explaining why so few Jews caught on to Jesus' identity (since *supposedly* he wished this kept secret).

19. [Necessary for body to be missing?]—Were later notions that Jesus' body was missing a countering of Gnosticism (Chap. 4, above)? See Mt 28:9; Lk 24:36–43; Jn 20:27.

20. Jeffery Lowder, "Historical Evidence and the Empty Tomb Story," *JHC* 8:2 (2001): 259ff.

21. [Not expecting resurrection]—Jesus' "predictions" of resurrection were introduced after the fact—see Chap. 8 §1; below, Chap. 20 ("Festinger's Failure ..."). Also, since Matthew's account that a theft was feared is fictional, it cannot be applied to show that a resurrection *hoax* was anticipated.

22. Peter Carnley, *The Structure of Resurrection Belief* (Oxford: Clarendon, 1987), 56; Lowder, *Evidence*, 287f.

23. [Beyond historical reconstruction]—Did belief in Jesus' resurrection arise among his followers from their struggle with cognitive dissonance: that Jesus died without accomplishing the messianic mission? Then, to address this disconfirmation, did they come to believe that Jesus' presence still (so to speak) "abode among them" *spiritually*? Then, when circulated, was this misconcretized into word of *physical* appearances—first to those most worthy (as the kerygma specifies)? See discussion below, Chap. 20. In *Kingdom and Community* (Englewood Cliffs, NJ: Prentice-Hall, 1975), 39–43, John Gager discusses cognitive dissonance primarily respecting proselytizing.

<u>24</u>. [Failure of the argument]—Even were we dealing here with differing nouns, they could still be synonymous (cf. English: "court," "tribunal"), not references to different institutions. Supporting this position is full discussion by Raymond Brown, *The Death of the Messiah* (New York: Doubleday, 1994), 342–48. If different courts *are* presupposed, presumably Joseph's council was the *boule* (he is a *bouleutes* = council member) and the body trying Jesus the *synedrion* (Sanhedrin); see Ellis Rivkin, "Beth Din, Boulé, Sanhedrin," *HUCA* 46 (1975): 181–99. But Mark's Greek must be heeded literally—speaking of Joseph as an "honorable *councilor*," not respected member of *the "council"*—so we do not have different *nouns* inferable as different courts.

25. [Snakes]—Also credited to St. Patrick.

Chapter 14

1. Krister Stendahl, *Paul Among Jews and Gentiles* (Philadelphia: Fortress, 1976), 37.
2. Suetonius, *On the Life of the Caesars*, "Claudius," 25.
<u>3</u>. [Trickling back to Rome]—Rom 16:3f. shows Priscilla and Aquila, together with Jews and other Jewish-Christians, taking advantage of this opportunity.
4. Cf. James Walters, *Ethnic Issues in Paul's Letter to the Romans* (Valley Forge, PA: Trinity, 1994), passim.
5. Cf. William Campbell, "The Rule of Faith in Romans 12:1–15:13," *Pauline Theology 3: Romans*, David Hay and E. Elizabeth Johnson, eds. (Minneapolis: Fortress, 1995), 264.
6. J. Paul Sampley, "Romans in a Different Light," Hay and Johnson, *Theology*, 119.
7. Samuel Sandmel, *The Genius of Paul* (Philadelphia: Fortress, 1979), 36.
8. Cf. N. T. Wright, "Romans and the Theology of Paul," Hay and Johnson, *Theology*, 60.
9. Cf. E. Elizabeth Johnson, "Romans 9–11: Faithfulness and Impartiality," Hay and Johnson, *Theology*, 218.
10. Terence Donaldson, "'Riches for the Gentiles' (Rom. 11:12): Israel's Rejection and Paul's Gentile Mission," *JBL* 112 (1993): 89.
11. Johnson, "Faithfulness and Impartiality," Hay and Johnson, *Theology*, 227, 232.
12. Peter Stuhlmacher, *Paul's Letter to the Romans* (Louisville, KY: Westminster/John Knox, 1994), 167, 177.
13. Douglas Moo, "The Theology of Romans 9–11," Hay and Johnson, *Theology*, 245.
14. Cf. Johnson, "Faithfulness and Impartiality," Hay and Johnson, *Theology*, 213 n. 12.
15. Heikki Räisänen, "Romans 9–11 and the 'History of Early Christian Religion,'" *Texts and Contexts*, T. Fornberg and D. Hellholm, eds. (Oslo: Scand. Univ., 1997), 751–52; E. Elizabeth Johnson, *The Function of Apocalyptic and Wisdom Traditions in Romans 9–11* (Atlanta: Scholars Press, 1989): 176–205.
16. *Epistle of Barnabas* 14.
17. Johnson, "Faithfulness and Impartiality," Hay and Johnson, *Theology*, 214f.

Chapter 15

1. A more extensive treatment of this subject appears in my contribution, under the title "Destabilizing the Tale of Judas Iscariot: A Vehicle for Enhancing Christian-Jewish Understanding," in *A Festschrift in Honor of the Rabbinate of Walter Jacob* (Pittsburgh: Rodef Shalom Press, 2001), 109–49.

2. [Iscariot]—The surname perhaps came into use to distinguish this Judas from another—e.g., "Judas ... son of James, and Judas *Iscariot*" in Luke 6:16 (cf. Acts 1:13); or "Judas (*not* Iscariot)" in John 14:22. What did "Iscariot" mean? Best guesses are the Hebrew *ish Keriyot* = "a man of *Keriyot*" (in Judea)—making Judas the only non-Galilean disciple; or *ish kir-yat*_____ ="a man of the city of _____."

3. Joshua Trachtenberg, *The Devil and the Jews* (New Haven: Yale, 1943), passim.

4. Hyam Maccoby, *Judas Iscariot and the Myth of Jewish Evil* (New York: Macmillan, 1992), 3.

5. [Papias]—A second-century bishop of Hierapolis (*HE* 3.36.2).

6. Zech 11:12f.

7. [Elsewhere in Paul's writings]—Jesus "was delivered *to death* for our misdeeds" (Rom 4:25); God "*gave up* [His own Son] for us all" (Rom 8:32); Christ "*gave himself* [to death] for me" (Gal 2:20).

8. Origen, *C.Cels.* 2.11.

9. William Klassen, *Judas* (Minneapolis: Augsburg/Fortress, 1996), 3.

10. Among those treating this problem long ago, I recommend: Ernest Best, "Discipleship in Mark," *SJT* 23 (1970): 323–37; Seán Freyne, "At Cross Purposes," *Furrow* 33 (1982): 331–39; David Hawkin, "Incomprehension of the Disciples in the Marcan Redaction," *JBL* (1972): 491–500; Werner Kelber, "Mark 14:32–42: Gethsemane, Passion Christology, and Discipleship Failure," *ZNW* 62 (1971): 166–87; Elizabeth Malbon, "Fallible Followers," *Semeia* 28 (1983): 29–48; Joseph Tyson, "The Blindness of the Disciples in Mark," *JBL* 80 (1961): 261–68.

11. [Weakness of "Criteria"]—The criterion of *Multiple Attestation* also fares poorly. Besides the Synoptists, John recounts the Judas saga, but writing almost thirty years after Mark how could he not have heard of it? Paul is cited (1 Cor 11:23) but only in mistranslation.

12. Regarding the first entry, recall (from Chap. 13, above) that verses after Mk 16:8 are by a post-Marcan hand.

13. Maccoby, *Myth*, 25 (emphasis added), 180 n. 10.

14. John Robertson, *Jesus and Judas* (London: Watts, 1927), 40.

15. Robertson, *Judas*, 33. See E. P. Sanders, *Jesus and Judaism* (Philadelphia: Fortress, 1985), 98ff.; *The Historical Figure of Jesus* (London: Penguin, 1993), 120ff.

16. John Donahue, *Are You the Christ?* (Missoula: SBL, 1973), 206f.

17. Cf. G. Schneider, "Die Verhaftung Jesu," *ZNW* 63 (1972): 196; K. G. Kuhn, "Jesus in Gethsemane," *EvTh* (n.s.) 12 (1952–53): 261.

18. Mk 8:31f.; 9:31; 10:32f.; cf. 9:12b.

19. See Brian Incigneri, *The Gospel to the Romans* (Leiden: Brill, 2003), passim.

20. Klassen, *Judas*, 90.

21. [Pieces of silver]—Even Jewish biblical motifs more divergent than parallel could "substantiate" Gospel episodes: Joseph is one *of* twelve, not a leader outside them; and Judah's intent was to keep Joseph alive! Also, the sale prices differ. Yet details that correlate suffice irrespective of others that do not.

22. Maccoby, *Myth*, 25, 180 n. 10.

23. See Martin Goodman, *Rome and Jerusalem* (London: Allen Lane, 2007), passim.

24. Above, Chaps. 10, 12; also Fig. 21.1.

25. Pinchas Lapide, *Wer War Schuld an Jesu Tod?* (Gütersloh: Mohn, 1987), 15.

26. [Correctives]—See Mt 13:18 and Lk 8:11 (cf. Mk 4:13); Mt 16:9 (cf. Mk 8:17end–18); Mt 16:17ff. (placed *before* 16:23); Mt 26:31: "because of me" (cf. Mk 14:27); Mt 26:33: "because of you" (cf. Mk 14:29); Lk 22:31–33 (cf. Mk 14:29).

27. [Later hand]—Conjecture here is that two passages softening the image of Peter (Mk 14:28 and 16:7), the second fulfilling the first, were introduced into Mark before Matthew used him. Mark reads well, if not better, without either or both. The former is omitted in the Fayum fragment (a papyrus text discovered in Al-Fayyum, Egypt, paralleling Mk 14:26–31). Matthew 28:7 has to repair the latter verse twice: eliminating "and Peter" as redundant and changing "as *he* told you" (a mistake since Jesus told *men*, not women—*and* in Mk 14:28, no less!) to "lo, I [the angel] have told you." That 16:7 is troublesome in these respects speaks against its original presence.

28. Mk 8:35; 10:38; 13:9ff.

29. [Geographical errors]—E.g., 7:31 (towns are encountered in reverse order); 11:1 (Jesus follows an implausible route).

30. Mk 12:42; 15:16; P. Feine, J. Behm. and W. Kümmel, *Introduction to the New Testament* (Nashville: Abingdon, 1966), 70; Ralph Martin, *Mark* (Grand Rapids: Zondervan, 1976), 64. Cf. 6:27, 7:4,8; 15:39,44,45.

31. For more on Rome as Mark's provenance, see (besides Incigneri, above) John Donahue and Daniel Harrington, *The Gospel of Mark* (Collegeville, MN: Liturgical, 2002), passim; Benjamin Bacon, *Is Mark a Roman Gospel?* (Cambridge: Harvard, 1919); Raymond Brown, *The Death of the Messiah* (New York: Doubleday, 1994), 9 n. 8.

Chapter 16

1. [Lost sheep]—The "lost sheep" balance out "Gentiles" (10:5–6), so entire peoples are meant, as Matthew's editor wants his audience to believe. But had Jesus himself said this, would *he* mean it the same way—or that only *some* sheep had gotten lost (can a shepherd lose an entire flock?)?

2. Eusebius (fourth-century), *HE* 3.39.16; emphasis added.

3. ["Fulfil"]—Meaning to bring the intentions of God's covenant to their fullest and ultimate fruition.

4. Adapting Dale Allison, *The New Moses* (Minneapolis: Fortress, 1993), 268.

5. [Extensiveness of Matthew's use of Mark]—Matthew draws on the substance of 606 of Mark's 661 verses (William Barclay, *The Gospel of Matthew* 1 [Philadelphia: Westminster, 1958], xviii; I thank James Somerville for this reference).

6. See Graham Stanton, "The Origin and Purpose of Matthew's Gospel," *ANRW* II.25.3, H. Temporini and W. Haase, eds. (Berlin: de Gruyter, 1985), 1908–10.

7. Mt 4:18–22; 9:9; cf. 10:1–4.

8. F. W. Beare, "The Mission of the Disciples and the Mission Charge: Matthew 10 and Parallels," *JBL* 89 (1970): 9; cf. Morna Hooker, "Uncomfortable Words: The Prohibition of Foreign Missions (Mt. 10:5–6)," *ET* 82 (1970–71): 364; Lucien Legrand, *Unity and Plurality* (Maryknoll, NY: Orbis Books, 1990), 51ff.

9. Shortened so as to clarify our pedagogical purpose.

10. Eta Linnemann, *Parables of Jesus* (London: SPCK, 1966), 95.

11. Joachim Jeremias, *Parables of Jesus* (Englewood Cliffs, NJ: Prentice Hall, 1979), 178.

<u>12</u>. [Allegorization]—Lifted from Isaiah's "Song of the Vineyard" (LXX 5:7), the vineyard "is the *house of Israel*," but Matthew changes it to mean the "kingdom of God."

<u>13</u>. [Solely to Gentiles]—This is understood in the broadest and theoretical sense: impatience and disappointment with Jews as a people. Naturally, *individual* Jews—amenable to converting or open to be persuaded—would be accepted.

14. Douglas Hare and Daniel Harrington, "Make Disciples of All the Gentiles," *CBQ* 37 (1975): 359–69; Hare, *The Theme of Jewish Persecution of Christians* (Cambridge: University, 1967), 148; Kenneth Clark, "The Gentile Bias in Matthew," *JBL* 66 (1947): 165–72; Amy-Jill Levine, "To All the Gentiles: A Jewish Perspective on the Great Commission," *RE* 103 (2006), 147–48; Hooker, "Uncomfortable Words," 363 n. 2. Cf. Ulrich Luz, *Matthew 8–20* (Minneapolis: Fortress, 2001), ad loc.

15. Anthony Saldarini, *Matthew's Christian-Jewish Community* (Chicago: Univ. of Chicago, 1994); J. A. Overman, *Matthew's Gospel and Formative Judaism* (Minneapolis: Fortress, 1990); David Sim, *The Gospel of Matthew and Christian Judaism* (Edinburgh: T&T Clark, 1998); W. D. Davies and Dale C. Allison, *A Critical and Exegetical Commentary on the Gospel According to Saint Matthew* (ICC, rev.) 3 vols. (Edinburgh: T. & T. Clark, 1988–97), Vol. 3, ad loc.

16. Quoted, sequentially, are Jeremias, *Parables*, 70; Charles Dodd, *The Parables of the Kingdom* (New York: Scribner's, 1961), 99; J. Dominic Crossan, *In Parables* (Santa Rosa, CA: Polebridge, 1992), 90; Charles Carlston, *The Parables of the Triple Tradition* (Philadelphia: Fortress, 1975), 44; Hare, *Persecution*, 153.

17. M. Eugene Boring, "The Gospel of Matthew," *NIB* 8, L. Keck, ed. (Nashville: Abingdon, 1995), 105; John Meier in Raymond Brown and John Meier, *Antioch and Rome* (New York: Paulist, 1983), 12–27. In D. Balch, ed., *Social History of the Matthean Community* (Minneapolis: Fortress, 1991): William Schoedel, "Ignatius and ... the Gospel of Matthew in Antioch," 129; Rodney Stark, "Antioch As the Social Situation for Matthew's Gospel," 189ff.

18. Meier, *Antioch*, 46ff.

19. William Farmer, "The Post-Sectarian Character of Matthew and Its Post-War Setting in Antioch of Syria," *PRS* 3 (1976): 235–47; Menachem Stern, "The Jewish Diaspora," *The Jewish People in the First Century*, eds. S. Safrai and M. Stern (Philadelphia: Fortress, 1974), 140ff.

20. *War* VII.iii.2–4; 46–62 / VII.v.2; 100–11. Similarly, Damascus in 66: *War* II.xx.2; 559–61.

21. Brown, *Antioch*, 9.

22. Meier, "Gospel of Matthew," *ABD* 4: 625.

23. Meier, *Antioch*, 32.

24. [Other matters]—Would a knowledgeable Jew not know who Mark's "scribes" were (Chap. 5, n. 13), substitute Sadducees for Herod or Herodians, or appear to lump Sadducees' teachings with those of Pharisees, their opposites (16:6)?

25. S. van Tilborg, *The Jewish Leaders in Matthew* (Leiden: Brill, 1972), 171.

26. David Balch, "The Greek Political Topos *Peri Nomon* and Matthew 5:17,19 and 16:19," in Balch, ed., *Social History*, 79.

27. [Luke's assessment of Matthew]—Most of those who accept the "Q" hypothesis will not likely believe that Luke knew Matthew's Gospel.

Chapter 17

1. [Jesus at twelve]—Josephus tells a similar story about himself, at age fourteen (*Life* ii; 7–12). Lucan/Josephan parallels are not necessarily coincidental, one reason I am open to dating Luke after 94 (date of Josephus' *Antiquities*). See Steve Mason, *Josephus and the New Testament* (Peabody, MA: Hendrickson, 1992), 185–229.

2. Lk 19:47; 20:1; 21:37.

3. ["Saul"]—I submit that Luke improvised this name on the basis of Phil 3:5, where the *genuine* Paul identifies himself as "of the tribe of Benjamin" (whose most characteristic name had been "Saul," ancient Israel's first king; see 1 Sa 9:1ff.).

4. Acts 17:2; 18:4; 19:8.

5. Acts 22:17; 26:21; cf. 24:12.

6. Acts 22:19f.; 26:10f.; cf. 7:58.

7. See Jacob Jervell, *Luke and the People of God* (Minneapolis: Augsburg, 1972), 44–46. Also 9:42; 12:24; 13:43; 14:1; 17:10ff.; (19:20).

8. Ernst Haenchen, *The Acts of the Apostles* (Philadelphia: Westminster, 1971), 193, then 189.

9. Howard Teeple, "The Historical Beginnings of the Resurrection Faith," *Studies in New Testament*, D. Aune, ed. (Leiden: Brill, 1972): 108ff.; 120.

10. It is "not proper to assume ... that Acts 21:20 refers to ... additional converts *when that is the very point that needs to be proved*" (Jack Sanders, "The Salvation of the Jews in Luke-Acts," in *Luke-Acts: New Perspectives from the Society of Biblical Literature*, C. Talbert, ed. [New York: Crossroad, 1984]), 112.

11. Sanders, "Salvation," 116.

12. Stephen Wilson, *The Gentiles and the Gentile Mission in Luke-Acts* (Cambridge: Univ. Press, 1973), 251.

13. Joseph Tyson, "The Jewish Public in Luke-Acts," *NTS* 30 (1984): 583.

14. Norman Beck, *Mature Christianity in the 21st Century* (New York: Crossroad, 1994), 207.

Chapter 18

1. W. F. Moulton, A. S. Geden, and H. K. Moulton, *A Concordance to the Greek New Testament*, 6th rev., I. H. Marshall, ed. (London: T. & T. Clark, 2002), under *Ioudaios* (Jew) and related forms; also, James Strong, *The New Strong's Exhaustive Concordance of the Bible* (Nashville: Nelson, 1991), under *Jew* and related forms.

2. Kaufmann Kohler, "New Testament," *JE* 9 (1905), 251.

3. Raymond Brown, *The Community of the Beloved Disciple* (New York: Paulist, 1979), 40.

4. R. Alan Culpepper, "The Gospel of John and the Jews," *RE* 84 (1987): 285.

5. Cf. Brown, *The Gospel According to John*, AB 29–29A (Garden City: Doubleday, 1966 & 1970), xxxii–ix.

6. Gerhard von Rad, Karl Kuhn, and Walter Gutbrod, "*Ioudaios*," *TDNT*, G. Kittel and G. Friedrich, eds., G. Bromiley, trans., 3 (Grand Rapids: Eerdmans, 1965), 356-391. E.g., Alexandria's Jewish philosopher, Philo, and Josephus— writing from Rome—used forms of "Israel" or "Hebrews" when referring to Jews of *biblical* times, but "Jews" when addressing their own day.

7. [Occasionally used "Jews"]—The author of the Hebrew underlying 1 Maccabees used "Israel" to refer to his fellow people but "Jews" when showing his own people referred to *by* Gentiles or mentioned *to* Gentiles.

8. [World-at-large]—Compare "the Jews" in 7:1–3 with "the world" in vv. 4, 7; also "the world" in 15:18–25 compared with the third-person plurals (referring to *the Jews*)—especially to "their" in the last verse; and possibly even 18:20, which parallels "the world" with places "where *the Jews* come together."

9. Gutbrod, "*Israel*," *TDNT*, 379.

10. Norman Beck, *Mature Christianity in the 21st Century* (New York: Crossroad, 1994), 207.

11. [Yavneh]—The Judean coastal town said to become the center of Jewish leadership and study after the Second Temple's fall.

12. Reuven Kimelman, "*Birkat Ha-Minim* and the Lack of Evidence for an Anti-Christian Jewish Prayer in Late Antiquity," E. P. Sanders et al., eds., *Jewish and Christian Self-Definition,* 2 (Philadelphia: Fortress, 1981), 228ff.; 232ff.; cf., also, Lawrence Schiffman, "At the Crossroads: Tannaitic Perspectives on the Jewish-Christian Schism,"151ff. Regarding the version from medieval Egyptian fragments, see Solomon Schechter, "Genizah Specimens," *JQR* o.s. 10 (1898): 657, 659.

13. Kimelman, "Lack of Evidence," 235 n. 58.

14. Rudolf Bultmann, *The Gospel of John*, G. R. Beasley-Murray, R. W. N. Hoare, and J. L. Riches, trans. (Philadelphia: Westminster, 1971), 86. Cf. Culpepper, *Anatomy of the Fourth Gospel* (Philadelphia: Fortress, 1983), 126–31.

15. Terry Schram, *The Use of Ioudaios [Jew] in the Fourth Gospel* (Netherlands: Utrecht State Univ., 1974), 138.

16. Cf. Schram's "tree diagram," *Ioudaios*, 133.

17. Schram, *Ioudaios*, 165. The discussion immediately below draws, and then expands, upon Schram, 132ff.; 200ff.

18. Wilbert Howard, "The Gospel According to St. John: Exegesis," *IB* 8 (Nashville: Abingdon, 1952), 600; cf. Jn 8:31,43.

19. See fuller discussion in Amy-Jill Levine, *The Misunderstood Jew* (San Francisco: Harper, 2006), 161ff.

Chapter 19

1. On substitute terminology, see Catherine Wessinger, "Millennialism With and Without the Mayhem," in Thomas Robbins and Susan Palmer, *Millennium, Messiahs, and Mayhem* (New York: Routledge, 1997), 47–59.

2. Paul Boyer's conceptualization of concentric circles (2ff.) is here implemented differently; see *When Time Shall Be No More* (Cambridge, MA: Belknap, 1992), 331.

3. ["Antichrist"]—Appears only in 1 and 2 John referring to Gnostic (Chap. 4) preachers denying that God had become man in Jesus and that the man Jesus was the Christ.

4. [Expecting Jesus' return]—*Newsweek* (Nov. 1, 1999): 68–69, 71. Sixty-one percent of Americans anticipate Jesus' return eventually: *U.S. News and World Report* (Dec. 19, 1994): 62, 64.

5. [Antichrist's rise]—Ably assisted by a "false prophet" (Rev 13:11).

6. [Ten nations]—If member nations of the European Union do not now number ten, it is presumed that they will by the necessary time (e.g., by mergers, subdivisions, etc.).

7. Derived/misinterpreted from Jer 30:7; Dan 12:1; Mt 24:9,14ff.,19ff.

8. Derived/misinterpreted from Dan 7:25; 9:27; 12:7; Rev 12:14; 13:5; cf. 2 Thes 2:4.

9. Derived/misinterpreted from 1 Cor 15:52; 1 Thes 4:16f.; 2 Thes 2:1; Mt 24:30,40f.; Jn 14:3; Tit 2:13.

10. "Pre-wrathists": the faithful are raptured before God's outpouring of wrath—during the Tribulation's last quarter; "partialists": while *established* faithful Christians are raptured before the Tribulation begins, these *new* believers must wait until the Tribulation starts or even until its end.

11. ["Eternity"]—Is "beyond history," i.e., not a dispensation but the state that follows all seven of them.

12. [Reestablished Jewish State]—Relying here on Jer 32:37, Ezek 37:3,10ff.; 39:25ff.; and Isa 11:12; Zech 12:6.

13. [Tribulation's first half]—Derived from Dan 9:27: "he" (inferred to be the Antichrist) "shall make a ... covenant ... for one week [seven *years*]; and for [the last] half of the week he shall cause sacrifice and offering to *cease*"—meaning that *before* the seven-years' midpoint sacrifices *are* operational but only in a rebuilt Temple (#3).

14. Lawrence Wright, "Forcing the End," *The New Yorker* (July 20, 1998): 42–53.

15. [Red heifer]—This must be born in Israel, perfectly healthy, without defect, never having worked, and by age three shows no hair of another color. It is then slaughtered and burned in fire with specified ingredients. Its ashes, placed in a vessel with pure water, produce the "water of purification" needed to cleanse anyone intent on entering the Temple Mount—hence its requirement for any rebuilding to commence.

16. E.g., Tim LaHaye and Jerry Jenkins, *Left Behind* (Spanish Fork, UT: Tyndale, 1996–2005).

17. ["Magog"]—Magog spelled backwards (without vowels) yields G-G-M in Hebrew. Substituting for these the Hebrew letters *preceding* each yields B-B-L = "Babylon," Revelation's designation for Rome.

18. *Newsweek* (Nov. 1, 1999): 68, 71; almost 20 percent expect to see the world end (*Time*, July 1, 2002): 41ff.

19. [Misinterprets texts]—E.g., the context of Mt 24:39–42 is those *perishing* in Noah's Flood, so the man from the field *left behind* is *saved*(!), not vice versa. 1 Cor 15 defends resurrection from the dead, not the Rapture. 1 Thes 4 focuses not on the Rapture but on assuaging fear that the deceased have forfeited salvation (those "caught up ... in the clouds to meet the Lord" are *first* the dead—reassuring Paul's readers that the deceased *will* participate in the Second Coming, greeting and escorting Jesus to earth). Is the man of lawlessness (2 Thes 2) not the Antichrist but a fomenter of disaster for Jerusalem's Jews during Rome's siege in 70, such as John of Gischala (Larry Pechawer, *Leaving the Rapture Behind* [Joplin, MO: Mireh, 2003], Ch. 14)?

20. Mk 13:32ff.; Mt 24:36,43f.; Lk 12:39f.; Acts 1:7; 1 Thes 5:2ff.; 2 Pet 3:10; Rev 3:3; 16:15.

21. This composite of misapplied texts is culled, *sequentially*, from Lk 13:28 (cf. Mt 8:11); Mt 13:43 (5:20); (Mk 1:15 & par); Mk 12:34; Mt 7:21; Mk 4:11,14; Mt 13:24.

22. 1 Thes 4:17; Jn 14:3; Rev 20:4.

23. [Calvary]—Site of Jesus' execution (Golgotha).

24. [Seedliners]—This material is furnished by, and used by permission of, the Anti-Defamation League of B'nai B'rith at their website: www.adl.org/learn/ext_us/ Christian_Identity.asp?LEARN_Cat=Extremism&LEARN_SubCat=Extremism_ in_America&xpicked=4&item=Christian_ID.

25. [Ten lost tribes]—Constituting the Northern Kingdom of Israel and deported by the conquering Assyrians in 721 BCE.

26. Jews are so classified by Christian Identity (Michael Barkun, "Millenarians and Violence," Robbins and Palmer, *Millennium*, 259 n.1).

27. Philip Lamy, "Secularizing the Millennium," Robbins and Palmer, *Millennium*, 109, 111.

28. [Protocols / Elders of Zion]—A late nineteenth-century fraudulent tract of a purported plan for Jewish world domination, produced by an anonymous Russian secret police operative. It largely plagiarized an 1864 French satire on Napoleon III having nothing to do with Jews. Yet it continues as a pretext and justification for antisemitism today.

29. Variously: Jessica Stern, *Terror in the Name of God* (New York: HarperCollins, 2003), 10; Lamy, "Secularizing," 109; Barkun, "Millenarians," 252.

30. Jack Van Impe with R. Campbell, *Israel's Final Holocaust* (Nashville: Thomas Nelson, 1979), 9, quoted by Boyer, *Time*, 189.

31. Menelaus sold out the integrity of the priesthood in 171 BCE, also arranging execution of the "anointed" high priest Onias III who resisted Hellenization.

Antiochus maintained relations with Jewish Hellenizers for the seven years of 171–164 BCE.

32. See Dan 7:8; 8:9,25; 11:21,36; 12:1; 2 Thes 2:3ff.; Mt 24:15; Rev 13:3ff.

33. Appeal here is to Gen 49:17; Jer 8:16,17; Ezek 21:25; and Dan 11:37.

Chapter 20

1. www.jewsforjudaism.org/web/mainpages/missionary_cult_challenge.html.

2. [Two-Covenant Theology]—Discussed above, in Chap. 14 (end), and below, in Chap. 21.

3. Respectively, Art. IV. 23, *The Willowbank Declaration on the Christian Gospel and the Jewish People*, adopted April 29, 1989, at The Consultation on the Gospel and the Jewish People (Singapore/Wheaton IL); Moishe Rosen, "Do Jews Need Christ to Be Saved?" *Jews for Jesus Newsletter* 7 (1989): 2.

4. L. Festinger, H. Riecken, and S. Schachter, *When Prophecy Fails*, repr. (New York: Harper & Row, 1964), 25ff.

5. Cited from the video, *The Target Is You* (New York: T.V. & Film Institute, 1988).

6. Festinger, *Prophecy*, 4, then 7.

7. Festinger, *Prophecy*, 28.

8. Festinger, *Prophecy*, 25.

9. A factor H. M. Orlinsky never raises in his classic Goldenson Lecture, "The So-Called 'Suffering-Servant' in Isaiah 53" (Cincinnati: HUC, 1964).

10. At one time James Cohn collaborated with me on this exercise which I here substantially revise for this new designated purpose.

11. [Good enough for Jews today]—This is apt for youngsters to *say*, but naturally today's Judaism differs markedly from the faith and practice of the pre-rabbinic Jesus.

12. "What Evangelical Christians Should Know about Jews for Jesus; a confidential report: not to be distributed to non-Christians" (one-page statement, n.d.).

13. For the full originals: D. M. Eichhorn, *Evangelizing the American Jew* (Middle Village, NY: Jonathan David, 1978), 189ff.

14. As detailed by Dan Sherbok Cohn, *Messianic Judaism* (London: Cassell, 2000), esp. chapters 1–2.

15. Quoted throughout this paragraph is Dennis Prager, "Is There Such a Thing As a 'Jew for Jesus'?" *Ultimate Issues* (Oct–Dec 1989), 6.

16. See Ellen Kamentsky, *Hawking God* (Sapphire Press, 1992).

Chapter 21

1. Letter to the Grand Duchess Christina of Tuscany (1615).

2. Cf. Philip Jenkins, *The Next Christendom* (New York: Oxford, 2002).

3. [As Greek as Hebraic]—Tending in this direction are Thomas Longstaff, "Nazareth and Sepphoris," *ATR* 11 (1990): 8–15; J. Dominic Crossan, *The Historical Jesus* (San Francisco: Harper & Row, 1991); Burton Mack, *A Myth of Innocence* (Philadelphia: Fortress, 1988); Howard Kee, "Early Christianity in the Galilee," in *The Galilee in Late Antiquity*, ed. Lee Levine (New York,

JTS, 1992); Richard Batey, *Jesus and the Forgotten City: New Light on Seppho-ris and the Urban World of Jesus* (Grand Rapids: Eerdman's, 1991).

4. The concept and position of Seán Freyne, *Galilee, Jesus and the Gospels* (Philadelphia: Fortress, 1988). See also Mark Chancey, *The Myth of a Gentile Galilee* (Cambridge: Univ. Press, 2002); E. P. Sanders, "Jesus in Historical Context," *TT* 50 (1993): 429–48; John Meier, "The Present State of the 'Third Quest' for the Historical Jesus," *Bib* 80 (1999): 483–86.

5. See Amy-Jill Levine, *The Misunderstood Jew* (San Francisco: Harper, 2007).

6. See Philipp Vielhauer, "On the Paulinism of Acts," Leander Keck and J. Louis Martyn, eds., *Studies in Luke-Acts* (Nashville: Abingdon, 1966): 33–50.

7. See discussion in J. D. Crossan, *The Birth of Christianity* (San Francisco: Harper, 1998), 111–14.

8. See Michael Cook, *Mark's Treatment of the Jewish Leaders* (Leiden; Brill, 1978).

9. See Daniel Boyarin, *Border Lines* (Philadelphia: Univ. of Pennsylvania, 2004).

Chapter 22

1. It appears in the writings of a German, Wilhelm Marr, around 1878.

2. This entire paragraph, not only the quotation, is indebted to Samuel Sandmel, *Anti-Semitism in the New Testament?* (Philadelphia: Fortress, 1978), xx.

3. [Mother]—I use the parent/offspring image despite reservations with it; see previous chapter.

Chapter 23

1. Assoc. Press: Apr. 8, 2006; 1:02 p.m. EDT.

2. [Seven scholars]—Four were Roman Catholic (Mary Boys, Philip Cunningham, Lawrence Frizella, and John Pawlikowski); three were Jewish (Paula Fredriksen, Amy-Jill Levine, and I). Eugene Fisher, Assoc. Dir., Secretariat for Ecumenical & Interreligious Affairs, USCCB, foresaw what might be coming, as did Eugene Korn of the ADL.

3. [Radioactive]—A term I remember as first applied in this sense by A. James Rudin.

4. [Racially important]—An *"Anschauungsunterricht für Rassenunterschiede"* ("an instruction for racial distinction"); see discussion in the *Allgemeine Jüdische Wochenzeitung* (June 6, 1980).

5. H. R. Trevor-Roper, *Hitler's Secret Conversations, 1941–1944* (New York: Octagon, 1972), 457.

6. [Declaration / commentaries]—Referenced here is Section 4 of the *"Nostra Aetate* Declaration on the Relation of the Church to Non-Christian Religions," proclaimed by Pope Paul VI (Oct. 28, 1965). Later commentaries are "Vatican Guidelines and Suggestions for Implementing the Conciliar Declaration Nostra Aetate" (Dec. 1, 1974); and "Notes on the Correct Way to Present the Jews and Judaism in Preaching and Catechesis in the Roman Catholic Church" (Jun. 24, 1985). Both of the latter were the work of the Vatican Commission for Religious Relations with the Jews.

7. [Cincinnati's campus]—HUC-JIR has campuses also in New York, Los Angeles, and Jerusalem.

8. [Other seminaries]—See Chap. 1 n. 6. The Reconstructionist Rabbinical College (Philadelphia) requires a course in Christianity, although not intensively New Testament textually based. The Jewish Theological Seminary of America offers New Testament on an elective basis.

9. [The cape's names]—Portugal's Bartholomeu Dias, becoming the first European to reach the cape (1488), named it the Cape of Storms (*Cabo das Tormentas*). Portugal's John II renamed it the Cape of Good Hope (*Cabo da Boa Esperança*) because optimism was engendered by the opening of a sea route to India and the East.

Selected Bibliography

Works of Central Importance

Numbers within { } represent a graduated program of further reading, on the wide gamut of subjects treated. Novice readers would do better to start with books numbered with a 1, while interested readers with more background should gauge themselves accordingly (i.e., from 1 through 4). The sequencing is purely for pedagogical reasons and represents no statement of relative value. Books not sequenced are also, in my view, of superior merit; hence their inclusion.

Allison, D. C. *The New Moses: A Matter of Typology*. Minneapolis: Fortress, 1993.

Allison, D. C., and W. D. Davies. *A Critical and Exegetical Commentary on the Gospel According to Saint Matthew*. 3 vols. Edinburgh: T. & T. Clark, 1988–97.

Bacon, Benjamin W. *The Beginnings of Gospel Story*. New Haven: Yale Univ. Press, 1909.

{4} Balch, David, ed. *Social History of the Matthean Community*. Minneapolis: Fortress, 1991.

{1} Barkun, Michael. "Militias, Christian Identity and the Radical Right." *CC* (Aug. 2–9, 1995): 738–40.

{3} Beare, F. W. "The Mission of the Disciples and the Mission Charge: Matthew 10 and Parallels." *JBL* 89 (1970): 1–13.

{3} Beck, Norman. *Mature Christianity in the 21st Century*. New York: Crossroad, 1994.

Best, Ernest. "Discipleship in Mark." *SJT* 23 (1970): 323–37.

{4} Black, C. *The Disciples According to Mark*. Sheffield: JSOT, 1989.

{4} Boyarin, Daniel. *Border Lines: The Partition of Judeo-Christianity*. Philadelphia: Univ. of Pennsylvania, 2004.

{1} Boyer, Paul. *When Time Shall Be No More*. Cambridge, MA: Belknap, 1992.

{3} Brown, Raymond. *The Birth of the Messiah*. Garden City, NY: Doubleday, 1977.

{4} ———. *The Death of the Messiah*. New York: Doubleday, 1994.

{4} ——. *The Gospel According to John*. AB 29–29A. Garden City: Doubleday, 1966–1970.

——. "Not Jewish Christianity and Gentile Christianity, But Types of Jewish/Gentile Christianity." *CBQ* 45 (1983): 74–79.

{2} Brown, Raymond E., and John P. Meier. *Antioch and Rome*. New York: Paulist, 1983.

Bultmann, Rudolf, G. R. Beasley-Murray, R. W. N. Hoare, and J. L. Riches, trans. *The Gospel of John*. Repr. Philadelphia: Westminster, 1971.

——. *History of the Synoptic Tradition*. Repr. Oxford: Blackwell, 1963.

Carlston, Charles E. *The Parables of the Triple Tradition*. Philadelphia: Fortress, 1975.

Carnley, Peter. *The Structure of Resurrection Belief*. Oxford: Clarendon, 1987.

{4} Chancey, Mark. *The Myth of a Gentile Galilee*. Cambridge: Univ. Press, 2002.

{3} Clark, Kenneth. "The Gentile Bias in Matthew." *JBL* 66 (1947): 165–72.

{3} Cohen, S. J. D. *The Beginnings of Jewishness*. Berkeley: Univ. of California Press, 1999.

{1} Cook, Michael. "Jesus and the Pharisees." *JES* 15 (1978): 440–61.

——. *Mark's Treatment of the Jewish Leaders*. Leiden: Brill, 1978.

{2} ——. "The Problem of Jewish Jurisprudence and the Trial of Jesus." In Philip Cunningham, ed., *Pondering the Passion: What's at Stake for Christians and Jews?* Lanham: Sheed & Ward, 2004, 13–25.

——. "Rabbinic Judaism and Early Christianity." *RE* 84 (1987): 201–21.

{3} Crossan, J. D. *The Birth of Christianity*. San Francisco 1998.

——. *The Historical Jesus*. San Francisco 1991.

——. *In Parables*. Santa Rosa, CA: Polebridge, 1992.

Culpepper, R. Alan. *Anatomy of the Fourth Gospel*. Philadelphia: Fortress, 1983.

{2} Dodd, Charles H. *The Parables of the Kingdom*. New York: Scribner's, 1961.

{4} Donahue, John R. *Are You the Christ?* Missoula: SBL, 1973.

{4} Donahue, John R., and Daniel J. Harrington. *The Gospel of Mark*. Collegeville: Liturgical, 2002.

{1} Ehrman, Bart. *Jesus*. Oxford: Univ. Press, 1999.

{1} Eichhorn, M. D. *Evangelizing the American Jew*. Middle Village, NY: Jonathan David, 1978.

{3} Enslin, Morton. "'Luke' and Paul." *JAOS* 58 (1938): 81–91.

{3} ——. "Once Again, Luke and Paul." *ZNW* 61 (1970): 253–71.

Farmer, William. "The Post-Sectarian Character of Matthew and Its Post-War Setting in Antioch of Syria." *PRS* 3 (1976): 235–47.

Feine, P., J. Behm, and W. Kümmel. *Introduction to the New Testament*. Nashville: Abingdon, 1966.

{1} Festinger, Leon, H. Riecken, and S. Schachter. *When Prophecy Fails*. Repr. New York: Harper & Row, 1964.

{3} Fredriksen, Paula. *From Jesus to Christ*. New Haven: Yale Univ. Press, 1988.

Freyne, Seán. "At Cross Purposes." *Furrow* 33 (1982): 331–39.

——. *Galilee, Jesus and the Gospels*. Philadelphia: Fortress, 1988.

{2} Funk, R. W., and the Jesus Seminar. *The Acts of Jesus*. San Francisco: Harper, 1998.

{2} Funk, R. W., and R. W. Hoover. *The Five Gospels*. New York: Macmillan, 1993.

{2} Funk, R. W., B. Scott, and J. R. Butts, eds. *The Parables of Jesus*. Sonoma, CA: Polebridge, 1988.

{2} Gager, John. *Kingdom and Community*. Englewood Cliffs, NJ: Prentice-Hall, 1975.

{2} ——. *The Origins of Anti-Semitism*. New York: Oxford Univ. Press, 1983.

{3} Goodman, Martin. *Rome and Jerusalem*. London: Allen Lane, 2007.

Haenchen, Ernst. *The Acts of the Apostles*. Philadelphia: Westminster, 1971.

{3} Hare, Douglas. *The Theme of Jewish Persecution of Christians in the Gospel According to St. Matthew*. Cambridge: University Press, 1967.

{3} Hare, Douglas, and Daniel Harrington. "Make Disciples of All the Gentiles." *CBQ* 37 (1975): 359–69.

{3} Hawkin, David. "Incomprehension of the Disciples in the Marcan Redaction." *JBL* 1972: 491–500.

Hay, David, and E. Elizabeth Johnson, eds. *Pauline Theology 3: Romans*. Minneapolis: Fortress, 1995.

{2} Hengel, Martin. *Crucifixion*. Philadelphia: Fortress Press, 1977.

{3} Hooker, Morna. "Uncomfortable Words: The Prohibition of Foreign Missions (Mt. 10:5–6)." *ET* 82 (1970–71): 361–365.

{2} Horsley, R. A., and J. S. Hanson. *Bandits, Prophets, and Messiahs*. Minneapolis: Winston, 1985.

{4} Incigneri, Brian J. *The Gospel to the Romans*. Leiden: Brill, 2003.

Jeremias, Joachim. *Parables of Jesus*. Englewood Cliffs, NJ: Prentice Hall, 1979.

Kelber, Werner, "Mark 14:32–42: Gethsemane, Passion Christology, and Discipleship Failure." *ZNW* 62 (1971): 166–87.

Kelber, Werner, and John R. Donahue, eds. *The Passion in Mark*. Philadelphia: Fortress, 1976.

{4} Kimelman, Reuven. "*Birkat Ha-Minim* and the Lack of Evidence for an Anti-Christian Jewish Prayer in Late Antiquity." In E. P. Sanders et al., eds., *Jewish and Christian Self-Definition*, 2. London: SCM, 1981, 226–244.

{2} Klassen, William. *Judas*. Minneapolis: Augsburg/Fortress, 1996.

Knox, John. "Acts and the Pauline Letter Corpus." In L. E. Keck and J. L. Martyn, eds. *Studies in Luke-Acts*. Philadelphia: Fortress, 1980, 279–287.

{3} Levine, Amy-Jill. *The Misunderstood Jew*. San Francisco: Harper, 2007.

{3} ——. "To All the Gentiles: A Jewish Perspective on the Great Commission," *RE* 103 (2006): 139–58.

{3} Levine, L. I., ed. *The Galilee in Late Antiquity*. New York: JTS, 1992.

{1} Linnemann, Eta. *Parables of Jesus*. London: SPCK, 1966.

{3} Lowder, Jeffery. "Historical Evidence and the Empty Tomb Story." *JHC* 8:2 (2001): 251–93.

{4} Lyons, William. "On the Life and Death of Joseph of Arimathea." *JSHJ* 2 (2004): 29–53.

{2} Maccoby, Hyam. *Judas Iscariot and the Myth of Jewish Evil*. New York: Macmillan, 1992.

Marshall, I. H. *Last Supper and Lord's Supper*. Grand Rapids: Eerdmans, 1980.

Mason, Steve. *Josephus and the New Testament*. Peabody: Hendrickson, 1992.

Meeks, W. A. *The First Urban Christians*. New Haven: Yale Univ. Press, 1983.

{2} Meier, J. P. *A Marginal Jew*. 3 vol. New York: Doubleday, 1991–2003.

{2} ——. "The Present State of the 'Third Quest' for the Historical Jesus." *Bib* 80 (1999): 459–87.

{3} Miller, Robert. *The Jesus Seminar and Its Critics*. Santa Rosa, CA: Polebridge, 1999.

{2} Neusner, Jacob, W. S. Green, and E. Frerichs, eds. *Judaisms and Their Messiahs at the Turn of the Christian Era*. Cambridge: University Press, 1987.

{2} O'Toole, R. "Last Supper." *ABD*. New York: Doubleday, 1992.

{3} Orlinsky, H. M. "The So-Called 'Suffering-Servant' in Isaiah 53." Goldenson Lecture at Hebrew Union College, Cincinnati, 1964.

Overman, J. A. *Matthew's Gospel and Formative Judaism*. Minneapolis: Fortress, 1990.

{1} Pechawer, Larry. *Leaving the Rapture Behind*. Joplin, MO: Mireh, 2003.

Räisänen, Heikki. "Romans 9–11." In T. Fornberg and D. Hellholm, eds., *Texts and Contexts*. Oslo: Scandinavian Univ. Press, 1997.

Rivkin, Ellis. "Beth Din, Boulé, Sanhedrin." *HUCA* 46 (1975): 181–99.

{3} ——. "Defining the Pharisees: The Tannaitic Sources," *HUCA* 40, 41 (1969–70): 205–49.

{2} ——. *A Hidden Revolution*. Nashville: Abingdon, 1978.

{1} ——. *What Crucified Jesus?* Nashville: Abingdon, 1984.

{1} Robbins, Thomas, and Susan Palmer, eds. *Millennium, Messiahs, and Mayhem*. New York: Routledge, 1997.

{4} Robertson, John. *Jesus and Judas*. London: Watts, 1927.

{1} Roetzel, C. J. *The World That Shaped the New Testament*. Rev. Louisville, KY: Westminster John Knox, 2003.

Safrai, S., and Menachem Stern, eds. *The Jewish People in the First Century*. Philadelphia: Fortress, 1974.

Saldarini, Anthony. *Matthew's Christian-Jewish Community*. Chicago: Univ. of Chicago Press, 1994.

{1} Sanders, E. P. *The Historical Figure of Jesus*. London: Penguin, 1993.

{3} ——. *Jesus and Judaism*. Philadelphia: Fortress, 1985.

{3} ——. "Jesus in Historical Context." *TT* 50 (1993): 429–48.

{2} ——. *Judaism: Practice and Belief 63 BCE–66 CE*. Philadelphia: Trinity, 1992.

{3} Sanders, Jack. "The Salvation of the Jews in Luke-Acts." In C. Talbert, ed., *Luke-Acts: New Perspectives From the Society of Biblical Literature*. New York: Crossroad, 1984. 104-128.

{1} Sandmel, Samuel. *Anti-Semitism in the New Testament?* Philadelphia: Fortress, 1978.

{1} ——. *A Jewish Understanding of the New Testament*. Repr. Woodstock: Jewish Lights, 2005.

{4} Schiffman, Lawrence. "At the Crossroads: Tannaitic Perspectives on the Jewish-Christian Schism." In E. P. Sanders et al, eds. *Jewish and Christian Self-Definition*, 2. London: SCM, 1981, 115–156.

Schneider[-Shapiro], Roxanne. *Teaching Jewish Children About Jesus: Is the Advice of Our Sages Still Sage Advice?* M.A. Thesis at HUC-JIR Cincinnati, 1999.

Schram, Terry. *The Use of Ioudaios [Jew] in the Fourth Gospel*. Netherlands: Utrecht State Univ., 1974).

{3} Segal, Alan F. *Paul the Convert*. New Haven: Yale Univ. Press, 1990.

{2} Seltzer, Robert. *Religions of Antiquity*. New York: Macmillan, 1989.

Sim, David C. *The Gospel of Matthew and Christian Judaism*. Edinburgh: T&T Clark, 1998.

Soards, Marion. "The Question of a Premarcan Passion Narrative." In Raymond Brown, ed. *The Death of the Messiah* 2. New York: Doubleday: 1994, 1492–1524.

Stanton, Graham. "The Origin and Purpose of Matthew's Gospel." In H. Temporini and W. Haase, eds. *ANRW* II.25.3. Berlin: de Gruyter, 1985.

Stendahl, Krister. *Paul Among Jews and Gentiles*. Philadelphia: Fortress, 1976.

Stuhlmacher, Peter. *Paul's Letter to the Romans*. Louisville, KY: Westminster/John Knox, 1994.

{1} Tatum, W. B. *In Quest of Jesus*. Nashville: Abingdon, 1999.

{2} Tyson, Joseph. "The Blindness of the Disciples in Mark." *JBL* 80 (1961): 261–68.

{2} ——. "The Jewish Public in Luke-Acts." *NTS* 30 (1984): 574–83.

van Tilborg, S. *The Jewish Leaders in Matthew*. Leiden: Brill, 1972.

{3} Vielhauer, Philipp. "On the Paulinism of Acts." In Leander Keck and J. Louis Martyn, eds., *Studies in Luke-Acts*. Nashville: Abingdon, 1966: 33–50.

von Rad, Gerhard, Karl Kuhn, and Walter Gutbrod, "*Ioudaios*." In *TDNT*. G. Kittel and G. Friedrich, eds., G. Bromiley, trans. 3. Grand Rapids: Eerdmans, 1965, 356-391.

{3} Weber, Timothy. *The Road to Armageddon*. Grand Rapids: Baker, 2004.

Weinstock, Harris. "Shall Jesus of Nazareth Be Taught in the Jewish Sabbath School?" Petition, 1899. The Jacob Rader Marcus Center of the American Jewish Archives (Cincinnati).

{2}   White, L. Michael. *From Jesus to Christianity*. San Francisco: Harper, 2004.

Wilken, Robert. *John Chrysostom and the Jews*. Berkeley: Univ. of California Press, 1983.

{3}   Wilson, Stephen G. *The Gentiles and the Gentile Mission in Luke-Acts*. Cambridge: Univ. Press, 1973.

{1}   Wright, Lawrence. "Forcing the End." *The New Yorker* (July 20, 1998): 42–53.

Modern Author Index

References to pages may be to "Figures" they contain
Bold indicates authors are *quoted* on pages listed

Scripture Index

References to pages may be to "Figures" they contain
Bold indicates biblical texts that are *quoted* on pages listed

Gospel Dynamics Index

References to pages may be to "Figures" they contain
Bold indicates especially important listings

Subject Index

References to pages may be to "Figures" they contain
"*cf.* #" = consult *Gospel Dynamics Index by number*
Bold indicates especially important listings

A

Abraham, 80, 102, 106, **165–166**, 172, 175, 207
activists, 43, 45–50, 315[nn.4,14], 316[n.18]
Adam, xxi, 245–246
adoptionism, 105
Agrippa. *See* Herod Agrippa
allegorizing (of parables), 57, **197–202**, 207, 208, 275, 317[n.31], 328[n.12]
angels, 19, 22, 80, 89, 97–103 passim, 319[n.4], 327[n.27]
Anti-Defamation League (ADL), **246**, 247, 296, 306, 332[n.24], 334[n.2]
anti-Judaism, xvi, 277, **278–288**
  different from antisemitism, 279–281
  in John, 76, 220–229 passim
  in Luke-Acts, 215–217, 321[n.8]
  in Mark, 90, 122, **133–144**, 186, **273–274**
  in Matthew, 194–207 passim
  Paul and, 170–174, 175
  SUMMARY POINTS on: **278–279**
antichrist. *See under* millennialism
Antioch, 33, 111, **202–206**, 208, 312[n.3]
antisemitism, 174, 219, 229, 237, 244, 251, **278–288**, 296, 302, 332[n.28]
  different from anti-Judaism, 279–281
apocalyptic, -ticist(s), xviii, **xxii**, 23, **46–52** passim, 56, 273, 316[n.20]
apocrypha
  Christian, xviii, **xix**, 23, 54, 191, 314[n.5], 316[n.25]
  Jewish, xviii, **xix**, 65
apostles (different from "disciples"), xviii, xxiii
archaeology, 269
Archelaus, 41–42, 96, 102, 320[n.11]
Armageddon. *See under* millennialists, post-trib; *also* pre-trib
atonement. *See under* Christianity: theology

B

baptism, 110, 118
  Jesus' adult, 95–96, **105**
    "moment of manifestation" (in Mk), 95–96
  mystery cults and, 37
  trinitarian formula for, 200, 209
Bar Kokhba, 14, 33, 43, 315[n.4]
Barabbas episode, 76, 90, 116, 122, 131, 134, **143**, 144, 146, 274
  aims, 141
  blood-curse inserted into, **195–196**
  illogic of, 123, 140–141, 142, 322[n.10]
  "king of the Jews" in, 136, 139–140
bet din. See Sanhedrin: Talmud
Bethlehem. *See under* infancy narratives
bibliolatry, 257–258, 267–268
birkat ha-minim (malediction against heretics), 112, 174, 220–225
blasphemy
  charged against Jesus, 84, 121–122, 136–137, 143, 314[n.6]; *cf.* #92
  displaced "sedition," **126**, 144, **145**, 147; *cf. #44, 55*
  inserted into paralytic's healing, **147–148**, 274
  latest layer of Sanhedrin construct, 132
  post-70 CE retrojection, **126**; *cf. #57*
blind(folded) Jews, xiv–xvi, 3, 91, 173, 278; *cf. #88*. See also *Synagoga*

T

talmud, xviii, xx. *See also* rabbinic
     literature
tanakh, xviii, xix
Tarsus, 19, 37, 70, 281. *See also* Mithraism
temple, first, 42, 111, 127, 235
temple, second, 42–51 passim, 110–120
     passim, 316n.19
   threatened by Jesus, **55–56**, 134, 143,
     219
temple, third (hypothetical
     "tribulational"), 235–243 passim,
     331n.13
temple, fourth (hypothetical "millennial"),
     240, 243
text plots, 24
Titus (general/emperor), 50, 204, 313n.3
   marched Judean captives through
     Rome, 186, 190, 191
Toledot Yeshu, 16
torah, xix, 42, 44, 45, 50, 69, 70, 85, 170
"traditions of the elders"/"... of my
     fathers," 44
trinity, xx, 109, 200, 209, 258,
triumphalism. *See* supersessionism
"two covenant theology." *See under*
     dialogue
typology, xviii, **xx**, 24, 124, **126**, **127**,
     194; *cf. #70–100*

V

Vatican Council, Second. See *Nostra
     Aetate*

vicarious suffering. *See under* Christianity:
     theology
virgin birth. *See under* infancy narratives:
     definitions

W

woman/women
   Canaanite (Syrophoenician), 192
   first to discover tomb empty/see
     resurrected Jesus, 156–157
   flee tomb, 150, 155; *cf. #15*
   Gentile, of faith, 201, 207
   keeping vigil, 153, 189
   Mary (*see under* infancy narratives:
     personages)
   Mary Magdalene (*see* Mary
     Magdalene)
   visiting tomb Easter Sunday, 153
   wasting costly ointment, 153
   why no interaction by Joseph of
     Arimathea with, 152
   within Matthew's genealogy, 97, 105,
     107; *cf. #43*
Word. *See under* John, Gospel of: motifs

Y

Yavneh (Jamnia), 224, 330n.11
Yeshu, Yeshua, Yehoshua, 5, 16, 64, 258,
     262, **264**

Z

Zealots. *See* activists

Notes

Notes

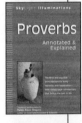

Ecology/Environment

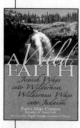

A Wild Faith: Jewish Ways into Wilderness, Wilderness Ways into Judaism
By Rabbi Mike Comins; Foreword by Nigel Savage 6 x 9, 240 pp, Quality PB, 978-1-58023-316-3 **$16.99**

Ecology & the Jewish Spirit: Where Nature & the Sacred Meet
Edited by Ellen Bernstein 6 x 9, 288 pp, Quality PB, 978-1-58023-082-7 **$18.99**

Torah of the Earth: Exploring 4,000 Years of Ecology in Jewish Thought
Vol. 1: Biblical Israel & Rabbinic Judaism; Vol. 2: Zionism & Eco-Judaism
Edited by Rabbi Arthur Waskow Vol. 1: 6 x 9, Quality PB, 978-1-58023-086-5 **$19.95**
Vol. 2: 6 x 9, 336 pp, Quality PB, 978-1-58023-087-2 **$19.95**

The Way Into Judaism and the Environment *By Jeremy Benstein, PhD*
6 x 9, 288 pp, Quality PB, 978-1-58023-368-2 **$18.99**; HC, 978-1-58023-268-5 **$24.99**

Graphic Novels/Graphic History

The Adventures of Rabbi Harvey: A Graphic Novel of Jewish Wisdom and Wit in the
Wild West *By Steve Sheinkin* 6 x 9, 144 pp, Full-color illus., Quality PB, 978-1-58023-310-1 **$16.99**

Rabbi Harvey Rides Again: A Graphic Novel of Jewish Folktales Let Loose in the
Wild West *By Steve Sheinkin* 6 x 9, 144 pp, Full-color illus., Quality PB, 978-1-58023-347-7 **$16.99**

Rabbi Harvey vs. the Wisdom Kid: A Graphic Novel of Dueling
Jewish Folktales in the Wild West *By Steve Sheinkin*
Rabbi Harvey's first book-length adventure—and toughest challenge.
6 x 9, 144 pp, Full-color illus., Quality PB, 978-1-58023-422-1 **$16.99**

The Story of the Jews: A 4,000-Year Adventure—A Graphic History Book
By Stan Mack 6 x 9, 288 pp, Illus., Quality PB, 978-1-58023-155-8 **$16.99**

Grief/Healing

Facing Illness, Finding God: How Judaism Can Help You and
Caregivers Cope When Body or Spirit Fails *By Rabbi Joseph B. Meszler*
Will help you find spiritual strength for healing amid the fear, pain and chaos of
illness. 6 x 9, 208 pp, Quality PB, 978-1-58023-423-8 **$16.99**

Midrash & Medicine: Healing Body and Soul in the Jewish Interpretive
Tradition *Edited by Rabbi William Cutter, PhD; Foreword by Michele F. Prince, LCSW, MAJCS*
Explores how midrash can help you see beyond the physical aspects of healing to
tune in to your spiritual source.
6 x 9, 352 pp, Quality PB, 978-1-58023-484-9 **$21.99**

Healing from Despair: Choosing Wholeness in a Broken World
By Rabbi Elie Kaplan Spitz with Erica Shapiro Taylor; Foreword by Abraham J. Twerski, MD
5½ x 8½, 208 pp, Quality PB, 978-1-58023-436-8 **$16.99**

Healing and the Jewish Imagination: Spiritual and Practical Perspectives on
Judaism and Health *Edited by Rabbi William Cutter, PhD*
6 x 9, 240 pp, Quality PB, 978-1-58023-373-6 **$19.99**

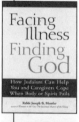

Grief in Our Seasons: A Mourner's Kaddish Companion *By Rabbi Kerry M. Olitzky*
4½ x 6½, 448 pp, Quality PB, 978-1-879045-55-2 **$15.95**

Healing of Soul, Healing of Body: Spiritual Leaders Unfold the Strength & Solace
in Psalms *Edited by Rabbi Simkha Y. Weintraub, LCSW*
6 x 9, 128 pp, 2-color illus. text, Quality PB, 978-1-879045-31-6 **$16.99**

Mourning & Mitzvah, 2nd Edition: A Guided Journal for Walking the Mourner's
Path through Grief to Healing *By Rabbi Anne Brener, LCSW*
7½ x 9, 304 pp, Quality PB, 978-1-58023-113-8 **$19.99**

Tears of Sorrow, Seeds of Hope, 2nd Edition: A Jewish Spiritual Companion
for Infertility and Pregnancy Loss *By Rabbi Nina Beth Cardin*
6 x 9, 208 pp, Quality PB, 978-1-58023-233-3 **$18.99**

A Time to Mourn, a Time to Comfort, 2nd Edition: A Guide to Jewish
Bereavement *By Dr. Ron Wolfson; Foreword by Rabbi David J. Wolpe*
7 x 9, 384 pp, Quality PB, 978-1-58023-253-1 **$21.99**

When a Grandparent Dies: A Kid's Own Remembering Workbook for Dealing
with Shiva and the Year Beyond *By Nechama Liss-Levinson, PhD*
8 x 10, 48 pp, 2-color text, HC, 978-1-879045-44-6 **$15.95** *For ages 7–13*

Congregation Resources

A Practical Guide to Rabbinic Counseling
Edited by Rabbi Yisrael N. Levitz, PhD, and Rabbi Abraham J. Twerski, MD
Provides rabbis with the requisite knowledge and practical guidelines for some of the most common counseling situations.
6 x 9, 432 pp, HC, 978-1-58023-562-4 **$40.00**

Professional Spiritual & Pastoral Care: A Practical Clergy and Chaplain's Handbook
Edited by Rabbi Stephen B. Roberts, MBA, MHL, BCJC
An essential resource integrating the classic foundations of pastoral care with the latest approaches to spiritual care, specifically intended for professionals who work or spend time with congregants in acute care hospitals, behavioral health facilities, rehabilitation centers and long-term care facilities.
6 x 9, 480 pp, HC, 978-1-59473-312-3 **$50.00**

Reimagining Leadership in Jewish Organizations: Ten Practical Lessons to Help You Implement Change and Achieve Your Goals
By Dr. Misha Galperin
Serves as a practical guidepost for lay and professional leaders to evaluate the current paradigm with insights from the world of business, psychology and research in Jewish demographics and sociology. Supported by vignettes from the field that illustrate the successes of the lessons as well as the consequences of not implementing them.
6 x 9, 192 pp, Quality PB, 978-1-58023-492-4 **$16.99**

Empowered Judaism: What Independent Minyanim Can Teach Us about Building Vibrant Jewish Communities
By Rabbi Elie Kaunfer; Foreword by Prof. Jonathan D. Sarna
6 x 9, 224 pp, Quality PB, 978-1-58023-412-2 **$18.99**

Building a Successful Volunteer Culture: Finding Meaning in Service in the Jewish Community *By Rabbi Charles Simon; Foreword by Shelley Lindauer; Preface by Dr. Ron Wolfson*
6 x 9, 192 pp, Quality PB, 978-1-58023-408-5 **$16.99**

The Case for Jewish Peoplehood: Can We Be One?
By Dr. Erica Brown and Dr. Misha Galperin; Foreword by Rabbi Joseph Telushkin
6 x 9, 224 pp, HC, 978-1-58023-401-6 **$21.99**

Finding a Spiritual Home: How a New Generation of Jews Can Transform the American Synagogue *By Rabbi Sidney Schwarz*
6 x 9, 352 pp, Quality PB, 978-1-58023-185-5 **$19.95**

Inspired Jewish Leadership: Practical Approaches to Building Strong Communities
By Dr. Erica Brown 6 x 9, 256 pp, HC, 978-1-58023-361-3 **$27.99**

Jewish Pastoral Care, 2nd Edition: A Practical Handbook from Traditional & Contemporary Sources *Edited by Rabbi Dayle A. Friedman, MSW, MAJCS, BCC*
6 x 9, 528 pp, Quality PB, 978-1-58023-427-6 **$30.00**

Jewish Spiritual Direction: An Innovative Guide from Traditional and Contemporary Sources
Edited by Rabbi Howard A. Addison, PhD, and Barbara Eve Breitman, MSW
6 x 9, 368 pp, HC, 978-1-58023-230-2 **$30.00**

Rethinking Synagogues: A New Vocabulary for Congregational Life
By Rabbi Lawrence A. Hoffman, PhD 6 x 9, 240 pp, Quality PB, 978-1-58023-248-7 **$19.99**

Spiritual Community: The Power to Restore Hope, Commitment and Joy
By Rabbi David A. Teutsch, PhD
5½ x 8½, 144 pp, HC, 978-1-58023-270-8 **$19.99**

Spiritual Boredom: Rediscovering the Wonder of Judaism By Dr. Erica Brown
6 x 9, 208 pp, HC, 978-1-58023-405-4 **$21.99**

The Spirituality of Welcoming: How to Transform Your Congregation into a Sacred Community By Dr. Ron Wolfson 6 x 9, 224 pp, Quality PB, 978-1-58023-244-9 **$19.99**

Social Justice

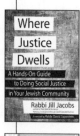

Where Justice Dwells
A Hands-On Guide to Doing Social Justice in Your Jewish Community
By Rabbi Jill Jacobs; Foreword by Rabbi David Saperstein
Provides ways to envision and act on your own ideals of social justice.
7 x 9, 288 pp, Quality PB Original, 978-1-58023-453-5 **$24.99**

There Shall Be No Needy
Pursuing Social Justice through Jewish Law and Tradition
By Rabbi Jill Jacobs; Foreword by Rabbi Elliot N. Dorff, PhD; Preface by Simon Greer
Confronts the most pressing issues of twenty-first-century America from a deeply Jewish perspective. 6 x 9, 288 pp, Quality PB, 978-1-58023-425-2 **$16.99**

There Shall Be No Needy Teacher's Guide 8½ x 11, 56 pp, PB, 978-1-58023-429-0 **$8.99**

Conscience
The Duty to Obey and the Duty to Disobey
By Rabbi Harold M. Schulweis
Examines the idea of conscience and the role conscience plays in our relationships to government, law, ethics, religion, human nature, God—and to each other.
6 x 9, 160 pp, Quality PB, 978-1-58023-419-1 **$16.99**; HC, 978-1-58023-375-0 **$19.99**

Judaism and Justice
The Jewish Passion to Repair the World
By Rabbi Sidney Schwarz; Foreword by Ruth Messinger
Explores the relationship between Judaism, social justice and the Jewish identity of American Jews. 6 x 9, 352 pp, Quality PB, 978-1-58023-353-8 **$19.99**

Spirituality/Women's Interest

New Jewish Feminism
Probing the Past, Forging the Future
Edited by Rabbi Elyse Goldstein; Foreword by Anita Diamant
Looks at the growth and accomplishments of Jewish feminism and what they mean for Jewish women today and tomorrow.
6 x 9, 480 pp, HC, 978-1-58023-359-0 **$24.99**

The Divine Feminine in Biblical Wisdom Literature
Selections Annotated & Explained
Translation & Annotation by Rabbi Rami Shapiro
5½ x 8½, 240 pp, Quality PB, 978-1-59473-109-9 **$16.99**
(A book from SkyLight Paths, Jewish Lights' sister imprint)

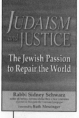

The Quotable Jewish Woman
Wisdom, Inspiration & Humor from the Mind & Heart
Edited by Elaine Bernstein Partnow
6 x 9, 496 pp, Quality PB, 978-1-58023-236-4 **$19.99**

The Women's Haftarah Commentary
New Insights from Women Rabbis on the 54 Weekly Haftarah Portions, the 5 Megillot & Special Shabbatot
Edited by Rabbi Elyse Goldstein
Illuminates the historical significance of female portrayals in the Haftarah and the Five Megillot. 6 x 9, 560 pp, Quality PB, 978-1-58023-371-2 **$19.99**

The Women's Torah Commentary
New Insights from Women Rabbis on the 54 Weekly Torah Portions
Edited by Rabbi Elyse Goldstein
Over fifty women rabbis offer inspiring insights on the Torah, in a week-by-week format.
6 x 9, 496 pp, Quality PB, 978-1-58023-370-5 **$19.99**; HC, 978-1-58023-076-6 **$34.95**

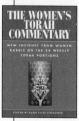

See Passover for *The Women's Passover Companion: Women's Reflections on the Festival of Freedom* and *The Women's Seder Sourcebook: Rituals & Readings for Use at the Passover Seder.*

Inspiration

God of Me: Imagining God throughout Your Lifetime
By Rabbi David Lyon Helps you cut through preconceived ideas of God and dogmas that stifle your creativity when thinking about your personal relationship with God. 6 x 9, 176 pp, Quality PB, 978-1-58023-452-8 **$16.99**

The God Upgrade: Finding Your 21st-Century Spirituality in Judaism's 5,000-Year-Old Tradition *By Rabbi Jamie Korngold; Foreword by Rabbi Harold M. Schulweis* A provocative look at how our changing God concepts have shaped every aspect of Judaism. 6 x 9, 176 pp, Quality PB, 978-1-58023-443-6 **$15.99**

The Seven Questions You're Asked in Heaven: Reviewing and Renewing Your Life on Earth *By Dr. Ron Wolfson* An intriguing and entertaining resource for living a life that matters. 6 x 9, 176 pp, Quality PB, 978-1-58023-407-8 **$16.99**

Happiness and the Human Spirit: The Spirituality of Becoming the Best You Can Be *By Rabbi Abraham J. Twerski, MD* Shows you that true happiness is attainable once you stop looking outside yourself for the source. 6 x 9, 176 pp, Quality PB, 978-1-58023-404-7 **$16.99**; HC, 978-1-58023-343-9 **$19.99**

A Formula for Proper Living: Practical Lessons from Life and Torah *By Rabbi Abraham J. Twerski, MD* 6 x 9, 144 pp, HC, 978-1-58023-402-3 **$19.99**

The Bridge to Forgiveness: Stories and Prayers for Finding God and Restoring Wholeness *By Rabbi Karyn D. Kedar* 6 x 9, 176 pp, Quality PB, 978-1-58023-451-1 **$16.99**

The Empty Chair: Finding Hope and Joy—Timeless Wisdom from a Hasidic Master, Rebbe Nachman of Breslov *Adapted by Moshe Mykoff and the Breslov Research Institute* 4 x 6, 128 pp, Deluxe PB w/ flaps, 978-1-879045-67-5 **$9.99**

The Gentle Weapon: Prayers for Everyday and Not-So-Everyday Moments— Timeless Wisdom from the Teachings of the Hasidic Master, Rebbe Nachman of Breslov *Adapted by Moshe Mykoff and S. C. Mizrahi, together with the Breslov Research Institute* 4 x 6, 144 pp, Deluxe PB w/ flaps, 978-1-58023-022-3 **$9.99**

God Whispers: Stories of the Soul, Lessons of the Heart *By Rabbi Karyn D. Kedar* 6 x 9, 176 pp, Quality PB, 978-1-58023-088-9 **$15.95**

God's To-Do List: 103 Ways to Be an Angel and Do God's Work on Earth *By Dr. Ron Wolfson* 6 x 9, 144 pp, Quality PB, 978-1-58023-301-9 **$16.99**

Jewish Stories from Heaven and Earth: Inspiring Tales to Nourish the Heart and Soul *Edited by Rabbi Dov Peretz Elkins* 6 x 9, 304 pp, Quality PB, 978-1-58023-363-7 **$16.99**

Life's Daily Blessings: Inspiring Reflections on Gratitude and Joy for Every Day, Based on Jewish Wisdom *By Rabbi Kerry M. Olitzky* 4½ x 6½, 368 pp, Quality PB, 978-1-58023-396-5 **$16.99**

Restful Reflections: Nighttime Inspiration to Calm the Soul, Based on Jewish Wisdom *By Rabbi Kerry M. Olitzky and Rabbi Lori Forman-Jacobi* 4½ x 6½, 448 pp, Quality PB, 978-1-58023-091-9 **$16.99**

Sacred Intentions: Morning Inspiration to Strengthen the Spirit, Based on Jewish Wisdom *By Rabbi Kerry M. Olitzky and Rabbi Lori Forman-Jacobi* 4½ x 6½, 448 pp, Quality PB, 978-1-58023-061-2 **$16.99**

Kabbalah/Mysticism

Jewish Mysticism and the Spiritual Life: Classical Texts, Contemporary Reflections *Edited by Dr. Lawrence Fine, Dr. Eitan Fishbane and Rabbi Or N. Rose* Inspirational and thought-provoking materials for contemplation, discussion and action. 6 x 9, 256 pp, HC, 978-1-58023-434-4 **$24.99**

Ehyeh: A Kabbalah for Tomorrow *By Rabbi Arthur Green, PhD* 6 x 9, 224 pp, Quality PB, 978-1-58023-213-5 **$18.99**

The Gift of Kabbalah: Discovering the Secrets of Heaven, Renewing Your Life on Earth *By Tamar Frankiel, PhD* 6 x 9, 256 pp, Quality PB, 978-1-58023-141-1 **$16.95**

Seek My Face: A Jewish Mystical Theology *By Rabbi Arthur Green, PhD* 6 x 9, 304 pp, Quality PB, 978-1-58023-130-5 **$19.95**

Zohar: Annotated & Explained *Translation & Annotation by Dr. Daniel C. Matt; Foreword by Andrew Harvey* 5½ x 8½, 176 pp, Quality PB, 978-1-893361-51-5 **$15.99**
(A book from SkyLight Paths, Jewish Lights' sister imprint)

See also *The Way Into Jewish Mystical Tradition* in The Way Into... Series.

Meditation

Jewish Meditation Practices for Everyday Life
Awakening Your Heart, Connecting with God
By Rabbi Jeff Roth
Offers a fresh take on meditation that draws on life experience and living life with greater clarity as opposed to the traditional method of rigorous study.
6 x 9, 224 pp, Quality PB, 978-1-58023-397-2 **$18.99**

The Handbook of Jewish Meditation Practices
A Guide for Enriching the Sabbath and Other Days of Your Life
By Rabbi David A. Cooper Easy-to-learn meditation techniques.
6 x 9, 208 pp, Quality PB, 978-1-58023-102-2 **$16.95**

Discovering Jewish Meditation, 2nd Edition
Instruction & Guidance for Learning an Ancient Spiritual Practice
By Nan Fink Gefen, PhD 6 x 9, 208 pp, Quality PB, 978-1-58023-462-7 **$16.99**

Meditation from the Heart of Judaism
Today's Teachers Share Their Practices, Techniques, and Faith
Edited by Avram Davis 6 x 9, 256 pp, Quality PB, 978-1-58023-049-0 **$16.95**

Ritual/Sacred Practices

The Jewish Dream Book: The Key to Opening the Inner Meaning of
Your Dreams *By Vanessa L. Ochs, PhD, with Elizabeth Ochs; Illus. by Kristina Swarner*
Instructions for how modern people can perform ancient Jewish dream practices and dream interpretations drawn from the Jewish wisdom tradition.
8 x 8, 128 pp, Full-color illus., Deluxe PB w/ flaps, 978-1-58023-132-9 **$16.95**

God in Your Body: Kabbalah, Mindfulness and Embodied Spiritual Practice
By Jay Michaelson
The first comprehensive treatment of the body in Jewish spiritual practice and an essential guide to the sacred.
6 x 9, 272 pp, Quality PB, 978-1-58023-304-0 **$18.99**

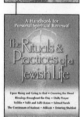

The Book of Jewish Sacred Practices: CLAL's Guide to Everyday &
Holiday Rituals & Blessings *Edited by Rabbi Irwin Kula and Vanessa L. Ochs, PhD*
6 x 9, 368 pp, Quality PB, 978-1-58023-152-7 **$18.95**

Jewish Ritual: A Brief Introduction for Christians
By Rabbi Kerry M. Olitzky and Rabbi Daniel Judson
5½ x 8½, 144 pp, Quality PB, 978-1-58023-210-4 **$14.99**

The Rituals & Practices of a Jewish Life: A Handbook for Personal Spiritual
Renewal *Edited by Rabbi Kerry M. Olitzky and Rabbi Daniel Judson*
6 x 9, 272 pp, Illus., Quality PB, 978-1-58023-169-5 **$18.95**

The Sacred Art of Lovingkindness: Preparing to Practice
By Rabbi Rami Shapiro 5½ x 8½, 176 pp, Quality PB, 978-1-59473-151-8 **$16.99**
(A book from SkyLight Paths, Jewish Lights' sister imprint)

Science Fiction/Mystery & Detective Fiction

Criminal Kabbalah: An Intriguing Anthology of Jewish Mystery &
Detective Fiction *Edited by Lawrence W. Raphael; Foreword by Laurie R. King*
All-new stories from twelve of today's masters of mystery and detective fiction—sure to delight mystery buffs of all faith traditions.
6 x 9, 256 pp, Quality PB, 978-1-58023-109-1 **$16.95**

Mystery Midrash: An Anthology of Jewish Mystery & Detective Fiction
Edited by Lawrence W. Raphael; Preface by Joel Siegel
6 x 9, 304 pp, Quality PB, 978-1-58023-055-1 **$16.95**

Wandering Stars: An Anthology of Jewish Fantasy & Science Fiction
Edited by Jack Dann; Introduction by Isaac Asimov
6 x 9, 272 pp, Quality PB, 978-1-58023-005-6 **$18.99**

More Wandering Stars: An Anthology of Outstanding Stories of Jewish Fantasy and
Science Fiction *Edited by Jack Dann; Introduction by Isaac Asimov*
6 x 9, 192 pp, Quality PB, 978-1-58023-063-6 **$16.95**

Spirituality/Prayer

Making Prayer Real: Leading Jewish Spiritual Voices on Why Prayer Is Difficult and What to Do about It *By Rabbi Mike Comins*
A new and different response to the challenges of Jewish prayer, with "best prayer practices" from Jewish spiritual leaders of all denominations.
6 x 9, 320 pp, Quality PB, 978-1-58023-417-7 **$18.99**

Witnesses to the One: The Spiritual History of the *Sh'ma*
By Rabbi Joseph B. Meszler; Foreword by Rabbi Elyse Goldstein
6 x 9, 176 pp, Quality PB, 978-1-58023-400-9 **$16.99**; HC, 978-1-58023-309-5 **$19.99**

My People's Prayer Book Series: Traditional Prayers, Modern Commentaries *Edited by Rabbi Lawrence A. Hoffman, PhD*
Provides diverse and exciting commentary to the traditional liturgy. Will help you find new wisdom in Jewish prayer, and bring liturgy into your life. Each book includes Hebrew text, modern translations and commentaries from all perspectives of the Jewish world.
Vol. 1—The *Sh'ma* and Its Blessings
  7 x 10, 168 pp, HC, 978-1-879045-79-8 **$29.99**
Vol. 2—The *Amidah* 7 x 10, 240 pp, HC, 978-1-879045-80-4 **$24.95**
Vol. 3—*P'sukei D'zimrah* (Morning Psalms)
  7 x 10, 240 pp, HC, 978-1-879045-81-1 **$29.99**
Vol. 4—*Seder K'riat Hatorah* (The Torah Service)
  7 x 10, 264 pp, HC, 978-1-879045-82-8 **$23.99**
Vol. 5—*Birkhot Hashachar* (Morning Blessings)
  7 x 10, 240 pp, HC, 978-1-879045-83-5 **$24.95**
Vol. 6—*Tachanun* and Concluding Prayers
  7 x 10, 240 pp, HC, 978-1-879045-84-2 **$24.95**
Vol. 7—Shabbat at Home 7 x 10, 240 pp, HC, 978-1-879045-85-9 **$24.95**
Vol. 8—*Kabbalat Shabbat* (Welcoming Shabbat in the Synagogue)
  7 x 10, 240 pp, HC, 978-1-58023-121-3 **$24.99**
Vol. 9—Welcoming the Night: *Minchah* and *Ma'ariv* (Afternoon and Evening Prayer) 7 x 10, 272 pp, HC, 978-1-58023-262-3 **$24.99**
Vol. 10—Shabbat Morning: *Shacharit* and *Musaf* (Morning and Additional Services) 7 x 10, 240 pp, HC, 978-1-58023-240-1 **$29.99**

Spirituality/Lawrence Kushner

I'm God; You're Not: Observations on Organized Religion & Other Disguises of the Ego
6 x 9, 256 pp, Quality PB, 978-1-58023-513-6 **$18.99**; HC, 978-1-58023-441-2 **$21.99**

The Book of Letters: A Mystical Hebrew Alphabet
Popular HC Edition, 6 x 9, 80 pp, 2-color text, 978-1-879045-00-2 **$24.95**
Collector's Limited Edition, 9 x 12, 80 pp, gold-foil-embossed pages, w/ limited-edition silkscreened print, 978-1-879045-04-0 **$349.00**

The Book of Miracles: A Young Person's Guide to Jewish Spiritual Awareness
6 x 9, 96 pp, 2-color illus., HC, 978-1-879045-78-1 **$16.95** For ages 9–13

The Book of Words: Talking Spiritual Life, Living Spiritual Talk
6 x 9, 160 pp, Quality PB, 978-1-58023-020-9 **$18.99**

Eyes Remade for Wonder: A Lawrence Kushner Reader *Introduction by Thomas Moore*
6 x 9, 240 pp, Quality PB, 978-1-58023-042-1 **$18.95**

God Was in This Place & I, i Did Not Know: Finding Self, Spirituality and Ultimate Meaning 6 x 9, 192 pp, Quality PB, 978-1-879045-33-0 **$16.95**

Honey from the Rock: An Introduction to Jewish Mysticism
6 x 9, 176 pp, Quality PB, 978-1-58023-073-5 **$16.95**

Invisible Lines of Connection: Sacred Stories of the Ordinary
5½ x 8½, 160 pp, Quality PB, 978-1-879045-98-9 **$15.95**

Jewish Spirituality: A Brief Introduction for Christians
5½ x 8½, 112 pp, Quality PB, 978-1-58023-150-3 **$12.95**

The River of Light: Jewish Mystical Awareness
6 x 9, 192 pp, Quality PB, 978-1-58023-096-4 **$16.95**

The Way Into Jewish Mystical Tradition
6 x 9, 224 pp, Quality PB, 978-1-58023-200-5 **$18.99**; HC, 978-1-58023-029-2 **$21.95**

Life Cycle

Marriage/Parenting/Family/Aging

The New Jewish Baby Album: Creating and Celebrating the Beginning of a Spiritual Life—A Jewish Lights Companion
By the Editors at Jewish Lights; Foreword by Anita Diamant; Preface by Rabbi Sandy Eisenberg Sasso
A spiritual keepsake that will be treasured for generations. More than just a memory book, *shows you how—and why it's important*—to create a Jewish home and a Jewish life. 8 x 10, 64 pp, Deluxe Padded HC, Full-color illus., 978-1-58023-138-1 **$19.95**

The Jewish Pregnancy Book: A Resource for the Soul, Body & Mind during Pregnancy, Birth & the First Three Months *By Sandy Falk, MD, and Rabbi Daniel Judson, with Steven A. Rapp* Medical information, prayers and rituals for each stage of pregnancy. 7 x 10, 208 pp, b/w photos, Quality PB, 978-1-58023-178-7 **$16.95**

Celebrating Your New Jewish Daughter: Creating Jewish Ways to Welcome Baby Girls into the Covenant—New and Traditional Ceremonies *By Debra Nussbaum Cohen; Foreword by Rabbi Sandy Eisenberg Sasso* 6 x 9, 272 pp, Quality PB, 978-1-58023-090-2 **$18.95**

The New Jewish Baby Book, 2nd Edition: Names, Ceremonies & Customs—A Guide for Today's Families *By Anita Diamant* 6 x 9, 320 pp, Quality PB, 978-1-58023-251-7 **$19.99**

Parenting as a Spiritual Journey: Deepening Ordinary and Extraordinary Events into Sacred Occasions *By Rabbi Nancy Fuchs-Kreimer, PhD*
6 x 9, 224 pp, Quality PB, 978-1-58023-016-2 **$17.99**

Parenting Jewish Teens: A Guide for the Perplexed
By Joanne Doades Explores the questions and issues that shape the world in which today's Jewish teenagers live and offers constructive advice to parents.
6 x 9, 176 pp, Quality PB, 978-1-58023-305-7 **$16.99**

Judaism for Two: A Spiritual Guide for Strengthening and Celebrating Your Loving Relationship *By Rabbi Nancy Fuchs-Kreimer, PhD, and Rabbi Nancy H. Wiener, DMin; Foreword by Rabbi Elliot N. Dorff, PhD*
Addresses the ways Jewish teachings can enhance and strengthen committed relationships. 6 x 9, 224 pp, Quality PB, 978-1-58023-254-8 **$16.99**

The Creative Jewish Wedding Book, 2nd Edition: A Hands-On Guide to New & Old Traditions, Ceremonies & Celebrations *By Gabrielle Kaplan-Mayer*
9 x 9, 288 pp, b/w photos, Quality PB, 978-1-58023-398-9 **$19.99**

Divorce Is a Mitzvah: A Practical Guide to Finding Wholeness and Holiness When Your Marriage Dies *By Rabbi Perry Netter; Afterword by Rabbi Laura Geller*
6 x 9, 224 pp, Quality PB, 978-1-58023-172-5 **$16.95**

Embracing the Covenant: Converts to Judaism Talk About Why & How
By Rabbi Allan Berkowitz and Patti Moskovitz 6 x 9, 192 pp, Quality PB, 978-1-879045-50-7 **$16.95**

The Guide to Jewish Interfaith Family Life: An InterfaithFamily.com Handbook
Edited by Ronnie Friedland and Edmund Case
6 x 9, 384 pp, Quality PB, 978-1-58023-153-4 **$18.95**

A Heart of Wisdom: Making the Jewish Journey from Midlife through the Elder Years
Edited by Susan Berrin; Foreword by Rabbi Harold Kushner
6 x 9, 384 pp, Quality PB, 978-1-58023-051-3 **$18.95**

Introducing My Faith and My Community: The Jewish Outreach Institute Guide for the Christian in a Jewish Interfaith Relationship
By Rabbi Kerry M. Olitzky 6 x 9, 176 pp, Quality PB, 978-1-58023-192-3 **$16.99**

Making a Successful Jewish Interfaith Marriage: The Jewish Outreach Institute Guide to Opportunities, Challenges and Resources *By Rabbi Kerry M. Olitzky with Joan Peterson Littman*
6 x 9, 176 pp, Quality PB, 978-1-58023-170-1 **$16.95**

A Man's Responsibility: A Jewish Guide to Being a Son, a Partner in Marriage, a Father and a Community Leader *By Rabbi Joseph B. Meszler*
6 x 9, 192 pp, Quality PB, 978-1-58023-435-1 **$16.99**; HC, 978-1-58023-362-0 **$21.99**

So That Your Values Live On: Ethical Wills and How to Prepare Them
Edited by Rabbi Jack Riemer and Rabbi Nathaniel Stampfer
6 x 9, 272 pp, Quality PB, 978-1-879045-34-7 **$18.99**

Holidays/Holy Days

Prayers of Awe Series

An exciting new series that examines the High Holy Day liturgy to enrich the praying experience of everyone—whether experienced worshipers or guests who encounter Jewish prayer for the very first time.

We Have Sinned—Confession in Judaism: Ashamnu and Al Chet
Edited by Rabbi Lawrence A. Hoffman, PhD
A varied and fascinating look at sin, confession and pardon in Judaism, as suggested by the centrality of *Ashamnu* and *Al Chet*, two prayers that people know so well, though understand so little. 6 x 9, 250 pp (est), HC, 978-1-58023-612-6 **$24.99**

Who by Fire, Who by Water—Un'taneh Tokef
Edited by Rabbi Lawrence A. Hoffman, PhD 6 x 9, 272 pp, HC, 978-1-58023-424-5 **$24.99**

All These Vows—Kol Nidre
Edited by Rabbi Lawrence A. Hoffman, PhD 6 x 9, 288 pp, HC, 978-1-58023-430-6 **$24.99**

Rosh Hashanah Readings: Inspiration, Information and Contemplation
Yom Kippur Readings: Inspiration, Information and Contemplation
Edited by Rabbi Dov Peretz Elkins; Section Introductions from Arthur Green's These Are the Words
Rosh Hashanah: 6 x 9, 400 pp, Quality PB, 978-1-58023-437-5 **$19.99**
Yom Kippur: 6 x 9, 368 pp, Quality PB, 978-1-58023-438-2 **$19.99**; HC, 978-1-58023-271-5 **$24.99**

Reclaiming Judaism as a Spiritual Practice: Holy Days and Shabbat
By Rabbi Goldie Milgram 7 x 9, 272 pp, Quality PB, 978-1-58023-205-0 **$19.99**

The Sabbath Soul: Mystical Reflections on the Transformative Power of Holy Time
Selection, Translation and Commentary by Eitan Fishbane, PhD
6 x 9, 208 pp, Quality PB, 978-1-58023-459-7 **$18.99**

Shabbat, 2nd Edition: The Family Guide to Preparing for and Celebrating the Sabbath
By Dr. Ron Wolfson 7 x 9, 320 pp, Illus., Quality PB, 978-1-58023-164-0 **$19.99**

Hanukkah, 2nd Edition: The Family Guide to Spiritual Celebration
By Dr. Ron Wolfson 7 x 9, 240 pp, Illus., Quality PB, 978-1-58023-122-0 **$18.95**

Passover

My People's Passover Haggadah
Traditional Texts, Modern Commentaries
Edited by Rabbi Lawrence A. Hoffman, PhD, and David Arnow, PhD
A diverse and exciting collection of commentaries on the traditional Passover Haggadah—in two volumes!
Vol. 1: 7 x 10, 304 pp, HC, 978-1-58023-354-5 **$24.99**
Vol. 2: 7 x 10, 320 pp, HC, 978-1-58023-346-0 **$24.99**

Freedom Journeys: The Tale of Exodus and Wilderness across Millennia
By Rabbi Arthur O. Waskow and Rabbi Phyllis O. Berman
Explores how the story of Exodus echoes in our own time, calling us to relearn and rethink the Passover story through social-justice, ecological, feminist and interfaith perspectives. 6 x 9, 288 pp, HC, 978-1-58023-445-0 **$24.99**

Leading the Passover Journey: The Seder's Meaning Revealed,
the Haggadah's Story Retold *By Rabbi Nathan Laufer*
Uncovers the hidden meaning of the Seder's rituals and customs.
6 x 9, 224 pp, Quality PB, 978-1-58023-399-6 **$18.99**

Creating Lively Passover Seders, 2nd Edition: A Sourcebook of Engaging Tales,
Texts & Activities *By David Arnow, PhD* 7 x 9, 464 pp, Quality PB, 978-1-58023-444-3 **$24.99**

Passover, 2nd Edition: The Family Guide to Spiritual Celebration
By Dr. Ron Wolfson with Joel Lurie Grishaver 7 x 9, 416 pp, Quality PB, 978-1-58023-174-9 **$19.95**

The Women's Passover Companion: Women's Reflections on the Festival of Freedom
Edited by Rabbi Sharon Cohen Anisfeld, Tara Mohr and Catherine Spector; Foreword by Paula E. Hyman
6 x 9, 352 pp, Quality PB, 978-1-58023-231-9 **$19.99**; HC, 978-1-58023-128-2 **$24.95**

The Women's Seder Sourcebook: Rituals & Readings for Use at the Passover Seder
Edited by Rabbi Sharon Cohen Anisfeld, Tara Mohr and Catherine Spector
6 x 9, 384 pp, Quality PB, 978-1-58023-232-6 **$19.99**

Sacred Texts—SkyLight Illuminations Series

Offers today's spiritual seeker an enjoyable entry into the great classic texts of the world's spiritual traditions. Each classic is presented in an accessible translation, with facing pages of guided commentary from experts, giving you the keys you need to understand the history, context and meaning of the text.

CHRISTIANITY

Celtic Christian Spirituality: Essential Writings—Annotated & Explained
Annotation by Mary C. Earle; Foreword by John Philip Newell
Explores how the writings of this lively tradition embody the gospel.
5½ x 8½, 176 pp, Quality PB, 978-1-59473-302-4 **$16.99**

Desert Fathers and Mothers: Early Christian Wisdom Sayings—
Annotated & Explained
Annotation by Christine Valters Paintner, PhD
Opens up wisdom of the desert fathers and mothers for readers with no previous knowledge of Western monasticism and early Christianity.
5½ x 8½, 176 pp (est), Quality PB, 978-1-59473-373-4 **$16.99**

The End of Days: Essential Selections from Apocalyptic Texts—
Annotated & Explained
Annotation by Robert G. Clouse, PhD
Helps you understand the complex Christian visions of the end of the world.
5½ x 8½, 224 pp, Quality PB, 978-1-59473-170-9 **$16.99**

The Hidden Gospel of Matthew: Annotated & Explained
Translation & Annotation by Ron Miller
Discover the words and events that have the strongest connection to the historical Jesus.
5½ x 8½, 272 pp, Quality PB, 978-1-59473-038-2 **$16.99**

The Infancy Gospels of Jesus: Apocryphal Tales from the Childhoods of Mary and Jesus—Annotated & Explained
Translation & Annotation by Stevan Davies; Foreword by A. Edward Siecienski, PhD
A startling presentation of the early lives of Mary, Jesus and other biblical figures that will amuse and surprise you.
5½ x 8½, 176 pp, Quality PB, 978-1-59473-258-4 **$16.99**

John & Charles Wesley: Selections from Their Writings and Hymns—
Annotated & Explained
Annotation by Paul W. Chilcote, PhD
A unique presentation of the writings of these two inspiring brothers brings together some of the most essential material from their large corpus of work.
5½ x 8½, 288 pp, Quality PB, 978-1-59473-309-3 **$16.99**

The Lost Sayings of Jesus: Teachings from Ancient Christian, Jewish, Gnostic and Islamic Sources—Annotated & Explained
Translation & Annotation by Andrew Phillip Smith; Foreword by Stephan A. Hoeller
This collection of more than three hundred sayings depicts Jesus as a Wisdom teacher who speaks to people of all faiths as a mystic and spiritual master.
5½ x 8½, 240 pp, Quality PB, 978-1-59473-172-3 **$16.99**

Philokalia: The Eastern Christian Spiritual Texts—Selections
Annotated & Explained *Annotation by Allyne Smith; Translation by G. E. H. Palmer, Phillip Sherrard and Bishop Kallistos Ware*
The first approachable introduction to the wisdom of the Philokalia, the classic text of Eastern Christian spirituality.
5½ x 8½, 240 pp, Quality PB, 978-1-59473-103-7 **$16.99**

The Sacred Writings of Paul: Selections Annotated & Explained
Translation & Annotation by Ron Miller
Leads you into the exciting immediacy of Paul's teachings.
5½ x 8½, 224 pp, Quality PB, 978-1-59473-213-3 **$16.99**

Sacred Texts—continued

CHRISTIANITY—continued

Saint Augustine of Hippo: Selections from *Confessions* and Other Essential Writings—Annotated & Explained
Annotation by Joseph T. Kelley, PhD; Translation by the Augustinian Heritage Institute
Provides insight into the mind and heart of this foundational Christian figure.
5½ x 8½, 272 pp, Quality PB, 978-1-59473-282-9 **$16.99**

Saint Ignatius Loyola—The Spiritual Writings: Selections Annotated & Explained *Annotation by Mark Mossa, SJ*
Draws from contemporary translations of original texts focusing on the practical mysticism of Ignatius of Loyola.
5½ x 8½, 288 pp, Quality PB, 978-1-59473-301-7 **$16.99**

Sex Texts from the Bible: Selections Annotated & Explained
Translation & Annotation by Teresa J. Hornsby; Foreword by Amy-Jill Levine
Demystifies the Bible's ideas on gender roles, marriage, sexual orientation, virginity, lust and sexual pleasure.
5½ x 8½, 208 pp, Quality PB, 978-1-59473-217-1 **$16.99**

Spiritual Writings on Mary: Annotated & Explained
Annotation by Mary Ford-Grabowsky; Foreword by Andrew Harvey
Examines the role of Mary, the mother of Jesus, as a source of inspiration in history and in life today.
5½ x 8½, 288 pp, Quality PB, 978-1-59473-001-6 **$16.99**

The Way of a Pilgrim: The Jesus Prayer Journey—Annotated & Explained
Translation & Annotation by Gleb Pokrovsky; Foreword by Andrew Harvey
A classic of Russian Orthodox spirituality.
5½ x 8½, 160 pp, Illus., Quality PB, 978-1-893361-31-7 **$14.95**

GNOSTICISM

Gnostic Writings on the Soul: Annotated & Explained
Translation & Annotation by Andrew Phillip Smith; Foreword by Stephan A. Hoeller
Reveals the inspiring ways your soul can remember and return to its unique, divine purpose.
5½ x 8½, 144 pp, Quality PB, 978-1-59473-220-1 **$16.99**

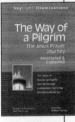

The Gospel of Philip: Annotated & Explained
Translation & Annotation by Andrew Phillip Smith; Foreword by Stevan Davies
Reveals otherwise unrecorded sayings of Jesus and fragments of Gnostic mythology.
5½ x 8½, 160 pp, Quality PB, 978-1-59473-111-2 **$16.99**

The Gospel of Thomas: Annotated & Explained
Translation & Annotation by Stevan Davies; Foreword by Andrew Harvey
Sheds new light on the origins of Christianity and portrays Jesus as a wisdom-loving sage.
5½ x 8½, 192 pp, Quality PB, 978-1-893361-45-4 **$16.99**

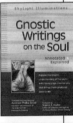

The Secret Book of John: The Gnostic Gospel—Annotated & Explained
Translation & Annotation by Stevan Davies
The most significant and influential text of the ancient Gnostic religion.
5½ x 8½, 208 pp, Quality PB, 978-1-59473-082-5 **$16.99**

Spirituality

The Jewish Lights Spirituality Handbook: A Guide to Understanding, Exploring & Living a Spiritual Life   *Edited by Stuart M. Matlins*
What exactly is "Jewish" about spirituality? How do I make it a part of my life? Fifty of today's foremost spiritual leaders share their ideas and experience with us.
6 x 9, 456 pp, Quality PB, 978-1-58023-093-3 **$19.99**

The Sabbath Soul: Mystical Reflections on the Transformative Power of Holy Time   *Selection, Translation and Commentary by Eitan Fishbane, PhD*
Explores the writings of mystical masters of Hasidism. Provides translations and interpretations of a wide range of Hasidic sources previously unavailable in English that reflect the spiritual transformation that takes place on the seventh day.
6 x 9, 208 pp, Quality PB, 978-1-58023-459-7 **$18.99**

Repentance: The Meaning and Practice of *Teshuvah*
By Dr. Louis E. Newman; Foreword by Rabbi Harold M. Schulweis; Preface by Rabbi Karyn D. Kedar
Examines both the practical and philosophical dimensions of *teshuvah*, Judaism's core religious-moral teaching on repentance, and its value for us—Jews and non-Jews alike—today.   6 x 9, 256 pp, HC, 978-1-58023-426-9 **$24.99**

Aleph-Bet Yoga: Embodying the Hebrew Letters for Physical and Spiritual Well-Being
By Steven A. Rapp; Foreword by Tamar Frankiel, PhD, and Judy Greenfeld; Preface by Hart Lazer
7 x 10, 128 pp, b/w photos, Quality PB, Lay-flat binding, 978-1-58023-162-6 **$16.95**

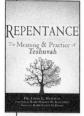

A Book of Life: Embracing Judaism as a Spiritual Practice
By Rabbi Michael Strassfeld 6 x 9, 544 pp, Quality PB, 978-1-58023-247-0 **$19.99**

Bringing the Psalms to Life: How to Understand and Use the Book of Psalms
By Rabbi Daniel F. Polish, PhD 6 x 9, 208 pp, Quality PB, 978-1-58023-157-2 **$16.95**

Does the Soul Survive? A Jewish Journey to Belief in Afterlife, Past Lives & Living with Purpose   *By Rabbi Elie Kaplan Spitz; Foreword by Brian L. Weiss, MD*
6 x 9, 288 pp, Quality PB, 978-1-58023-165-7 **$16.99**

Entering the Temple of Dreams: Jewish Prayers, Movements and Meditations for the End of the Day   *By Tamar Frankiel, PhD, and Judy Greenfeld*
7 x 10, 192 pp, illus., Quality PB, 978-1-58023-079-7 **$16.95**

First Steps to a New Jewish Spirit: Reb Zalman's Guide to Recapturing the Intimacy & Ecstasy in Your Relationship with God   *By Rabbi Zalman M. Schachter-Shalomi with Donald Gropman* 6 x 9, 144 pp, Quality PB, 978-1-58023-182-4 **$16.95**

Foundations of Sephardic Spirituality: The Inner Life of Jews of the Ottoman Empire
By Rabbi Marc D. Angel, PhD 6 x 9, 224 pp, Quality PB, 978-1-58023-341-5 **$18.99**

God & the Big Bang: Discovering Harmony between Science & Spirituality
By Dr. Daniel C. Matt 6 x 9, 216 pp, Quality PB, 978-1-879045-89-7 **$18.99**

God in Our Relationships: Spirituality between People from the Teachings of Martin Buber   *By Rabbi Dennis S. Ross* 5½ x 8½, 160 pp, Quality PB, 978-1-58023-147-3 **$16.95**

Judaism, Physics and God: Searching for Sacred Metaphors in a Post-Einstein World
By Rabbi David W. Nelson 6 x 9, 352 pp, Quality PB, inc. reader's discussion guide, 978-1-58023-306-4 **$18.99**; HC, 352 pp, 978-1-58023-252-4 **$24.99**

Meaning & Mitzvah: Daily Practices for Reclaiming Judaism through Prayer, God, Torah, Hebrew, Mitzvot and Peoplehood *By Rabbi Goldie Milgram*
7 x 9, 336 pp, Quality PB, 978-1-58023-256-2 **$19.99**

Minding the Temple of the Soul: Balancing Body, Mind, and Spirit through Traditional Jewish Prayer, Movement, and Meditation *By Tamar Frankiel, PhD, and Judy Greenfeld*
7 x 10, 184 pp, Illus., Quality PB, 978-1-879045-64-4 **$18.99**

One God Clapping: The Spiritual Path of a Zen Rabbi *By Rabbi Alan Lew with Sherril Jaffe*
5½ x 8½, 336 pp, Quality PB, 978-1-58023-115-2 **$16.95**

The Soul of the Story: Meetings with Remarkable People
By Rabbi David Zeller 6 x 9, 288 pp, HC, 978-1-58023-272-2 **$21.99**

Tanya, the Masterpiece of Hasidic Wisdom: Selections Annotated & Explained
Translation & Annotation by Rabbi Rami Shapiro; Foreword by Rabbi Zalman M. Schachter-Shalomi
5½ x 8½, 240 pp, Quality PB, 978-1-59473-275-1 **$16.99**

These Are the Words, 2nd Edition: A Vocabulary of Jewish Spiritual Life
By Rabbi Arthur Green, PhD 6 x 9, 320 pp, Quality PB, 978-1-58023-494-8 **$19.99**

Judaism / Christianity / Interfaith

Christians & Jews—Faith to Faith: Tragic History, Promising
Present, Fragile Future *By Rabbi James Rudin*
A probing examination of Christian-Jewish relations that looks at the major
issues facing both faith communities. 6 x 9, 288 pp, HC, 978-1-58023-432-0 **$24.99**

Religion Gone Astray: What We Found at the Heart of Interfaith
By Pastor Don Mackenzie, Rabbi Ted Falcon and Imam Jamal Rahman
Probes more deeply into the problem aspects of our religious institutions—specifically exclusivity, violence, inequality of men and women, and homophobia—to
provide a profound understanding of the nature of what divides us.
6 x 9, 192 pp, Quality PB, 978-1-59473-317-8 **$16.99***

Getting to the Heart of Interfaith: The Eye-Opening, Hope-Filled
Friendship of a Pastor, a Rabbi and an Imam
By Rabbi Ted Falcon, Pastor Don Mackenzie and Imam Jamal Rahman
Presents ways we can work together to transcend the differences that have divided
us historically. 6 x 9, 192 pp, Quality PB, 978-1-59473-263-8 **$16.99***

How to Do Good & Avoid Evil: A Global Ethic from the Sources of Judaism
By Hans Küng and Rabbi Walter Homolka 6 x 9, 224 pp, HC, 978-1-59473-255-3 **$19.99***

Claiming Earth as Common Ground: The Ecological Crisis through the Lens of
Faith *By Rabbi Andrea Cohen-Kiener* 6 x 9, 192 pp, Quality PB, 978-1-59473-261-4 **$16.99***

Modern Jews Engage the New Testament: Enhancing Jewish Well-Being in a
Christian Environment *By Rabbi Michael J. Cook, PhD* 6 x 9, 416 pp, HC, 978-1-58023-313-2 **$29.99**

The Changing Christian World: A Brief Introduction for Jews
By Rabbi Leonard A. Schoolman 5½ x 8½, 176 pp, Quality PB, 978-1-58023-344-6 **$16.99**

Christians & Jews in Dialogue: Learning in the Presence of the Other
By Mary C. Boys and Sara S. Lee
6 x 9, 240 pp, Quality PB, 978-1-59473-254-6 **$18.99**; HC, 978-1-59473-144-0 **21.99***

Disaster Spiritual Care: Practical Clergy Responses to Community, Regional and
National Tragedy *Edited by Rabbi Stephen B. Roberts, BCJC, and Rev. Willard W. C. Ashley Sr., DMin, DH*
6 x 9, 384 pp, HC, 978-1-59473-240-9 **$40.00***

How to Be a Perfect Stranger, 5th Edition: The Essential Religious Etiquette
Handbook *Edited by Stuart M. Matlins and Arthur J. Magida*
6 x 9, 432 pp, Quality PB, 978-1-59473-294-2 **$19.99***

InterActive Faith: The Essential Interreligious Community-Building Handbook
Edited by Rev. Bud Heckman with Rori Picker Neiss
6 x 9, 304 pp, Quality PB, 978-1-59473-273-7 **$16.99**; HC, 978-1-59473-237-9 **$29.99***

Introducing My Faith and My Community
The Jewish Outreach Institute Guide for the Christian in a Jewish Interfaith Relationship
By Rabbi Kerry M. Olitzky 6 x 9, 176 pp, Quality PB, 978-1-58023-192-3 **$16.99**

The Jewish Approach to Repairing the World (*Tikkun Olam*)
A Brief Introduction for Christians *By Rabbi Elliot N. Dorff, PhD, with Rev. Cory Willson*
5½ x 8½, 256 pp, Quality PB, 978-1-58023-349-1 **$16.99**

The Jewish Connection to Israel, the Promised Land: A Brief Introduction for
Christians *By Rabbi Eugene Korn, PhD* 5½ x 8½, 192 pp, Quality PB, 978-1-58023-318-7 **$14.99**

Jewish Holidays: A Brief Introduction for Christians *By Rabbi Kerry M. Olitzky and
Rabbi Daniel Judson* 5½ x 8½, 176 pp, Quality PB, 978-1-58023-302-6 **$16.99**

Jewish Ritual: A Brief Introduction for Christians *By Rabbi Kerry M. Olitzky and
Rabbi Daniel Judson* 5½ x 8½, 144 pp, Quality PB, 978-1-58023-210-4 **$14.99**

A Jewish Understanding of the New Testament *By Rabbi Samuel Sandmel;
Preface by Rabbi David Sandmel* 5½ x 8½, 368 pp, Quality PB, 978-1-59473-048-1 **$19.99***

Righteous Gentiles in the Hebrew Bible: Ancient Role Models for Sacred
Relationships *By Rabbi Jeffrey K. Salkin; Foreword by Rabbi Harold M. Schulweis; Preface by Phyllis Tickle*
6 x 9, 192 pp, Quality PB, 978-1-58023-364-4 **$18.99**

We Jews and Jesus: Exploring Theological Differences for Mutual Understanding
By Rabbi Samuel Sandmel; Preface by Rabbi David Sandmel
6 x 9, 192 pp, Quality PB, 978-1-59473-208-9 **$16.99**

*A book from SkyLight Paths, Jewish Lights' sister imprint

Theology/Philosophy/The Way Into... Series

The Way Into... series offers an accessible and highly usable "guided tour" of the Jewish faith, people, history and beliefs—in total, an introduction to Judaism that will enable you to understand and interact with the sacred texts of the Jewish tradition. Each volume is written by a leading contemporary scholar and teacher, and explores one key aspect of Judaism. *The Way Into...* series enables all readers to achieve a real sense of Jewish cultural literacy through guided study.

The Way Into Encountering God in Judaism
By Neil Gillman
For everyone who wants to understand how Jews have encountered God throughout history and today.
6 x 9, 240 pp, Quality PB, 978-1-58023-199-2 **$18.99**; HC, 978-1-58023-025-4 **$21.95**
Also Available: **The Jewish Approach to God:** A Brief Introduction for Christians
By Neil Gillman
5½ x 8¼, 192 pp, Quality PB, 978-1-58023-190-9 **$16.95**

The Way Into Jewish Mystical Tradition
By Lawrence Kushner
Allows readers to interact directly with the sacred mystical text of the Jewish tradition. An accessible introduction to the concepts of Jewish mysticism, their religious and spiritual significance and how they relate to life today.
6 x 9, 224 pp, Quality PB, 978-1-58023-200-5 **$18.99**; HC, 978-1-58023-029-2 **$21.95**

The Way Into Jewish Prayer
By Lawrence A. Hoffman
Opens the door to 3,000 years of Jewish prayer, making available all anyone needs to feel at home in the Jewish way of communicating with God.
6 x 9, 208 pp, Quality PB, 978-1-58023-201-2 **$18.99**

Also Available: **The Way Into Jewish Prayer Teacher's Guide**
By Rabbi Jennifer Ossakow Goldsmith
8½ x 11, 42 pp, PB, 978-1-58023-345-3 **$8.99**
Visit our website to download a free copy.

The Way Into Judaism and the Environment
By Jeremy Benstein
Explores the ways in which Judaism contributes to contemporary social-environmental issues, the extent to which Judaism is part of the problem and how it can be part of the solution.
6 x 9, 288 pp, HC, 978-1-58023-268-5 **$24.99**

The Way Into *Tikkun Olam* (Repairing the World)
By Elliot N. Dorff
An accessible introduction to the Jewish concept of the individual's responsibility to care for others and repair the world.
6 x 9, 320 pp, HC, 978-1-58023-269-2 **$24.99**; 304 pp, Quality PB, 978-1-58023-328-6 **$18.99**

The Way Into Torah
By Norman J. Cohen
Helps guide in the exploration of the origins and development of Torah, explains why it should be studied and how to do it.
6 x 9, 176 pp, Quality PB, 978-1-58023-198-5 **$16.99**

The Way Into the Varieties of Jewishness
By Sylvia Barack Fishman, PhD
Explores the religious and historical understanding of what it has meant to be Jewish from ancient times to the present controversy over "Who is a Jew?"
6 x 9, 288 pp, HC, 978-1-58023-030-8 **$24.99**

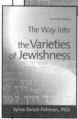

Theology/Philosophy

From Defender to Critic: The Search for a New Jewish Self
By Dr. David Hartman
A daring self-examination of Hartman's goals, which were not to strip halakha of its authority but to create a space for questioning and critique that allows for the traditionally religious Jew to act out a moral life in tune with modern experience. 6 x 9, 336 pp, HC, 978-1-58023-515-0 **$35.00**

Our Religious Brains: What Cognitive Science Reveals about Belief, Morality, Community and Our Relationship with God
By Rabbi Ralph D. Mecklenburger; Foreword by Dr. Howard Kelfer; Preface by Dr. Neil Gillman
This is a groundbreaking, accessible look at the implications of cognitive science for religion and theology, intended for laypeople. 6 x 9, 224 pp, HC, 978-1-58023-508-2 **$24.99**

The Other Talmud—*The Yerushalmi:* Unlocking the Secrets of The Talmud of Israel for Judaism Today   *By Rabbi Judith Z. Abrams, PhD*
A fascinating—and stimulating—look at "the other Talmud" and the possibilities for Jewish life reflected there. 6 x 9, 256 pp, HC, 978-1-58023-463-4 **$24.99**

The Way of Man: According to Hasidic Teaching
By Martin Buber; New Translation and Introduction by Rabbi Bernard H. Mehlman and Dr. Gabriel E. Padawer; Foreword by Paul Mendes-Flohr
An accessible and engaging new translation of Buber's classic work—available as an e-book only. E-book, 978-1-58023-601-0 Digital List Price **$14.99**

The Death of Death: Resurrection and Immortality in Jewish Thought
By Rabbi Neil Gillman, PhD   6 x 9, 336 pp, Quality PB, 978-1-58023-081-0 **$18.95**

Doing Jewish Theology: God, Torah & Israel in Modern Judaism   *By Rabbi Neil Gillman, PhD*
6 x 9, 304 pp, Quality PB, 978-1-58023-439-9 **$18.99**; HC, 978-1-58023-322-4 **$24.99**

A Heart of Many Rooms: Celebrating the Many Voices within Judaism
By Dr. David Hartman   6 x 9, 352 pp, Quality PB, 978-1-58023-156-5 **$19.95**

The God Who Hates Lies: Confronting & Rethinking Jewish Tradition
By Dr. David Hartman with Charlie Buckholtz   6 x 9, 208 pp, HC, 978-1-58023-455-9 **$24.99**

Jewish Theology in Our Time: A New Generation Explores the Foundations and Future of Jewish Belief   *Edited by Rabbi Elliot J. Cosgrove, PhD; Foreword by Rabbi David J. Wolpe; Preface by Rabbi Carole B. Balin, PhD*   6 x 9, 240 pp, HC, 978-1-58023-413-9 **$24.99**

Maimonides—Essential Teachings on Jewish Faith & Ethics: The Book of Knowledge & the Thirteen Principles of Faith—Annotated & Explained
Translation and Annotation by Rabbi Marc D. Angel, PhD
5½ x 8½, 224 pp, Quality PB Original, 978-1-59473-311-6 **$18.99***

Maimonides, Spinoza and Us: Toward an Intellectually Vibrant Judaism
By Rabbi Marc D. Angel, PhD   6 x 9, 224 pp, HC, 978-1-58023-411-5 **$24.99**

A Touch of the Sacred: A Theologian's Informal Guide to Jewish Belief
By Dr. Eugene B. Borowitz and Frances W. Schwartz
6 x 9, 256 pp, Quality PB, 978-1-58023-416-0 **$16.99**; HC, 978-1-58023-337-8 **$21.99**

Traces of God: Seeing God in Torah, History and Everyday Life   *By Rabbi Neil Gillman, PhD*
6 x 9, 240 pp, Quality PB, 978-1-58023-369-9 **$16.99**

Your Word Is Fire: The Hasidic Masters on Contemplative Prayer
Edited and translated by Rabbi Arthur Green, PhD, and Barry W. Holtz
6 x 9, 160 pp, Quality PB, 978-1-879045-25-5 **$15.95**

I Am Jewish
Personal Reflections Inspired by the Last Words of Daniel Pearl
Almost 150 Jews—both famous and not—from all walks of life, from all around the world, write about many aspects of their Judaism.
Edited by Judea and Ruth Pearl   6 x 9, 304 pp, Deluxe PB w/ flaps, 978-1-58023-259-3 **$18.99**
Download a free copy of the *I Am Jewish Teacher's Guide* at www.jewishlights.com.

Hannah Senesh: Her Life and Diary, The First Complete Edition
By Hannah Senesh; Foreword by Marge Piercy; Preface by Eitan Senesh; Afterword by Roberta Grossman
6 x 9, 368 pp, b/w photos, Quality PB, 978-1-58023-342-2 **$19.99**

*A book from SkyLight Paths, Jewish Lights' sister imprint

About Jewish Lights

People of all faiths and backgrounds yearn for books that attract, engage, educate, and spiritually inspire.

Our principal goal is to stimulate thought and help all people learn about who the Jewish People are, where they come from, and what the future can be made to hold. While people of our diverse Jewish heritage are the primary audience, our books speak to people in the Christian world as well and will broaden their understanding of Judaism and the roots of their own faith.

We bring to you authors who are at the forefront of spiritual thought and experience. While each has something different to say, they all say it in a voice that you can hear.

Our books are designed to welcome you and then to engage, stimulate, and inspire. We judge our success not only by whether or not our books are beautiful and commercially successful, but by whether or not they make a difference in your life.

For your information and convenience, at the back of this book we have provided a list of other Jewish Lights books you might find interesting and useful. They cover all the categories of your life:

Bar/Bat Mitzvah
Bible Study / Midrash
Children's Books
Congregation Resources
Current Events / History
Ecology / Environment
Fiction: Mystery, Science Fiction
Grief / Healing
Holidays / Holy Days
Inspiration
Kabbalah / Mysticism / Enneagram

Life Cycle
Meditation
Men's Interest
Parenting
Prayer / Ritual / Sacred Practice
Social Justice
Spirituality
Theology / Philosophy
Travel
Twelve Steps
Women's Interest

Stuart M. Matlins, Publisher

Or phone, fax, mail or e-mail to: **JEWISH LIGHTS Publishing**
Sunset Farm Offices, Route 4 • P.O. Box 237 • Woodstock, Vermont 05091
Tel: (802) 457-4000 • Fax: (802) 457-4004 • www.jewishlights.com
Credit card orders: (800) 962-4544 (8:30AM–5:30PM EST Monday–Friday)
Generous discounts on quantity orders. SATISFACTION GUARANTEED. Prices subject to change.